THE PRUDHOMME
FAMILY COOKBOOK

By Chef Paul . . .

Chef Paul Prudhomme's Louisiana Kitchen

THE PRUDHOMME FAMILY COOKBOOK

Old-time Louisiana Recipes by the eleven Prudhomme brothers and sisters and Chef Paul Prudhomme

WILLIAM MORROW AND COMPANY, INC., NEW YORK

Library of Congress Cataloging-in-Publication Data

Prudhomme, Paul.
  The Prudhomme family cookbook: old-time Louisiana recipes/by the eleven Prudhomme brothers and sisters and Chef Paul Prudhomme.
    p. cm.
  Includes index.
  ISBN 0-688-07549-5
  1. Cookery, American—Louisiana style. I. Title.
TX715.P949 1987
641.59763—dc19   87-18345
                                                                    CIP

Printed in the United States of America

Book-of-the-Month Records® offers recordings on
compact discs, cassettes and records. For information and
catalog write to BOMR, Department 901, Camp Hill, PA 17012.

BOOK DESIGN BY LINEY LI

For Mom and Dad and Saul

Acknowledgments

This cookbook would not be, were it not for the talent, enthusiasm, and hard work of the following people. We would like to recognize them and offer our warmest thanks.

We deeply appreciate Paulette Rittenberg, who worked diligently, testing and re-testing all our recipes to make them clear and workable for today's cook in a home kitchen. Her patience and palate are remarkable.

Myra Peak has earned our respect and gratitude for organizing, writing, and editing this book. Her skill, dedication to detail, and craftsmanship with the written word are unexcelled.

Lois Diaville transcribed hundreds of hours of family interviews, assisted Myra in editing and proofing recipes, and proofread every word of the galleys with Leslie Capo.

Sharon Courtney assisted Paulette in the test kitchen and entered all the recipes into the computer.

Photographer Tom Jimison took exceptional shots for the book jacket.

We are grateful, too, to the staffs of all the K-Paul's Louisiana Enterprises companies for their unflagging practical assistance and moral support.

We all owe a huge debt of gratitude to our editor at William Morrow & Company, Narcisse Chamberlain. Her wonderful enthusiasm, sharp wit, and unerring eye for language (French as well as English) are unsurpassable. Thank you, Narcisse.

THE PRUDHOMMES

Contents

Contents

Introduction

When I was eight years old, I remember a family gathering. I was sitting away to the side, just listening, because you were not seen at eight years old when adults were talking—you didn't say anything unless somebody asked you something, and you didn't walk in front of the adults. So I was sitting in the corner daydreaming, and I overheard a conversation about a relative who had been a cook in the navy during World War II. He was now working in New Orleans as a cook, and he was making one hundred fifty dollars a week! In 1948, that was a huge amount of money. And I had this wonderful image of me dressed in white with a big hat on and making one hundred and fifty dollars a week—that would be the fantasy of my life.

I think the reason this was so attractive to me was that for several years I had already been cooking some of my own food; I'd cook pork chops and other things I really liked, and liked cooked a certain way. Cooking and food were a major part of my family life. And for me, cooking something that was good and making it better than I had tasted it before was really important.

I had the inspiration of a family that had nothing but food as their pleasure and as their entertainment and as their most important thing in life. My mom and dad were sharecroppers, which meant they farmed on someone else's land and gave the landowner a percentage of the cash crops they raised. We were very poor, and we lived off the land. The greatest, most prideful thing I'd hear my dad say when I was growing up was that, "Well, we don't have nothing else, but we have plenty to eat." But it hadn't always been that way.

To understand the importance of food in our lives, you have to go into a part of the family history before I was born because, from what I've heard other members of the family talk about, we were so poor that there were times when there wasn't enough food, or there wasn't the right kind of food. Dad had only one mule back then, he and Mom had a big family to feed, and they were the only ones capable of working. When my oldest sister, Darilee, was seven years old, there were six kids. Everybody had to work as best they could—Mom had to work in the fields with Dad, and that left my brothers and sisters to take care of each other. I think it's hard for people to understand the pain and frustration of parents working year after year trying to raise this huge family and just sort of making an incredibly slow climb up a very steep mountain to try to get out of poverty and to get beyond just barely being able to feed the family properly.

As each one of the brothers and sisters got old enough—and old enough was eight or nine years old—they began to help Mom and Dad with the farm work. Each time that happened, it seemed to give the family some kind of relief because there were so many close together that came to that age. As more people were able to work, Dad could go to bigger plots of land. He moved frequently during the early years, always trying to find a place to sharecrop that had a better house for the family and better soil to farm and more acreage to farm. The family kept up this slow but steady climb for more than twenty years, until World War II.

The war years were watershed years, because several of the boys were in the service and their allotment checks were sent home to the family. Dad used that money to buy cattle and chickens and hogs and horses and mules, and by shrewd trading and bartering, he was able to use the money to make more money. And when the boys returned home, I remember so well, Dad paid back every cent that had been sent home by each one. He was really proud of that.

By the time I came along and was growing up, the family was really well off for that area of the country. But I've heard Mom and Dad and my brothers and sisters talk about when there just was not enough to go around. I think it's impossible for someone who's never been hungry to understand what it is not to have enough food. There were times when the family had to put water and sugar in the milk to make it go further, and when there was no meat for days because there weren't enough chickens to kill and there was no meat left from the last butchering. If you live through those kinds of times, you remember it always—you can never forget it.

As things progressed and the family got better off, we still didn't have money for clothes and automobiles and other things, but we could produce enough food to feed the family well. And food became our pride—we even had enough to feed other people. My family fed other families who didn't farm for a living, who lived in the city and didn't have enough to eat. My brothers and sisters could have their friends over at the house, and there was enough food for them.

Mom and Dad loved having lots of people over to eat. We were often between fifteen and twenty people on weekdays and over thirty people on weekends. I remember my mom saying to my sisters and sisters-in-law when the house was full of people, "Well, we'll have to put the little pots in the big pots today!" No one could stretch food like my mom: She could take one old hen and a little bit of Cajun andouille sausage and make an incredible gumbo. Then she made a big potato salad and cooked some fresh vegetables from the garden,

Mom Prudhomme

and she could feed twenty people wonderfully. Mom kept track one time for a period of almost ten months, and we never sat down to a meal with only members of the family present! So food was our way of sharing with others and our social identity and our entertainment, as well as our nourishment.

Over the years, we became like rich people, we were like the elite. What made us wealthy was that we had a storehouse full of food, and we had a hundred and fifty or two hundred chickens in the yard, thirty or forty hogs, and cows and calves and horses. And we had land that really produced well. That was rich for us; that was like a person today having two or three cars, a nice big house, a hundred thousand dollars in the bank, and huge insurance policies. That's why there was so much pride in being able to say, "Well, we don't have nothing else, but we have plenty to eat."

In 1951, when I was eleven years old, Bobby and I were the only children still at home, so Dad couldn't farm sixty acres of land anymore. Ours had always been a people and animal farm, no machines of any kind, so our farming days were over. Mom and Dad sold everything they had accumulated over the years—tools, farm animals, and equipment—for six thousand dollars. That was an enormous amount of money for us, and Dad took four thousand dollars and used it as a down payment on a grocery store in the nearby town of Opelousas.

Mom and Dad loved the grocery store. We cooked food for people to take home, and we cooked for people who couldn't afford to buy food. And my wanting to be a cook stayed with me the whole time. I even learned how to cut meat in our meat market. And that's where everything started for me—the farm and the grocery store—it was sort of a destined education for what would come later.

My book *Chef Paul Prudhomme's Louisiana Kitchen* covered the time from when I became a professional cook through 1984 at K-Paul's Louisiana Kitchen, the restaurant that K, my wife, and I own and operate in New Orleans. It dealt with the professionalism I had learned and with what I had learned as a cook, the touch of adding butter and the touch of adding herbs and other things that Cajun food doesn't have—making a sauce from a stock and cooking individual orders. It did not cover the old Cajun methods of cooking. I have wanted so much to do a book like *The Prudhomme Family Cookbook* because, at K-Paul's, I had to change from the way food had been at home, just wonderful country food. I couldn't sell food cooked in pork lard at the restaurant, and I couldn't cook a pot of food at five o'clock in the evening and keep serving it until eleven o'clock that night. I had to create new ways to cook and yet try to keep the wonderful taste that I had grown up with. But what I did in New Orleans changed the food—in some cases making it better, and in some, just changing it.

When the idea for a family cookbook came from my sister Enola, it was just what I had been looking for to show people all over the nation what real Cajun food is. I wanted the recipes to be authentic, I wanted them to be real, and I wanted them to be simple. Every recipe wouldn't have to appeal to everybody. There are very old recipes in the book that you may never use, but that was not what was important. What was important to me was to document the recipes, to save them, and at the same time to tell something about life in Cajun country. With the enormous popularity of Cajun food, there are so many people doing Cajun food and Louisiana food, but without any idea of where it comes from. I wanted to show the roots of Cajun food, to show where it came from.

The Prudhomme Family Cookbook fulfills my desire to have a book that lets people see the way Cajun food originally was, and why it was that way, and why it was so important—to let them see that Cajun food came from people, real people, people who didn't have anything else. The book shows how surrounded our lives were with food and how important it was to us. So the book for me is a message, a part of history, and it's what I saw I had the opportunity to do—to show the public what Cajun was about.

It's important to understand how all the Prudhommes made this book together. We wanted recipes that were carefully researched and carefully tested, and we wanted to do the best we could to reproduce them the way they were thirty to sixty years ago. So I went, with the staff that would do the manuscript for us, to each of my brothers' and sisters' houses and they cooked from fifteen to twenty recipes during our four or five days with each one. We wrote down everything that they did—and then we all sat down and joyfully ate the dishes they had cooked. After we finished at each one's house, we went back to New Orleans and took each recipe and tested it and tasted it and refined it and tried to get it where anybody, anywhere could produce at least a close facsimile of the original dish.

My brothers and sisters don't all cook as much as they used to, now that most of their families are grown and away from home, but each one of them has lots of specialties—like a gumbo, or a sauce piquant, or a stew, or maque choux or boudin—that they love to do and remember really well; those are the ones we chose for the book. They all put their own personalities into their recipes to some extent—that's what Cajuns do!—but all the recipes have a base, a root, a background—and that base was my family and our mom and dad and the farm and what we had to eat. This whole book evolved from what we remember Mom fed us when we were kids.

Our Cajun food stems from the earth. We grew virtually everything that we ate—I mean *everything* that we ate, except the sugar and the rice and the flour, we grew ourselves. We had a perfect balance at the farm of what nature is. We started out by planting a seed and that seed grew into corn or cotton or potatoes or beans, and we took the plants and fed them to the animals; then the animals processed the food and we used the animal manure to replenish the nutrients in the fields by plowing it into the ground. When the animals reached a point where they no longer produced—if a chicken didn't lay eggs or a rooster couldn't fertilize eggs, or a mother hog was too old to have baby pigs—we killed them and turned them into food for the family. We also planted vegetables for the family to eat, and we always ate what was in season. We did can some vegetables for the times when we wouldn't have fresh vegetables, but we usually ate the things that were in season, day after day—and that's a difference, a strong difference, between now and when I was a kid.

We didn't have things all year round; so, for instance, when fresh corn was in season, we had corn every day, and three or four times a week we'd have maque choux, a really special corn dish. But each one was different because Mom used whatever ingredients were handy. So you might remember one maque choux that was really incredible that she had maybe put chicken or crawfish in—and that was the one you remembered and took into your life as you grew up and that's the one you like to cook now. Each of the Prudhommes remembers different things about Mom's cooking, and that's how we were able to make a book about it.

What I most want for you to do is to read all the introductions to the recipes. They are glimpses of what life was like in our great big Cajun farming family, and though they're short, all together, they'll give you a real picture. Then I hope you'll choose some of the simple old recipes to make, like Croquesignoles, Candied Yams, Potato Stew with Andouille Smoked Sausage, Crawfish Boulettes, Pork Backbone Stew, or Smothered Turnips and Potatoes. For some dishes, to get just the taste they should have, make the old-time ingredients like Ground Hot Pepper Vinegar and Cajun Home-Canned Spicy Tomatoes that are called for in quite a few recipes. You can stick to the less old-fashioned recipes if you want, but you'll be missing what I want so much for you to experience—what it was like to have dinner at my house years and years ago.

I've included the recipe for Blackened Redfish again in this book, as well as variations for blackened pork chops, chicken, and hamburgers, because of the enormous popularity of the blackening method of cooking. These are not old Cajun recipes; I created the blackening method to try to capture in a skillet the taste of fish or meat cooked over an open fire. I've provided more details about how to blacken because people all over the country have asked for additional information. There are other modern recipes in the family cookbook, too, but they are based on what all of us Prudhomme children learned growing up in our home with Mom and Dad—a home where fabulous food was an everyday happening.

You'll know right away when you see a historical recipe that we want to preserve—like Red Boudin, Paunce Bourré, or Bouilli. These recipes work, and if you can get really fresh ingredients, you will get a fantastic-tasting dish. But they are here primarily so people will know what those wonderful, very old ones were, so they won't be lost forever. That's so important to me. I think that when you have read this book and learned about my family, you'll understand why I wanted to make the book and help preserve the Cajun culture and my extraordinary heritage.

Mom, **Hazel Reed Prudhomme,** was one of eight children. Her parents had a big farm with lots of paid workers, and her family led a much more comfortable life than Dad's. When Mom first met Dad at a dance, she thought he was a country bumpkin, but she fell in love with him and married him in spite of her family's objections. Mom finished the tenth grade and she loved to read. She was the one who really wanted the children to go to school. And she was so talented. She was an awesome cook and a wonderful manager for all the family's needs. She worked right alongside Dad in the fields, especially during the first ten or fifteen years they were married. Mom made every stitch of the clothes we wore on her sewing machine,

Eli Prudhomme, Sr., and Hazel Reed Prudhomme

underwear on up—work denims and Sunday clothes. I remember when Ralph came home from the navy, she took the good wool material from his uniform and made me a little sailor suit with stars on the wide back collar, just like a real uniform. Boy, was I proud to wear that suit.

Dad, **Eli Prudhomme, Sr.,** had three brothers and five sisters. At one time, his parents had thousands of acres of land. The story in the family is that his dad donated ten thousand acres to the Catholic Church, and the family was left with so little land that most of his children had to become sharecroppers. Dad was unbelievably resourceful and extremely hard-headed. In the early years when times were so tough, Mom's family wanted to help, but Dad was too proud and wouldn't accept help from anyone, even family. He wanted to care for his family himself, and over the years he did a better and better job of it. He was a tireless worker. After finishing up with our crops, he'd hire out to help other people with theirs; he worked in canefields and cotton fields and at the sweet-potato processing plant. He was a pretty fair barber, a skilled butcher, and had a fine reputation as a horse and mule trainer. He was also the family dentist and doctor.

Dad taught my brothers and sisters and me about life—and Mom just loved us.

THE PRUDHOMME
FAMILY COOKBOOK

GLOSSARY

& NOTES FROM OUR TEST KITCHEN

Some of our definitions, comments, and other information in this alphabetical glossary come straight from Paul's book *Chef Paul Prudhomme's Louisiana Kitchen* because he stated them the best way he knew how there, and they have stood the test of time. We think it would be unfair (unacceptable!) for us to cross-reference you back to that book when you need the information right here—so, "repetition be damned!" Some of the information has been revised because of more study and work since the first book. And then there are a lot of new entries in the glossary, because this is a Cajun book, with all sorts of interesting things to know about, plus tips about ingredients and cooking that came out of our test kitchen.

Andouille: The most popular Cajun smoked pure pork sausage. Pronounced ahn-*doo*-ee.

Beans and Peas, Dried: See pages 304, 310, 312, and 314. They often don't cook the way you expect them to, and there are different ways to treat them.

Beignet: A square, fried doughnut that has no hole. The Prudhomme beignets are more round and more cakelike than the famous New Orleans beignets. Pronounced bin-*yea*.

Bisque: A Cajun soup, sometimes served over rice, usually made with crawfish or shrimp, and made with a fairly dark roux. Pronounced bisk.

Boucherie: Boucherie literally means butchering—but in Louisiana it means a festive, communal gathering at which several hogs and a steer are killed and the meat is dressed out and prepared for curing or refrigerating. There is always a wonderful feast featuring fresh pork and all the trimmings—potato salad, candied yams, gumbo, and lots of desserts. Boucheries can last for several days and they're always held in midwinter when it is quite cold. Most of the work of the boucherie is done outdoors so the meat can be kept cold. Pronounced *boo*-shuh-*ree*.

Boudin: A Cajun sausage with rice mixed into the stuffing. The most popular type is white boudin, made with pork and usually just referred to as boudin; if pork blood is added, it becomes red boudin. Several other meats or seafood can also be used. Pronounced *boo*-dan, with only a hint of the "n" on the end.

Bouilli: A classic Cajun soup made with the internal organs of beef. Pronounced boo-*yee*.

Boulette: The name the Prudhommes use for meatballs or anything formed into a sphere and then cooked, usually fried. Pronounced boo-*let*.

Butter: We recommend using unsalted butter because it's generally a superior product. And because salted butter has an unpredictable amount of salt, it's easier to control the overall salt level in a dish by using unsalted butter. When cooking over high heat, butter alone is often not the right choice. See **Margarine** and **Oil.**

Cajun French: A distinctive, colorful, and wonderfully musical dialect of the French language spoken by South Louisiana Acadians. The roots of Cajun French are almost four hundred years old, having begun in southern France, moved to Acadia (in Canada), and then to South Louisiana. (When Paul visits southern France, his Cajun French is recognized by the locals as a very old, antiquated style of speaking similar to that used by their grandparents.) Cajun French is less widely heard in Louisiana today, as Cajuns have continued to assimilate into mainstream American culture since World War II. Since the use of Cajun French was discouraged in Louisiana schools when the middle and younger Prudhomme children were growing up, Mom and Dad made a conscious effort to speak English to them so they would have an easier time in school. At one time during this period, anyone who spoke Cajun French was often looked down upon. But Cajuns never lost pride in their language, and Dad Prudhomme, for one, wouldn't ever admit to anyone outside the immediate family that he could understand English—he knew just enough to be able to speak to the younger children.

Attempts are now being made to revive Cajun French in Louisiana. In 1968 the legislature established the Council for the Development of French in Louisiana (CODOFIL) to do any and all things necessary to accomplish the development, utilization, and preservation of the French language as found in Louisiana. In recent years, at least two Cajun French dictionaries have been written and should be helpful in preserving the language. Some of the younger Prudhomme family members are now learning the language of their grandparents in school.

We've done our best to spell correctly all Cajun words and phrases that we've used, but we've not always had a written source for reference. Cajun French has never been considered a written language. Rather, it is a spoken language that began taking on its own flavor and rules of usage as soon as the speakers left southern France. Even in different locales in Cajun Louisiana, there are different terms for the same things. And since Cajun French was rarely written, spelling and grammatical inflections important in a written language were simply not a consideration. We'd love your input, especially if you consider yourself of Cajun descent, on how the terms we use for foods and folkways may differ from what you know. Let us hear from you!

Cocodrie: Alligator. Isn't that a wonderful word? Presumably, it derives from "crocodile." See page 208.

Cornmeal: All the family use yellow cornmeal only, and they prefer it freshly ground; it is widely available in rural areas of Louisiana.

Couche-couche: A breakfast food, basically a fried corn dough; see page 30.

Crabs/Crabmeat: Louisiana crabs are known as "blue crabs"—and the meat is unbelievably sweet and delicious. Lump crabmeat and peeled crawfish tails are the only seafoods we use that are precooked (actually, only blanched and sold in packages kept on ice).

Cracklins: Fried pieces of fresh pork fatback. Cracklins originally were a by-product of rendering lard, but now cracklins are made for cracklins—the lard is the by-product.

Crawfish: In Louisiana crawfish are readily available in three forms: live; fresh tails, blanched and "picked" (peeled) in 1-pound bags packed on ice; and frozen peeled tails (not preferred) in 1-pound bags. Since 1984, the demand for crawfish outside of Louisiana has grown enormously, and all three forms of crawfish are shipped to markets throughout the country—and even to Paris. However, Louisianians still eat most of the crawfish produced here each season. In 1986, 100 million pounds of crawfish were sold on the commercial market, and of that total, about 73 percent were bought and eaten in Louisiana (the overwhelming majority in South Louisiana). Louisiana has both natural or wild crawfish (primarily from the Atchafalaya Basin, Louisiana's great natural wilderness area) and farm-raised crawfish. Each year the production figures for farm-raised crawfish grow stronger, and the state is aggressively marketing the wonderful little creatures nationally and internationally.

If you purchase live crawfish and blanch and peel them yourself, be sure to save the fat—the orange substance in the head that is also attached to the upper part of the tail. It adds incredible richness to crawfish dishes and can often be substituted for some or all of the butter in a recipe. It's wonderful!

A note of caution: Crawfish don't freeze well, and especially not the fat. The oils in the fat, since they freeze poorly, turn rancid quickly and will give your crawfish dishes a fishy taste.

Peeled crawfish tails and lump crabmeat are the only seafoods we use that are precooked, and by that we mean only blanched. This means that if you, or your source of supply, does it right, the crawfish are plunged into boiling water and left for only a few seconds, just until they turn red.

Do not substitute shrimp for crawfish unless the recipe indicates that either may be used.

In Louisiana the pronunciation is crawfish, and the spelling is the same—notwithstanding the "crayfish" spelling acceptable elsewhere.

Croquesignole: Croquesignole means doughnut in Cajun French. The family make theirs approximately square, without a hole, and cakelike in texture. Pronounced *crook*-sin-*yawl*.

Etouffée: Literally translated, "smothered." In Cajun cooking it signifies covering food with a liquid, and the terms etouffée and smothered are interchangeable. Vegetables as well as meats and seafood can be "etoufféed." Pronounced *ay*-too-*fay*. In French Louisiana, we don't put the accent on the first "e"—that would mean to smother a person!

Food Injector: A handy device for injecting liquids and semiliquids into meats. The Prudhomme family use them more and more to inject seasoning purées into meat, poultry, and game. The family also like to stuff meats the traditional way by cutting slits in the meat and filling the slits with various seasoned mixtures, but injectors provide a means for distributing the seasonings in a different way. Food injectors are readily available from cookware shops and are relatively inexpensive and easy to use. See page 157 for what we call our "Cajun deluxe" model.

Food Processor: For all recipes using the processor, we used only the steel cutting blade. A helpful tip: Paul and his chefs and cooks have observed again and again that a dull steel blade will make processed vegetables taste bitter. If your cutting blade has received a lot of use, get it professionally sharpened or buy a new one.

Fresh Fish: Freshness is a prerequisite for having the full, natural taste and texture in cooked fish that a fish has when it is alive and swimming. And since freezing destroys both the flavor and texture of fish, Paul's definition of fresh fish does not include anything that has *ever* been frozen. Find a reliable seafood market that will tell you honestly if the fish has ever been frozen. Many supermarkets and seafood stores sell fish and seafood as fresh, but what they really mean is that it is a safe product, not frozen at the time you buy it. Most of it has been frozen and then thawed and put in the display case. If you use local fish native to your area, you will have a better chance of getting really fresh fish.

Fricassée: A thick stew made with a brown roux. Classically, fricassées are made with cream, but the Prudhomme fricassées don't contain cream. Pronounced *free*-kah-*say*.

Green Onions: Many people call these scallions, and just as many call them green onions. Our recipes say green onions, because that's what we call them in Louisiana. They are common everywhere. What matters is that there should be plenty of fresh and tender edible green tops. All the family plant green onions year-round in their gardens. Some of them use both the white bulb and the green part, while others use the green part only.

Grillades: To the family, "grillades" denotes small pieces of lean boneless pork. The meat can be eaten freshly cooked or it can be cooked and canned in pork lard to preserve it for later use. Pronounced *gree*-yahds.

Gumbo: A Cajun soup almost always containing a cooked roux, and it is sometimes thickened with okra or gumbo filé. It usually contains a variety of seasoning vegetables and meats or seafood and is served over rice. Many people top their gumbo with gumbo filé. Pronounced *gum*-boe.

Gumbo Filé (Filé Powder): An herb, ground young sassafras leaves, often used as a flavoring and/or thickener in gumbos and other Cajun dishes. Pronounced *gum*-boe *fee*-lay.

Ham, Cure 81: The most consistent, best-tasting ham distributed nationally and readily available. It is smoke cured, not water cured, and it is not injected with water.

Jambalaya: A rice dish highly seasoned and strongly flavored with any combination of beef, pork, fowl, smoked sausage, ham (or tasso), or seafood, and often containing tomatoes. According to the *Acadian Dictionary* (Rita and Gabrielle Claudet, Houma, Louisiana, 1981), the word "jambalaya" ". . . comes from the French 'jambon' meaning ham, the African 'ya' meaning rice, and the Acadian [language] where everything is 'à la.'" Pronounced djum-buh-*lie*-yuh.

Lagniappe: A popular term in South Louisiana, "lagniappe" means "a little something extra"—a gift or a show of appreciation. There are lagniappes of information sprinkled throughout this book. Pronounced *lahn*-yap, or, occasionally, *lan*-yap.

Lard: The family used pork lard for almost all their cooking—for deep frying, pan frying, browning foods, making roux, preserving meat (grillades), and even greasing cake pans. Today, all twelve Prudhomme children have their special preferences for various types of fat, lard, or oil (and so do their spouses!), depending on the dish.

We call for pork lard in some recipes because it adds a flavor that a relatively bland vegetable oil just cannot.

Maque Choux: A sweet and highly seasoned corn dish. Some variations of maque choux are chicken maque choux and crawfish maque choux, both of which Mom Prudhomme used to make. The family also like to make maque choux soup. Pronounced mock-*shoe*.

Margarine: Margarine is not a substitute for butter, but there are times when margarine tastes better in a particular recipe. Bobby and others in the family also sometimes make roux with margarine instead of vegetable oil or pork lard. Paul often uses a combination of margarine and butter (or oil and butter) when he wants a buttery taste but is cooking with too intense a heat to use butter alone.

Measurements: Although the Prudhommes (to a person!) do not precisely measure ingredients (or, to be truthful, do not measure at all unless coerced, as for the cookbook recipes), when we retested each recipe in Paul's test kitchen (at least once and usually several times), we used calibrated measuring spoons, glass measuring cups (for liquids), and metal cups (for dry ingredients). Measurements in the recipes are always *level* unless otherwise specified.

    Flour: All flour in our recipes is *un*sifted unless specified sifted.

    Oven temperatures: When we give oven temperatures, we always mean a *preheated* oven.

Milk, Evaporated and Condensed: These two milk products are quite different: *Evaporated milk* contains about 74 percent water (whole milk contains about 87 percent), and sometimes it's desirable to have milk in this concentrated form. *Condensed milk* contains about 27 percent water, and it is usually sweetened with sugar. Its primary use is in desserts.

    Paul believes that the evaporated milk of today is much like Mom Prudhomme's canned milk, which she made from fresh cow's milk, so some of the recipes call for evaporated milk. Mom canned milk to take advantage of the times when the cows were producing a lot of milk—when they had new or young calves—and good milk. (At some times of the year, the cows ate bitterweeds, which grew periodically in the pasture, and the milk would take on the bitter taste and be undrinkable.) She cooked the fresh milk just long enough to reach the boiling point, then poured it into sterile jars, sealed them, and stored them in a dry place. Cream rose to the top of the canned milk just as it does on fresh milk. The shelf-life was two to three months.

Oil: When vegetable oil is specified in a recipe, any fresh (unused) cooking oil is acceptable. Paul generally prefers to use peanut oil for deep frying, especially when using a batter on the food; it gives a nutty taste more quickly than other liquid oils. He recommends vegetable oil for most pan frying, however, unless you specifically want to add the flavor that butter or pork lard imparts.

Use only fresh oil. The molecules in fresh oil are close together and relatively inactive. Food dropped into fresh hot oil acts like an irritant to the oil, which responds very quickly by immediately sealing the batter on fried foods or the surface of unbattered foods such as French fries. Then the oil cannot get to the food inside. All crumbs, drops of batter, salt, or water that fall or are released into the oil during frying separate the molecules and therefore weaken the oil's ability to seal the breading or batter. As a matter of fact, simply heating oil in the first place begins to break it down, and the more you reheat it, the less like the original oil it is. That's why you should change oil frequently, instead of putting it aside to be used again.

Okra: The Cajun name for okra is gombo févi, a popular vegetable in the southern states, brought over to this country by African slaves, who hid the seeds in their hair. The taste is wonderful, and it is served steamed, boiled, fried, pickled, or smothered with other vegetables like tomatoes and onions. In addition, it is used as a thickener in gumbos, soups, bisques, and stews. Okra varieties differ considerably in appearance, texture, and slipperiness—people who don't like this characteristic call it sliminess. Okra pods can be white or reddish in color, but are usually different shades of green. Sizes of pods range from one to eight inches long (the baby ones are just fantastic steamed!), and the pods can be soft to firm and smooth to deeply grooved. Much of today's okra, at least that grown in the United States, is a hybrid bred to reduce the slippery quality. There are cooking methods, too, that can eliminate this trait, but many southerners *like* to eat it slippery.

Ouaouaron: Frog. Another wonderful word. It sounds like the croaking of frogs. Try saying, fast: ooah-ooah-*rrow(n)*. See page 99.

Oysters: Louisiana oysters are wonderful!—but it's more important for oysters to be fresh than for them to come from Louisiana waters. If there are good native oysters where you live, those are the ones you want. If you buy shucked oysters in their liquor and the liquor is not called for in a recipe, be sure to reserve it when you drain the oysters and use it promptly in a seafood stock or in a cream sauce. It's far too delicious to waste.

Paunce Bourré: The Cajun term for stuffed pork stomach. The family always smoked paunce bourré, although not all Cajuns do. Pronounced pons-boo-*ray*.

Pecans: Pecans are usually specified in the recipes as "dry roasted." This is important for flavor. (And so is freshness.) Place shelled pecans—halves or pieces—in a large *un*greased roasting pan and roast in a 425° oven for 10 minutes, stirring occasionally. Mom Prudhomme roasted pecans in a cast-iron skillet outdoors over an open fire. The roasted pecans may be added either hot or cold to the other ingredients (unless a recipe specifies one or the other), and they can be stored in a covered container in the refrigerator.

Roasting gives pecans extra flavor by bringing the sugar and oil in them to the surface. When you roast chopped pieces rather than whole halves, much more of the surface is in contact with the heat of the pan. So, if a recipe calls for roasted pieces, chop up pecan halves *before* roasting. Recipes call sometimes for pieces, sometimes for halves, but it's worth remembering that shelled pecans packaged in pieces usually cost less than halves.

Peppers: Black (ground), red (ground cayenne and peter peppers), cayenne (fresh), banana (fresh), and bell peppers (fresh) were staples in Mom Prudhomme's kitchen in the early years. And later, the family began using other hot peppers like jalapeño, Tabasco, finger, and bird's-eye also. Paul uses all these, along with ground white pepper and other fresh varieties like serrano and poblano, at his restaurant.

With the exception of black pepper—which was bought in the form of peppercorns and ground in a coffee mill—the family grew all the peppers they used. Allie vividly remembers the peter peppers: "Talk about hot—just looking at them would burn your eyes!" And that was literally true, because the semitropical Louisiana sun beating down on the peppers caused them to emit fumes. The family roasted peter peppers in the oven, then took them outside to grind so the fumes wouldn't be in the house. Most of the family believe that the use of hot red pepper is a distinguishing characteristic of Cajun cooking. They also feel that hot red peppers have been so misused throughout the country that many people are understandably hesitant to use them. The family unanimously assert that if everyone could taste hot red peppers properly cooked, we'd have more exciting food cooked all over the nation. As you can tell by glancing through the recipes, peppers, especially ground red, are ever present!

There are many benefits of peppers, and of course "heat" is one of them. But the ultimate purpose of peppers is to achieve flavors, and these flavors are sensations in the palate that come at different times—when you first put a bite of food in your mouth, when you're chewing it, after you've swallowed it. Each kind of pepper works differently, and when they are balanced correctly, they achieve an "after-you-swallow" glow. They are also played off against the other ingredients in a dish. For example, in many recipes such as stuffings and sauces, we use the method of long cooking times of vegetables to bring out their natural sugars, which contrast so well with the peppers. And, as you'll note, we really *cook* the peppers, in particular ground red pepper, and this produces an entirely different result (a wonderful exciting taste) from adding a raw taste of pepper at the end of a dish (a painful burning sensation). Red pepper is so important to the family that they are still giving Paul a hard time for not talking more about it in his first book!

Po Boy: A very popular sandwich in New Orleans and other parts of South Louisiana, always made with French bread. The first po boy was created during the Depression years at a New Orleans bar located along the streetcar tracks near the Mississippi riverfront. Many longshoremen bought their lunch there, and the owner created a long sandwich big enough to fill a hungry working man and cheap enough for the "poor boys" in the depressed riverfront area to be able to buy them. They are a classic now. When the rounded heel ends of the loaf are used, part of the bread is plucked out and the hollow is slathered with flavored mayonnaise and stuffed with fried seafood; then it's called a "loaf" rather than a po boy. In addition to the traditional fixings used on other sandwiches, po boys are made with a glorious array of different ingredients: fried fish, fried shrimp, fried crawfish, fried oysters, fried softshell crabs, andouille and other smoked sausages, meatballs, roast beef and gravy, smothered potatoes, and mashed potatoes. And Paul is noted for making unusual and wonderful po boys with oysters Bienville, fish sauce piquant, and deep-fried smoked chicken breast.

Praline: The Louisiana praline is a candy patty popular in the South, made with sugar (especially brown sugar), nuts (especially pecans) or seeds, and sometimes butter and/or cream. Down here in Louisiana, praline is pronounced praw-*lean*. (Listen for the pronunciation and you'll be able to differentiate natives and tourists in South Louisiana.)

Rabbit: We strongly recommend that you use fresh rabbit, if possible. The popularity of the rabbit dishes at Paul and K's restaurant and in other restaurants throughout the country has resulted in more fresh rabbit being available, and frozen cut-up rabbit has been widely distributed for some years. Wild or game rabbit is quite different from domestic rabbit in taste and tenderness; the meat has a more distinctive taste and often is very tough. Louisianians marinate wild rabbit meat in an herbal oil and vinegar (or lemon) mixture to remove the gamy taste (the vinegar and/or lemon also help tenderize it), and then smother the meat in an etouffée. Game rabbit, too, is better when it is fresh, not frozen, but the Prudhomme family and many other Louisianians hunt for rabbit during the fall and winter and freeze the meat to use throughout the year.

Roux: A roux is a mixture of flour and oil. The cooking of flour and fat together to make roux is a process that seems to go back as far as the Prudhomme family ancestors of four hundred years ago. Traditionally, the fat used was animal fat (usually pork lard), although today various oils are used, and the roux was, and often still is, made by very slow cooking. Mom Prudhomme used to start with a paste of animal fat and flour and cook it for several hours. Paul remembers standing at the stove helping to stir the pot. Probably because of those memories, Paul over the years developed a way to cook roux so it can be made in a matter of minutes, over very high heat, and with very few exceptions, this is the method used in this book's recipes.

The basic reason for making a roux is for the taste and texture it lends to food. The taste and texture of roux are characteristic of many dishes that Louisiana Cajuns make. In fact, most of the Prud-homme brothers and sisters feel that knowing how to cook a roux is indispensable in Cajun cooking.

The first few times, making roux may seem difficult, and, cer-tainly, stirring together oil and flour at a temperature of about 400° has an element of danger in it. However, once you've made roux several times and become accustomed to handling the high tem-perature, you will find it to be extremely rewarding because of the uniqueness of the finished product—and, as lagniappe, you're sure to get praise from everyone who tastes your cooking!

How to Make a Roux

A few overall points may be helpful:

The usual proportion of oil to flour is fifty-fifty.

Roux can be made in advance, cooled, and then stored in an airtight jar for several days, in the refrigerator or at room tem-perature. (If you use a cast-iron skillet or pot, remove the roux promptly from the pot once it has cooled thoroughly; otherwise, the roux will begin picking up the flavor of iron.)

If you make the roux ahead, don't add any vegetables to it that may be called for in recipes. Those vegetables can be omitted from the recipe or, if desired, added to the roux when it is reheated and before it is added to the finished dish. Or the vegetables can be added to the dish after stirring in the premade roux.

Pour off excess oil from the surface of the roux and reheat it (preferred); or let it return to room temperature before using. For best results, add premade roux by spoonfuls to boiling stock or liq-uids, stirring until the roux is blended in before adding more.

A good rule of thumb for the amount of premade roux to use is as follows: Substitute the *same* amount of premade roux as the amount of flour called for to make the roux in the recipe. For example, if a recipe calls for making a roux with ⅓ cup oil and *½ cup flour*, then substitute *½ cup roux* for the oil and flour.

Since the family don't normally follow recipes but quite often make roux ahead, they use premade roux this way: They usually start with a little less roux than they think the finished dish will need. Then, about 30 minutes before the dish is done, they stir in more roux, as needed, to get the flavor and consistency they want.

Cajun cooks view roux as being essentially of two types—medium brown and black. And they classify meats as basically of two types—heavy, dark, somewhat strong-flavored ones, and light, white, sweet ones. They traditionally use light roux with dark meats and dark roux with light meats. This is because they know intuitively, whether they can verbalize it or not, that these particular combinations lead to wonderful-tasting food.

Paul's use of roux is based on these same traditions. In general, he uses light and medium brown roux in sauces or gravies for dark, heavy meats such as beef, game like venison, and dark-meat fowl such as duck and geese. They give a wonderful, toasted, nutty flavor to these sauces and gravies. And he uses dark red-brown and black roux in sauces and gravies for sweet, light, white meats such as pork, rabbit, veal, and all kinds of freshwater and saltwater fish and shellfish. In addition, Paul likes to use black roux in gumbos because the darkest roux results in the thinnest, best-tasting gumbos of all. But it takes practice to make a black roux without burning it, and a dark red-brown roux is certainly acceptable for any gumbo.

You'll notice that the family makes exceptions to these general guidelines in some recipes. These exceptions simply reflect their own preferences for the flavor of a particular roux with the combined flavors of the other ingredients in certain dishes. For example, Paul prefers the flavor of a medium red-brown roux in Crawfish Bisque, which is a lighter color than the roux he uses in most other seafood dishes. Ralph likes a medium brown roux instead of a darker one in his Fresh Fish in Brown Gravy.

You'll find, as you gain experience and skill in making roux, that you'll want to experiment with the endless combinations of roux colors and the flavors of other ingredients—especially meat—to find those combinations that excite your taste buds the most.

Several words of advice are essential:

1. Cooked roux is called Cajun napalm by the cooks at Paul and K's restaurant because it is extremely hot and sticks to your skin. *So* *be very careful* to avoid splashing it on you. It's best to use a *long*-handled metal whisk or wooden spoon. We advise having both a whisk and wooden spoon handy so you can switch utensils quickly if you're having difficulty stirring with one of them.

2. Always begin with a very clean skillet or pot, preferably one that is heavy, such as cast iron (and never a nonstick type); the cast iron should be well seasoned. If possible, use a skillet or pot with flared sides (without angular corners) because this makes stirring easier and thus makes it less likely the roux will burn. In addition, use a large enough skillet or pot so that the oil does not fill it by more than one fourth of its capacity. We have found that the best all-around pot for making the amount of roux called for in most of our recipes is a 2-quart, cast-iron Dutch oven with flared sides. We often call for this type of pot in our recipes, although sometimes we specify other sizes and shapes because they work better in some recipes.

3. The oil should be smoking hot or just short of it before the flour is added.

4. Once the oil is hot, move promptly to add the flour, not only because the oil will eventually burn, but because the quality of the oil starts breaking down as it continues to heat. Stir in the flour gradually (about a third at a time) and stir or whisk quickly and *constantly* to avoid burning the mixture. (Flour has moisture in it, and adding it to hot oil often creates steam—another good reason for using long-handled whisks or spoons.)

5. If black specks appear in the roux as it cooks, it has burned; discard it (place it in a heatproof container to cool before discarding), then start the roux over again—*c'est la vie!*

6. As soon as the roux reaches the desired color, remove it from the heat. Unless you are making the roux ahead, stir in any vegetables called for (they help to stop the browning process and enhance the taste of the finished dish), and continue stirring until the roux stops getting darker, usually about 3 minutes.

7. While cooking roux (bringing it to the desired color), if you feel it is darkening too fast, immediately remove it from the heat and continue whisking constantly until you have control of it; don't ever hesitate to do this. And lower the heat whenever you feel it is necessary.

8. Occasionally, every member of the family (even Paul!) has trouble with a roux not coming out just right—that is, it "breaks" instead of dissolving when it hits hot stock or water. This doesn't happen often, and it is always surprising and somewhat perplexing when it does. We are not sure of all the reasons, but it seems most often to be related to variations in the moisture and gluten contents of flour at different times of the year; even batches of flour with the same brand name can vary. And there are also regional variations in flour that may account for some of the problems. We've also noticed that we can predict when we're running into trouble with a roux if, during the final stages of cooking it, we see a *blue* smoke coming off the roux surface instead of the clear smoke you see when oil is just beginning to smoke. When a roux breaks for us, even after trying it for a second time, we find it's best to use less intense heat or change to a different brand of flour. And if this happens repeatedly during a certain time of the year, you may want to do what Paul's roux makers at the restaurant do—switch to using a high-gluten flour for a while.

9. Care and concentration are essential for you to be successful with this fast method of making roux. Especially the first few times you make a roux, be certain that any possible distractions—including children—are under control. In addition, have all cooking utensils and required vegetables or seasoning mixtures prepared ahead of time and near at hand before you start cooking.

Sauce Piquant: Piquant to a Cajun means "it's hot and 'hurts like a sticker in your tongue.'" Sauce piquant is a favorite family dish made with any type of fish, meat, fowl, game, or seafood. If you don't hover between pleasure and pain when you eat it, chances are you haven't made your sauce piquant hot enough!

Seasoning Mixes: Many of the recipes in this book have ingredients listed under the separate heading of **Seasoning mix.** When all the seasonings are well combined together ahead of time in a small bowl, they are convenient to handle and to distribute evenly in a dish as you cook it. You just measure out portions of the mix with measuring spoons (measure *level*)—rather than having to measure different amounts of each seasoning for different steps in the recipe—and the final amount of each seasoning is controlled. It's not unusual for Paul's recipes to have eight or more seasonings, and many of the other family members use several, too; so you can see that measuring them needs to be convenient if it's going to be right.

The seasoning mixes in this book are specially calibrated for every recipe. In Paul and K's restaurant they use Louisiana Cajun Magic®, the brand name of seven different blends of herbs, spices, and salt, which Paul created for different kinds of foods. He made the blends originally to teach his cooks to produce a *consistent* taste each time in dishes cooked to order. Cajun Magic is now distributed nationally.

Shrimp: Shrimp with their heads as well as shells are readily available in Louisiana and are becoming more widely available in many parts of the country, especially in the South and on both coasts. If possible, buy shrimp with heads on and use the heads and shells to make seafood stock. If you can't purchase shrimp with heads on, buy the tails unshelled—which is possible almost anywhere—and use the shells for stock. Shrimp fat, the orange substance in the heads, makes shrimp dishes rich, full, sweet tasting, and wonderful!

Shrimp are not a substitute for crawfish, but many Louisiana recipes work well with either shellfish. All recipes assume fresh, uncooked shrimp. Never use frozen shrimp.

Slow Sandwich: Our term for any uninteresting sandwich that leaves you wishing you hadn't wasted the calories—and we do suggest a remedy: **Ground Hot Pepper Vinegar Mayonnaise** (page 335). There is no Cajun French translation for slow sandwich because Cajun cooking *never* leaves you wishing you hadn't wasted the calories.

Squirrel: There are no domestic squirrels raised for meat and sold commercially, which means you'll need to be a hunter, or know one, to have squirrel meat. As with both wild and domestic rabbit, we strongly recommend you use it immediately fresh rather than freezing it, though families in rural areas do hunt squirrel and freeze the meat to use throughout the year. Squirrels are not very meaty, but they are very tasty. They add a unique and excellent flavor to gravies, gumbos, and jambalayas.

Stocks: Cooking with stocks definitely gives depth, adds new dimensions, and makes more exciting the taste of almost any dish. And especially when the time is taken to make a *rich* stock, it can actually make the difference between a good dish and a fantastic one. So, the general rule of thumb is to use stock whenever possible. In some rare cases, however, we have found the reverse to be true—that is, it's better to use water—so we occasionally call for using water instead of stock in a recipe. For example, the gravy in Elden and Odelia Mae's Meatballs in Brown Gravy is actually *too* rich when made with stock. Paul always tells people who ask him for one simple key to better cooking that they can improve their cooking dramatically by using stocks rather than water, and he encourages them to use them even for vegetables and rice.

Making stock is simple. Use the ingredients you commonly have in your kitchen. Whenever possible, use the meat or poultry bones, seafood shells or carcasses, and vegetable trimmings that are provided by the ingredients in the recipe you are making. But it's also easy to purchase at a very reasonable price such stock-making items as chicken backs and necks, beef marrow or soup bones, pork neck bones. And if you have a fish market available, you should easily be able to obtain fresh fish carcasses.

When possible, use shrimp stock in shrimp dishes, rabbit stock in rabbit dishes, beef in beef dishes . . . but you *can* make substitutions such as a general seafood stock for shrimp stock, beef stock for turtle stock, and chicken stock for rabbit stock. And you may develop personal preferences as you experiment; for example, we like the taste of seafood stock with alligator meat and chicken stock in frogs' legs dishes.

There are very few no-no's when making stocks: Don't use bell peppers, spices, or livers. There is no set rule regarding amounts of ingredients to use in making stock, but we've provided proportions that work well. Because stock is really quite simple to make, you can multiply at will the ingredients for the basic 1-quart recipe if you need just a few quarts of stock. Use the large-yield **Basic Turducken Stock** recipe, page 115, as a general guide when making extra-large quantities of stock.

To Make 1 Quart of Basic Stock

About 2 quarts cold water
Vegetable trimmings from the recipe(s) you are cooking, *or*
1 medium onion, unpeeled and quartered

1 large clove garlic, unpeeled and halved
1 rib celery
Bones and any excess meat (excluding livers) from
    meat or poultry, or shells or carcasses from
    seafood, used in the recipe(s) you are cooking, *or*

For Fowl and Game Stocks: 1½ to 2 pounds backs,
    necks and/or bones from chickens, guinea hens,
    ducks, geese, rabbits, etc.

For Beef or Turtle Stock: 1½ to 2 pounds beef
    shank (preferred) or other beef or turtle bones

For Pork Stock: 1½ to 2 pounds pork neck bones
    (preferred) or other pork bones

For Seafood Stock: 1½ to 2 pounds rinsed shrimp
    heads and/or shells, or crawfish heads and/or
    shells, or crab shells (2½ to 3 quarts), or rinsed
    fish carcasses (heads and gills removed), or any
    combination of these. (You can substitute oyster
    liquor for all or part of the seafood stock called
    for in a recipe.)

NOTE: If desired, you can first roast meat bones and vegetables at 350° until thoroughly browned, then use them to make your basic stock. When you brown the bones and vegetables, the natural sugar in both caramelizes on the surface, which gives the stock a fuller taste and adds color when it dissolves in the stock water.

Always start with *cold* water—enough to cover the other ingredients. Place all ingredients in a stockpot or a large saucepan. Bring to a boil over high heat, then gently simmer at least 4 hours, preferably 8, replenishing the water as needed to keep about 1 quart of liquid in the pot. The pot may be uncovered or you can set a lid on it askew. Strain, cool, and refrigerate until ready to use. **NOTE:** Remember, if you are short on time, that using a stock simmered 20 to 30 minutes is far better than using just water in any recipe.

To Make a Rich Stock

Strain the basic stock, then continue simmering it until evaporation reduces the liquid by half or more. For example, if your recipe calls for 1 cup of rich stock, start it with at least 2 cups of strained basic stock. Rich stocks are needed when a sauce requires lots of taste but only a limited amount of liquid. They are also excellent for general use.

Tasso: A very highly seasoned, intensely smoked Cajun ham. Pronounced *tah*-so.

Ti Salé: A type of salt pork preserved with salt that has ground red pepper mixed in with it. See page 17. Pronounced tee-sah-*lay*.

Tomato Sauce: In all recipes calling for canned tomato sauce, we used *un*seasoned canned crushed tomatoes or tomato sauce.

Turducken®: Paul and K coined the term by combining the names of the fowl in this dish: turkey, duck, and chicken. It is served at their restaurant every Thanksgiving—and it is awesome!

Turtle Meat: In Louisiana, turtle meat (both fresh and frozen) is available in many seafood markets and specialty food stores. If it's scarce in your area, try Chinatown markets before you give up looking for it. In South Louisiana, turtle meat is sold boned or bone-in, and often the meat is repacked in the shell. See page 103.

Utensils: Paul believes that there are very few occasions when the pot or pan is going to make a tremendous difference in the quality of the finished dish, and the rest of the family heartily agree. The recipes give advice, when necessary, and cast-iron or other heavy pots are often recommended. No cook likes thin "tinny" equipment. But Paul's advice to a new beginning cook in the kitchen is exactly what his brothers and sisters would say: Spend your time and money looking for the best ingredients you can find. Then, as you become more at ease with cooking and with handling ingredients, you can consider more expensive and sophisticated equipment. Although all the family members take pride in their pots and pans, it wasn't until later in life that most of them could afford anything fancy or expensive. It was always the food and the respect they showed it that counted most, and it still does. As Paul says, if you're accustomed to your pots and pans—whatever they're made of—you know what to expect from them and these will be the most successful to use in your own kitchen. However, he recommends *not* using nonstick skillets and pans unless specifically called for.

BREADS & BREAKFAST

PAINS ET DÉJEUNERS

ELI AND SUE'S RECIPE

Crusty Houseboat Biscuits

Makes about 16 biscuits

Eli says the family usually ate homemade breads for breakfast and for supper, and they usually had fresh butter, syrup, and milk with them. Eli doesn't cook a lot at home; he does most of his cooking on their houseboat. He doesn't camp so much now, but at one time he and four or five friends went to the houseboat to fish and duck hunt almost every weekend. He usually cooks rabbits, ducks, alligator, frogs, and fish at the houseboat, and he always makes biscuits to go with whatever he cooks.

Eli's houseboat biscuits really look and taste "country." The recipe is actually Eli's, but there's a friendly difference of opinion between Eli and Sue over who makes the best biscuits in the family. He first learned to make biscuits from Sue (which might account for the difference of opinion), but then he learned to make this variation. Eli starts cooking his biscuits on top of the stove and finishes them in the oven, which gives them extra crustiness on the bottom.

5¾ sifted cups self-rising flour, *in all* (see **NOTE**)
¼ cup sugar
3 tablespoons baking powder
1 teaspoon salt
¾ cup vegetable oil, *in all*
1¾ cups cold water
2 tablespoons unsalted butter, *in all*, melted

NOTE: Be sure to sift the flour, even if it's labeled "presifted."

Place oven shelf at highest level possible and preheat oven to 450°.

In a large mixing bowl, sift together *5 cups* of the flour with the sugar, baking powder, and salt; stir well. Very gradually dribble ¼ *cup* of the oil over the surface, just a few drops at a time, and gently mix oil droplets in until they make small balls of moist flour about the size of rice kernels before adding more; then stir until these "kernels" are well distributed throughout the mixture. Gradually add the water, stirring until well mixed, but do not overbeat.

Place ¼ *cup* more oil in a heavy 10½-inch skillet (preferably cast iron) and set aside.

Place the remaining ¾ *cup* flour in a medium-size bowl and set aside.

Divide dough in half. (You can leave both halves in the bowl. Each half is enough dough for a skilletful, or about 8 biscuits.) Working with one half of the dough, pinch off one eighth (a heaping ⅓ cup) and, with floured hands, shape into biscuits about ½ inch high and 3 inches in diameter. Dredge biscuits in the reserved flour, shake off excess, and arrange in a single layer in the skillet, placing 7 biscuits around the edge and 1 biscuit in the center. Turn biscuits over to coat both sides completely with oil, pushing them down a little if necessary so they will fit snugly together.

Place skillet over high heat and cook until oil is bubbling strongly and dough on bottom is starting to cook, 2 to 2½ minutes, being very careful not to let the biscuit bottoms scorch. (**NOTE:** If your burner produces a very high heat, this will take less time.) Immediately transfer skillet to the highest oven rack and bake at 450° until biscuits are done—light brown on top and evenly golden brown on bottom—about 14 minutes, being careful not to let bottoms burn. Brush *1 tablespoon* of the butter on top, turn biscuits over with a metal spatula, and cook until tops of biscuits (now on skillet bottom) have browned, 3 to 4 minutes more (see **Lagniappe**). Remove from oven and immediately turn biscuits over onto a plate. Serve immediately.

For the second batch, wipe the skillet clean, add the remaining ¼ *cup* oil to the skillet, and cook as you did the first batch. **NOTE:** If the biscuit bottoms on the first batch weren't nice and crusty, cook the second batch a few seconds longer on top of the stove before baking.

···············**LAGNIAPPE**···············
To test doneness, remove one biscuit from skillet; the bottom should be evenly golden brown and the inside should be cooked through and have a dense, cakelike consistency.

RALPH AND MARY ANN'S RECIPE

Ralph and Mary Ann's Cornbread
(Pain de Maïs)

Makes 8 servings

Each of the children had chores to do, and Ralph and Calvin (who were in the middle group of children) took turns, a week at a time, getting up to do the early morning work: First, they made a fire in the wood stove (and, if it was cold, another fire in the fireplace) and then ground the coffee beans. (Mom Prudhomme bought green coffee beans and parched them outside in a cast-iron skillet.) After taking Mom a cup of coffee (Dad didn't drink coffee), they started the cornbread for breakfast and went out to milk the cows.

The family ate cornbread for breakfast and for supper, never for dinner. Ralph can remember one year when they were so poor that they had hot chocolate made with water to drink and cornbread to eat for supper—and that was all.

One of Ralph's favorite memories (he remembers a lot about the early days) is of Dad making what he called "corn flakes." He would mix up a batter with cornmeal, rub a cast-iron skillet with lard, and heat the skillet until it was really hot. Then he'd take a little spoonful of the batter and drop it into the skillet and mash it flat. Ralph says the edges of the pieces would curl up just like corn flakes, and he declares, "They're one of the best things I've ever tasted." But he hasn't been successful in making them himself. He's certain of one thing— that Dad used water and not milk to make the flakes because "there were too many milk drinkers in the family to use much of it for cooking."

This is everything a true country cornbread should be—and it's delicious.

1 cup sifted yellow cornmeal
½ cup all-purpose flour
2 tablespoons sugar
1 tablespoon baking powder

1 teaspoon salt
½ teaspoon baking soda
5 tablespoons vegetable oil, *in all*
½ cup milk
¼ cup water
1 large egg

In a medium-size bowl, combine the cornmeal, flour, sugar, baking powder, salt, and baking soda, mixing well and breaking up any lumps. Add 2 *tablespoons* of the oil, the milk, water, and egg, stirring vigorously just until well beaten, 30 to 40 seconds. Do not overbeat.

Place the remaining 3 *tablespoons* of oil in an 8-inch cast-iron skillet; heat pan in a preheated 425° oven until oil is hot, about 2 minutes. Carefully remove hot skillet from oven and pour in the cornbread batter. Bake at 425° until done and golden brown, about 18 minutes. Then place under broiler about 2 inches from heat source and broil a few seconds until top is dark golden brown. Immediately turn bread over onto a serving plate and serve while still warm.

RALPH AND MARY ANN'S RECIPE

Golden Yeast Rolls
(Pain de Froment)

Makes 2 dozen rolls

The aroma of fresh yeast rolls baking reminds Mary Ann of her mom more than any other thing; she made yeast rolls every day, just as Mom Prudhomme did. Ralph loves to eat Mary Ann's yeast rolls with milk and with pear preserves on top, "just like at Mom and Dad's." And, like many of the other family members, he likes potato sand-

wiches, *especially if they're made with homemade yeast rolls. He loves to cut open a roll, spread cold* **Smothered Potatoes** *(page 299) on one side, and top them with the other piece of roll.*

These crusty rolls are easy to make. The bottom crust comes out essentially fried (delicious!) and contrasts nicely with the delicate, airy interior. And these rolls make a really special sandwich bread.

½ pound (2 sticks) unsalted butter
6 cups all-purpose flour, *in all*
2 (¼-ounce) packages dry yeast
¼ cup sugar
1½ teaspoons salt
2½ cups hot water (105° to 115°)
Vegetable oil or additional butter, to oil hands

Melt the butter in a small saucepan over medium heat. Remove from heat and let cool about 5 minutes. Skim foam from the top and discard. Pour into a large glass measuring cup and set aside in a warm place if not using immediately.

In a large mixing bowl, combine *2½ cups* of the flour with 4 tablespoons of the melted butter. (Ladle out and use the top butter-fat; don't use the butter solids at the bottom of the measuring cup.) Add the yeast, sugar, and salt, and mix with your hands until butter is very well distributed, using fingertips to break up lumps until mixture is the consistency of coarse meal with only very tiny lumps remaining. (This is an important step in getting the dough to rise properly, and it takes about 5 minutes.) Gradually add the hot water, stirring until the batter is free of large lumps. Stir in *3 cups* more flour, 1 cup at a time, mixing until flour is thoroughly incorporated before adding more. After the third cup is mixed in, stir vigorously about 1 minute more.

Turn dough out onto a flat surface floured with the remaining ½ *cup* flour; gently knead dough by hand for about 30 seconds. Place in a large greased bowl and then invert dough so top is greased. Cover with a dry towel. Let stand in a warm place (90° to 100°) until doubled in size, about 50 minutes. (Place in a slightly warmer place if dough hasn't doubled in 1 hour.)

Oil hands generously with oil or butter and spend a few seconds gently caressing down the dough (Mary Ann is a gentle person, so she doesn't punch down the dough) and coaxing it away from sides, continuing to oil hands as needed. Coat the bottoms of two 13 × 9-inch baking pans with 2 tablespoons each of the butter (use top butterfat). Pinch off dough to make 24 rolls. (An easy way to do this is to measure out a scant ¼ cup for each roll using a greased ¼-cup measuring cup; there's no need to shape the portions into rolls—the portions will smooth out as they rise and bake.) Place 12 rolls in each pan, arranging them evenly in the pan. Cover each pan with a towel. Let rolls rise just until almost doubled in size, about 30 minutes.

Bake at 350° until done and evenly golden brown on tops and bottoms, 30 to 35 minutes. (**Note:** After the first 15 minutes of baking, brush some of the remaining top butterfat on the rolls, using about 1½ teaspoons per pan.) Remove from oven and brush tops of rolls again, using about 1½ teaspoons more butter per pan. Serve while piping hot. Turn rolls over onto a plate to cool if not eaten immediately.

· · · · · · · · · · · · · ·LAGNIAPPE· · · · · · · · · · · · · ·

To test doneness, carefully remove one roll from pan; bottom should be evenly golden brown, and when bottom and sides are gently squeezed they should spring back into place. In high-humidity areas, store in paper bags or a bread box (instead of airtight containers) so the bread can breathe.

· ·

ALLIE AND ETELL'S RECIPE

Homemade Yeast Bread or Rolls
(Pain de Froment)

Makes 1 dozen large rolls or a
13 × 9-inch pan of bread

Mom Prudhomme made yeast rolls almost every day for dinner at midday, and all the family remember well that incomparable aroma of homemade yeast bread—there's no better smell. They also remember that they couldn't jump around in the house while the dough was rising; Mom was always afraid the rolls would "fall." Sometimes, when it was cold, she put the dough on the fireplace hearth to get it to rise.

Allie says she doesn't like to measure out ingredients for bread, she just likes to wing it. She remembers vividly the first cornbread she made with measured ingredients: "I would have thrown it out the door, but I was afraid it would hit a dog and kill it or at least break its legs."

This recipe makes wonderful, nice big rolls that can be eaten as rolls or sliced for bread. They're distinctly different from Ralph and Mary Ann's yeast rolls (see preceding recipe), not only because of their size, but also because they have a lighter crust and a slightly stronger yeast flavor. Be sure to try them the old-time way, with butter and cane syrup!

2 cups hot milk (105° to 115°)
1 tablespoon sugar
2⅛ teaspoons salt
2 (¼-ounce) packages dry yeast
6½ cups all-purpose flour, *in all*
6 tablespoons unsalted butter, melted
¼ teaspoon vanilla extract
1 tablespoon vegetable oil

In a large bowl combine the hot milk, sugar, salt, and yeast. Let sit 5 to 10 minutes; stir until yeast granules are thoroughly dissolved. Add *2 cups* of the flour, *5 tablespoons* of the butter, and the vanilla. Mix by hand until well blended and most of the flour lumps are broken up. Let sit about 15 minutes. Add *3½ cups* more flour and mix a few seconds by hand until blended, then continue mixing vigorously for 1 minute more.

Turn out onto a surface floured with the remaining *1 cup* flour. Knead by hand for about 2 minutes. Form into a smooth ball and place in a large clean bowl. Drizzle the oil on top of the dough and knead in the bowl about 30 seconds more; form dough again into a smooth ball. Cover with a dry towel. Let stand in a warm place (90° to 100°) until doubled in size, about 1 hour. (Place in a slightly warmer place if dough hasn't doubled in 1 hour.)

Punch down dough and divide into 12 equal portions (about 3¾ ounces each). Roll dough by hand into balls, making tops smooth by stretching dough and tucking edges under. Place in a greased 13 × 9-inch baking pan, pressing rolls down to fit snugly against each other and sides of pan. Cover with towel again and let rise until almost doubled in size, about 50 minutes.

Bake at 425° until golden brown on top, 20 to 25 minutes. Rotate pan, reduce heat to 300°, and bake until done, about 15 minutes more. Remove from oven and sprinkle a few drops of water on tops of rolls to soften the crust. Brush tops with the remaining *1 tablespoon* butter. Let cool 5 to 10 minutes before removing from pan, then turn rolls over onto a platter. You can serve them piping hot (and they're delicious), but we've found they are even better if you let them sit about 45 minutes.

· · · · · · · · · · · · ·**LAGNIAPPE**· · · · · · · · · · · · · ·

To test doneness, carefully remove one roll from pan; bottom should be evenly golden brown, and when bottom and sides are gently squeezed they should spring back into place. In high-humidity areas, store in paper bags or a bread box (instead of airtight containers) so the bread can breathe.

Couche-Couche

Makes 4 to 6 breakfast servings

Couche-couche is a simple, old-time breakfast food that has always been popular in Cajun country. The family had couche-couche for breakfast and occasionally for their evening meal, supper, which was always light.

Mom Prudhomme served couche-couche, which is basically a fried corn dough, with milk over it, and the family liked to add **Fig Preserves** *(page 349) or cane syrup. But Allie says the family's favorite way to eat couche-couche was with "caille" or clabbered milk— milk fresh from the cow that has sat at room temperature until it clabbers, that is until a white, rather thick, curdlike substance has formed on top. The top white part is caille; the bottom part is the whey, or water, which is discarded. Paul says caille is the first step in making cheese.*

Mom also made couche-couche with leftover cornbread, and Paul remembers that he always got to stir the pot. Debbie (Elden and Odelia Mae's daughter) fondly remembers Versie's couche-couche from when she was a little girl. Malcolm and Versie both say a cast-iron skillet is a "must" for cooking couche-couche. Be sure to read the **Lagniappe** *at the end of the recipe before you begin cooking to learn more about what to look for when making the bottom crust.*

2 cups yellow cornmeal
1 teaspoon salt
1⅔ cups hot tap water, *in all*
⅓ cup corn oil or other vegetable oil
Milk
Cane syrup or fruit preserves, optional

Combine the cornmeal and salt in a large bowl, mixing well. Gradually add *1⅓ cups* of the water, stirring until well blended. Set aside.
    In a large heavy skillet (preferably cast iron), heat the oil over

medium-high heat until hot, 4 to 5 minutes. (**Note:** If your burner produces a very high heat, turn it down a bit.) Carefully spoon the cornmeal into the hot oil and spread it evenly over the pan bottom. Cook *without stirring* (this is the key to success—*don't* stir!) until a thick well-browned crust forms on the bottom, 6 to 7 minutes, being careful not to let the mixture burn (see **Lagniappe**).

Once the thick bottom crust has formed, turn cornmeal over by forkfuls. Add the remaining ⅓ *cup* water evenly over the top and cook until no oil remains in the pan bottom and cornmeal is uniformly golden and fluffy, 3 to 4 minutes more, turning chunks occasionally and carefully with the fork so mixture stays lumpy. The finished couche-couche should still be quite moist.

Remove from heat and serve immediately in bowls with milk poured over the top. Add fruit preserves or syrup, if desired.

Note: To reheat leftovers, sprinkle a little water on top and reheat uncovered in a skillet.

·············LAGNIAPPE·············

The browned parts from the initial crust taste best and are really what make the dish so good, so be sure to disturb the mixture as little as possible until that first crust forms. Test crust by using a fork to lift up very small chunks from 3 or 4 different spots and peek underneath; make certain you press chunks back in place as quickly as possible. If the undercrust looks scorched, don't be alarmed—it may *look* charred, but probably is not. Taste it immediately and discard only any small spots that are bitter.

DARILEE AND SAUL'S RECIPE

Beignets

Makes about 2 dozen beignets

*A beignet is a fried doughnut that has no hole and is usually sprin-
kled with powdered sugar. Mom Prudhomme made beignets for
special occasions—like rainy days or to serve with coffee for special
company at night after supper. She didn't serve them with powdered
sugar. Darilee says Mom liked to have beignets with scrambled eggs
because they go so well together.*

*Our beignets make a wonderful snack or dessert. They're not as
sweet as most doughnuts, but you can sweeten them, as Darilee does,
with cane syrup: She puts a little syrup on each dessert plate first,
then puts the beignets to the side so each person can sop up the syrup
with them.*

*Beignets are a local and a tourist favorite in New Orleans, where
they're always served with powdered sugar on top. There is a famous
French Quarter café in New Orleans that serves beignets and café au
lait around the clock, twenty-four hours a day, seven days a week.
Beignets and café au lait make a fine breakfast and are the perfect
late-night ending to a special evening on the town.*

2 cups all-purpose flour
2 tablespoons baking powder
1 tablespoon sugar
1½ teaspoons salt
1 cup plus 2 tablespoons milk, *in all*
2 tablespoons vegetable oil
1 large egg
Vegetable oil for frying
Cane syrup, molasses, or powdered sugar, optional

In a large mixing bowl, combine the flour, baking powder, sugar,
salt, ½ *cup* of the milk, the 2 tablespoons oil, and the egg; mix until
well blended and any big lumps of flour and baking powder are

broken up. Add the remaining ½ *cup plus 2 tablespoons* milk, stirring vigorously until only tiny lumps remain and batter is the consistency of a pancake batter, about 5 minutes.

In a deep skillet or deep fryer, heat at least 1½ inches of oil to 350°. Slide batter by large tablespoonfuls into the hot oil (use another tablespoon to push batter off). Fry in single-layer batches until dark golden brown on both sides and centers are cooked, 4 to 6 minutes, turning at least once. Do not crowd. (Maintain temperature as close to 350° as possible.) Drain on paper towels and serve immediately as is, or with cane syrup or molasses, or sprinkled with powdered sugar.

ABEL AND JO'S RECIPE

Croquesignoles

Makes about 2 dozen doughnuts

Croquesignole, pronounced "crook-sin-yawl," means doughnut in Cajun French. These doughnuts have a wonderful cake texture, and if you have a sweet tooth they can be made sweeter by sprinkling them with powdered sugar or by glazing.

Mom Prudhomme and Jo's mom cooked these for special occasions or on rainy days when the families couldn't work in the fields. Jo learned this recipe from her mother, but Calvin says they are just like Mom Prudhomme's. She made them every March 19 for Calvin's birthday because he loved them—he still does! She made the other children their favorites, too, for their birthdays. When Mom got sick, Allie carried on the tradition of preparing a birthday dish for Calvin, but she switched from croquesignoles to a cherry cake.

6 tablespoons unsalted butter, melted and cooled
    slightly
1 large egg
1 tablespoon plus ½ teaspoon baking powder

1 teaspoon dry yeast
1 teaspoon vanilla extract
¼ teaspoon salt
¼ teaspoon ground cloves
¼ teaspoon ground nutmeg
¾ cup cane syrup
¼ cup evaporated milk
3 cups all-purpose flour, *in all*
Vegetable oil for deep frying
Glaze (recipe follows) or powdered sugar, optional

In a large bowl of an electric mixer, combine the butter, egg, baking powder, yeast, vanilla, salt, ground cloves, and nutmeg; beat on medium speed a few seconds until well blended, pushing sides down with a rubber spatula. Add the syrup and milk; beat about 2 minutes, pushing sides down as needed. Add 2¼ *cups* of the flour, half at a time, beating a few seconds on low speed until all the flour is mixed in; then increase speed to high and beat about 1 minute more.

Spoon the dough onto a flat surface floured with ½ *cup* of the flour. Flour your hands and knead dough fairly gently for about 1 minute. Add the remaining ¼ *cup* flour and knead about 1 minute more. Lightly flour board again, if necessary, then roll dough into a rectangular shape about ⅜ inch thick. Cut into rectangles 2 inches by 2½ inches. Score each rectangle twice, making each cut about 1 inch long.

Heat 1 inch of oil in a deep skillet or deep fryer to 375°. Carefully slide a single layer of the dough rectangles into the hot oil and fry until dark golden brown on both sides and cooked in the centers, about 4 minutes, turning at least once with a spatula. Do not crowd. (Adjust heat to maintain oil's temperature as close to 375° as possible.) Drain on paper towels. **NOTE:** If you prefer a crispier doughnut, fry at 350° for about 4 minutes; to get a cookie effect, fry at 300° for about 13 minutes.

If desired, glaze (recipe follows) or sprinkle with powdered sugar while still hot. Let sit, uncovered, about 1 hour before serving. Store, covered, at room temperature for the first 2 days, then refrigerate. (You surely will not need to know how to store them—they'll all be eaten quickly. But we thought we'd provide the information so that if an emergency arose—e.g., you had to leave town quickly, and didn't remember to put them in the suitcase—you wouldn't come home to stale croquesignoles!)

Glaze

½ cup powdered sugar
2 teaspoons evaporated milk, at room temperature
¼ teaspoon vanilla extract

Combine the ingredients in a small bowl, mixing well. Immediately spread on hot doughnuts. Makes enough to glaze 2 dozen doughnuts.

PAUL AND K'S RECIPE

Sweet-Potato Omelet

Makes 6 breakfast or light supper servings

It's best to use sweet potatoes when they're in season—July through November—when they're at the peak of flavor.

Seasoning mix:
1½ teaspoons salt
¼ teaspoon white pepper
¼ teaspoon onion powder
¼ teaspoon garlic powder
¼ teaspoon dry mustard
¼ teaspoon ground red pepper (preferably cayenne)
¼ teaspoon black pepper

2 (6- to 8-ounce) sweet potatoes, baked just until fork
    tender
1 tablespoon dark brown sugar
1 (5- to 7-ounce) white potato, baked just until fork
    tender
6 eggs
½ cup evaporated milk or heavy cream
⅓ cup chicken fat or vegetable oil
¾ cup diced tasso (preferred) or other smoked ham
    (preferably Cure 81)
½ cup julienned onions (see **NOTE**)
¼ cup julienned green bell peppers (see **NOTE**)
½ cup julienned yellow squash (see **NOTE**)
½ cup julienned zucchini (see **NOTE**)
½ cup shelled young sweet peas

NOTE: To julienne squashes, cut peelings ⅛ inch thick and cut these into strips ⅛ inch wide and 2 inches long; use only strips that have skin on one surface. Cut onions and bell peppers into similar strips.

Combine the seasoning mix ingredients thoroughly in a small bowl, breaking up any lumps.

Peel the baked sweet potatoes and cut into ½-inch dice; place in a small bowl and combine with the brown sugar, coating well. Peel the baked white potato, cut into ½-inch dice, and place in a separate bowl.

In a medium-size bowl, beat the eggs with a metal whisk until frothy. Mix in the milk or cream, blending well.

Meanwhile, heat the serving plates in a 250° oven.

In a 10-inch ovenproof skillet, 2 inches deep, heat the fat over high heat until hot, 1 to 2 minutes. Add the tasso and white potatoes and cook about 1 minute, stirring occasionally. Add the onions, bell peppers, and the seasoning mix and sauté about 3 minutes, stirring occasionally and scraping pan bottom well. Stir in the squash, zucchini, and peas and continue cooking about 3 minutes, stirring occasionally and scraping the pan bottom well. Stir in the sweet potatoes and cook and stir about 2 minutes more.

Whisk the egg mixture briefly again and add it to the skillet. Cook about 30 seconds while pushing the mixture toward the center of the pan with a spatula. Distribute all ingredients evenly in the pan, remove from heat, and place under a broiler, 4 to 5 inches from heat source. Cook until eggs are almost set and beginning to brown around the edges, about 2 minutes; the time will vary depending on how close your heat source is to the omelet. Remove from broiler and let pan sit a minute or two, so eggs will finish cooking by residual heat. Then serve immediately on heated plates.

DARILEE AND SAUL'S RECIPE

Café au Lait

Makes 2 (8-ounce) glasses

Darilee says that the family had this "café au lait" for breakfast and for supper at times when they didn't have enough milk and when they just couldn't afford to buy coffee. They browned the sugar first and added water to the mixture to stretch the little bit of milk they had. As you will see, the recipe contains no coffee.

Darilee says that while she was growing up (she is one of the first children) they never had coffee-milk or the traditional café au lait. Paul says that by the time he came along, Mom Prudhomme did serve the children real café au lait, but the mixture for them was about seventy-five percent milk, twenty-five percent coffee, and lots of sugar for lagniappe. The family served café au lait the traditional way, in glasses rather than cups.

Be sure to try this old-time Cajun version of café au lait. Then, if you'd like to make the real thing that is served in New Orleans, use your favorite dark-roast coffee (in New Orleans, the favorite is a blend of dark-roast coffee and chicory) and make it strong. *(South Louisiana coffee is so strong that people say the spoon will stand up in the cup.) Then put sugar in each cup (you'll want to use more than you normally do), and heat some milk (you need the same amount of milk as you have coffee) to the boiling point. Finally—and this is crucial—*

pour from the coffeepot and the milk pan both at the same time into the cups. If you pour it correctly, the café au lait should have a foamy head. Then, sit back and enjoy New Orleans café au lait.

One added touch that will make you feel you're in the heart of Louisiana: Serve the café au lait with **Beignets** (page 32).

2 cups milk, or 1½ cups evaporated milk mixed with
   ½ cup water
½ cup sugar

Place the milk (or evaporated milk and water) in a 2-quart saucepan and set aside.

Heat an 8-inch cast-iron or other small heavy skillet over high heat about 1 minute. Add the sugar and cook about 1 minute, stirring constantly. Reduce heat to medium high and cook about 3 minutes, stirring constantly, until sugar melts and turns to a rich bubbly brown. (Be careful not to overcook it or it will burn.) Carefully and quickly add the caramelized sugar to the milk (the milk will steam up and the sugar will crystallize). Place over low heat and cook until the sugar dissolves into the milk and mixture is hot, about 4 minutes, stirring constantly. Remove from heat and serve immediately.

· · · · · · · · · · · · ·**LAGNIAPPE**· · · · · · · · · · · · · ·
To clean the skillet easily, heat water in it; the sugar will dissolve in the water.

FISH & SEAFOOD

POISSONS

RALPH AND MARY ANN'S RECIPE

Fresh Fish Two O'Clock Bayou
(Poisson Frais de Bayou à Deux Heures)

Makes 2 to 3 main-dish servings

Ralph loves to fish for bass in Two O'Clock Bayou, and he named this dish for that special place. He cooks his catch of the day in his screened-in outdoor kitchen while Mary Ann prepares the rest of the meal inside the house.

Ralph says, "Mom made this dish, too, but I learned how to cook it from watching Dad. Dad was like a cat. He loved fish, him!" When Dad Prudhomme made it, he put in all the ingredients at once except the flour and then added just a pinch of flour at a time if he wanted to change the consistency of the gravy.

"When someone who doesn't like fish tastes this," says Ralph, "I'll tell you what, they come back for more!"

Fresh (never frozen) freshwater bass is delicate in flavor and delicious; we hope it's available in your area. If it isn't, use your favorite fresh (never frozen) freshwater or saltwater fish.

Seasoning mix:
½ teaspoon salt
¼ teaspoon plus ⅛ teaspoon ground red pepper (preferably cayenne)
¼ teaspoon black pepper

1 pound fresh white-fleshed fish fillets ½ to ¾ inch
thick, cut into about 4 pieces (see **NOTE**)
4 tablespoons unsalted butter
¼ cup very finely chopped onions
¼ cup very finely chopped celery
¼ cup very finely chopped green bell peppers
¾ cup hot **Rich Seafood Stock** (page 19; see **NOTE**)
1 tablespoon all-purpose flour

½ cup finely chopped green onions (tops only)
About 1½ to 2 cups hot **Basic Cooked Rice**
(page 252)

NOTE: If you fillet the fish yourself, save the bones to make the stock. Otherwise, buy an extra ½ pound of fillets for making the stock.

Combine the seasoning mix ingredients thoroughly and use a *rounded ½ teaspoon* of it to sprinkle lightly and evenly on both sides of the fish pieces. Let fish sit for 1 hour at room temperature. Reserve remaining seasoning mix to finish the dish.

In a large skillet, heat the butter over high heat until half melted. Add the onions, celery, bell peppers, and the *remaining* seasoning mix; sauté about 2 minutes, stirring occasionally. Add *½ cup* of the stock and the flour, stirring until well blended. Reduce heat and simmer until liquid is almost evaporated, about 3 minutes, stirring frequently.

Stir in the remaining *¼ cup* stock, then add the fish in a single layer and sprinkle the green onions evenly over the top. Cover and cook just until fish is cooked, about 5 minutes, shaking pan occasionally. Do not overcook. Remove from heat and serve immediately with rice, spooning some of the gravy over the fish and rice.

RALPH AND MARY ANN'S RECIPE

Fresh Fish in Brown Gravy
(Poisson Frais dans une Sauce Rouillée)

Makes 2 to 3 main-dish servings

Now that Ralph has retired, he fishes with a rod and reel for the sport of it and for the fresh fish. Even as a teenager he liked to go off by himself and fish with a cane pole for hours. Dad thought he was a little strange spending so much time in the woods alone hunting and fishing—and cooking whatever he caught—but Ralph also stump fished and barrel fished with Dad and the other boys.

Stump fishing is a little scary. Dad and the boys walked along the edges of streams, and, when they saw fish holes in the banks or in the ridged cypress tree trunks that reach down into stream or swamp water, they reached into the holes to pull out the fish. They just had to hope they'd get a fish and not a snake. Usually they got catfish, which like to burrow into the banks and hole up in the tunnels created by the cypress trees.

Barrel fishing requires an area of shallow, rather clear water (there were numerous spots like this near the family home) and a barrel with both ends open. Dad and the boys liked to barrel fish because it's simple, safe, and productive. Two boys held a barrel up until they spotted a fish, then they quickly shoved one end of the barrel down around the fish, pushing the barrel into the soft water bottom so the fish couldn't get out. Then they reached down and grabbed it.

Ralph uses freshwater bass in this recipe, and the bass stock he makes is exceptional. But use your favorite fish that is locally available, fresh, and has never been frozen.

Seasoning mix:
1¼ teaspoons salt
½ teaspoon ground red pepper (preferably cayenne)
⅛ teaspoon black pepper

¼ cup very finely chopped onions
About 5 cups hot **Rich Seafood Stock** (page 19; see
    Note)
⅓ cup vegetable oil
½ cup all-purpose flour
½ teaspoon very finely chopped garlic
½ cup finely chopped green onions (tops only)
1 pound fresh white-fleshed fish fillets ½ to ¾ inch
    thick, cut into about 4 pieces and at room
    temperature (see **Note**)
About 1½ to 2 cups hot **Basic Cooked Rice**
    (page 252)

NOTE: If you fillet the fish yourself, save the bones to make the stock. Otherwise, buy an extra ½ pound of fillets for making the stock.

Combine the seasoning mix ingredients in a small bowl and set aside. Place the onions in a bowl and the hot stock in a large measuring cup so each will be ready to add quickly when needed.

In a large heavy skillet with rounded sides, heat the oil over high heat for about 1 minute. Turn heat to low and use a long-handled metal whisk or wooden spoon to gradually stir the flour into the hot oil. Cook, whisking constantly or stirring briskly, until smooth; then cook about 1 minute, whisking or stirring constantly. Stir in the seasoning mix, increase heat to high, and cook until roux is medium brown, about 3 minutes more, whisking or stirring constantly and being careful not to let it scorch or splash on your skin. Immediately stir in the reserved onions and then gradually and carefully (it will steam up) stir in *4 cups* of the stock.

❋See page 12 for more about making roux.

Add the garlic and bring to a boil, continuing to stir until roux is well blended into the mixture. Reduce heat and simmer about 8 minutes, stirring and scraping pan bottom frequently. Add the green onions and cook about 5 minutes, stirring frequently. **NOTE:** If gravy gets extremely thick, thin it with a little more stock or water.

Add the fish in a single layer and coat all pieces well with gravy. Cover pan, reduce heat to low, and cook just until fish pieces are done, 8 to 10 minutes, stirring once or twice (stir gently so fish pieces won't break up) and scraping pan bottom well each time you stir. Do not overcook fish. Add a little more stock or water if gravy gets too thick, but the finished gravy should be creamy.

Remove from heat and serve immediately with rice, spooning some of the gravy over the rice and fish.

CALVIN AND MARIE'S RECIPE

Fresh Fish Sauce Piquant
(Sauce Piquante de Poisson Frais)

Makes 6 to 8 main-dish servings

Before Dad Prudhomme retired, he didn't believe in fishing with a cane pole or a rod and reel—it took far too long to catch enough fish to feed a family the size of his. By far the most productive method was to fish with a seine, a large rectangular net that has sinkers or weights along one side and floats along the opposite side. The net hangs vertically in the water and encloses the fish when the ends are brought together. One of Dad's brothers made him a seine about 100 feet long. Dad and one of the older boys held the seine by either end and swooped it down into the water, pulling it along for several yards, then they walked the seine, still in the water, to the shore and pulled it up and emptied it. The areas they fished in Cajun country were so dense with fish back then that the seine always held more than the family could use, so they could pick and choose the kind of fish and the size they preferred.

Calvin makes sauce piquant with all types of meat and game, and he also makes it with fish. Sauce piquant traditionally is made using a slow cooking method. He says that "when you cook sauce piquant, you should cook the vegetables and seasonings until you can no longer identify them." The sauce is even better if made a day ahead. Add the fish when you reheat the sauce and cook just until the fish pieces are cooked through. Calvin serves sauce piquant over rice and sometimes with French bread.

Calvin raises his own cayenne peppers and grinds them himself. His homegrown cayenne pepper is hotter than the cayenne we are able to buy. So, while we call for 1 tablespoon ground red pepper (store bought), Calvin uses only 1 teaspoon of his homegrown kind. Remember, "piquant" by definition has to be hot. This dish is so good, we want you to try it even if you insist on cutting the amount of red pepper in half!

This dish is cooked for fairly long periods of time over high heat. If

your gas burner or electric cooking element produces a very high heat, or if your pot is not a heavy one, you will need to adjust the temperature down.

3 pounds cleaned (heads removed), bone-in
    (preferred) gaspergou or freshwater or farm-raised
    catfish, or 3 pounds freshwater or farm-raised
    catfish fillets, or other freshwater or saltwater
    fish, cut crosswise into 2-inch pieces (see **NOTE**)

Seasoning mix:
1 tablespoon ground red pepper (preferably cayenne)
2½ teaspoons salt
2 teaspoons black pepper

2 cups finely chopped onions
1 tablespoon vegetable oil
1 tablespoon all-purpose flour
1½ cups finely chopped green bell peppers
½ cup finely chopped celery
¼ cup finely chopped garlic
3½ cups, *in all*, **Basic Seafood Stock** (page 18)
2 (8-ounce) cans tomato sauce
1 tablespoon lemon juice
Hot **Basic Cooked Rice** (page 252) or French bread

NOTE: If you can't get very fresh and never frozen (even for a few hours!) gaspergou, use freshwater or farm-raised catfish or your favorite local fish instead, because if gaspergou is even a few hours old, an oil taste, not unlike castor oil, develops as the fish cooks.

If you use gaspergou, rinse it well under cool water, making sure to wash away the black or red blood vessel that runs along the spinal column. (You can use a brush to remove it, and it's important to do so because it imparts a bad taste.)

    Thoroughly combine the seasoning mix ingredients in a small bowl. Sprinkle 2 *teaspoons* of the mix evenly on the fish, working it in with your hands and using it all. Refrigerate fish until ready to cook.

Place onions in a bowl and have handy to add to roux quickly when needed. In a heavy 6-quart saucepan, combine the oil with the flour, stirring until smooth; cook over high heat until roux is medium brown, 5 to 7 minutes, stirring briskly with a long-handled wooden spoon and being careful not to let it scorch or splash on your skin. Remove from heat and immediately add the onions, mixing thoroughly.

✳See page 12 for more about making roux.

Return to high heat and cook about 1 minute, stirring constantly. Add the bell peppers, celery, and garlic, stirring well. Add *1 cup* of the stock and the remaining *1 tablespoon plus 2½ teaspoons* seasoning mix, stirring well. Bring to a boil and continue boiling about 5 minutes, stirring occasionally and scraping pan bottom well. Reduce heat to low and stir in the tomato sauce; cook about 50 minutes, stirring occasionally and making sure mixture doesn't scorch. Add *1 cup* more stock and cook about 25 minutes, stirring occasionally. Add *1 cup* more stock, stirring well; cook and stir about 20 minutes. Stir in the lemon juice and cook and stir about 15 minutes.

Now add the fish, cover pan, and increase heat to high. Bring to a boil, stirring occasionally and being careful not to break up the fish. Stir in the remaining *½ cup* stock, reduce heat to low, and re-cover pan; cook about 20 minutes more (or a little longer if fish isn't cooked through at thickest parts), stirring occasionally. **NOTE**: Fish vary in the amount of water they give off. If the sauce is watery, remove the fish when it is done and let the sauce continue cooking uncovered a few minutes more.

Remove from heat and skim any fat from the surface. Serve immediately over rice or in bowls with French bread for dipping in the sauce.

ELI AND SUE'S RECIPE

Cajun Fried Catfish with Sweet Hushpuppies

(Barbue Frit avec des Boules de Pain de Maïs)

Makes 6 main-dish servings

Eli says that when the family wanted a good, big fish dinner, Mom and Dad loaded the fish, corn flour, pork lard, seasonings, and pots in the wagon, hitched up the horses, and headed for the woods near the house to cook. He says they ended up within rock-throwing distance of the house, but there was "just something about cooking fish outdoors."

Mom enjoyed these outings because Dad did the cooking. He and the boys cleaned the fish, used wire to hang a big pot from a tree limb, and built a wood fire under the pot. Dad determined when the pork lard was hot enough for frying by dropping a match into it; if the match lit, the lard was hot enough. Elden remembers Dad draining the fried fish on green moss. All the family agree that fish always seemed to taste better when it was cooked outdoors.

Eli and Sue's fried catfish has a nice crunchy crust. Sue fries it for an unusually long time by modern standards, which usually call for cooking fish just until flaky. We found her method makes the crust crunchier and keeps the fish moister for a longer time than quick frying. When we tested the recipe, we discovered that something we had found to be true about many vegetables was also true for fish— that they're delicious cooked for a very long time or a very short time, but they're really terrible cooked for a medium length of time or anything between long term and short term.

Eli and Sue's hushpuppy recipe is unusual in that the only liquid in the batter is from one egg; yet the hushpuppies come out wonderfully moist. Be sure to make the batter well ahead of frying the fish, since the batter needs to sit about two hours (but not more than three) before the hushpuppies are fried.

1½ pounds freshwater catfish fillets about ½ inch
    thick, cut into pieces 3 inches long
    Seasoning mix:
1 tablespoon garlic powder
2 teaspoons salt
1½ teaspoons black pepper
1 teaspoon ground red pepper (preferably cayenne)

2 tablespoons **Ground Hot Pepper Vinegar,** vinegar
    only (page 357)
2 tablespoons prepared mustard
1 large egg
1 cup milk
About 3 cups pork lard (preferred) or vegetable oil
    for pan frying
1½ cups corn flour (see **NOTE**)
Sweet Hushpuppies (recipe follows)

NOTE: Corn flour is available at most health food stores.

Place the fish pieces in a large bowl or pan. Combine the seasoning mix ingredients thoroughly in a small bowl. In a separate bowl, combine *1 tablespoon* of the seasoning mix with the Ground Hot Pepper Vinegar (vinegar only) and mustard, mixing well. Reserve the remaining seasoning mix. Spread the vinegar and mustard mixture evenly over the fish, working it in with your hands to coat all pieces well. Set aside.

In a medium-size bowl, beat the egg until frothy. Beat in the milk and *1 teaspoon* of the seasoning mix.

In a large plastic bag, combine the corn flour and the remaining *1 tablespoon plus ½ teaspoon* seasoning mix, mixing well. Soak one batch of fish in the egg and milk mixture for a couple of minutes, making sure all pieces are thoroughly coated. Add the fish pieces to the seasoned flour and dredge thoroughly. (Dredging the fish in a bag instead of in a pan or bowl seems to help more corn flour adhere to the fish, and that results in a thicker crust.) Let sit about 5 minutes.

Meanwhile, in a large heavy skillet, heat pork lard ½ inch deep over high heat to 300°. (If using vegetable oil, heat to 280°.) Add the fish to the hot lard without shaking off excess flour, making sure all fish pieces lie flat in the skillet. Fry until dark golden brown on the bottom, about 11 minutes in lard, or 16 minutes in oil. (Meanwhile, soak another batch of fish in the egg and milk mixture.) Turn fish and cook until second side is dark golden brown, about 6 minutes more for either lard or oil. Do not crowd. (Maintain temperature for lard as close to 300° as possible, and 280° for oil.) Drain on paper towels and serve immediately with the hushpuppies.

Sweet Hushpuppies

1 cup all-purpose flour
½ cup sugar
½ cup yellow cornmeal
2 tablespoons baking powder
¼ teaspoon salt
⅛ teaspoon ground red pepper (preferably cayenne)
1 cup very finely chopped onions
½ cup very finely chopped green bell peppers
½ cup very finely chopped green onions (tops only)
1 egg, beaten
Pork lard (preferred) or vegetable oil for pan frying

In a large bowl, combine the flour, sugar, cornmeal, baking powder, salt, and pepper; mix well, breaking up any lumps. Add the onions, bell peppers, green onions, and egg, stirring until thoroughly blended. **NOTE**: Mixture will be very dry at this point, but it will get moister as it sits. Cover and refrigerate for about 2 hours, but no longer than 3 hours or the batter will get too moist.

In a large skillet over high heat, heat lard ½ inch deep to 350°. (If using vegetable oil, heat to 330°.)

If using lard, slip the batter by tablespoonfuls (or use a small ice-cream scoop) into the hot lard and fry in batches until cooked through and dark golden brown on all sides, about 5 minutes total, turning at least once.

If cooking in oil, once the oil reaches 330°, turn off heat momentarily and slip the hushpuppies into the hot oil. Then turn heat to low and fry in batches until dark golden brown on all sides, about 4 minutes total, turning at least once. Continue for remaining batches, being sure to return lard to 350° each time, and oil to 330°.

Drain on paper towels and blot the tops with more paper towels. Serve while piping hot. Makes 2 to 3 dozen hushpuppies.

DARILEE AND SAUL'S RECIPE

Baked Fresh Fish with Crabmeat Red Gravy
(Poisson Frais Rôti avec une Sauce Rouge de Viande de Crabe)

Makes 8 to 10 main-dish servings

Mom baked fish occasionally, but the family preferred it fried. Darilee likes to bake fish in a spicy hot red gravy that she makes with her Cajun Home-Canned Spicy Tomatoes. The family always canned tomatoes while they were in season, and they added their own fresh cayenne peppers. Canning summer vegetables like tomatoes, corn, and beans was a major project for the family. Everyone helped. The married children usually came home to help and close friends of Mom's would also come for a day or two.

Make Darilee's red gravy (without the crabmeat) the day before you bake the fish.

Seasoning mix:
2¼ teaspoons salt
2¼ teaspoons ground red pepper (preferably cayenne)
1½ teaspoons black pepper

¼ cup vegetable oil
1 cup finely chopped onions

1 cup finely chopped green bell peppers

2 pints **Cajun Home-Canned Spicy Tomatoes** (page 359)

¼ cup finely chopped garlic

2 cups **Basic Seafood Stock** (page 18)

½ cup finely chopped green onions (tops and bottoms)

1 pound lump crabmeat (picked over)

5 (10- to 12-ounce) fresh white-fleshed fish fillets or
   steaks about ½ inch thick, cut in half crosswise
   (see **NOTE**)

2 tablespoons unsalted butter, melted

Hot **Basic Cooked Rice** (page 252), optional

NOTE: Use your favorite local freshwater or saltwater fish.

Combine the seasoning mix ingredients in a small bowl, mixing well. Set aside.

Combine the oil and onions in a 5½-quart saucepan or large Dutch oven; sauté over high heat until onions start to brown, about 6 minutes, stirring frequently. Stir in the bell peppers and *1 tablespoon plus 1 teaspoon* of the seasoning mix (reserve the remaining mix) and cook about 3 minutes, stirring and scraping pan bottom frequently. Add the tomatoes and garlic, stirring and scraping pan bottom well; cook about 3 minutes, stirring occasionally. Stir in the stock and green onions. Bring to a boil, stirring and scraping pan bottom occasionally. Continue boiling about 10 minutes, stirring occasionally.

Remove from heat and transfer mixture to a bowl. Let cool slightly, then cover and refrigerate until well chilled, preferably overnight. **NOTE:** It's important to have the sauce very cold or it will become too watery in the final cooking. Put it on ice to speed the process if you're in a hurry.

Place chilled sauce in a 17 × 11-inch ungreased pan (2½ inches deep). Gently stir in the crabmeat, being careful not to break up lumps and distributing crabmeat and sauce evenly in pan. Arrange fish on top in a single layer. Brush top of fish with the melted butter, then sprinkle with the remaining *2 teaspoons* seasoning mix. Bake at 475° just until fish is cooked (flaky) and sauce is heated through, about 20 minutes. Do not overcook. Remove from oven and serve immediately as is or with rice.

Shrimp Etouffée
(Etouffée de Chevrettes)

Makes 6 main-dish servings

Louisianians make shrimp etouffée when crawfish are not in season, and shrimp make a fine etouffée. The chief difference is that if the crawfish have a lot of yellow-orange fat on them, a crawfish etouffée is generally much richer.

"Etouffée" means smothered, and in Louisiana cooking it means covered with a liquid; but those are the only constants. Recipes for etouffée vary greatly in South Louisiana—even among members of the Prudhomme family. Some, like Paul, say an etouffée must have a cooked roux as a thickener; some, like J.C. and Sis, use cornstarch as a thickener; and some Cajuns we know use no thickener at all. Some of the family, like Calvin and Marie and J.C. and Sis, say etouffée must have tomatoes or a tomato sauce—and Calvin says Mom always used her homemade sweet tomato sauce in her etouffée; others, like Paul, say it does not contain tomatoes. And, of course, they all have their favorite seasoning vegetables. But you can be sure with Prudhomme family etouffées that they're all Cajun, they're all spicy, and they're all wonderful.

¼ pound (1 stick) unsalted butter
2 cups chopped onions
1 cup chopped celery
1 cup chopped green bell peppers
½ teaspoon minced garlic
1 tablespoon tomato paste
½ cup chopped fresh parsley
½ cup chopped green onions (tops only)
1½ teaspoons salt
¾ teaspoon ground red pepper (preferably cayenne)
¾ teaspoon black pepper

2 cups **Rich Seafood Stock** (page 19)
1½ pounds peeled medium shrimp
2 teaspoons cornstarch dissolved in 1 tablespoon
      water
3 cups hot **Basic Cooked Rice** (page 252)

Melt the butter in a 4-quart saucepan over high heat. Add the onions, celery, bell peppers, and garlic; sauté until onions start to brown, about 6 minutes, stirring occasionally. Add the tomato paste, stirring until well blended. Add the parsley, green onions, salt, and red and black peppers, stirring well; cook about 5 minutes, stirring frequently. Stir in the stock and bring to a boil, stirring occasionally. Reduce heat to maintain a simmer, cover pan, and cook about 25 minutes, stirring occasionally.

   Now add the shrimp and cook just until shrimp are pink, about 6 minutes, stirring occasionally. Add the cornstarch, stirring well. Turn heat to high and bring to a boil. Remove from heat and serve immediately over rice, allowing ½ cup rice and about ¾ cup etouffée for each serving.

CALVIN AND MARIE'S RECIPE

Crawfish Etouffée
(Etouffée d' Écrevisses)

Makes 4 main-dish servings

Mom Prudhomme made crawfish etouffée occasionally, but the family liked boiled crawfish best. "Crawfish boils" are huge get-togethers with lots of people and hundreds of pounds of boiled crawfish, and they are major social events in South Louisiana. There's nothing like them for good fun and good eating!

   Crawfish boils are virtually always held outdoors. The crawfish are cooked in big pots of highly seasoned boiling water. (There are commercial crawfish-boil mixtures of herbs and spices available, and some folks use a mixture of salt, red pepper, and fresh sliced or halved lemons or oranges.) Almost everyone adds small new red potatoes, corn on the cob, whole small onions, lots of garlic heads, and even smoked sausage to the seasoned water with the crawfish. Everything is boiled together and everything, including the garlic, tastes unbelievably wonderful. The crawfish are usually served on picnic tables covered with lots of newspaper or, as Mom and Dad Prudhomme did, on grass sacks spread on the ground. Forget about plates and silverware. The only way to peel crawfish is with your fingers, and you eat them as you peel them. Then all you need is a nice cold drink—icy cold beer is the favorite at Louisiana crawfish boils—and you're set for a feast.

Somehow you have to save enough crawfish to make crawfish etouffée the next day. Paul says etouffées are best made at the height of crawfish season, which usually begins in mid-March and lasts about eight weeks. That's when crawfish are at their best—when they're the fattest (and the fat is what makes a good crawfish dish superb), the texture is at its finest, and the taste is, as Paul says, "just spectacular!"

Calvin and Marie use catsup in their recipe because it is more like the home-canned sweet sauce that Mom used than any commercial tomato sauce. We made the recipe in our test kitchen with margarine and with butter and found that margarine produces a better taste for this particular recipe.

1 cup finely chopped onions, *in all*
2 teaspoons vegetable oil
1 tablespoon all-purpose flour

Seasoning mix:
1 teaspoon salt
½ teaspoon ground red pepper (preferably cayenne)
¼ teaspoon black pepper

6 tablespoons margarine, *in all*
⅓ cup finely chopped celery
⅓ cup finely chopped green bell peppers
2 teaspoons very finely chopped garlic
1 teaspoon catsup

2 tablespoons finely chopped green onions (tops only)
1½ tablespoons finely chopped fresh parsley
1 pound peeled crawfish tails
1 cup hot **Basic Seafood Stock** (page 18)
3 cups hot **Basic Cooked Rice** (page 252)

Place ⅓ *cup* of the onions in a small bowl and have handy to add quickly to the roux when called for.

Heat the oil in an 8-inch cast-iron skillet over high heat for about 1 minute. Stir in the flour with a long-handled wooden spoon until smooth. Continue cooking until the roux is medium brown, 1 to 2 minutes more, stirring vigorously and being careful not to let mixture scorch or splash on your skin. Remove from heat and immediately stir in the reserved ⅓ cup onions. Continue stirring until mixture stops sizzling, about 2 minutes.

✸See page 12 for more about making roux.

Thoroughly combine the seasoning mix ingredients in a small bowl and set aside.

In a heavy 5½-quart saucepan or large Dutch oven, heat *4 tablespoons* of the margarine over high heat until half melted. Add the remaining ⅔ *cup* onions, the celery, and bell peppers; cook until onions start to brown, about 6 minutes, stirring frequently. Reduce heat to low and add the roux, stirring until well blended. Add the garlic and catsup and cook and stir about 1 minute. Stir in the seasoning mix, the green onions, and parsley; cook about 2 minutes, stirring and scraping pan bottom frequently.

Now stir in the crawfish and sauté about 1 minute, stirring constantly. Add the hot stock and the remaining 2 *tablespoons* margarine and cover pan. Turn heat to high and cook until margarine is melted and mixture is hot, about 2 minutes, shaking the pan constantly in a back-and-forth motion (versus stirring). Do not overcook crawfish. Remove from heat and serve immediately over rice.

ABEL AND JO'S RECIPE

Cajun Fried Crawfish
(Écrevisses Frites)

Makes 3 to 4 main-dish or 6 appetizer servings

The older children say they didn't have crawfish very often when they were young, but Paul remembers having crawfish frequently when he was growing up. (One of his earliest memories is of pulling up his fishing line and finding a crawfish hanging on to the bait.) All the family liked crawfishing in nearby ditches and swampy areas, and Dad and the older boys seined for crawfish in the rice fields, where they flourish.

Paul says that when the season began, the family had fried crawfish two or three times right away. Then, when the crawfish got really fat, they had crawfish boils every Saturday afternoon. If there were any tails left over from a crawfish boil, Dad loved them fried, and he loved fried whole soft-shell crawfish for breakfast. Malcolm remembers this from when he was in the Korean War and brought his buddies home to visit. Paul likes to say that "a Cajun anticipates the beginning of crawfish season as much as he does his wedding night!"

Abel and Jo serve fried crawfish as an appetizer, for snacks, or as a main course with French fries or hot French bread. They are also very good mixed into a green salad for lunch. Their fried crawfish have a wonderful corn flavor and are nice and crunchy. Serve them with Ground Hot Pepper Vinegar Mayonnaise, if you like, because the pepper vinegar taste enhances the crawfish flavor in a special way. The mayonnaise is best made a few days before using.

Soaking Mixture:

1 cup evaporated milk
1 egg, beaten
1½ teaspoons ground red pepper (preferably
    cayenne)
1 teaspoon salt
½ teaspoon garlic powder

1 pound peeled crawfish tails

2 cups corn flour (see **NOTE**)

2 teaspoons salt

2 teaspoons garlic powder

1 teaspoon white pepper

1 teaspoon ground red pepper (preferably cayenne)

1 teaspoon black pepper

Vegetable oil for deep frying

Ground Hot Pepper Vinegar Mayonnaise (page
    335), optional

NOTE: Corn flour is available at most health food stores.

In a large bowl, combine the soaking mixture ingredients, stirring until thoroughly blended. Stir in the crawfish, being sure each is well coated. Cover and refrigerate overnight. (Stir occasionally.)

Remove crawfish from refrigerator, stir well, then let sit about 30 minutes at room temperature before frying.

Meanwhile, in a pan (pie and cake pans work well), combine the corn flour, salt, garlic powder, and the peppers, mixing thoroughly.

In a deep skillet or deep fryer, heat at least 1½ inches of oil to 385°. Just before frying, with a slotted spoon, drain any liquid from just enough crawfish to fry a small batch and place them in the flour mixture. Dredge well and let sit about 5 minutes in the flour. Then shake off excess flour and carefully slip crawfish one at a time into the hot oil. Fry until crawfish are cooked and well browned, about 5 minutes, stirring once to make sure crawfish aren't sticking together. Do not crowd. (Maintain oil's temperature as close to 385° as possible.) Drain on paper towels.

Repeat procedure with remaining crawfish. Serve immediately as is, or with Ground Hot Pepper Vinegar Mayonnaise.

ENOLA AND SHELTON'S RECIPE

Eggplant and Crabmeat Casserole with Cheese Sauce
(Casserole de Brème et Crabe avec une Sauce de Fromage)

Makes 6 main-dish or 18 appetizer servings

Mom Prudhomme cooked eggplant in the summer when it was fresh in the garden. She made eggplant dressing and smothered eggplant, and she cooked it in dirty rice and in fried ground beef. Enola often uses eggplant as a base for seafood casseroles, which she tops with cheese sauce. Store-bought cheese was a real rarity for the family, so it was an extra-special treat. Dad bought a five-pound stick of cheese once a year when he sold the first bale of cotton the family produced on the land they farmed as sharecroppers.

This casserole makes a fine appetizer, side dish, or main course. It is rich and spicy, so Enola and Shelton serve it with relatively bland foods, a roast chicken or vine-ripened tomatoes and a green vegetable. And we like to serve it on crisply fried slices of eggplant.

> **Seasoning mix:**
> 2⅛ teaspoons salt
> 1¼ teaspoons ground red pepper (preferably cayenne)
> 1 teaspoon black pepper
> ½ teaspoon garlic powder
> ½ teaspoon dried thyme leaves

¼ pound (1 stick) plus 2 tablespoons unsalted butter, *in all*
5 cups peeled and chopped eggplant, *in all*, about 1
    (1-pound) eggplant
2 cups finely chopped onions
3 cups thinly sliced mushrooms
2 cups finely chopped green bell peppers, *in all*

1¼ cups finely chopped celery, *in all*
1 teaspoon minced garlic
1¾ cups, *in all*, **Basic Seafood Stock** (page 18)
1 cup finely chopped green onions
About ½ cup very fine dry bread crumbs, *in all*
1 pound lump crabmeat (picked over)
Cheese Sauce (recipe follows)

Combine the seasoning mix ingredients thoroughly in a small bowl.

In a large skillet, melt *1 stick* of the butter over high heat until half melted. Add *3 cups* of the eggplant and the onions; sauté about 3 minutes, stirring occasionally. Add the seasoning mix, stirring well; cook about 6 minutes, stirring only occasionally and scraping pan bottom well each time you stir. **NOTE**: Be sure to allow sediment to stick to pan bottom before stirring; this browning gives a lot of flavor to the dish. If mixture sticks so much you're afraid it might burn, add 1 to 2 tablespoons of stock or water; but don't overdo the liquid—the mushrooms will throw off liquid quickly after they're added, which will make it easy to scrape off any remaining sediment.

Add the mushrooms, *1 cup* of the bell peppers, and *½ cup* of the celery, stirring and scraping pan bottom well. Cook about 8 minutes, stirring and scraping pan bottom frequently. Stir in the garlic and cook about 1 minute, scraping pan bottom as needed. Add *1 cup* of the stock, stirring until sediment on pan bottom is dissolved.

Now reduce heat and simmer about 10 minutes, stirring and scraping occasionally. Add the remaining *¾ cup* stock and cook and stir about 5 minutes. Add the green onions and the remaining *2 cups* eggplant, *1 cup* bell peppers, and *¾ cup* celery, stirring well. Stir in *4 tablespoons plus 2 teaspoons* of the bread crumbs and remove from heat.

Place the crabmeat in an ungreased 2-quart ovenproof casserole. Add the eggplant mixture, stirring well and being careful not to break up crabmeat lumps. Spread mixture fairly evenly in the dish and dot the top with the remaining *2 tablespoons* butter; then sprinkle the top evenly with the remaining *3 tablespoons plus 1 teaspoon* bread crumbs. Bake at 350° for about 25 minutes. Then increase oven temperature to 475° and continue baking until bubbly dark brown on top, about 15 minutes more.

Meanwhile, make the Cheese Sauce and set aside at least 5 minutes. Then serve immediately.

To serve, the prettiest presentation is to broil individual portions as follows: Mound each serving of the casserole mixture in the center of an individual heat-resistant serving dish and top with sauce. Place the dishes under a hot broiler for a few seconds until the sauce is brown and bubbly. Or simply serve the sauce (thinned if necessary, as described below) spooned on top of portions of the casserole mixture. Allow 1 cup of the casserole and 6 tablespoons sauce for a main-course serving and one-third that amount for an appetizer.

Cheese Sauce

¼ pound (1 stick) unsalted butter
3 tablespoons all-purpose flour
½ cup finely chopped onions
½ teaspoon salt
½ teaspoon onion powder
½ teaspoon garlic powder
½ teaspoon ground red pepper (preferably cayenne)
1 cup **Basic Seafood Stock** (page 18)
1½ cups (one 12-ounce can) evaporated milk, plus
    extra milk or water to thin the sauce
1½ cups grated Cheddar cheese

In a large skillet, melt the butter over medium-low heat. Add the flour and stir until smooth. Add the onions, salt, onion powder, garlic powder, and red pepper. Increase heat to high and cook about 3 minutes, stirring occasionally. Add the stock and the 1½ cups of milk; bring to a boil, stirring frequently. Reduce heat to maintain a strong simmer and cook until mixture thickens and flour cooks, about 8 minutes, stirring almost constantly so mixture doesn't scorch.

Remove from heat and add the cheese, stirring until cheese is melted. Let sit until casserole finishes baking. **NOTE:** If sauce gets too thick as it sits, thin with more evaporated milk (preferred) or milk or water—and gently reheat. Makes about 2⅔ cups.

Cajun Shrimp and Crabmeat Spaghetti

(Macaroni avec Chevrettes et Viande de Crabe)

Makes 6 main-dish servings

Calvin and Marie are avid campers. They belong to two camping groups, "The Cruising Cajun Club" and "The Retiree Club," and they've camped all over the United States in their new motor home. One of the things they most enjoy about camping is "spreading the good taste of Cajun" around the nation. It's not unusual for them to prepare gumbos, jambalayas, and sauce piquants for old and new friends while they're camping, and they love to share recipes. Several campground managers have given them standing invitations to come back because they love the "lagniappe" of Calvin and Marie's gumbos and jambalayas and sauce piquants.

A few years ago on a trip near the Louisiana Gulf coast, they spent the day crabbing and shrimping with other camping friends, and the group caught dozens of big blue Louisiana crabs and many pounds of fat Louisiana shrimp. That evening everyone got together and cooked a huge pot of shrimp and crabmeat spaghetti with the fresh-from-the-Gulf seafood. Calvin and Marie knew immediately that they had discovered a great new recipe to share around the country.

The sauce is best if made a day or so in advance, but don't add the shrimp and crabmeat. When you reheat the sauce, add the seafood and cook just until the shrimp are pink and plump.

Calvin and Marie's tomato sauce in this recipe is really versatile. You can make it with the shrimp and crabmeat, or you can use it as an all-purpose basic sauce without adding any seafood or meat. Substitute meat stock for the seafood stock if you want to serve the sauce over a dish such as meat loaf or Eli and Sue's **Bell Peppers Stuffed with Rice Dressing** (page 259). The sauce even makes a terrific thick tomato soup for cold days!

5 tablespoons unsalted butter

2 cups finely chopped onions

1 cup finely chopped green bell peppers

½ cup finely chopped celery

1¼ teaspoons ground red pepper (preferably
cayenne)

¾ teaspoon black pepper

3 (8-ounce) cans tomato sauce

4 cups **Basic Seafood Stock** (page 18)

2 tablespoons finely chopped garlic

2 tablespoons plus 2 teaspoons salt, *in all*

¾ cup catsup

1 pound peeled small shrimp

1 pound lump crabmeat (picked over)

4 quarts hot water

2 tablespoons vegetable oil

1 pound fresh spaghetti, or about ⅔ pound dry, each
strand cut or broken in half

Finely grated Parmesan cheese (preferably imported),
optional

In a 5½-quart saucepan or large Dutch oven, heat the butter over high heat until half melted. Add the onions, bell peppers, celery, and red and black peppers; cook about 10 minutes, stirring occasionally. Reduce heat to medium low and stir in the tomato sauce; cook about 4 minutes, stirring occasionally. Add the stock, garlic, and 2 *teaspoons* of the salt, stirring well. Cover and bring to a boil over high heat, stirring frequently. Reduce heat and simmer, covered, about 15 minutes, stirring occasionally. Add the catsup, stirring well; cover and return to a boil over high heat. Remove cover, reduce heat, and simmer about 20 minutes, stirring frequently so mixture doesn't scorch. Reduce heat and cook at a slow simmer until mixture is a thick tomato soup consistency, about 40 minutes more, stirring occasionally.

Now add the shrimp and crabmeat to the sauce, stirring well. Turn heat to high and cook just until shrimp are plump and pink, about 5 minutes, stirring occasionally. Do not overcook.

Meanwhile, in a 6-quart saucepan, combine the hot water, the remaining 2 *tablespoons* salt, and the oil. Cover pan, place over high heat, and bring to a boil. When water reaches a rolling boil, add small amounts of spaghetti at a time to the pan, breaking up oil patches as you drop spaghetti in. Return to boiling and cook uncovered to al dente stage (about 4 minutes if fresh, 7 minutes if dry); do not overcook. During this cooking time, use a wooden spoon or spaghetti spoon to lift spaghetti out of the water and shake strands back into the boiling water. It may be an old wives' tale, but this procedure seems to improve the texture of the spaghetti. Then immediately drain spaghetti into a colander; stop its cooking by running cold water over it. (If you used dry spaghetti, first rinse with hot water to wash off starch.) After the spaghetti has cooled thoroughly, 2 to 3 minutes, pour a liberal amount of vegetable oil in your hands and toss spaghetti. Set aside still in the colander.

Heat the serving plates in a 250° oven.

Serve immediately, with the sauce and spaghetti tossed together, or with the sauce spooned over the spaghetti. **NOTE**: If you toss them together, be sure to arrange some of the shrimp on top of each serving. Sprinkle cheese on top, if desired.

· · · · · · · · · · · · ·**LAGNIAPPE**· · · · · · · · · · · · ·

To test doneness of spaghetti, cut a strand in half near the end of cooking time. When done, there should be only a speck of white in the center, less than one-fourth the diameter of the strand.

ELDEN AND ODELIA MAE'S RECIPE

Crawfish Boulettes
(Boulettes d'Écrevisses)

Makes about 3 dozen boulettes or 12 appetizer servings

Boulette is the family's name for meatballs or anything formed into a round ball. Paul says that in boulettes of any type, seventy to eighty percent of the mixture used to be the main ingredient, such as crawfish. Other ingredients included onions, seasonings, and some type of binder like bread crumbs, mashed potatoes, mashed sweet potatoes, or flour. The mixture before it's fried, Paul says, was and is, in essence, a dressing.

When we were cooking with Elden and Odelia Mae, Paul asked her if she remembered the first time she had cooked with Mom Prudhomme. Odelia Mae said, "Yes, it's been a long time, boy! I was fifteen years old, because that's how old I was when I married Elden, and I stayed more with Mom Prudhomme than I did with my own mother. I was always hanging over her shoulder watching every little thing she did so I could cook like her. Forget about sitting and rocking on a front porch when we visited Elden's folks, I wanted to cook with Mom Prudhomme."

Odelia Mae learned well. She's widely known as an excellent Cajun cook, and she still cooks Cajun dishes the way Mom did. She also does all her own canning the way Mom did.

Elden and Odelia Mae's crawfish boulettes make an outstanding appetizer or hors-d'oeuvre, and they're a fine addition to a seafood platter. The good tastes of Louisiana crawfish and fresh, barely cooked bell peppers complement each other particularly well in boulettes. And the boulette mixture makes a delicious stuffing for bell peppers; we have provided a lagniappe recipe for deep-fried crawfish-stuffed peppers. They can serve as a main course or as part of a seafood platter.

Crawfish boulette mixture:

1 pound peeled crawfish tails, in all

Seasoning mix:

2 teaspoons salt
1 teaspoon black pepper
½ teaspoon ground red pepper (preferably cayenne)

¼ pound (1 stick) plus 4 tablespoons unsalted butter, *in all*
2½ cups very finely chopped onions, *in all*
1¼ cups very finely chopped green bell peppers, *in all*
1 tablespoon plus 1 teaspoon **Ground Hot Pepper
Vinegar,** peppers only (page 357; see **NOTE**)
4 small bay leaves
1 teaspoon dried thyme leaves
1 cup finely chopped green onions (tops only)
½ cup very finely chopped fresh parsley
1 tablespoon plus 2 teaspoons minced garlic
1 pound potatoes, peeled and coarsely chopped
   (about 2¾ cups chopped)
1 egg
½ cup very fine dry bread crumbs, lightly toasted and
   cooled

Seasoned flour:

2 cups all-purpose flour
1½ teaspoons ground red pepper (preferably cayenne)
1 teaspoon salt
1 teaspoon black pepper

Egg and milk wash:

1 egg, beaten
1½ cups milk

Vegetable oil for frying
Salt to sprinkle on hot boulettes

NOTE: If your Ground Hot Pepper Vinegar peppers are very hot, use your own judgment on how much of the peppers to use.

Mince *half* the crawfish tails by hand or in a food processor; cover and refrigerate minced and whole tails separately until ready to use.

Combine the seasoning mix ingredients thoroughly in a small bowl.

Place *4 tablespoons* of the butter in a large skillet over medium heat. Add *1 cup* of the onions and sauté until onions start to brown, about 5 minutes, stirring occasionally. Add the remaining *1 stick* butter and 1½ *cups* onions, ½ *cup* of the bell peppers, the Ground Hot Pepper Vinegar peppers, and the seasoning mix, stirring well. Reduce heat to medium low and cook about 3 minutes, stirring occasionally.

Add the bay leaves and thyme, stirring well; cook about 10 minutes, stirring occasionally and scraping pan bottom well each time. Stir in the green onions, parsley, and garlic. Cook about 5 minutes more, stirring occasionally. Remove from heat and let sit about 5 minutes. Remove and discard bay leaves and let vegetables cool at least 20 minutes more, still in the skillet.

Meanwhile, boil the potatoes until tender; drain well and immediately put them through a ricer or food mill. Place in a large bowl and mix vigorously with a fork until very creamy and stiff, about 2 minutes. (This brings out the starch, which will help bind the boulette mixture.)

To the skillet containing the cooled vegetables, add the egg, bread crumbs, the minced crawfish and the *remaining* crawfish tails, and ¾ *cup* bell peppers, mixing well. Add this mixture to the mashed potatoes, mixing well. Set aside.

In a pan (loaf, cake, and pie pans work well), combine the seasoned flour ingredients, mixing well.

In a medium-size bowl, beat together the ingredients of the egg and milk wash until well blended.

Heat oil 1½ inches deep in a large skillet or deep fryer to 365°.

Form the crawfish mixture into 1-ounce boulettes (round balls) that are about 1½ inches in diameter, making sure each boulette contains some of the whole crawfish; place on a greased cookie sheet. Dredge each boulette in the seasoned flour, coating thoroughly, then let soak in the egg and milk wash a couple of minutes. Just before frying, drain the boulettes, then dredge again in the flour, coating well and shaking off excess. Fry the boulettes in batches until golden brown and crusty, about 9 minutes total, turning occasionally. Adjust heat as needed to maintain oil as close to 365° as possible. Do not crowd. Drain on paper towels, then salt lightly and serve immediately.

Deep-Fried Crawfish-Stuffed Bell Peppers

Makes 10 to 12 stuffed pepper halves

We floured the stuffed bell peppers twice to give them a crusty top after they're fried. When the crawfish boulette mixture is stuffed into the bell pepper halves and fried, the wonderful mashed potato taste of the mixture is even more apparent than in the fried boulettes. That, combined with the crawfish and bell pepper tastes and textures, makes these really special!

Seasoning mix:
1 teaspoon salt
½ teaspoon ground red pepper (preferably cayenne)
½ teaspoon black pepper

5 to 6 medium-to-large green bell peppers, about 7
    ounces each, cut in half lengthwise, cored, and
    seeded
1 recipe crawfish boulette mixture (preceding recipe)
Vegetable oil for frying
1 recipe seasoned flour (preceding recipe)
1 recipe egg and milk wash (preceding recipe)

In a small bowl, combine the seasoning mix ingredients thoroughly and sprinkle some of the mix evenly on the inside of each bell pepper half, using about ⅛ teaspoon for each one.

Fill each bell pepper half with about ½ cup of the crawfish boulette mixture, packing it firmly.

Heat oil 1½ inches deep in a large skillet or deep fryer to 365°.

Dredge each stuffed bell pepper half lightly in the seasoned flour, then coat with the egg and milk wash and let soak a minute or so. Just before frying, drain, then dredge again lightly in the flour, shaking off excess. Fry the stuffed bell pepper halves in the hot oil, stuffing side up, until the batter is dark crusty brown, about 2 minutes. Adjust heat as needed to maintain oil as close to 365° as possible. (**NOTE:** The top of the stuffing will fry to a dark crusty brown without your having to turn over the bell pepper halves. The peppers themselves will stay quite crunchy and will have little if any crust on them.) Drain, stuffing side down, on paper towels and serve immediately.

Garfish Boulettes
(Boulettes de Poisson Armé)

Makes about 14 boulettes or 4 to 7 appetizer servings

Every now and then during the summer, Dad and one of his brothers loaded up both their families in wagons, with quilts and blankets and fishing and cooking gear, and headed for the Atchafalaya River to catch garfish. The two families (Dad's brother had nine children and Dad had twelve) camped out for a night or two on the banks of the river.

The men and older boys set out trotlines (fishing lines fixed at both ends, with baited hooks between) and "ran the lines" periodically to collect the fish that were caught on the hooks. Abel says they sometimes caught hundreds of pounds of fish, especially garfish. They cleaned them and had a huge fish fry right on the banks of the river. If they caught more than they could eat, Dad smoked some to take home and carried lots of the fresh fish home to neighbors and friends. He also barbecued garfish and often dried it to preserve it for later use. The family ate pieces of dried garfish as a snack, sort of like beef jerky, and Mom sometimes used it in okra dishes.

Enola learned to make garfish boulettes from Dad. She and Shelton like to serve them as an appetizer with tartar sauce or as part of a seafood platter with baked potatoes and **Coleslaw** *(page 321). You can substitute any very firm-fleshed fish for the garfish, as long as it's fresh and has never been frozen.*

1 pound very fresh (never frozen) garfish fillets (see **NOTE**), or any
    very firm-fleshed fish available fresh in your area
3 tablespoons unsalted butter
¾ cup finely chopped onions, *in all*
½ cup finely chopped green bell peppers, *in all*
2 teaspoons ground red pepper (preferably cayenne)
1 teaspoon salt, *in all*
¼ teaspoon black pepper
1 bay leaf
¾ teaspoon dried sweet basil leaves
½ teaspoon minced garlic
⅓ cup finely chopped green onions (tops only)
8 ounces new red potatoes, peeled (about 6 small to medium)
1 egg

> **Seasoned flour:**
> ½ cup all-purpose flour
> ¼ teaspoon salt
> ¼ teaspoon ground red pepper (preferably cayenne)
> ⅛ teaspoon black pepper

Vegetable oil for frying
Tartar sauce, optional

NOTE: If you can't get *very* fresh and never frozen garfish (even for a
few hours!), don't use garfish, because the boulettes will be strong-
flavored and rubbery, just perfect to play tennis with.

Cut the garfish into chunks and put through a food mill to separate
fibers from meat. Discard fibers. Set meat aside.

    In a large skillet, combine the butter, *½ cup* of the onions, *¼ cup*
of the bell peppers, *¼ teaspoon* of the salt, and the red and black
peppers. Place over high heat and cook until onions are browned, 5
to 7 minutes, stirring occasionally. Remove from heat and add the
remaining *¼ cup* onions, *¼ cup* bell peppers, and *¾ teaspoon* salt,
and the bay leaf, basil, and garlic, stirring well. Place over low heat
and cook about 3 minutes, stirring frequently. Stir in the green
onions and remove from heat. Transfer mixture to a large plate or

shallow bowl, spreading it out to cool. Let sit about 15 minutes.

Meanwhile, boil the potatoes until tender. Drain potatoes and immediately process them in a food processor about 30 seconds until very creamy and smooth.

Remove and discard bay leaf from the cooled vegetable mixture and place mixture in a large bowl. Stir in the egg, then the reserved garfish, and then the potatoes, mixing well each time before adding the next ingredient.

Combine the seasoned flour ingredients thoroughly in a medium-size bowl.

Heat oil at least 1¼ inches deep in a deep skillet or a deep fryer to 360°.

Have a bowl of water handy to moisten hands, as needed. Using moistened hands—or a 1½-ounce manual-release ice-cream scoop that's been oiled—measure out enough garfish mixture to form 1½-ounce boulettes that are 1½ inches in diameter; place boulettes on a greased cookie sheet. **NOTE**: If you're using an ice-cream scoop or a scale to weigh the portions, you can wait to shape the mixture into boulettes until just before dredging the boulettes in flour.

Just before frying, dredge the boulettes well in the seasoned flour. Shake off excess flour and fry in batches in the hot oil until dark golden brown and cooked through, about 4 minutes, turning at least once. Do not crowd. Drain on paper towels and serve while piping hot, allowing 2 or 3 boulettes per serving.

PAUL AND K'S RECIPE

Redfish Cornbread Boulettes

Makes about 2 dozen boulettes or 8 appetizer servings

These boulettes are sweet and spicy. To save time, make the cornbread a day ahead if you like, or use leftover cornbread.

Seasoned flour:

¾ cup all-purpose flour

¼ teaspoon salt

¼ teaspoon white pepper

¼ teaspoon ground red pepper (preferably cayenne)

¼ teaspoon black pepper

¾ pound redfish fillets, *in all* (preferred), or your
    favorite local firm-fleshed freshwater or
    saltwater fish, cut into ½-inch pieces (2 cups)

3 eggs, *in all*

4 tablespoons unsalted butter

½ cup finely chopped onions

½ cup finely chopped bell peppers (preferably a
    mixture of red and green, for color)

¼ cup finely chopped celery

¾ teaspoon ground red pepper (preferably cayenne)

½ teaspoon black pepper

¾ cup chopped green onions

1½ tablespoons minced fresh parsley

¾ teaspoon salt

¾ teaspoon minced garlic

½ teaspoon white pepper

½ teaspoon dried sweet basil leaves

3 tablespoons plus 1 teaspoon evaporated milk

2 cups finely crumbled **Bobby's Cornbread** (page
    278) or leftover cornbread (see **Note**)

Vegetable oil for frying

Ground Hot Pepper Vinegar Mayonnaise (page
    335; add the optional sugar) or tartar sauce

Note: If you use Bobby's Cornbread, be sure to make his sweetened
version. If you use leftover unsweetened cornbread, add 2 *tablespoons plus ½ teaspoon sugar* to the redfish mixture.

Combine the seasoned flour ingredients thoroughly in a pan (loaf,
cake, and pie pans work well). Set aside.
    In a food processor, process ¾ *cup* of the fish pieces with *1 of the*

eggs for several seconds, until fish is minced and mixture is thick. Place the mixture and the remaining *1¼ cups* fish pieces in a large bowl. Set aside.

In a 2-quart saucepan, combine the butter, onions, bell peppers, celery, and red and black peppers. Cook over medium heat about 6 minutes, stirring and scraping pan bottom frequently. Reduce heat to low and add the green onions, parsley, salt, garlic, white pepper, and basil, stirring well; cook about 3 minutes more, stirring and scraping occasionally. Remove from heat and immediately add the vegetable mixture to the fish, stirring well. Stir in the remaining 2 *eggs*, then the evaporated milk, then the cornbread, and *2 table-spoons plus ½ teaspoon sugar*, if cornbread is not sweet.

Have a bowl of water handy to moisten hands, as needed. Using moistened hands, form fish mixture into 1-ounce (2-tablespoon) boulettes. A ⅛-cup (1-ounce) measuring cup works well for this, or use an ice-cream scoop 1¾ inches in diameter. (Dip the cup or scoop in water before measuring each portion.) Place the 1-ounce portions on a greased cookie sheet and do the final shaping by hand just before you dredge the boulettes in flour.

Heat oil at least 1½ inches deep in a deep fryer or deep skillet to 360°. Just before frying, dredge each boulette well in the seasoned flour, shaking off excess. Fry in batches in the hot oil until golden brown, about 2 minutes. (Maintain oil's temperature as close to 360° as possible.) Do not crowd. Drain on paper towels and serve immediately as is, or with Ground Hot Pepper Vinegar Mayonnaise or tartar sauce as a dip.

POULTRY & GAME

VOLAILLES ET GIBIERS

J.C. AND SIS'S RECIPE

Company Fried Chicken

(Poulet Frit pour Compagnie)

Makes 4 main-dish servings

Mom Prudhomme cooked fried chicken only when someone, like Dad, had an "envie," a yen, for it. For Mom and Dad to feed their large group of children, plus the numerous friends who visited daily, they had to manage their resources exceedingly well. Fried chicken broke all the rules of good management: It required a fairly young bird, one that was still either producing eggs or fathering baby chickens. It produced no rich gravy or sauce to serve over rice or potatoes, so the chicken didn't "stretch" to make more food for a meal. And, as Calvin pointed out, it was tough to find a way to cut one small frying chicken into twelve or sixteen pieces, so you had to use two chickens.

What Mom and Dad didn't know (or never let on that they knew) was that the younger children actually had fried chicken fairly often. When they left the younger children with Ralph as baby-sitter, to visit friends or shop, maybe once a week, he killed a chicken or two, and he usually fried it. All the children knew Mom and Dad wouldn't approve, but Ralph was a terrific cook, and the fried chicken was awfully good!

J.C. and Sis serve their fried chicken for Sunday dinner when their children and grandchildren visit. Sis, too, worries about how well fried chicken can feed a large group, so she usually makes rice dressing and also **Candied Yams** *(page 283) as a "backup" because J.C. is so partial to them.*

Season the chicken a day ahead, cover, and refrigerate until ready to cook.

1 (3½- to 4-pound) fryer, cut into 8 pieces

> **Seasoning mix:**
> 2 teaspoons salt
> 1½ teaspoons black pepper
> 1 teaspoon ground red pepper (preferably cayenne)

Seasoned flour:

1½ cups all-purpose flour

1½ teaspoons salt

1 teaspoon black pepper

¾ teaspoon red pepper (preferably cayenne)

Seasoned egg wash:

2 large eggs

3 tablespoons evaporated milk

½ teaspoon salt

¼ teaspoon ground red pepper (preferably cayenne)

Vegetable oil for pan frying

Remove excess fat from the chicken pieces and place pieces in a large bowl. Combine the seasoning mix ingredients thoroughly and sprinkle evenly on the chicken, working the mix in with your hands. Cover and refrigerate overnight. Leave chicken refrigerated until ready to fry.

In a paper or plastic bag (Ziploc bags work well), combine the seasoned flour ingredients, mixing well. Set aside.

Combine the egg wash ingredients in a medium-size bowl, mixing well with a metal whisk. Dip chicken pieces in the mixture, coating well. Let excess drip off, then dredge pieces well in the flour, and let sit in the flour about 15 minutes. (Prepare only enough chicken pieces to cook in one batch to this point.)

Meanwhile, in a large deep skillet, heat oil 1¼ inches deep to 350°. When chicken pieces have been in the flour for 15 minutes, shake off excess flour and fry chicken (large pieces and skin side down first) until cooked through and dark golden brown on both sides, about 5 to 8 minutes per side. Do not crowd. (Adjust heat as needed to maintain about 350°.) Drain on paper towels. Repeat procedure for remaining pieces. Serve immediately.

PAUL AND K'S RECIPE

Fried Chicken Marinated in Ground Hot Pepper Vinegar

Makes 8 main-dish servings

Marinate the chicken for twenty-four hours before frying. Fried chicken usually gets oily after sitting, but this nicely different chicken stays crunchy and is actually at its best about an hour after it's fried.

Seasoning mix:
1 tablespoon salt
2 teaspoons sweet paprika
1½ teaspoons onion powder
1 teaspoon garlic powder
1 teaspoon gumbo filé (filé powder)
1 teaspoon dried thyme leaves
½ teaspoon dried sweet basil leaves
¼ teaspoon white pepper
¼ teaspoon ground red pepper (preferably cayenne)
¼ teaspoon black pepper

2 (2½- to 3-pound) fryers, each cut into 8 pieces
1 pint **Ground Hot Pepper Vinegar** (page 357)
Vegetable oil for pan frying
3 cups all-purpose flour
2 cups milk
2 eggs, beaten

Combine the seasoning mix ingredients thoroughly in a small bowl.
    Remove excess fat from the chicken pieces and place chicken in a very large bowl. Sprinkle pieces lightly and evenly on both sides with a total of *1 tablespoon plus 1 teaspoon* of the seasoning mix, patting it in with your hands and coating all the pieces. (Reserve remaining mix to finish the dish.) Pour the pepper vinegar over the chicken,

76

working it in with your hands and making sure all the pieces have some of the ground peppers on them.

Cover and refrigerate for 24 hours, turning chicken pieces over and stirring mixture at least 4 times so that all the pieces soak in the liquid for several hours and the ground peppers are redistributed. This is important to ensure that the chicken will be evenly seasoned. Keep refrigerated until just before ready to fry.

In a very large skillet or deep fryer, heat oil ¾ inch deep over high heat to 360°, about 10 minutes.

Meanwhile, in a pan (cake and loaf pans work well), thoroughly combine the flour with the remaining 2 *tablespoons plus* ¾ *teaspoon* seasoning mix.

In a large bowl, beat together the milk and eggs until well blended.

Remove chicken from refrigerator. Dredge and fry chicken pieces in batches. Just before dredging each batch, check to see if the ground peppers are clumped together; if so, rub pieces to distribute peppers evenly. Dredge the chicken (let juice drip off first, but leave bits of ground pepper on) in the seasoned flour, coating thoroughly. Shake off excess flour, then drop the pieces, a few at a time, into the milk mixture and let soak a couple of minutes.

Drain each piece well, then dredge again in the flour and shake off excess flour. Carefully slide each piece of chicken into the hot oil. Fry until dark golden brown on both sides and meat is cooked, 6 to 8 minutes per side. (**NOTE**: Fry equal-size pieces together and skin side down first. Maintain temperature as close to 360° as possible.) Drain on paper towels. Repeat procedure for remaining pieces.

Let sit uncovered at room temperature for 1 hour before serving.

ABEL AND JO'S RECIPE

Baked Chicken
(Poule Rôtie)

Makes 6 main-dish servings

Jo's family lived just across the road from the Prudhomme family. Her parents were sharecroppers, also, and the two families were good friends. Mom Prudhomme and Jo's mother often talked about cooking, and when Jo and Abel married, Jo already knew a lot about Mom Prudhomme's cooking.

Neither Mom Prudhomme nor Jo's mom baked chicken very often because they had to make one chicken serve a lot of people, so they usually cooked it in a gumbo or a stew, or smothered it, with the broth or gravy served over rice. As Calvin said, when you cook one chicken to feed twelve children, you have to be real clever to cut it up so there's a piece for everyone. But both families did sometimes have baked chicken for special occasions like Thanksgiving and Easter.

Abel and Jo stuff slits in the chicken meat with a vegetable-and-spice mixture before baking so that all the carved meat will have the flavor of the seasonings. The pan gravy, with all the vegetables and herbs in it, is delicious spooned over the meat. Stuff the chicken and season it the day before baking, then cover and refrigerate until ready to use.

1 (5- to 6-pound) stewing chicken

Stuffing:
¼ cup very finely chopped onions
2 teaspoons salt
1½ teaspoons minced garlic
1 teaspoon ground red pepper (preferably cayenne)

    Seasoning mix:
    1 teaspoon salt
    1 teaspoon onion powder
    1 teaspoon garlic powder

½ teaspoon ground red pepper (preferably cayenne)
½ teaspoon black pepper

¼ cup plus 1 tablespoon vegetable oil, *in all*
1 cup very finely chopped onions
¾ cup very finely chopped green bell peppers
½ cup very finely chopped celery
3 cups **Rich Chicken Stock** (page 19)
½ cup finely chopped green onions (tops only)
¼ cup coarsely chopped fresh parsley

Remove all visible fat from the chicken and trim the excess fatty skin from the neck area. In a small bowl, combine the stuffing ingredients, mixing very well.

With a small knife, cut about 12 to 16 slits in the chicken, all the way to the bone, to form pockets; make most of the pockets in the meatiest parts, and make each pocket about 1 inch long. (Be careful not to cut slits all the way through the cavity wall.) Fill each pocket with some of the stuffing, using it all; or rub any excess stuffing over the surface of the chicken.

Combine the seasoning mix ingredients thoroughly and sprinkle the mix evenly over the chicken, using it all and pressing it in by hand. Cover chicken and refrigerate overnight. Keep refrigerated until just before ready to bake.

Place ¼ *cup* of the oil in a heavy ovenproof 8- to 10-quart saucepan or large Dutch oven with as broad a bottom as possible. Drain chicken and rub well inside and out with the remaining *1 tablespoon* oil. Place chicken in saucepan, breast side up; cover and bake at 400° for 1 hour. Remove pan from oven and turn chicken over; return to oven and bake uncovered for 20 minutes. Remove pan from oven. Skim most of the fat (amount will vary depending on fattiness of chicken) from the pan juices. (Remove chicken from pan to make this easier to do.)

Turn chicken breast side up again in pan. Place the onions, bell peppers, and celery around the chicken. Return pan to oven and continue baking uncovered about 10 minutes. Turn chicken over again and stir pan juices well. Add the stock and sprinkle the green onions and parsley over the chicken. Cover pan and continue baking until chicken is tender, about 1 hour more. (**NOTE:** Remember that a stewing chicken is not as tender as a fryer; the cooked meat will still be very firm, but it shouldn't be tough.) Transfer chicken to a serving platter and cover loosely with aluminum foil; set aside.

Place the pan with the drippings over high heat and reduce the pan gravy to about 2 cups, about 20 minutes, stirring occasionally. Skim fat off gravy if desired and serve immediately, spooning the gravy over carved chicken pieces.

ALLIE AND ETELL'S RECIPE

Sticky Chicken
(Poulet Collant)

Makes 4 main-dish servings

Allie remembers that the family had chicken fairly often, but they had to cook only the older chickens that were no longer productive—hens that no longer produced eggs and roosters that could no longer breed. So the chickens they used had to cook for a long time in a gravy or broth. Calvin has this wonderful story about those old chickens: He says that during the first eight or nine years of Mom and Dad's marriage, the family moved so often that, each moving time, the older, experienced, chickens would just lie down and cross their legs, ready to be picked up and loaded on the wagon to move to a new home. (The reason for all the moving was that Dad was always looking for a location to sharecrop on better soil and for a better house for the family.)

Allie and Etell both cook "sticky chicken," but Allie says Etell is the expert. They call it that because "it is sticky—and you just have to lick your fingers afterward." The slightly sweet gravy is rich and perfect over rice, and it's also good with any of the family cornbread recipes.

*Allie serves her **Bread and Butter Pickles** (page 361) on the side when she has sticky chicken. She makes the pickles exactly the way Mom Prudhomme's sister, "Nanza" (Darilee's godmother Louisa Reed), did.*

Season the chicken the day before, cover, and refrigerate until ready to cook. This dish is cooked for fairly long periods of time over high heat. If your gas burner or electric cooking element produces a very high heat, or if your pot is not a heavy one, you will need to adjust the temperature down.

1 (3- to 3½-pound) fryer, cut up

Seasoning mix:
1 tablespoon sugar
2 teaspoons salt
1 teaspoon ground red pepper (preferably cayenne)

½ cup vegetable oil
1½ cups finely chopped onions
¾ cup finely chopped green bell peppers
1 tablespoon all-purpose flour
2½ cups, *in all*, **Basic Chicken Stock** (page 18)
½ teaspoon minced garlic
Hot **Basic Cooked Rice** (page 252) and/or
    cornbread

Remove all excess fat from the chicken pieces and place chicken in a large bowl. Combine the seasoning mix ingredients in a small bowl, mixing well. Sprinkle the pieces evenly on both sides with *1 tablespoon plus 1 teaspoon* of the mixture, working it in with your hands. Cover well and refrigerate overnight. Reserve remaining seasoning mix to finish the dish.

In a heavy 6-quart saucepan or large Dutch oven, with as broad a bottom as possible, heat the oil for about 2 minutes over high heat. Drain the chicken pieces and add them all to the pan, in a single layer. Turn each piece to coat with oil and start to cook skin side down first. Cook until well browned on both sides, about 20 minutes, turning only occasionally and allowing pieces to stick and build up a little crust before turning. Scrape pan bottom only if sediment is getting dark brown; if necessary, transfer any very brown bits of sediment to a plate.

Remove pan from heat and transfer chicken to the plate with the sediment. Pour the hot oil from the pan into a glass measuring cup, leaving as much sediment as possible in the pan. Return 1 tablespoon of the hot oil to the pan and add the onions and bell peppers. Return pan to high heat and cook about 1 minute, scraping pan bottom constantly to loosen sediment. Add 2½ tablespoons more hot oil to the pan, then stir in the flour. (Discard any remaining oil in the measuring cup.) Continue cooking about 3 minutes, stirring and scraping pan bottom constantly. Reduce heat, or remove pan from heat momentarily if mixture seems close to burning, still scraping pan bottom constantly.

Now stir in *1½ cups* of the stock and scrape pan bottom until all sediment is dissolved. Cook until mixture is a rich brown color and noticeably thicker, about 7 minutes, stirring occasionally. Stir in the garlic and the remaining 2 *teaspoons* seasoning mix, then add the plateful of chicken pieces and drippings. Add the remaining *1 cup* stock and continue cooking until liquid has reduced to a gravy, about 10 minutes more, stirring occasionally.

Remove from heat and serve immediately over rice and/or with cornbread.

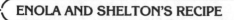

ENOLA AND SHELTON'S RECIPE

Chicken Smothered with Okra and Tomatoes
(Poule Etouffée avec Gombo Févi et Tomates)

Makes 6 to 8 main-dish servings

Enola learned to cook chicken smothered with okra and tomatoes from Mom Prudhomme, and she still cooks it just like Mom did. The only difference now is that she goes to a store to buy the ingredients. "When I was living at home with Mom and Dad, if we needed something to cook, we didn't go to the store, we went outside to the yard or the garden." Mom cooked this smothered chicken during the summer and early fall when the garden was full of tomatoes and okra.

Of course, the family always raised the chickens. Dad made a wire contraption with a crook on one end to catch chickens with. Enola says, "All we had to do to get a fresh chicken was to walk out into the yard and feed the chickens some shelled corn. While they were all milling around eating the corn, we just chose one, snagged its leg with the wire, and picked it up and wrung its neck. Then we cleaned it and got it ready for cooking, all within an hour or so."

The sauce in this old country recipe comes out very, very thick, which is how Mom served it at home—and she always served it over rice, naturally! If you would like a thinner sauce, add a little hot stock or water to the finished dish.

Season the chicken the day before, then cover and refrigerate until ready to cook. This dish is cooked for fairly long periods of time over high heat. If your gas burner or electric cooking element produces a very high heat, or if your pot is not a heavy one, you will need to adjust the temperature down.

1 (2½- to 3-pound) fryer, cut up

Seasoning mix:
1 tablespoon plus ¾ teaspoon salt
1 tablespoon plus ½ teaspoon ground red pepper (preferably cayenne)
1 teaspoon black pepper

1 cup all-purpose flour
1 cup vegetable oil, *in all*
3 pounds okra, sliced ¼ inch thick (15 cups sliced), *in all*
4 tablespoons unsalted butter
1½ cups chopped onions
1 cup chopped green bell peppers
2 cups, *in all*, **Basic Chicken Stock** (page 18)
4 cups peeled and coarsely chopped vine-ripened tomatoes
1½ teaspoons minced garlic
½ cup chopped green onions (tops only)
3½ tablespoons light brown sugar, optional
About 6 cups hot **Basic Cooked Rice** (page 252)

Trim any visible fat from the chicken pieces and place chicken in a large bowl. Combine the seasoning mix ingredients thoroughly and sprinkle *1 tablespoon* of the mix evenly over the meat, working it in by hand. Cover well and refrigerate overnight. Reserve remaining seasoning mix to finish the dish.

Place the flour in a pan (cake and pie pans work well). In a large heavy skillet, heat *½ cup* of the oil over high heat until hot, about 2 minutes. Just before frying, dredge the chicken pieces very lightly in the flour. Fry the chicken pieces in the hot oil (skin side down and large pieces first) until cooked through and dark golden brown on both sides, about 7 minutes per side. Drain on paper towels. When cool enough to handle, bone the chicken and cut it into bite-size pieces.

In a heavy 6-quart saucepan or Dutch oven (preferably cast iron), heat *7 tablespoons* of the oil over high heat until a piece of okra placed in it sizzles around the edges, about 3 minutes. Stir in *10 cups* of the okra and fry until about half the okra slices are browned, about 12 minutes, stirring occasionally and scraping pan bottom well. You will need to stir more often toward the end of the cooking time as the mixture becomes dry; if necessary, remove pan from heat momentarily and scrape well so mixture doesn't scorch.

Now add the butter, onions, bell peppers, and the remaining *1 tablespoon plus 2¼ teaspoons* seasoning mix and *1 tablespoon* oil, stirring well. Cook about 5 minutes, stirring almost constantly and scraping browned sediment from pan bottom. Add *½ cup* of the stock and the remaining *5 cups* okra, scraping until pan bottom is free of sediment. Continue cooking about 5 minutes, stirring and scraping constantly. Add *½ cup* more stock; cook until okra is no longer stringy and mixture is a little mushy, about 7 minutes, stirring and scraping constantly.

Next, stir in the tomatoes and the remaining *1 cup* stock and scrape pan bottom clean. Stir in the garlic. Bring to a boil, stirring occasionally. Reduce heat and simmer about 10 minutes. Add the cut-up chicken and continue cooking until okra is cooked and flavors marry, about 20 minutes, stirring frequently so mixture doesn't scorch. Stir in the green onions. Stir in the sugar, if desired.

Remove from heat and cover pan; let sit covered for about 20 minutes before serving. Then serve immediately, allowing about 1 cup of the smothered chicken, okra, and tomato mixture spooned over about ¾ cup rice for each serving.

MALCOLM AND VERSIE'S RECIPE

Chicken Maque Choux
(Maque Choux de Poule)

Makes 6 to 8 main-dish servings

Paul says a family custom he remembers well was "maque choux night." Mom and Dad invited friends and their children over for supper and Mom cooked chicken maque choux or crawfish maque choux. She made other dishes, too, but the meal was called a maque choux. Since a typical supper for the family was just hot bread with preserves or syrup and milk, a company supper was a big occasion.

Versie learned to cook chicken maque choux from her own mother. We noticed that Versie's cooked corn stays especially crisp. She thinks it's because she uses very fresh corn—which is sweet and juicy—and because of the way she cuts the kernels from the cob: She takes one shallow layer of corn off (halfway through the kernels), then cuts another layer off, and then she scrapes the cob to get all the milk out.

When Versie cooked her chicken maque choux for the cookbook, we were impressed by how good the corn maque choux was by itself; she smothers it first alone. Then we were just as impressed by how good the smothered chicken was. We almost hated to see her put the two together. But when she stirred the corn and the chicken together and the flavors married, we knew this was what Versie had been working toward—and the combination is heavenly.

Season the chicken a day ahead, cover well, and refrigerate until ready to cook. This dish is cooked for fairly long periods of time over high heat. If your gas burner or electric element produces a very high heat, or if your pot is not a heavy one, you will need to adjust the temperature down.

Seasoning mix:
1 tablespoon plus 2 teaspoons salt
1½ teaspoons ground red pepper (preferably cayenne)
½ teaspoon garlic powder
½ teaspoon black pepper

2 (2- to 2½-pound) fryers, each cut into 8 pieces (use
    necks and giblets, too)
⅔ cup vegetable oil, *in all*
3½ cups finely chopped onions, *in all*
1½ cups finely chopped green bell peppers, *in all*
1 pound tomatoes, peeled and puréed with ½ cup
    water in a blender or food processor
2¼ cups, *in all*, **Rich Chicken Stock** (page 19)
2 quarts fresh corn cut off the cob (about nineteen 8-
    inch cobs) or frozen corn kernels
1 teaspoon sugar
Hot **Basic Cooked Rice** (page 252), optional

Combine the seasoning mix ingredients thoroughly in a small bowl. Set aside.

Remove excess fat from the chicken pieces. Place chicken pieces, necks, and giblets on a flat surface. Sprinkle *1 tablespoon plus 2 teaspoons* of the seasoning mix on the meat and work it in with your hands, including under any loose skin. Cover and refrigerate overnight.

In a heavy 6-quart saucepan or large Dutch oven, place *⅓ cup* of the oil over medium heat; heat until oil sizzles when you add a piece of onion, about 4 minutes. Add *1½ cups* of the onions and sauté for about 2 minutes, stirring occasionally. Add *1 cup* of the bell peppers; cook for about 10 minutes, stirring occasionally. Add the tomato purée and cook for about 5 minutes, stirring occasionally. Add *2 cups* of the stock, the corn, sugar, and the remaining *2½ teaspoons* seasoning mix. Bring to a boil over high heat, stirring occasionally and scraping pan bottom well so the mixture doesn't scorch. When mixture begins to boil, remove from heat and set aside.

In a heavy 12-quart roaster or large, heavy rectangular pan, heat the remaining *⅓ cup* oil over medium-high heat about 1 minute. Add all chicken pieces except giblets (in a single layer if possible); cook until chicken starts to brown on underside, 3 to 4 minutes. Turn pieces over and cook about 4 minutes, stirring and scraping pan bottom occasionally. Continue cooking until oil and browned sediment become a "rusty gravy," about 25 minutes, frequently scraping pan bottom well as sediment starts to stick, and turning chicken often as it sticks to pan. The sediment will become a rusty color. Add the remaining ¼ *cup* stock and cook about 5 minutes, continuing to turn chicken pieces and scrape pan. (This continuous browning of the sediment is what makes the gravy so good!)

Now sprinkle the remaining 2 *cups* onions and ½ *cup* bell peppers over the chicken. Reduce heat to medium and lightly stir to loosen chicken from pan bottom, but don't scrape. Add the giblets; cook about 4 minutes, stirring infrequently and scraping only lightly. (**NOTE**: The sediment should be dark rusty brown by now. Any browned sediment stuck to pan bottom that you can't scrape off at this point will readily loosen after you cover pan and cook it longer.) Cover pan, reduce heat to low, and cook for about 7 minutes.

Remove cover, stir, and scrape pan bottom lightly, then stir in the corn mixture. Re-cover pan, increase heat to medium, and cook until chicken and corn flavors marry, about 5 minutes, stirring and scraping occasionally. Remove cover and cook and stir for about 10 minutes more.

Remove from heat and serve immediately as is or Cajun style over rice.

MALCOLM AND VERSIE'S RECIPE

Chicken Sauce Piquant
(Sauce Piquante de Poule)

Makes 8 main-dish servings

Mom Prudhomme usually made sauce piquant with chicken or rabbit for company on Sundays and sometimes on Fridays with fresh turtle. But sauce piquant can be made with almost anything. All the Prudhommes and many other South Louisiana families make it with chicken, rabbit, squirrel, beef, turtle, alligator, shrimp, crabmeat, and every variety of fresh fish. Malcolm and Versie like to use a hen or stewing chicken rather than a fryer for chicken sauce piquant because hens have so much more flavor.

Season the chicken with the seasoning mix at least one day ahead, preferably two, then cover and refrigerate until ready to use. This dish is cooked for fairly long periods of time over high heat. If your gas burner or electric cooking element produces a very high heat, or if your pot is not a heavy one, you will need to adjust the temperature down.

1 (5½- to 6-pound) stewing chicken, cut up (use neck
    and giblets, too)

    Seasoning mix:
    1 tablespoon salt
    2 teaspoons ground red pepper (preferably cayenne)
    1 teaspoon garlic powder

⅓ cup vegetable oil
5½ cups, *in all*, **Rich Chicken Stock** (page 19)
5 cups finely chopped onions, *in all*
2 cups finely chopped green bell peppers, *in all*
1 tablespoon plus 1 teaspoon finely chopped garlic, *in all*
¼ pound (1 stick) unsalted butter
¾ cup finely chopped celery
1 (8-ounce) can tomato sauce
2 tablespoons catsup
¼ cup plus 1 teaspoon finely chopped cayenne
    peppers (preferred) or jalapeño peppers (see **NOTE**)
2 teaspoons black pepper
¾ teaspoon salt
About 6 cups hot **Basic Cooked Rice** (page 252)

NOTE: Fresh peppers can vary significantly in heat value, so start with one half the amount called for, then taste before adding more. Fresh jalapeños are preferred; if you have to use pickled ones, rinse as much vinegar from them as possible.

Remove excess fat from chicken pieces. Thoroughly combine the seasoning mix ingredients in a small bowl. Sprinkle the chicken and giblets with the mix; press it in by hand and rub some under any loose skin. Cover well and refrigerate at least overnight, preferably 2 days.

In a heavy 12-inch skillet, heat oil over medium-high heat about 3 minutes. Add chicken pieces (except neck and giblets), skin side down; have as many pieces as possible in contact with pan bottom so all will brown. Cook about 6 minutes without turning. Turn pieces over with tongs or a fork, but don't scrape pan bottom; cook about 5 minutes more. Turn chicken again and scrape pan bottom well; cook about 5 minutes more, scraping pan bottom frequently. Turn again and loosen any pieces stuck to pan, scraping well; cook again about 5 minutes, scraping pan bottom almost constantly.

Now carefully (it will steam up) add ½ *cup* of the stock to pan bottom and turn chicken pieces over, rubbing them on pan bottom to loosen some of the sediment; cook about 2 minutes. (Don't worry at this point if there's still some sediment sticking.) Turn pieces over once more and rub pan bottom with them again. By now, the oil in the pan bottom should be dark rusty brown. Remove from heat.

Now place chicken in a heavy, *heated*, 8-quart saucepan or large Dutch oven and pour the rusty gravy over the chicken. Turn heat to medium-high and add *3 cups* of the onions, *1 cup* of the bell peppers, and *1 teaspoon* of the garlic. Stir and scrape pan bottom well; cook about 5 minutes, stirring almost constantly and scraping pan bottom clean of browned sediment. Turn heat to high and add *2 cups* more stock, stirring and scraping pan bottom well. Bring stock to a boil, then reduce heat to very low and cover pan; cook about 15 minutes more. Stir well and turn over any pieces not submerged in liquid. Remove from heat and set pan aside, covered.

In a heavy 6-quart saucepan or large Dutch oven, melt the butter over medium heat. Add the celery and the remaining *2 cups* onions, *1 cup* bell peppers, and *1 tablespoon* garlic; cook about 20 minutes, stirring occasionally. Add the tomato sauce plus 8 ounces of water measured in the tomato-sauce can. Cook about 20 minutes, stirring occasionally (more often toward end of cooking time). Stir in the catsup and cook about 5 minutes more, stirring occasionally. Remove from heat and set aside.

Remove cover from the smothered chicken, tilt pan, and skim off all fat possible; place pan over medium heat. Add the neck, giblets, tomato-sauce mixture, the remaining *3 cups* stock, and the cayenne peppers, black pepper, and salt; stir well, cover and cook about 30 minutes, stirring once or twice. Reduce heat to low and cook until chicken is tender, about 30 minutes more, stirring occasionally.

Remove from heat, skim off fat, and serve immediately over rice.

PAUL AND K'S RECIPE

Chicken Chartres

Makes 6 very generous main-dish servings

Paul and K's French Quarter restaurant is still located on Chartres Street in the homey little building where they first opened it seven years ago. Paul created this chicken dish of multiple tastes and textures in honor of that picturesque, sometimes quiet, often lively French Quarter street. The combined tastes of baked chicken, classic New Orleans potatoes, and rich béarnaise sauce make an extraordinary dish, and the portions are Olympian.

Seasoning mix:
1 tablespoon plus 1½ teaspoons salt
1¼ teaspoons onion powder
1¼ teaspoons garlic powder
1 teaspoon white pepper
1 teaspoon black pepper
1 teaspoon ground cumin
½ teaspoon sweet paprika
¼ teaspoon ground red pepper (preferably cayenne)

3 (3- to 3½-pound) fryers
1½ cups finely chopped onions, *in all*
¼ pound (1 stick) plus 6 tablespoons unsalted
    butter, *in all*
Vegetable oil for deep frying
3 pounds russet potatoes, peeled and cut crosswise into slices ¼ inch thick
3 ounces sliced bacon, finely chopped (about ½ cup)
4 ounces ham, chopped (about ¾ cup)
1 cup **Basic Chicken Stock** (page 18)
1 recipe **Béarnaise Sauce** (page 339)
6 eggs

Combine the seasoning mix ingredients thoroughly in a small bowl.

Cut the leg-thigh pieces from the 3 chickens, slit the meat to the bone along the inner side, and bone meat along the length of the bones, leaving meat in one piece with the skin on. Split and bone the breasts lengthwise so you get two breast pieces per chicken, also with the skin on.

To prepare each portion, use one breast piece and one leg piece. Sprinkle the skin side of each breast piece with some of the seasoning mix, using a total of 2 *teaspoons* and patting it in by hand. In a roasting pan, lay each leg piece (skin side up) on top of a seasoned breast piece (skin side up). Tuck the edges of the leg meat and skin under the breast piece to form what will appear to be one piece of chicken. Season the chicken "halves" on both sides with a total of 1 *tablespoon* more seasoning mix, patting it in. Plump up each half so it is neatly formed and rounded, with the skin side up. Sprinkle ½ *cup* of the onions and 1 *stick* of the butter (in chunks) in the roasting pan around the chicken. Set aside.

In a deep-fat fryer with a fry-basket, heat the oil to 350° and fry the potatoes in small batches until they start to brown but are not completely cooked, about 5 minutes. Adjust heat as necessary to maintain the oil temperature at about 350°. Drain potatoes on paper towels, then place them in an ungreased 13 × 9-inch baking pan. Sprinkle potatoes evenly with 1 *tablespoon plus 1 teaspoon* of the seasoning mix and set aside.

In a large skillet, fry the bacon over high heat until brown. Add the ham and cook for 3 to 5 minutes, stirring frequently. Stir in the remaining 1 *cup* onions and continue cooking for 5 minutes, stirring occasionally. Remove from heat and, with a slotted spoon and draining well, spoon the bacon mixture on top of the potatoes. Add the stock and 2 *tablespoons* of the butter; stir until well mixed.

Place the pans containing the potatoes and the reserved chicken in the oven and bake at 400° until the chicken is done, 35 to 40 minutes. Stir the potatoes about every 10 minutes.

Meanwhile, make the béarnaise sauce and set aside.

When the chicken and potatoes are done, remove pans from oven. Transfer chicken to a heated platter and set aside. Spoon the potatoes into the pan containing the chicken drippings and toss the potatoes to coat them with the drippings; set aside.

Heat the serving plates in a 250° oven.

In a mixing bowl, beat the eggs and the remaining 1¾ *teaspoons* seasoning mix together with a metal whisk until frothy, about 30 seconds. Melt the remaining *4 tablespoons* butter in a large skillet (preferably a nonstick type) over high heat. Add about two thirds of the egg mixture to the skillet, then, with a slotted spoon, add the potato mixture to the pan, and then add the remaining egg mixture on top of the potatoes. Lower heat a little and cook until the omelet is done but not too firm. (Or you may prefer to scramble the mixture.) Remove from heat and cut the omelet into 6 wedges. Serve immediately.

To serve, for each serving place a wedge of the omelet (or a portion of the scrambled eggs) on a heated plate. Arrange a "half" chicken on top and then spoon about ¼ cup of the béarnaise sauce over all.

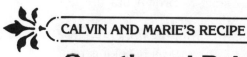

CALVIN AND MARIE'S RECIPE

Smothered Rabbit with Rusty Gravy
(Etouffée de Lapin dans une Sauce Rouillée)

Makes 4 to 6 main-dish servings

Smothered rabbit is actually rabbit etouffée, and for those of you who think the only good etouffée is a crawfish or shrimp etouffée, we say, "You must try this!" Almost everything that can be cooked can be smothered or etoufféed, according to the Prudhommes, and game and poultry are especially good smothered.

Calvin says he likes smothered dishes because the cooking method makes so much good rich gravy to serve over rice. To a Cajun, rice and gravy, and plenty of it, can't be beat. Calvin remembers well the first time he was served rice in a restaurant outside of Cajun country (in Mississippi). There was just one ice-cream scoop of rice on his plate and Calvin was very taken aback. He very nicely asked the waitress to go back to the kitchen and have three scoops of rice put on his plate. Now she was taken aback! When he went to the restaurant again the next day, the cook looked out from the kitchen and said really loudly, "Hey, that's the man who eats all that rice!"

The "rusty gravy" of Calvin and Marie's smothered rabbit is made with the browned sediment that forms while the rabbit is cooking. This dish is extraordinary in that only a few relatively simple ingredients produce a strikingly complex and fine taste. It is cooked for fairly long periods of time over high heat. If your gas burner or electric cooking element produces a very high heat, or if your pot is not a heavy one, you will need to adjust the temperature down.

Seasoning mix:

2 teaspoons salt

1½ teaspoons ground red pepper (preferably cayenne)

½ teaspoon black pepper

2 (2-pound) domestic rabbits, cut up

2 tablespoons vegetable oil

1 cup finely chopped onions

½ cup finely chopped green bell peppers

¼ cup finely chopped celery

2 tablespoons very finely chopped garlic

7 cups, *in all*, **Rich Rabbit** or **Chicken Stock** (page 19)

Hot **Basic Cooked Rice** (page 252) or hot **Crusty Houseboat Biscuits** (page 22)

Combine the seasoning mix ingredients thoroughly in a small bowl and set aside.

Bone just enough rabbit to yield a heaping ½ cup meat (one back thigh should be just right); chop the meat very finely and set aside.

Place the rabbit pieces (but not the chopped meat) in a heavy 8-quart saucepan. Sprinkle the seasoning mix on both sides of the meat, working it in with your hands and using it all. Add the oil to the bottom of the pan. Cover pan and cook over high heat about 5 minutes without stirring. Remove lid, turn meat over, and scrape pan bottom well. Re-cover pan and cook until meat is well browned and oil is a rusty color, about 20 minutes, stirring well every 2 to 3 minutes and turning meat occasionally. Be sure to let sediment stick before you stir.

Add the chopped rabbit meat, onions, bell peppers, celery, and garlic; cook until chopped meat is browned, about 5 minutes more, stirring and thoroughly scraping pan bottom almost constantly. (This continuous process of letting sediment stick and then scraping pan bottom is what makes the gravy so good.) Now add *2 cups* of the stock, stirring and scraping pan bottom clean. Cover pan and cook about 10 minutes, stirring and scraping occasionally. Stir in *1 cup* more stock, re-cover pan, and cook about 10 minutes, stirring occasionally. Stir in the remaining *4 cups* stock and cook until meat is tender and flavors marry, about 30 minutes more, stirring ocasionally.

Remove from heat and serve immediately over rice or with hot biscuits.

CALVIN AND MARIE'S RECIPE

Stuffed Rabbit Legs
(Lapin Piqûre à l'Ail)

Makes 4 main-dish servings

After the older children were grown, Dad and Mom managed to find more time for relaxing. About once a year, they loaded up the children who were still at home and a few supplies in the wagon and headed for the nearby forest to fish and hunt and live off the land in a way that was even more basic than their normal life. They took only staple foods like cornmeal, flour, lard, rice, and seasonings.

Dad and the boys set traps for game animals like rabbits, squirrels, and birds, and they seined for fish. Whatever they caught or trapped was what they had to eat, and as the boys all say, Mom sometimes had to make a "long gravy" if they were short on meat. But rabbits, squirrels, and turtles were plentiful in the woods back then, so the boys usually managed to get enough game for Mom to make a gumbo, etouffée, stew, or jambalaya. And fish were abundant, too. Dad always helped with the outdoor cooking, especially on camping trips, and he was the family expert at frying fish.

The children loved these vacations in the woods. At night, they slept under the wagon, just like their cowboy idols in the movies did, and during the day, they played hide-and-seek, swung on vines, and climbed trees. Bobby says it was important to know which trees to climb. Most of them were cedar or pine. Cedars were thin at the top and you could climb way up and make the whole tree swing back and forth. But if you climbed too far up on a pine, the top would snap off and pitch you to the ground. That was good enough reason to learn to distinguish between conifers!

All the children knew was that trips to the woods were great fun, a terrific vacation, but Paul says Mom and Dad had a more important purpose: They were teaching the children survival skills—how to fish and hunt, which trees burned the best, how to live off what you could find in the wild and not rely on the home storehouse of canned meats and vegetables.

Calvin and Marie rarely cook game rabbits now; they prefer domestic rabbit because the meat is much more tender and cooks more quickly. Calvin created this stuffed rabbit especially for the cookbook, calling on all he learned "growing up in a family where wonderful food was served three times a day." It's garlicky and delicious.

You will need to buy two whole rabbits: Cut off the back legs to stuff and use 4 ounces (½ cup) of the remaining meat in the stuffing itself. The leftover rabbit can be cooked in a gumbo or in any other way you would cook chicken. The rabbit tenderloin (that succulent strip of meat on either side of the backbone) is great boned and lightly sautéed in butter. You will need a food injector (page 5) to inject the vegetable purée into the meat.

1¼ cups, *in all*, **Rich Rabbit** or **Chicken Stock** (page 19)
¼ cup finely chopped onions
¼ cup finely chopped green bell peppers
2 tablespoons finely chopped celery
1 tablespoon minced garlic
2 teaspoons salt
1 teaspoon black pepper
½ teaspoon ground red pepper (preferably cayenne)

½ cup ground or very finely chopped rabbit meat (4 ounces)
¼ cup finely chopped green onions (tops only)
2 tablespoons very fine dry bread crumbs
4 back legs of domestic rabbit
Hot **Basic Cooked Rice** (page 252), optional

In a 1-quart saucepan, combine ¼ *cup* of the stock with the onions, bell peppers, celery, garlic, salt, and black and red peppers. Bring to a boil over high heat, stirring occasionally. Remove from heat and immediately transfer mixture to a blender. Blend on highest speed until mixture is a very smooth purée, pushing sides down with a rubber spatula as necessary so that every piece of vegetable gets puréed. (Be sure to make the mixture as smooth as possible so it won't stop up the food injector.)

In a small bowl, combine 2 *tablespoons* of the purée with the ground rabbit meat, green onions, and bread crumbs, mixing well. Set aside.

Make pockets in each back leg as follows: Place meat flat on a cutting board, with fleshier side up. With a paring knife, cut a slit along the thighbone—down to the bone but no deeper—about 3 inches long. With meat still lying flat, cut a horizontal pocket (that is, parallel to the cutting board) on each side of the thighbone. Make each pocket as large as possible without piercing through to the surface of the meat; this is easier to do if you start with the knife and then use your fingers to enlarge the pockets on either side.

Fill the pockets with the ground-meat mixture, packing it in well and using it all.

Put the remaining purée in a food injector and inject some of the purée into the meatiest part of each leg, making 3 to 5 injections in each side of the meat (don't inject purée into the stuffing) and using as much of the purée as possible. If you have a little left over that won't go through the injector, rub it over the surface of the meat.

Place the legs in a single layer, stuffing side up, in an ungreased 13 × 9-inch baking pan. Pour the remaining 1 *cup* stock around the meat and seal pan well with aluminum foil. Bake at 450° for about 20 minutes. Remove foil and continue baking until meat is done and browned on top, 30 to 35 minutes more. Remove from oven and serve immediately as is or with rice, spooning some of the pan drippings over the rice and meat.

ENOLA AND SHELTON'S RECIPE

Super Squirrel
(Écureuil dans une Sauce Rouillée)

Makes 4 to 6 main-dish servings

Game squirrels and rabbits are quite different, in taste and in size. Rabbits are very meaty and can be used in many dishes; they're excellent stewed, smothered, or cooked in gumbo, jambalaya, and sauce piquant. Squirrels are small animals with very little meat and, although they are good in gumbo and jambalaya, they are unquestionably best cooked in a gravy. Nothing makes a better gravy than several fresh squirrels—and squirrels are so small that it does take several to make even a few servings.

Enola's son, Sonny (who is a chef at Enola's restaurant), taught her how to cook this squirrel gravy. He likes to hunt, so he prepares this dish every fall in squirrel season. Sonny's favorite pastime, though, is fishing, and he learned how to fish from Dad Prudhomme. When Dad retired, he became an avid sport fisherman. In the spring, he would come by and pick up Sonny almost every Saturday morning to go fishing. Dad carried three rods and reels, fishing stoppers, worms, and three buckets on his fishing jaunts. He raised his own worms in a large washtub, but he taught Sonny how to get fishing worms out from under trees: What you do is lean over close to the ground and rub two sticks together to make a vibration; this makes the worms come up out of the ground! Sonny says Dad was all business when he was fishing. He sat on one of the three buckets and fished three lines at a time—and he insisted on quiet, no talking. Sonny says that's why Dad liked to take him along; he always was a quiet youngster.

Do try to find a source for fresh squirrel during hunting season (usually October and November in most states) to try this fine example of game cooking.

4 squirrels, cleaned and each cut into 6 to 8 pieces
    (about 2 pounds dressed meat)

Seasoning mix:
1 tablespoon salt
1 tablespoon ground red pepper (preferably cayenne)

1 tablespoon all-purpose flour
¼ pound (1 stick) margarine
4 cups finely chopped onions, *in all*
2 cups finely chopped green bell peppers
2 teaspoons minced garlic
About 3 cups **Basic Chicken Stock** (page 18)
¼ cup dry sherry
1 tablespoon Worcestershire sauce
½ cup finely chopped green onions (tops only)
¼ cup finely chopped fresh parsley
3 tablespoons unsalted butter
¾ cup finely chopped mushrooms
2 to 3 cups hot **Basic Cooked Rice** (page 252)
Smothered Potatoes (page 299), optional

Place the squirrel pieces in a large bowl. Combine the seasoning mix ingredients in a small bowl, mixing well. Sprinkle *1 tablespoon plus 1 teaspoon* of the seasoning mix evenly over the meat, working it in with your hands. Let meat sit about 30 minutes at room temperature.

Sprinkle the meat very lightly and evenly on both sides with the flour, working the flour in well with your hands; set aside.

Heat a very large heavy skillet (preferably cast iron) over high heat until very hot, about 4 minutes. Carefully add the margarine to the hot pan and heat until it is half melted. Add the squirrel pieces and cook until well browned, letting some of the pieces stick to the pan bottom before turning, about 4 minutes per side, stirring and scraping pan bottom occasionally. (The browned parts that stick to the pan bottom are essential to the flavor of the gravy.) Add *2 cups* of the onions and sauté about 2 minutes, stirring and scraping constantly. Add the bell peppers and garlic; cook about 10 minutes, stirring and scraping occasionally.

Now add *½ cup* of the stock, *1 teaspoon* seasoning mix, the sherry, Worcestershire, and the remaining *2 cups* onions, stirring well. Reduce heat to low and cook until most of the liquid has evaporated, about 10 minutes, stirring occasionally. Add ½ *cup* more stock and the green onions and parsley, stirring and scraping pan bottom well; cook about 10 minutes, stirring and scraping occasionally. Add *1 cup* more stock and the remaining *1 teaspoon* seasoning mix, stirring and scraping pan bottom well. Reduce heat to very low and cook until meat is tender, about 20 minutes more, stirring occasionally. (Meat from older squirrels may require longer cooking; if necessary, add more stock or water to cook meat until tender.) Remove from heat and set aside.

In a 1-quart saucepan, melt the butter over high heat. Add the mushrooms and sauté about 2 minutes, stirring frequently. Remove from heat and serve immediately.

For each serving, spoon a portion of meat and gravy over about ½ cup rice and top the meat with a portion of drained mushrooms. Serve Smothered Potatoes on the side, if desired.

DARILEE AND SAUL'S RECIPE

Frogs' Legs and Garlic Hopalong Cassidy
(Jambes de Ouaouarons dans une Sauce d'Ail)

Makes 8 main-dish servings

Several times each year, Dad and the boys went frogging so Mom Prudhomme could cook frogs' legs. They used a contraption that Dad had made—a metal pole with an insert called a frog grabber on the end. The metal insert opened up and when it touched a frog, it closed around the frog but didn't kill it. Sometimes, a frogging trip resulted in just a small catch, but occasionally, in good years, there were "beaucoup" frogs around. They could come home with sacks full of frogs. They were placed in an enclosure and kept there and fed "bugs and stuff." When Mom wanted to cook frogs' legs, the kids ran out to the frog pen and caught whatever number she needed.

Kids in South Louisiana had this really terrible joke going around that the toughest thing about eating frogs' legs was sitting by a window and watching the front half of the frogs hopping around in the yard—because you only cook the back legs!

Paul remembers well Mom cooking frogs' legs in a cast-iron pot and making a gravy with them. He says frogs' legs are like beans— you should either cook them for a long time or just a short time. If you try for a middle stage, they'll be tough.

Darilee and Saul's frogs' legs are spicy and tender. Season them the day before, cover, and refrigerate until ready to cook.

4 pounds frogs' legs

> **Seasoning mix:**
> 1 tablespoon plus 2½ teaspoons salt
> 1 tablespoon plus 1 teaspoon ground red pepper (preferably cayenne)
> 1 tablespoon black pepper

About 1 cup vegetable oil, *in all*
About 1 cup all-purpose flour
1½ cups chopped onions, *in all*
2 cups chopped green bell peppers, *in all*
About 7 cups, *in all*, **Rich Chicken Stock** (page 19)
6 tablespoons finely chopped garlic
2 cups chopped green onions (tops and bottoms)
1 cup chopped fresh parsley
4 cups hot **Basic Cooked Rice** (page 252)

If frogs' legs are not separated in two, cut them apart. Place in a large bowl.

Combine the seasoning mix ingredients thoroughly in a small bowl. Sprinkle *1 tablespoon plus ½ teaspoon* of the mix evenly over the meat, working it in with your hands. Cover and refrigerate overnight. (Reserve the remaining seasoning mix.)

In a 6-quart saucepan or large Dutch oven, heat oil ⅛ inch deep over high heat. Heat until oil sizzles when you sprinkle a drop of water in, about 6 minutes.

Meanwhile, place the flour in a pan (cake, pie, and loaf pans work well) with *1 tablespoon* seasoning mix, mixing well. Just before frying, dredge each frog leg well in the seasoned flour, shaking off excess. (Reserve leftover flour.) Sauté frogs' legs, a single layer at a time, in the hot oil just until very lightly browned, 1 to 2 minutes. Turn meat over and lightly brown on other side, about 1 minute more. Do not overcook or the meat will toughen. Transfer browned meat to a large bowl and fry remaining batches.

Pour the hot frying oil into a glass measuring cup, including as many of the browned particles in the pan as possible; if necessary, add fresh oil to make 1 cup and return the oil to the pan. Measure out the leftover flour and add more if necessary to yield ½ cup. Have ¾ *cup* of the onions handy. Add the ½ cup flour to the 1 cup hot oil in the pan. Place over high heat and cook until mixture is light to medium brown, about 2 minutes, stirring with a long-handled wooden spoon and scraping pan bottom constantly so roux doesn't scorch. Immediately add the reserved ¾ cup onions and cook about 2 minutes, stirring constantly. Add the remaining 2 *tablespoons* seasoning mix and *1 cup* of the bell peppers; cook about 2 minutes, stirring frequently.

✳ See page 12 for more about making roux.

Gradually add *6 cups* of the stock, stirring constantly until mixture is well blended. Bring to a boil, stirring occasionally. Add the frogs' legs, garlic, and the remaining ¾ *cup* onions and *1 cup* bell peppers, stirring well. Return to a boil. Cover pan, reduce heat, and simmer about 20 minutes, stirring frequently and scraping pan bottom well to make sure mixture doesn't scorch.

Now add the green onions and parsley, stirring well; simmer uncovered for about 15 minutes more, skimming any oil from surface as it develops and stirring and scraping pan bottom frequently. (**NOTE**: Add about 1 cup more stock or water if gravy gets too thick.) Remove from heat and let sit covered about 10 minutes more (or a little longer if meat isn't tender) before serving.

Serve over rice, allowing about ½ cup rice, ¾ cup sauce, and a portion of the frogs' legs for each serving.

Turtle Sauce Piquant
(Sauce Piquante de Tortue)

Makes 4 to 6 main-dish servings

Ralph's elderly black friend, Felix, taught him how to hunt turtles in the swampy areas right near home. To poke around in the mud, or in soft ground near old logs, Felix used a rod that was flat on one end and had a crook on the other. He poked with the flat end and used the crook end to pull up the turtles. Ralph figured Felix could tell when he had a turtle by the sound or by the feel of the rod. But when Ralph felt something and pulled, he just pulled up an old piece of wood. So he asked Felix what he was doing wrong and why Felix always got turtles and Ralph got only rotten wood. Felix thought this was pretty funny and he laughed.

Felix poked in the mud and then had Ralph hold his rod firmly in the same place and tell him what he felt.

"I don't know what I feel—sounds like a piece of wood or a turtle—either one."

"Push hard on the rod." Ralph did and the turtle moved.

"That thing moved!"

Felix just had to laugh at Ralph again and told him, "It's a turtle. Dig it up and haul it out."

When Ralph began coming home from the woods with sacks of turtles, Dad and the other Prudhomme boys wanted to catch them, too, so Felix taught them. Dad became an avid turtle hunter and even organized groups of friends to hunt on weekends. They would bring back their sacks of turtles, dump them in Dad's yard, sort them by the kind and size, and split up the catch.

Dad was innovative with making tools and coming up with better ways to help feed the family. As soon as a fairly productive source of turtles was established, he built a turtle pen. It was enclosed by pieces of tin sunk far into the ground. Turtles can burrow deep down into soil; the tin has to be there to hold them. He kept the dirt in the pen really wet, and when turtles were brought home, they were put in the pen and burrowed into the dirt and stayed alive. When Mom wanted turtle meat, there was a fresh supply. Dad just went out to the pen and used his turtle rod to poke around and pull them up. Sometimes the turtle supply was so good that Dad could sell some of them.

Mom made turtle soup, turtle stew, turtle etouffée, and turtle sauce piquant, especially on Fridays. The family never ate meat on Fridays, because they were Catholic, but they didn't consider turtle to be meat; it was thought of as more like seafood, as were frogs' legs.

Calvin enjoys cooking his recipe for turtle sauce piquant because it reminds him of Mom's good turtle dishes. It is cooked for fairly long periods of time over high heat. If your gas burner or electric cooking element produces a very high heat, or if your pot is not a heavy one, you will need to adjust the temperature down.

About 4 pounds bone-in turtle meat, or 3 pounds
    boneless turtle meat, or bone-in meat from a 6-
    to 8-pound whole turtle, including shell (see
    Note)
¾ cup vegetable oil
2 cups finely chopped onions
1 cup finely chopped green bell peppers
1 cup finely chopped celery
2 teaspoons minced garlic
4 cups **Rich Turtle** or **Beef Stock** (page 19)
2 (8-ounce) cans tomato sauce
2 tablespoons plus ½ teaspoon ground red pepper
    (preferably cayenne)
1¾ teaspoons salt
1 teaspoon black pepper
½ cup finely chopped green onions (tops only)
½ cup finely chopped fresh parsley
Hot **Basic Cooked Rice** (page 252)

Note: It's better to select one large turtle instead of more than one small turtle; otherwise, you will have a lot of small bones to deal with and you'll probably end up with less meat.

Trim any black skin, gristle, or anything else that doesn't look like meat or fat (the fat is yellowish-orange) from the turtle meat. Cut meat into about 1½ inch pieces.

Place the oil and meat in a 5½-quart saucepan or large Dutch oven over high heat. Cover pan and cook about 25 minutes, stirring only occasionally and scraping pan bottom well each time. Remove cover, stir well, and cook uncovered until all the meat is well browned and crisp, about 15 minutes, stirring only when sediment builds up on pan bottom, then scraping pan bottom well as you stir. Remove pieces of meat and browned particles as they finish browning. (**NOTE**: This sediment build-up enhances the flavor of the dish significantly. If the mixture begins sticking so much that you feel you are losing control of it, remove the pan from heat as needed and scrape well, then continue cooking.) Remove the pan from heat and, with a slotted spoon, transfer meat and any large pieces of fat or dark brown sediment to a bowl.

Stir pan bottom well to loosen any remaining browned sediment, then add to the pan the onions, bell peppers, celery, and garlic. Place pan over high heat and cook about 10 minutes, stirring and scraping pan bottom frequently. Stir in the stock, tomato sauce, red pepper, salt, and black pepper. Add the turtle meat and drippings, stirring well; cover and bring to a boil. Reduce heat and simmer about 1½ hours, stirring occasionally.

Now skim off any fat from the surface, then stir in the green onions and parsley. Re-cover pan and cook until meat is tender and starting to fall off the bone, about 10 minutes more. (**NOTE**: You may need to add more stock or water if the meat requires longer cooking; the finished gravy should be fairly thick and rich.) Remove from heat and skim off any fat. Serve immediately over rice.

If you have leftovers, don't be surprised if the heat of the pepper is toned down; if that happens, simply add more red pepper when you reheat. Simmer a few extra minutes to let the pepper cook into the sauce.

ABEL AND JO'S RECIPE

Cajun Fried Turkey
(D'inde Frite)

Makes about 10 main-dish servings

When the older Prudhomme children were youngsters, the family spent Christmas and Easter with their Prudhomme grandparents. Abel remembers that Dad's parents raised turkeys, geese, guinea hens, and ducks and that Grandma Prudhomme cooked all the different fowl for Christmas and Easter dinners. That was the only time the family had turkey in those early years. Later, Elden and Odelia Mae often brought a turkey with them from New Orleans when they came to visit at Thanksgiving and New Year's, but the family didn't ever raise turkeys, geese, or ducks.

Abel and Jo serve fried turkey fairly often for special company and on holidays. This is a relatively new dish in South Louisiana (created about seven years ago), and it's quite the rage. It originated in the Acadiana Parishes (Cajun country), as did many of South Louisiana's favorite and best dishes. The frying method produces a turkey with wonderfully moist meat that contrasts beautifully with the crunchy skin. Abel injects the turkey meat with a mixture of seasoning vegetables, spices, stock, and butter, so the meat is seasoned throughout. In Cajun country, almost everyone fries turkey in pork lard.

Abel and Jo serve candied yams or baked sweet potatoes, rice dressing, potato salad, and cranberry sauce with the turkey. (They use the turkey carcass to make an excellent stock for gumbo and soup.)

If at all possible, select a fresh (never frozen) turkey and one that has not been injected with butter, seasonings, or other flavorings. You will need a food injector (page 5) with a fairly large hole to inject the turkey with the seasoning purée. Do this a day ahead, then cover and refrigerate until ready to cook.

It is really best to fry the turkey outdoors, using a butane burner or other outdoor cooking equipment. Be sure to place the burner or other equipment on a concrete slab or some type of solid, level, and *nonslippery surface. (A few drops of oil will probably bubble over, so have some old towels handy for wiping up slippery spots.)*

Whether you fry the turkey indoors or out, you will need a heat source capable of producing a lot of heat quickly, so you can maintain a constant, moderately hot (350°) oil temperature while the turkey is frying.

And, while frying, you have to be very careful to avoid splashing or sloshing the very hot oil on you or anyone else close by. We cannot overstress this! Be certain that any possible distractions—including children—are under control. To avoid possible burns (we learned the hard way!), we strongly advise you to have a complete "dress rehearsal" (as described in the recipe) before you begin heating the large volume of oil.

Seasoning mix:
2 teaspoons salt
2 teaspoons ground red pepper (preferably cayenne)

1 (10- to 12-pound) dressed turkey, preferably fresh
    (never frozen), and not injected with butter,
    seasonings, or other flavorings
4 tablespoons unsalted butter
¾ cup finely chopped onions
¼ cup finely chopped celery
3 tablespoons minced garlic
2 tablespoons **Ground Hot Pepper Vinegar,** peppers only (page 357)
1 tablespoon plus 1 teaspoon salt
1 tablespoon ground red pepper (preferably cayenne)
1 teaspoon black pepper
½ cup **Basic Turkey** or **Chicken Stock** (page 18)
2 tablespoons Worcestershire sauce
About 5 gallons vegetable oil for frying

Thoroughly combine the seasoning mix ingredients in a small bowl and set aside.

To prepare the turkey: If your turkey comes with a metal prong that holds the cavity closed, remove and set it aside. Remove the giblets and neck from the turkey. (Remember to check both ends for the giblets—they can be packed in either or both places.) Place turkey and neck in a large pan. (Use giblets in another recipe.) If your turkey comes with a plastic "pop-up" doneness indicator, be sure to remove and discard it. Set pan aside.

In a large skillet, melt the butter over high heat until half melted. Add the onions and sauté about 3 minutes, stirring occasionally. Add the celery, garlic, Ground Hot Pepper Vinegar peppers, the 1 table-spoon plus 1 teaspoon salt, the 1 tablespoon red pepper, and the black pepper. Cook until mixture is a rich golden brown, about 3 minutes, stirring and scraping pan bottom frequently. Add the stock and Worcestershire and bring to a boil, stirring constantly. Remove from heat and immediately transfer mixture to a blender; blend on highest speed until mixture is a very smooth purée, pushing sides down as needed to make sure every bit of the vegetables is finely puréed (so it won't stop up the injector needle).

Rinse and drain turkey well. While purée is still hot, pour it into the food injector and inject the purée into the turkey: Insert to the bone or to the depth of the injector needle, without piercing through to the cavity. To fill the injection hole with the purée as much as possible, from bone to surface of bird, begin to draw the needle out as you inject the purée. Make holes about 2 inches apart and use most of the purée in the meatiest areas; be sure to inject some of the purée in the upper joint of the wing, too. Pour any remaining purée (the part that won't go through the injector) into the cavity of the turkey and rub it over the inner surface. Set turkey aside.

Sprinkle the reserved seasoning mix evenly over the bird and inside the cavity, rubbing it in by hand and using it all. Place the neck inside the cavity. Close the legs and tail together with the metal prong (or fold legs back into skin flaps, or tie legs together with kitchen twine). Cover and refrigerate overnight.

Equipment: Assemble all equipment and utensils before starting to fry the turkey. You will need:

1. A butane burner or other heat source with adjustable control capable of producing a strong flame.

2. A very deep pot (8-gallon size or larger) so the turkey will be totally submerged in hot oil with plenty of room left over—a depth of several extra inches for the oil to bubble in without bubbling over.

3. A large boiling or fry-basket (large enough for the turkey to fit inside with room to spare) that fits the pot; the turkey will be slipped into and lifted out of the bubbling hot oil in the basket.

4. A thermometer that reads up to at least 400° and has a long probe and clip so it can be left in the hot oil while the turkey fries.

5. Two strong and heatproof utensils (two 20-inch, or longer, barbecuing forks work well for this) to use for turning the turkey over in case it doesn't stay submerged in the oil. (Or you can weight the turkey down to keep it submerged while frying by inserting a long-handled heatproof fork securely under the metal prong or by pressing down on the turkey with a strong and heatproof utensil. But don't weight it down with anything so broad that it will keep a spot of skin from frying crisp.)

6. A large platter or pan lined with several thicknesses of paper bags to drain the turkey once it's fried.

7. Plenty of hot pads (potholders).

8. Old towels to place on the ground around the burner in case oil bubbles over and makes the surrounding area slippery.

Dress rehearsal: Let the turkey sit at room temperature for 1 hour before frying. Place the turkey on its back inside the boiling or fry-basket. Place the basket in the *empty* pot and measure the turkey's height in the pot with a ruler; be sure to include in the measurement the thickness of the basket bottom and any space between the basket bottom and the pan bottom. Remove basket and turkey from the pot. Place pot on the burner and fill it with oil at least up to the height of the total measurement made with the ruler. (Remember that the turkey itself, as well as the basket, will displace some of the oil, making the oil come up higher in the pot.)

Before heating the oil, have the "dress rehearsal." Drain off any liquid that has accumulated in or under the turkey and pat the turkey dry, so no water will get into the oil and make the oil pop when heated. Place the turkey in the basket, then rehearse in detal how you will maneuver the turkey throughout the cooking process.

First, practice slipping basket and turkey slowly and with total control into the cold oil, so the oil will slosh the least amount possible—and definitely not out of the pot! Then practice removing basket and turkey with no sloshing of oil. Also practice how you will turn the turkey over, if need be, while it's cooking. This run-through should help you determine how much sloshing of oil to expect so you can make any necessary adjustments in order to work safely and competently when the oil is hot. (Be sure to wear closed shoes and appropriate clothing—no bathing suits, please!—while frying the turkey.)

To fry the turkey: Remove basket and turkey from the cold oil. Heat the oil to 400°. *Very carefully and slowly* lower the basket containing the turkey into the hot oil. Immediately adjust flame or heat source down slightly and maintain a temperature lowered to as close to 350° as possible. You may have to adjust flame up again. Oil should be hot enough to bubble during frying but not so hot that it burns.

Make sure the turkey is either submerged completely while frying (weight it down if necessary), or turn it carefully, so oil doesn't slosh, about every 10 to 15 minutes. Let the turkey fry until the juices run clear when you insert a skewer into the breast meat. Or check doneness of meat by removing basket from hot oil and cutting the meat to the bone at the thigh-hip joint where meat is densest; the meat should look pink but not raw. Total frying time will be from 35 to 45 minutes. The fried turkey will look very dark brown when done. Don't be afraid that it has burned; this is the right color.

Carefully remove basket and turkey from the hot oil and place the turkey, breast side *down*, on a platter or pan lined with several thicknesses of paper bags and let drain about 5 minutes, then turn turkey over to drain and cool about 15 minutes more before slicing. Carve as you normally do and serve immediately.

PAUL AND K'S RECIPE

Turducken®
(K-Paul's Thanksgiving Dinner)

Makes 15 to 25 main-dish servings

Paul and K coined the term "turducken" by combining the names of the turkey, duck, and chicken used in the recipe. It's a lot of fun to let your guests think you're serving them a regular holiday turkey. When you begin to carve it, they will be surprised to see how you cut right through the "bones"!

Since the turducken takes 12 to 13 hours to cook, and then it needs to cool at least 1 hour before it's carved, you need to plan your time wisely. First, be sure your oven temperature control is accurate. If not, or if you're not sure, get it adjusted; or use a dependable oven thermometer to monitor and control the temperature. Otherwise, your turducken may take considerably fewer or more than 12 to 13 hours to cook. A good thing to know is that since you are roasting the turducken at such a low temperature (190°, assuming your oven is accurate), you can leave it to cook a couple of extra hours with no harm done. Once it's removed from the oven, turducken will stay hot for several hours.

The quickest way to prepare turducken is to get friends and family to make the dressings. If you're on your own, make the three dressings the day before boning the fowl and assembling the turducken. Cover the cooled dressings tightly and refrigerate them until well chilled before you stuff them in the meat. Bone the birds (be sure to save the bones and necks for making stock) and assemble the turducken the day before cooking—and family or friends can have fun helping you with this, too. Keep the turducken refrigerated until ready to cook.

If you make everything yourself, you need plenty of stock. The recipe on page 115 yields about 2 gallons. Bone the birds first and refrigerate them, so you can use the bones in the stock.

To stuff the turducken, you will need about 7 cups of the andouille dressing; about 4 cups cornbread dressing; and about 3 cups oyster dressing. But it's also good to have additional dressing to serve in bowls at the table, so the dressing recipes are for amounts that give you plenty of extra.

If you're inexperienced at boning fowl, start with the turkey. It's big, so you can more easily see the bone structure. After doing the turkey, boning the duck and chicken will go much faster.

Each time you do a turducken, it will become easier; it doesn't take magical cooking ability, it just takes care. What is magical is the way people who eat it will feel about your cooking!

Make the gravy after the turducken has finished cooking. We always serve **Candied Yams** (page 282 or 283) with turducken.

Andouille Smoked Sausage Dressing (page 265)
Cornbread Dressing (page 267)
Oyster Dressing (page 263)

1 (20- to 25-pound) turkey
1 (4- to 5-pound) domestic duckling
1 (3- to 3½-pound) chicken

Seasoning mix:
3 tablespoons salt
1 tablespoon plus 1½ teaspoons sweet paprika
1 tablespoon onion powder
1 tablespoon garlic powder
1 tablespoon ground red pepper (preferably cayenne)
1½ teaspoons white pepper
1½ teaspoons dried thyme leaves
¾ teaspoon black pepper

Sweet Potato Eggplant Gravy (page 342)
A small hammer
A 3-inch needle (a "carpet" needle with a curved tip works well)
Strong thread to sew up the fowl
1 (15 × 11-inch) baking pan at least 2½ inches deep
1 pan, larger than the 15 × 11-inch pan, into
    which the smaller pan will fit with room to spare

Make the three dressings. Cool, cover well, and refrigerate. Then bone the fowl. It's helpful to keep the following in mind:

1. Your goal is to end up with one large piece of essentially boneless turkey meat; the boned turkey will contain only the tip end of each leg bone and the bones of the first two joints of each wing. You will end up with one piece of completely boneless duck meat and one piece of completely boneless chicken meat.

2. Be careful not to pierce the skin of the birds except for the initial slits. Cuts in the skin tend to enlarge during cooking, making the turducken less attractive as well as dryer.

3. Allow yourself plenty of time, especially if you're a beginner. And even if you are experienced, approach the boning procedure with a gentle, careful touch; the meat is not tough and you want to end up with as much of it off the bone and in one piece as possible.

4. Bone one side of each bird—either the left or right—before doing the other side.

5. Use a very sharp knife and use mainly the tip; stay close to the bone at all times with the knife.

6. It's worth the time and effort!

To bone the turkey: Place the turkey, breast side down, on a flat surface. Make an incision the entire length of the spine through the skin and flesh.

Starting from the neck end and using the tip of the knife, follow as close to the bone as you can cut, carefully teasing the skin and meat away from the frame. Toward the neck end, cut through the meat to expose the shoulder blade; feel for it first and cut through small amounts of meat at a time if you have trouble locating it. Cut the meat away from around the bone and sever the bone at the joint so you can remove the shoulder blade.

Disjoint the wing between the second and third joint. Free the heavy drumstick of the wing and remove it; be careful to leave the skin intact. Continue teasing the meat away from the backbone, heading toward the thighbone and being careful to keep the "oyster" (the pocket of meat on the back) attached to the skin instead of leaving it with the bone.

Cut through the ball-and-socket joint to release the thighbone from the carcass. You should now be able to open up the bird more to see better what bones are left to deal with. Continue teasing the meat away from the carcass until you reach the center front of the breastbone. Then *very* carefully separate the skin from the breastbone at the midline without piercing the skin; go slowly because the skin is very thin at this point.

Repeat the same boning procedure on the other side of the turkey, with the turkey still breast side down. When both sides are finished, carefully remove the carcass.

Then remove the thighbone and leg bone on each side as follows: Being careful not to break through the skin, use a small hammer to break the leg bone completely across, about 2 inches from the tip end. Then manipulate both ends of the bone with your hands to be sure the break is complete. Leave the tip of the bone in, but remove the leg bone and thighbone as one unit. To do this, cut the meat away from around the thighbone first, using the knife tip. Then, holding the thighbone up with one hand, use the other hand to carefully cut the meat away from around the leg-thigh joint. (Don't cut through this joint, and don't worry if it seems as if you're leaving a lot of meat around the joint—it can't be helped and, besides, it will add flavor when you make the stock with the bones!) Then use the blade of the knife to scrape the meat away from the leg bone; remove the leg-thighbone. With your hands or the knife, one by one remove as many pin bones from the leg meat as possible. Then, if necessary, pull the tip of the leg bone to turn the meat to the inside, so the skin is on the outside and the bird looks like a turkey again. Refrigerate.

To bone the duck: Place the duck, breast side down, on a flat surface and follow the same procedure you used to bone the turkey, except this time you will remove all the bones instead of leaving in part of the wing and leg bones.

To bone each wing, cut off the first two joints of the wing (and save for stock), leaving the wing's drumstick; cut the meat from around the drumstick and remove this bone, being careful not to cut through the skin.

When you reach the thigh, follow the thigh-leg bone with the knife blade to release the bone as one unit, again being careful not to cut through the skin.

Trim some of the excess skin and fat from the neck area. Cut the skin into small pieces and reserve it for making the gravy; discard the fat. Refrigerate the duck and skin pieces.

To bone the chicken: Use precisely the same procedure to bone the chicken that you used for the duck.

To assemble the turducken: Spread the turkey, skin side down, on a flat surface, exposing as much meat as possible. Sprinkle the meat generously and evenly with a total of about 3 *tablespoons* of the seasoning mix, patting the seasoning in with your hands. (Be sure to turn the leg, thigh, and wing meat to the outside so you can season it, too.) Then stuff some of the cold **andouille dressing** into the leg, thigh, and wing cavities until full but not tightly packed. (If too tightly packed, the leg and wing may burst open during cooking.) Spread an even layer of dressing over the remaining exposed meat, about ½ to ¾ inch thick. You should use a total of about 7 *cups* dressing.

Place the duck, skin side down, on top of the andouille dressing, arranging the duck evenly over the dressing. Season the exposed duck meat generously and evenly with about 1 *tablespoon* more seasoning mix, pressing it in with your hands. Then spread the cold **cornbread dressing** evenly over the exposed duck meat, making the layer slightly less thick than the andouille dressing, about ½ inch thick. Use a total of about *4 cups* dressing.

Arrange the chicken, skin side down, evenly on top of the corn-bread dressing. Season the exposed chicken meat generously and evenly with about *1 tablespoon* more seasoning mix, pressing it in with your hands. Spread the cold **oyster dressing** evenly over the exposed chicken meat, making the layer about ½ inch thick. Use a total of about 3 cups dressing.

Enlist another person's help to carefully lift the open turducken into an ungreased 15 × 11-inch baking pan at least 2½ inches deep. (**NOTE**: This pan size is right because the turducken should fit snugly in the pan to stay in proper shape while cooking.) As you lift the turducken into the pan, fold the sides of the turkey together to close the bird. Have your helper hold the turkey closed while you sew up all openings on one side, making the stitches about 1 inch apart. When you finish sewing on the first side, turn the turducken over in the pan and sew closed any openings in the other side. Then tie the legs together just above the tip bones. Leave the turducken breast side up in the pan, tucking in the turkey wings.

Place the turducken pan in a slightly larger pan with sides at least 2½ inches high, so that the larger pan will catch the overflow of drippings during cooking. Season the exposed side of the turducken generously and evenly with about 2 *tablespoons* more seasoning mix, patting it in with your hands. Refrigerate until ready to bake. (Use any remaining seasoning mix in another recipe.)

Bake at 190° until done, 12 to 13 hours, or until a meat ther-mometer inserted through to the center reads 165°. (**NOTE**: There is no need to baste the turducken, but you will need to remove accu-mulated drippings from the turducken pan every few hours so that the lower portion of the turkey won't "deep fry" in the hot fat.) When done, remove the turducken from the oven and let it cool in its pan at least 1 hour.

Meanwhile, make the gravy with some of the pan drippings and the reserved duck skin.

With strong spatulas inserted underneath (remember there are no bones to support the bird's structure), carefully transfer the tur-ducken to a serving platter and present it to your guests before carv-ing. Then place the turducken on a flat surface to carve. (Or leave on the platter if it is large enough.) Be sure to make your slices crosswise so that each slice contains all three dressings and all three meats. It's easy to do this and still have servings of manageable size if you slice the turducken in half lengthwise, then cut servings crosswise to the desired thickness from one side of the turducken at a time.

Serve additional bowls of the dressing on the side.

Basic Turducken Stock

If you don't have a large enough stockpot, cut the recipe in half and make the stock in batches. You can use the vegetable trimmings (onions and celery, but not bell peppers) from the dressings and gravy you are preparing.

About 2½ gallons cold water (see **NOTE**)
Bones and necks from the turkey, duck, and chicken,
  or use 5 pounds backs, necks and/or bones and/
  or giblets (excluding livers) from turkeys and
  chickens
3 medium onions, unpeeled and quartered
½ stalk celery, separated into ribs
½ large head garlic, unpeeled and coarsely chopped

NOTE: Always start with cold water, enough to cover all the other ingredients.

Place all ingredients in a large stockpot. Bring to a boil over high heat, then gently simmer at least 4 hours, preferably 8, replenishing the water as needed to keep about 2 gallons of liquid in the pot. Strain, cool, and refrigerate until ready to use. Makes about 2 gallons. **NOTE:** Remember, if you are short on time, that using a stock simmered 20 to 30 minutes is far better than using just water in any recipe.

BEEF

VIANDE DE BÊTE

PAUL AND K'S RECIPE

Sunday Roast Beef

Makes 10 main-dish servings

This roast is really well seasoned and wonderfully juicy; the fennel seeds make it just a little different. It's perfect for Sundays and special occasions.

Stuff the roast the day before, cover well, and refrigerate until ready to cook. Paul and K like their beef medium rare. If you like yours medium or beyond, just extend the roasting time as directed at the end of the recipe.

1 (7½- to 8-pound) aged rib-eye roast, about 4 inches
    thick at thickest part

    Seasoning mix:
    2½ teaspoons salt
    2½ teaspoons white pepper
    1½ teaspoons dry mustard
    1½ teaspoons ground red pepper (preferably cayenne)
    1½ teaspoons black pepper
    1½ teaspoons whole fennel seeds
    1½ teaspoons onion powder

6 tablespoons unsalted butter
1½ cups finely chopped green bell peppers
1½ cups finely chopped onions
1½ cups finely chopped celery
1 tablespoon minced garlic

Trim the roast of all silver skin, trim off the USDA stamp, and trim the fat cap to about ¼ inch thick. Lay the roast, fat side up, in a 15 × 11-inch roasting pan (without rack) suitable for refrigerating.
    Combine the seasoning mix ingredients in a small bowl.
    Melt the butter over medium heat in a large heavy skillet until

half melted. Add *3 tablespoons plus 1 teaspoon* of the seasoning mix and the bell peppers and sauté about 3 minutes, stirring occasionally. Add the onions and celery and sauté about 3 minutes, stirring occasionally. Add the garlic and sauté about 1 minute more, stirring and scraping pan bottom well. Remove from heat and spread vegetable mixture on a large plate to cool and to stop the cooking process. Set aside.

Season the roast evenly on all sides with the remaining 2¼ *teaspoons* seasoning mix and then rub bottom of roast (side without fat cap) with ¼ cup of the vegetable mixture. Turn the roast fat side up and cut 10 to 12 deep slits (about 2 to 3 inches long) in the roast to form pockets. Cut the slits in the lengthwise direction, with the grain (so that when the meat is sliced, all the slices will contain some of the vegetable mixture), being careful not to cut through to the bottom. Set aside ¼ cup of the vegetable mixture. Stuff the pockets with·the remaining vegetable mixture, being sure to stuff it to the depths of the pockets. Spread the reserved ¼ cup vegetable mixture on the top and sides. Cover and refrigerate overnight. Keep refrigerated until just before ready to cook.

Bake the roast uncovered at 300° for about 2 hours and 20 minutes for a true rare (a cool red center) or about 2 hours and 35 minutes for medium rare. Remove from oven and transfer roast to a cutting board or platter; let sit 15 to 20 minutes before carving.

NOTE: If you start with your roast at room temperature, it will take considerably less cooking time—about 1 hour and 30 minutes for true rare and 1 hour and 40 minutes for medium rare. Cooking times will vary, too, if your roast is more or less than 4 inches thick. A trustworthy method is to use a meat thermometer inserted in the thickest part of the meat: A true rare will register 127°, medium rare 138°, medium 148°, medium well 158°—and any temperature in excess of 165° is considered well done.

Stuffed Beef Roast
(Rôti de Viande de Bête Piqûre à l'Ail)

Makes 6 to 8 main-dish servings

Beef certainly wasn't an everyday dish for the family. Dad usually killed a steer only in the winter, and he occasionally bought a beef soupbone or a package of mixed cuts of beef. But back when the oldest children were youngsters, Elden says that, in early summer every year, about ten families in the neighborhood would get together to have "boucheries quartiers," which means to divide up the butchering. One of the ten families would kill a young steer that weighed enough so it could be split up to make fresh meat for each family to use until the next boucherie. Then, each week, another one of the ten families killed a steer of the same size and split the meat the same way. Abel remembers that sometimes as many as sixteen families participated in boucheries together.

Even when the family had fresh beef, they rarely had it in the form of a roast, which Mom Prudhomme cooked only for a very special occasion. Bobby says she cooked it just like he does: "She stuffed it with the same ingredients; she cooked it covered; and she cooked it well done—and the pan juices were the gravy." All the family like beef cooked well done, but there's a difference between well done and dry as shoe leather. Cook the roast just until it is tender and the meat juices run clear, but no longer.

Stuff the roast a day ahead, cover well, and refrigerate until ready to cook. For this cooking procedure, it is important to have a layer of fat on the top of the meat. The fat bastes the roast as it cooks and adds to the flavor of the pan gravy.

1 (3- to 3½-pound) boneless beef rump roast (about
    1½ inches thick), with a layer of fat on top

Stuffing:
1 cup chopped onions
½ cup chopped green bell peppers

3 tablespoons unsalted butter, melted
1½ teaspoons minced garlic
1 teaspoon salt
1 teaspoon ground red pepper (preferably cayenne)
1 teaspoon black pepper

1½ cups **Basic Beef Stock** (page 18)
Salt for the gravy, to taste

Place the roast, fat side up, on a flat surface or in a pan suitable for refrigerating. With a large knife, make 6 to 12 deep slits in the top of the roast to form pockets that are roughly parallel to the grain (so that each serving will contain some of the stuffing), being careful not to cut through to the bottom. Make the slits about 3 inches long and fairly close together.

In a medium-size bowl, combine the stuffing ingredients, mixing thoroughly. Spoon the mixture into the pockets, using all but about 3 tablespoons; rub the remaining mixture on the top and sides of the roast. Cover well and refrigerate overnight. Keep the roast refrigerated until ready to cook.

Place the roast, fat side up, in a large Dutch oven or large heavy roasting pan. Pour the stock around the edges. Cover pan tightly or seal it snugly with aluminum foil. Bake at 350° just until meat is tender and juices run clear, from 1 hour to 1 hour and 30 minutes. The cooking time will vary according to the thickness of the roast.

Remove from oven and transfer roast to a serving platter. Skim fat from gravy and add salt to the gravy, if needed. Serve immediately, spooning gravy over each slice of meat.

RALPH AND MARY ANN'S RECIPE

Stuffed Smothered Steak
(Steak Piqûre à l'Ail et Etouffé)

Makes 8 to 10 main-dish servings

Ralph says that one source of fresh beef for the family was a neighborhood door-to-door meat man who butchered regularly and came by the house on Tuesdays and Thursdays. His steaks cost fifteen cents a pound, and mixed cuts of beef sold for ten cents a pound. For fifteen cents, Bobby says, Mom Prudhomme could buy enough ground beef for a meatloaf recipe that fed about twenty people.

Ralph and Mary Ann rub sugar and mustard on this stuffed steak to help it brown. You can taste just a nice hint of mustard after the steak is cooked. They, too, like beef well done, but not dry! If you take the steak out of the oven as soon as it's tender and the juices run clear, it will be beautifully moist.

Stuff the steak with the seasonings the day before, cover well, and refrigerate until ready to cook.

Stuffing:
½ cup finely chopped onions
¼ cup finely chopped green bell peppers
1 tablespoon very finely chopped garlic
2 teaspoons sugar
2 teaspoons salt
2 teaspoons prepared mustard
1 teaspoon ground red pepper (preferably cayenne)
1 teaspoon black pepper
1 teaspoon white vinegar

    Seasoned mustard:
    1 teaspoon prepared mustard
    1 teaspoon sugar
    ½ teaspoon salt
    ½ teaspoon black pepper

1 (4-pound) boneless sirloin or other good-quality
    boneless beef steak, about 2 inches thick
1 medium onion, peeled and cut into eighths (about
    ½ pound)
1 cup coarsely chopped green bell peppers
1½ cups **Basic Beef Stock** (page 18)
1 tablespoon all-purpose flour
Hot **Basic Cooked Rice** (page 252)

In a small bowl, combine the stuffing ingredients, mixing well. In a separate bowl, mix together the seasoned mustard ingredients.

Make 12 to 14 deep slits in the steak with a knife, to form pockets, being careful not to cut through to the bottom. Stuff the pockets fully with the stuffing mixture, using it all. Rub the surface of the steak thoroughly with the seasoned mustard. Cover well and refrigerate overnight. Keep refrigerated until ready to cook.

Place the steak, stuffing side up, and the juices it has given off in a heavy ovenproof 8-quart pan or large Dutch oven with as broad a bottom as possible, so the steak will lie flat. Sprinkle the onion and bell peppers on top of the meat and pour *1½ cups* of the stock around the edges and a little over the meat. Cover pan and bake at 300° for 1 hour. Remove lid, push any pieces of onion and bell pepper on the sides of the pan back into the liquid, and continue baking uncovered just until tender and juices run clear, about 1 hour and 45 minutes more. The cooking time will vary according to the thickness of the steak.

Remove pan from oven and transfer steak to a platter. Skim off and discard fat from the pan juices. Spoon out about 3 tablespoons of the pan juices into a small bowl and mix with the flour until smooth. Place pan over high heat and gradually stir in the flour mixture until well blended. Bring to a boil, then reduce heat and simmer until juices thicken a little and flour is cooked, about 10 minutes more, stirring and scraping pan bottom frequently.

Remove from heat and serve immediately with some of the pan gravy spooned over the meat and rice.

BOBBY'S RECIPE

Country Steak and Gravy
(Steak et Sauce de Campagne)

Makes 6 to 8 main-dish servings

Bobby says that later, when he was a youngster, the family had a regular source for fresh beef: Mom Prudhomme's sister and her husband owned a country store and Dad was their butcher. Every two weeks, Dad and Mom's brother-in-law began butchering at about one o'clock in the morning; they killed the steer and had the meat cut up and ready to sell by the time the store opened for business at seven o'clock. Dad always took fresh beef as payment for doing the butchering.

This steak and gravy is Bob's own creation, and one of our chefs who tasted it said, "I could get really serious about this food—it not only tastes country, it tastes 'Grandma'!"

When we tested and retested the recipe, we found that sirloin and other lean steaks don't work well for the cooking procedure. Shoulder steak and similar less expensive cuts are better because they have fat that adds flavor to the gravy and keeps the meat moist. Moreover, in the testing we were reminded of the dramatic difference in taste and texture when food is cooked covered rather than uncovered. It's the covered cooking that makes this steak and the gravy so good.

Season the meat a day ahead, cover well, and refrigerate until ready to cook.

This dish is cooked for fairly long periods of time over high heat. If your gas burner or electric cooking element produces a very high heat, or if your pot is not a heavy one, you will need to adjust the temperature down.

2½ pounds boneless beef shoulder steak (chuck,
    blade, or seven-bone steak) ½ inch thick, cut
    into about 10 pieces
    Seasoning mix:
2¼ teaspoons salt

2 teaspoons black pepper
1 teaspoon garlic powder
½ teaspoon ground red pepper (preferably cayenne)

Scant ½ cup vegetable oil
About 5 cups, *in all*, **Basic Beef Stock** (page 18)
½ cup plus 2 tablespoons all-purpose flour
1 cup chopped onions
⅔ cup chopped green bell peppers
¼ cup minced fresh parsley
1½ teaspoons black pepper
¼ teaspoon salt
Hot **Basic Cooked Rice** (page 252), mashed
     potatoes, or **Crusty Houseboat Biscuits** (page 22)

Place the meat in a large pan. Combine the seasoning mix ingredients thoroughly in a small bowl. Sprinkle the meat evenly with the
seasoning mix, working it in by hand and using it all. Cover well and
refrigerate overnight.

Heat the oil in a very large heavy skillet for about 1 minute over
high heat. Place the meat in the pan in a single layer and cook without turning until well browned on the underside, about 8 minutes.
Turn meat pieces over, reduce heat to medium high, and cook about
15 minutes, turning meat once or twice more and rotating pan if
necessary so it browns evenly.

Remove from heat and pour off ⅓ cup of the hot oil into a glass
measuring cup and set it aside. (It's okay if the ⅓ cup oil has some
sediment in it.) Return skillet with meat to low heat, add *1 cup* of
the stock, and stir until browned sediment is dissolved from pan
bottom. Stir in *3 cups* more stock, cover, and cook about 15 minutes,
stirring once or twice.

Meanwhile, make the roux. In a 2-quart cast-iron Dutch oven,
heat the reserved ⅓ cup oil over high heat until hot, about 3 minutes. Using a long-handled whisk or wooden spoon, gradually stir
the flour into the hot oil. Reduce heat to medium and cook, stirring
briskly or whisking constantly, until roux is medium brown, about 4
minutes, being careful not to let it scorch or splash on your skin.
Remove from heat and stir until roux stops getting darker, 1 to 2
minutes. Set aside.

✳See page 12 for more about making roux.

When the meat-and-stock mixture has cooked its last 15 minutes, add to the skillet the onions, bell peppers, parsley, pepper, and salt, stirring well. Add the roux by spoonfuls to the skillet (around the meat, not on it), stirring until well mixed before adding more. Cover and continue cooking about 25 minutes more (adjust heat if necessary to maintain a simmer), stirring and scraping pan bottom occasionally. **NOTE**: If gravy gets too thick, add a little stock or water, but keep in mind that the finished gravy is fairly creamy. See **Lagniappe.** Remove from heat and serve immediately.

··············**LAGNIAPPE**··············

At the end of the cooking time, try this experiment, which is a good method to use with any rich gravy or sauce. Spoon out about ½ cup of the gravy or sauce from the pan and add roughly 1 tablespoon stock or water to the ½ cup gravy. Taste, then compare the taste with the gravy in the pot. We find that gravies can sometimes cook down to be so rich that they actually "lock off" the wonderful flavors you're after. If your sample tastes better than what's in the pan, "open" the gravy back up by simply adding more stock or water.

ELI AND SUE'S RECIPE

Stuffed Beef Tongue
(Langue de Bête Piqûre à l'Ail)

Makes 4 main-dish servings

Paul says, "In the early years, the family had beef tongue only when we butchered, but later, when Dad had an 'envie,' a yen, for tongue, he went out and bought one. He seemed to like some things at certain times of the year—year after year—but beef tongue was one thing he loved at any season."

Mom Prudhomme cooked beef tongue just as Eli and Sue do, stuffing it first, then braising it until tender. Stuff the tongue with the seasonings the day before, cover well, and refrigerate until ready to cook.

1 (2-pound) fresh young beef tongue, unskinned (get
    butcher to skin it for you) or 1 (1- to 1½-pound)
    skinned and trimmed tongue

Stuffing:
3 tablespoons very finely chopped onions
3 tablespoons very finely chopped green bell peppers
2 tablespoons minced garlic
1½ teaspoons **Ground Hot Pepper Vinegar,** vinegar
    only (page 357)
1½ teaspoons prepared mustard
¾ teaspoon salt
½ teaspoon ground red pepper (preferably cayenne)
¼ teaspoon black pepper
¼ teaspoon **Ground Hot Pepper Vinegar,** peppers
    only (page 357; see **Note**)

2 tablespoons vegetable oil
4 cups **Basic Beef Stock** (page 18)
1 cup very finely chopped onions
1 cup chopped green bell peppers
½ cup coarsely chopped onions
½ ounce peeled garlic cloves, about 4 large
1 teaspoon salt
½ teaspoon black pepper
¼ teaspoon ground red pepper (preferably cayenne)
Hot **Basic Cooked Rice** (page 252), optional
Crusty Houseboat Biscuits (page 22), optional

Note: If your Ground Hot Pepper Vinegar peppers are exceptionally mild, you may want to use more.

If the tongue is not skinned, see the **Lagniappe** for how to skin and trim it.

In a small bowl, combine the stuffing ingredients, mixing thoroughly.

Place the skinned tongue on its side on a flat surface. With a knife, make 6 to 10 deep slits in the tongue to form pockets, being careful not to cut through to the bottom. Make the slits about 2 inches long and parallel to the length of the tongue so that when it is sliced, all the slices will contain stuffing. Fill the pockets with the stuffing mixture, using your fingers to pack it down and using as much as possible. Rub the outside of the meat thoroughly with any excess mixture, and turn the tongue stuffing side up. Cover well and refrigerate overnight. Keep refrigerated until ready to cook.

In a heavy 6-quart pan or a large Dutch oven with a broad enough bottom for the tongue to lie flat on its side, heat the oil over high heat about 1 minute. Place the tongue, stuffing side up, in the pan; cover and cook about 3 minutes. Turn meat over and scrape pan bottom well. (A sturdy spatula works well for scraping under the meat.) Re-cover pan and cook about 1 minute.

Now remove cover and cook about 1 minute, scraping pan bottom frequently. Add ½ *cup* of the stock and scrape pan bottom well; cook about 1 minute. Turn meat over, add ½ *cup* more stock, cover pan again, and cook about 5 minutes without stirring.

With pan still over high heat, transfer tongue to a plate and scrape the pan bottom clean. Add to the pan the remaining *3 cups* stock, the very finely chopped onions, bell peppers, coarsely chopped onions, garlic, salt, and black and red peppers, stirring well. Return meat to pan, stuffing side up; cover and cook about 10 minutes without stirring.

Now reduce heat to a simmer, remove cover and scrape pan bottom if needed, then re-cover pan and continue cooking until meat is tender, about 1 hour and 30 minutes, turning meat over at least once. Test for tenderness by inserting a fork into the tongue; when done and tender, it will still have a very solid feel to it, but the fork should come out without much effort. Remove pan from heat and mash garlic cloves in the gravy with a fork. Serve immediately.

To serve, slice meat crosswise into slices about ½ inch thick, making sure each serving contains some of the stuffing. Spoon the gravy over the meat and the rice or biscuits, if desired.

· · · · · · · · · · · · · ·**·LAGNIAPPE·**· · · · · · · · · · · · · ·

To skin the beef tongue, blanch it in boiling water for about 10 minutes. Then submerge it in a large bowl of ice water just a few seconds until cool enough to handle. Skin the tongue while still hot; as it cools it becomes harder to skin. Use a sharp boning or paring knife to peel away skin and trim fat and gristle from the thicker end. When finished, the meat will look more or less like a raw, lean beef loin. If necessary, blanch any trouble spots again, as needed, submerging just those spots in boiling water.

ELDEN AND ODELIA MAE'S RECIPE

Meatballs in Brown Gravy
(Boulettes dans une Sauce Rouillée)

Makes 6 to 8 main-dish servings

Elden says Dad Prudhomme built a long bench for the small children to sit on at the dinner table because "there were just too many kids to have separate chairs." (And, Elden says, the very small children slept four or five to a big bed.)

The family call meatballs "boulettes," and the children loved them, just the way kids still love meatballs today. Mom Prudhomme cooked ground-beef boulettes in brown gravy when she had mixed cuts or scraps of fresh beef. Odelia Mae serves spaghetti in a red sauce as a side dish with her nicely seasoned meatballs. (Yes, she serves rice, too!) The meatballs and gravy would make a fantastic po boy with **Ground Hot Pepper Vinegar Mayonnaise** (page 335).

3 pounds ground beef
3 slices white sandwich bread
3 cups very finely chopped green onions, *in all* (tops and bottoms)
2 cups very finely chopped onions, *in all*
⅔ cup very finely chopped green bell peppers, *in all*
¼ cup plus 2 tablespoons very finely chopped fresh parsley, *in all*
1 large egg
1 tablespoon plus 2 teaspoons very finely chopped garlic, *in all*
1 tablespoon plus ½ teaspoon salt, *in all*
1 tablespoon **Ground Hot Pepper Vinegar,** *in all,* peppers only (page 357; see **Note**)
2½ teaspoons black pepper, *in all*
2 teaspoons ground red pepper (preferably cayenne)
½ cup all-purpose flour
¾ cup vegetable oil
4 cups water, *in all*
About 6 cups hot **Basic Cooked Rice** (page 252)

Note: If your Ground Hot Pepper Vinegar peppers are very hot, use your own judgment on how much to use.

Put the meat in a very large mixing bowl. Wet the bread thoroughly under tap water, then squeeze out moisture and add the bread to the meat. Add *1½ cups* of the green onions, *1 cup* of the onions, *⅓ cup* of the bell peppers, *2 tablespoons* of the parsley, the egg, *2 teaspoons* of the garlic, *1 tablespoon* of the salt, *2 teaspoons* of the Ground Hot Pepper Vinegar peppers, *1½ teaspoons* of the black pepper, and the red pepper. Mix thoroughly by hand until bread has disappeared into the mixture. Form into 16 meatballs, each about 2½ inches in diameter.

Place the flour in a medium-size bowl and set aside.

In a heavy 6-quart saucepan or large Dutch oven, heat the oil over high heat for about 3 minutes. Brown meatballs in two batches. Just before browning each batch, dredge meatballs thoroughly in the flour, shaking off excess. Set aside 2 tablespoons of the flour. Cook each batch in the hot oil until dark brown and crisp on all sides, a total of 12 to 14 minutes, scraping pan bottom clean. (With a slotted spoon, remove and reserve browned particles that have stuck to the pan bottom.) Reduce heat if oil starts smoking excessively. Remove browned meatballs and as much browned sediment as possible to a platter and set aside.

Remove pan from heat and scrape pan bottom well again to loosen any remaining sediment. Pour the hot oil left in the pan into a large glass measuring cup, leaving as much sediment in the pan as possible. Return ⅓ cup of the oil (and as much of the sediment in the cup as possible) to the pan.

Combine the remaining 1½ *cups* green onions, *1 cup* onions, ⅓ *cup* bell peppers, and *1 tablespoon* garlic in a bowl and set aside. Place pan over medium heat. Add the 2 *tablespoons* reserved dredging flour and cook about 1 minute, stirring constantly and scraping pan bottom to loosen any sediment still sticking. Add the vegetable mixture and cook about 8 minutes, stirring and scraping pan bottom almost constantly. Add *1 cup* of the water and the remaining ¼ *cup* parsley, scraping until pan bottom is clean. Add the remaining *3 cups* water and the browned meatballs and reserved drippings to the pan.

Turn heat to high and bring to a strong boil, stirring occasionally. Reduce heat to medium and cook and stir about 5 minutes. Add the remaining *1 teaspoon* black pepper, *1 teaspoon* Ground Hot Pepper Vinegar peppers, and ½ *teaspoon* salt, stirring well. Cover, reduce heat, and simmer about 20 minutes more, stirring occasionally.

Remove from heat, remove cover, and let sit about 15 minutes. Skim fat from surface (tilt pan to do this) and serve meatballs and gravy over rice. Allow 2 meatballs and about ¾ cup rice topped with about ½ cup gravy for each serving.

DARILEE AND SAUL'S RECIPE

Beef Ribs Sauce Piquant
(Sauce Piquante de Côtes de Boeuf)

Makes 6 to 8 main-dish servings

Saul learned how to make sauce piquant from Calvin, and since then he and Calvin have made it regularly on their camping trips together. Calvin says that when he and Saul make sauce piquant, they don't taste it very often while it's cooking because they're usually having "toddies"—several toddies, since sauce piquant has to cook for quite a while.

Sauce piquant can be made relatively fast, but it just doesn't taste the same as it does when it's simmered for a long time. Old-timers like Saul as well as younger Cajuns like Paul all say sauce piquant is better that way, and Saul even says, "The longer you cook it, the better it is."

This dish is cooked not only for fairly long periods of time, but also over high heat. If your gas burner or electric cooking element produces a very high heat, or if your pot is not a heavy one, you will need to adjust the temperature down.

Seasoning mix:
2 tablespoons ground red pepper (preferably cayenne)
1 tablespoon plus 2 teaspoons salt
1 tablespoon plus 1 teaspoon black pepper

5 pounds very meaty bone-in beef short ribs (have
    your butcher cut them into about 2 × 2-inch
    pieces)
About 3 tablespoons vegetable oil, *in all*
4 cups chopped onions
3 cups chopped green onions (tops and bottoms)
1½ cups chopped celery
1 cup chopped green bell peppers

½ cup finely chopped fresh parsley

1 (8-ounce) can tomato sauce

¾ cup **Cajun Home-Canned Spicy Tomatoes** (page 359)

2 tablespoons minced garlic

About 3 quarts, *in all*, **Basic Beef Stock** (page 18)

Additional ground red pepper (preferably cayenne), optional (see **NOTE**)

Hot **Basic Cooked Rice** (page 252)

NOTE: It may be necessary to add extra ground red pepper to achieve a true sauce piquant if your home-canned tomatoes were made with relatively mild peppers. (Remember, sauce piquant is supposed to be hot!)

In a small bowl, thoroughly combine the seasoning mix ingredients. Place the meat on a flat surface and sprinkle it evenly with the seasoning mix, working it in by hand and using it all.

Just barely cover the bottom of a heavy 12-quart kettle or very large Dutch oven (with as broad a bottom as possible) with oil. (About 2 *tablespoons* of oil will probably do; the oil should definitely be less than ⅛ inch deep.) Heat the oil over high heat until hot, about 3 minutes. Add the ribs to the pan, arranging them so as many of them touch the pan bottom as possible; cook until all ribs are *very* well browned on all surfaces, 35 to 45 minutes, turning meat infrequently at first, but more often once the browning process has started. (**NOTE:** Be sure to scrape pan bottom well, especially toward the end of the cooking time, as the browned sediment sticks to the pan more and more. This browning procedure is an essential part of the final taste of the dish; if the meat gives off a lot of juice, or if the pan bottom is small, you might need more time to brown the meat, but it's worth taking the time!) Remove the pan from heat and transfer the meat with a slotted spoon to a bowl. Set aside. The meat will taste wonderful at this point—but don't eat it yet!

If you have more than about 3 tablespoons of fat left in the pan, drain off the excess, leaving as much sediment in the pan as possible. To the pan add the onions, green onions, celery, bell peppers, parsley, tomato sauce, spicy tomatoes, and garlic. Place over high heat and cook about 5 minutes, stirring occasionally. Cover pan and continue cooking over high heat about 20 minutes, stirring as needed and scraping pan bottom well each time to make sure mixture is not sticking excessively. (If mixture is sticking, reduce heat.) Reduce heat to low and cook covered until mixture is well browned, about 10 minutes more, stirring and scraping pan bottom as needed.

Remove pan from heat and spoon off all but about 1 tablespoon fat, leaving as much sediment in the pan as possible. (**NOTE**: You may not have any fat left in the pan; if not, add 1 tablespoon fresh oil.) Place pan over high heat and cook mixture again about 5 minutes, stirring and scraping pan bottom as needed. Reduce heat to medium and add *2 cups* of the stock, scraping pan bottom clean. Cook uncovered until mixture starts to stick, about 20 minutes, stirring and scraping occasionally. Stir in *1 cup* more stock, stirring until any sediment is dissolved, then stir in *2 cups* more stock and add the reserved meat. Cook about 30 minutes, scraping pan bottom as needed.

NOTE: The meat should stay almost covered with liquid—but it doesn't need to be completely covered—for the remaining cooking time. If a lot of the meat is not covered with liquid after you add each amount of stock called for next, add just enough extra stock or water to bring the liquid up to the proper level—keeping in mind that the finished sauce should be quite rich and, although not creamy-thick, not watery either.

Now, add *3 cups* more stock, stirring and scraping well. Taste the liquid and, if desired, add more red pepper. Cook about 15 minutes, stirring and scraping as needed. Add *2 cups* more stock, stirring well. Return mixture to a boil. Then, if meat is tender, remove from heat and skim off fat. Conduct the taste experiment described in the **Lagniappe** to see if you are satisfied with the taste, then serve immediately over rice.

If meat is not tender, cover pan and cook until tender, stirring as needed. (**NOTE**: Since you're covering the pan, you probably will not need to add more stock or water.) Remove from heat and skim. Do the taste test, then serve immediately over rice.

If you have leftovers, don't be surprised if the heat level of the peppers tones down. If that happens, simply add more red pepper as you reheat and cook a few extra minutes to let the pepper cook into the sauce.

···············**LAGNIAPPE**··············

At the end of the cooking time, try this experiment, which is a good method to use with any rich gravy or sauce. Spoon out about ½ cup of the gravy or sauce from the pan and add roughly 1 tablespoon stock or water. Taste, then compare the taste with the liquid in the pot. We find that gravies and sauces can sometimes cook down to be so rich that they actually "lock off" the wonderful flavors you're after. If your sample tastes better than what's in the pan, "open" the gravy or sauce back up by simply adding more stock or water.

ENOLA AND SHELTON'S RECIPE

Cabbage Rolls
(Rouleaux de Chou)

Makes 4 main-dish servings

When cabbage was in season, Mom made the best of it and cooked cabbage rolls often. She filled them with a variety of stuffings, including pork, rice, chicken, beef—even cornbread dressing. The family loved them, whatever they were stuffed with.

Enola's cabbage rolls are really special—rich, sweet, and spicy hot—and they're good to serve to people who think they don't like cabbage! If you like a lot of cabbage flavor, you can double or even triple the number of leaves used to make each roll. Rice is perfect to serve on the side.

Seasoning mix:
2½ teaspoons salt
2 teaspoons ground red pepper (preferably cayenne)

1 teaspoon garlic powder
1 teaspoon black pepper

1 large head green cabbage (about 3 pounds), or
    enough to yield 6 to 8 or more large leaves plus 2
    packed cups of shredded cabbage
About 4 tablespoons unsalted butter, *in all*
2 cups chopped onions
¾ pound ground chuck
1 cup **Rich Beef** or **Chicken Stock** (page 19)
2 (8-ounce) cans tomato sauce, *in all*
1 cup chopped green bell peppers
½ cup chopped green onions (tops only)
¼ cup chopped celery
2 tablespoons finely chopped fresh parsley
½ teaspoon minced garlic

Thoroughly combine the seasoning mix ingredients in a small bowl and set aside.

Discard any outer leaves of the cabbage that are soiled or torn. Then carefully remove at least 6 leaves (use the largest possible), being careful not to tear them. It's a good idea to save 2 to 3 additional leaves in case you have extra stuffing. Set aside.

Finely shred enough of the remaining cabbage to yield 2 packed cups; set aside. (Use remaining cabbage in another recipe or steam and serve with butter at another meal.)

Trim the thick stem end from each cabbage leaf and steam the leaves until tender enough to fold, 5 to 10 minutes. (Or, if you prefer, parboil them.) Drain leaves and set aside.

In a heavy 6-quart saucepan or large Dutch oven, melt *2 tablespoons plus 1 teaspoon* of the butter over medium-high heat. Add the onions and sauté until many of the onion pieces are dark brown, 10 to 12 minutes, stirring frequently. Remove from heat and with a slotted spoon transfer onions to a bowl. Return pan to high heat without wiping it. Add the meat to the pan and cook until browned, 3 to 4 minutes, stirring frequently and breaking up meat chunks. Remove pan from heat and with a slotted spoon transfer meat to the same bowl with the onions.

Pour the fat from the pan into a glass measuring cup and return 2 tablespoons fat to the pan. (If necessary, add more butter to make up the balance.) Add the shredded cabbage to the pan, place over high heat, and cook until cabbage starts to get soft, about 5 minutes, stirring and scraping pan bottom frequently. Add the stock, *1 can* of the tomato sauce, the bell peppers, green onions, celery, parsley, minced garlic, seasoning mix, and the reserved onions and meat, mixing well. Cook until mixture is fairly dry, about 12 minutes more, stirring occasionally. Remove from heat.

Working on a flat surface, fill each wilted cabbage leaf with one sixth (about ½ cup) of the filling. Fold the cabbage leaf, envelope style, and, if desired, tie with kitchen twine or secure with toothpicks. (If ½ cup filling is too much for the size of the leaves, make additional rolls with the reserved extra leaves.) Place the cabbage rolls, seam side up, in a greased 8 × 8-inch baking pan, arranging them so they fit snugly together.

Pour the remaining *1 can* tomato sauce evenly over the top of the rolls, coating each one thoroughly with the sauce. Seal the pan well with aluminum foil, being careful not to let foil touch the rolls or that spot may scorch. Bake at 425° until cabbage leaves are very tender, about 1 hour and 30 minutes.

Remove from oven and serve immediately. For each serving, allow 1½ cabbage rolls with sauce.

PORK

VIANDE DE COCHON

ABEL AND JO'S RECIPE

Andouille Smoked Sausage in Red Gravy
(Andouille dans une Sauce Rouge)

Makes 4 main-dish servings

When Mom and Dad Prudhomme retired from the family grocery store, Abel and Jo bought it. Then Abel made all the sausages and boudins for the store, and he quickly became well known in Opelousas for his excellent products. He's still making fine sausages; now he runs Paul and K's andouille and tasso plant.

Mom made sausage in red gravy "wonderfully," according to Paul, who says, "She used homemade smoked pork sausage in it and served the dark red gravy over rice." Abel and Jo serve sausage in red gravy often, usually over rice, but occasionally over macaroni or spaghetti— and even over (yes, over!) potato salad.

Select sausage of the best quality you can find since it is the dominant taste of the dish. Abel makes an excellent stock for red gravy (and other dishes) in a pressure cooker; he uses browned bones for the stock.

This dish is cooked for fairly long periods of time over high heat. If your gas burner or electric cooking element produces a very high heat, or if your pot is not a heavy one, you will need to adjust the temperature down.

6 tablespoons unsalted butter
1½ pounds andouille smoked sausage (preferred) or
    any other good smoked pure pork sausage, such
    as Polish sausage (kielbasa), cut into 2-inch pieces
3 packed cups, *in all*, julienned onions (see **NOTE**)
6½ cups, *in all*, **Basic Pork** or **Beef Stock** (page 18)
1½ teaspoons ground red pepper (preferably cayenne)
¾ teaspoon salt

½ cup finely chopped celery
½ cup finely chopped green bell peppers
1 teaspoon minced garlic
1 (8-ounce) can tomato sauce
¼ cup finely chopped fresh parsley
1 cup, *in all*, finely chopped green onions (tops only)
About 3 cups hot **Basic Cooked Rice** (page 252),
    noodles or spaghetti, or potato salad, such as
    Sweet and Seasoned Potato Salad (page 327)

NOTE: Julienne strips should be 1½ × ¼ × ¼-inch.

Melt the butter in a heavy 8-quart pan or large Dutch oven over high heat until pan bottom is well coated with butter. Add the sausage in a single layer and cover pan; cook without stirring until sausage is well browned on the bottom, about 7 minutes. Turn sausage over and sprinkle 2 *packed cups* of the onions on top of it. Re-cover pan and cook without stirring until sausage and onions in contact with pan bottom are well browned, and until there is a buildup of dark brown sediment, about 7 minutes.

Add ¾ *cup* of the stock and scrape the pan bottom clean. Add the pepper and salt, stirring and scraping pan bottom well and turning sausage again. Re-cover pan and cook about 2 minutes, stirring and scraping once. Add the celery, bell peppers, and garlic, stirring well. Re-cover pan and cook about 3 minutes, stirring and scraping once or twice.

Add the tomato sauce, stirring well. Continue cooking uncovered about 5 minutes, stirring and scraping occasionally. Add ½ *packed cup* more onions, stirring well. Cook until large puddles of fat have broken out of the mixture and the remaining tomato mixture is thick, about 8 minutes, allowing the sediment to build up on the pan bottom before stirring. (Stir only if the mixture is sticking excessively to the pan bottom.)

Stir in the parsley and ½ *cup* of the green onions. Add 3¼ *cups* more stock, scraping pan bottom clean; cook until liquid has reduced to a thick, dark red gravy, about 20 minutes, stirring occasionally (more often toward the end of cooking time). Stir in the remaining 2½ *cups* stock, ½ *packed cup* onions, and ½ *cup* green onions; bring to a boil, then reduce heat, and simmer until gravy is noticeably thicker but still juicy, about 15 minutes more, stirring frequently.

Remove from heat and serve immediately, allowing about ¾ cup rice mounded in the center of each plate surrounded by about ¾ cup gravy and 3 to 4 pieces of sausage.

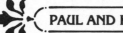

PAUL AND K'S RECIPE

Salt Meat in Red Gravy

Makes 8 main-dish servings

Dad Prudhomme made homemade salt meat for Mom to use as a seasoning meat. He cut slabs of pork belly into large pieces to fit the crockery jars he used for curing. He rubbed each piece with as much salt as possible and laid them in the jars with more salt between the layers. After several weeks the meat was cured, and the streaks of lean in the pork belly were a dark red color, like pastrami. He also made **Ti Salé** *(page 171).*

For many years, homemade salt meat was a staple in Cajun kitchens, but few people make it today because it's readily available in supermarkets and called salt pork, though it rarely contains any lean to speak of. Salt meat is traditionally used as a seasoning meat for beans, peas, and other vegetables, but in Cajun cooking it is also eaten as a main-course meat and called poor man's meat because it's inexpensive.

The Prudhomme family, like most Cajun families, love starches. Mom typically served a bean dish and a dried-pea dish, both over rice, as well as bread, and sometimes potato salad, too, with salt meat in red gravy. What Mom Prudhomme just naturally knew, that a meal like this would feed her family well with almost no meat, is common knowledge now. Combine those good starches, especially rice and beans, and you're putting together something that adds up to real protein.

The red tomato gravy is loaded with fresh vegetables and leftovers are terrific.

Seasoning mix:
2 tablespoons sugar
2½ teaspoons dried sweet basil leaves
2 teaspoons onion powder
2 teaspoons gumbo filé (filé powder)
2 teaspoons dried thyme leaves
1 teaspoon garlic powder
1 teaspoon ground red pepper (preferably cayenne)
1 teaspoon sweet paprika
½ teaspoon white pepper
½ teaspoon dried oregano leaves

8 cups water, *in all*
2 pounds salt pork, as meaty as possible, cut into
      pieces about 1 inch thick by 3 inches long by ½
      inch wide (see **Note**)
½ pound (2 sticks) unsalted butter, *in all*
4 cups chopped onions, *in all*
3 cups chopped celery
2 cups chopped green bell peppers
1 (8-ounce) can tomato sauce
3 cups **Basic Pork Stock**, *in all* (page 18)
5 cups peeled and chopped tomatoes
2 bay leaves
Salt to taste
Hot **Basic Cooked Rice** (page 252) or spaghetti (see **Note**)

Note: Salt pork with lean in it is fairly rare in the average super-market. It's worth seeking out a specialized pork butcher to get a lean cut. If serving over spaghetti, cut the salt pork into bite-size pieces.

Combine the seasoning mix ingredients thoroughly in a small bowl. Set aside.
   Bring 4 *cups* of the water to a boil in a 4-quart saucepan over high heat. Add the salt pork, cover pan, and cook about 5 minutes. Remove from heat and drain off water, leaving meat in the pan. Add the remaining 4 *cups* water to the pan; cover and bring to a boil.

Remove from heat and drain very well. Set aside.

In a 5½-quart pan or large Dutch oven, melt *1 stick* of the butter over high heat. Add *2 cups* of the onions and sauté until onions are dark brown, 10 to 12 minutes, stirring occasionally. Remove from heat and transfer onion-and-butter mixture to a bowl; set aside.

In the same pan, melt the remaining *1 stick* butter over high heat. Add half the drained meat (make sure it's well drained or it will pop fiercely!) to the pan in a single layer. Cover pan with lid askew and cook, without stirring, until meat is well browned, about 3 minutes. Turn meat over and scrape the pan bottom well. Place lid askew and cook about 1 minute. Add the remaining meat and *2 cups* onions, stirring well. Add the celery, bell peppers, and tomato sauce, stirring well and scraping pan bottom clean of any browned sediment. Cover pan tightly and cook about 2 minutes without stirring. Stir well, re-cover pan, and cook about 3 minutes without stirring. Then stir again, re-cover pan, and cook about 3 minutes more without stirring. Remove lid and cook about 5 minutes more, stirring and scraping pan bottom frequently.

Now stir in the seasoning mix and cook uncovered about 5 minutes, stirring frequently and scraping pan bottom well. Add *1 cup* of the stock, the tomatoes, bay leaves, and the reserved browned onion mixture, stirring well. Cover pan and bring to a strong boil, stirring occasionally. Reduce heat and simmer covered about 20 minutes, stirring frequently. Add the remaining *2 cups* stock and continue simmering until meat is tender and flavors marry, about 40 minutes more, stirring and scraping fairly often so mixture doesn't scorch.

Remove from heat and skim off fat. Discard bay leaves and add salt, if needed. Serve immediately over rice or spaghetti.

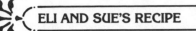

Cracklins
(Gratons)

Makes about 2½ quarts cracklins

Cold weather was the time for boucheries, and the Prudhomme children all got to stay home from school because a boucherie was a family affair. All the married children came home to help. Dad raised a special breed of hogs for lard, "old-fashioned lard-type hogs," according to our food encyclopedia, versus "desirable meat-type hogs," which were used for fresh pork and to make sausage, tasso, grillades, and andouille. About two or three months before the time for a boucherie, Dad penned up two of the lard hogs and force-fed them with corn to make them get extra fat. They were penned in a small enclosure and the hog trough was kept full of corn around the clock.

Cracklins were a by-product of rendered hog lard back then. The family used about forty to fifty gallons of lard a year, and it took at least two huge hogs to produce that much. Mom and Dad stored it in five- and ten-gallon crockery jars. Today, the roles have switched: Lard is a by-product of cracklins—which are wonderful! Eli remembers helping to cook cracklins when he was a boy, but he says, "What I'm really an expert on is eating cracklins!" Now he and Sue make cracklins often, but they make them for the cracklins, not for the lard, though they do store the lard in quart or gallon jars and use it for cooking. (It makes really crisp fried potatoes!) Eli says to cook cracklins only on dry days "because they just don't turn out as good on humid days."

Cracklins are made from fresh fatback—unsmoked and uncured, very fatty bacon. (In North Louisiana, where Sue grew up, fatback is called pork rind.) It's best to use fatback from young pigs because the cracklins will be more tender. Use a cast-iron pot; cracklins tend to stick less in cast iron.

If you haven't tasted fresh cracklins, you haven't tasted cracklins, period! Perfect cracklins are almost a lost art. They're blistered on the outside (the blisters help tenderize them) and they crumble and melt in your mouth. Try cracklins and sweet potatoes together—they're fantastic.

145

You will have about 2 to 3 quarts of lard left over, which can be used for cooking. Let it cool, then strain it into jars, and store in the refrigerator.

About 1 cup pork lard (preferred) or vegetable oil
8 pounds pork fatback (preferably with some lean
    meat in it), cut into ¾-inch cubes (see **Note**)
A bowl of water or a sprinkler bottle full of water
About 2 tablespoons salt, to season the hot cracklins

Note: Be sure to get very fresh fatback that has never been frozen; if possible, get fatback from a young pig. Chill well before cutting (it will cut more easily) and cut so there is lean meat in every piece.

In an 8-quart Dutch oven (preferably cast iron), heat lard ¼ inch deep over high heat until hot but not smoking, about 3 minutes. Carefully slip the pieces of fatback into the hot fat and stir well. Cook until all cracklins are golden brown, about 55 minutes, stirring occasionally (more often toward end of cooking time) and scraping pan bottom well each time so cracklins won't stick. **Note:** After cooking a few minutes, there will be enough fat in the pan to measure the temperature with a thermometer. If using lard, don't let the temperature go above about 330°; if using oil, don't let it go above about 400°.

Continue to cook about 5 minutes more while using a slotted spoon to scoop spoonfuls of cracklins out of the lard; sprinkle them with several drops of water to form white blisters on the surface of the pieces and return to the pot. **Note:** Work carefully and do not burn yourself. Sprinkle only a few drops of water at first so you can judge how much—if any—popping of the oil to expect. When we retested the recipe for the book, our fat did not pop much, but if yours pops excessively and you are afraid of getting burned, continue to cook the cracklins until done, as described below, and skip this step of sprinkling with water.

Then continue cooking until done (see **Lagniappe** for how to test for doneness), about 15 minutes more, sprinkling water every few seconds—one small handful at a time, carefully and directly onto the cracklins in the pan—to make more white blisters on the skins. Eli likes them blistered a lot!

Drain on paper towels and, while still piping hot, salt generously on all sides. Serve immediately. Store leftovers in an airtight container.

···············**LAGNIAPPE**···············

To test for doneness, remove a few cracklins of different sizes or shapes from the hot fat and let drain a couple of minutes, then cut in half. When done, the cracklins should be cooked through and should not look greasy on the inside.

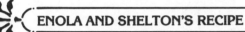

ENOLA AND SHELTON'S RECIPE

Baked Pork Backbone
(Reintier de Cochon Rôti)

Makes 4 to 6 main-dish servings

Enola didn't like working in the fields, but Mom Prudhomme didn't mind outside work, so Enola began to cook for the family when she was twelve years old. She stayed home each morning and gathered fresh vegetables from the garden, then killed a chicken or used whatever meat Mom had on hand to prepare dinner, and got lots of hot water ready by 11:30 sharp, when the rest of the family returned from the fields, washed up, and ate dinner. Then the others all headed back to the field work, and Enola cleaned up the kitchen, made the beds, and did the washing.

Enola and Shelton's baked pork backbone is a simple and tasty country dish. The cooked vegetables in the gravy have a nice crunchiness and the gravy is delicious served over **Smothered Potatoes** *(page 299). Because the backbone pieces are quite bony, everyone gets a heaping plateful.*

In the country at local stores, it is possible to buy pork "back-bone" as a roast or cut into pieces, but pigs are no longer butchered this way commercially. What the term means is the unsplit spine of the pig, cut out separately, with some meat left attached. Except for an occasional loin roast (saddle), the animal is now always split down the spine. If your market does its own butchering, ask for whole backbone crosscut into pieces. Otherwise, bone-in cuts such as pork loin fingers or country-style pork ribs will work admirably.

Seasoning mix:
1 tablespoon salt
2½ teaspoons ground red pepper (preferably cayenne)
1 teaspoon garlic powder
½ teaspoon black pepper

6 pounds meaty pork backbone (have your butcher
    cut it into 2-inch squares), bone-in pork loin
    fingers, or country-style pork ribs
About ¼ cup melted pork lard (preferred) or
    vegetable oil
1 cup chopped onions
1 cup chopped green bell peppers
1 cup **Basic Pork** or **Chicken Stock** (page 18)

Combine the seasoning mix ingredients thoroughly in a small bowl. Place the pork pieces in an ungreased 15 × 11-inch baking pan. Rub the lean meaty areas of the pork lightly with the lard so they won't dry out during baking. Sprinkle the seasoning mix evenly on both sides of the meat pieces, pressing it in by hand and using it all. Turn pieces fattest side up and arrange in a single layer, as nearly as possible. (Fat side up will also help keep the meat from getting dry.)

Bake at 525° until the fat on the pork pieces is crisp and browned, 20 to 25 minutes. Reduce oven temperature to 300° and remove pan from oven momentarily. Sprinkle the onions and bell peppers evenly over the meat, then pour the stock over all. Return pan to oven and bake at 300° until meat is cooked through and tender, about 1 hour. Remove from oven and serve immediately.

Baked Pork Chops with Onion Gravy

Makes 6 main-dish servings

Behind the family home was about 300 acres of forest, a common woodland for hunting and fishing as well as the source of firewood for all the families living nearby. The Prudhommes used an enormous amount of firewood each year for cooking and for heating the house in winter. Dad periodically took the four oldest boys to the woods for a week at a time to cut, haul, and stack wood.

The fellows cut the trees down with a crosscut saw, trimmed the limbs, and cut the trunks and limbs into pieces that could be pulled by the mules back to the house, to be cut up later and split with axes, splitting wedges, and mauls. There was always a pile of uncut wood and a stack of stove wood next to the house, and the stove wood was continually replenished by the boys when they found some time to cut and split more pieces. Most of them also earned spending money by selling firewood. Dad let them use the equipment and the mules and wagon, and they sold the wood in town for seventy-five cents a cord.

Ralph and Mary Ann serve these delicious pork chops and gravy with rice or mashed potatoes. Ralph says when Mom Prudhomme cooked rice, the kids fought over who would get the bottom part that had scorched slightly in the pan. Mom loved it, too. The family call the scorched rice "gratin," and they eat it with milk.

Seasoning mix:
2½ teaspoons salt
2¼ teaspoons ground red pepper (preferably cayenne)
1¼ teaspoons black pepper

12 (½-inch-thick) pork chops, about 2¾ pounds (see **NOTE**)
About 3½ tablespoons margarine, *in all*
4 cups coarsely chopped onions, *in all*
1 teaspoon very finely chopped garlic
3 cups **Basic Pork Stock** (page 18)
Hot **Basic Cooked Rice** (page 252) or mashed potatoes

NOTE: Choose fairly fatty chops so the meat will stay moist while baking.

Combine the seasoning mix ingredients thoroughly in a small bowl. Sprinkle the mix evenly on both sides of the chops, pressing it in by hand and using it all. Cover and refrigerate overnight.

Grease a very large heavy skillet generously with margarine and heat over high heat until hot, about 3 minutes. Add the chops in batches and cook until well browned, about 3 minutes per side. As chops finish browning, transfer to a 15 × 11-inch ungreased baking pan.

In the same (unwiped) skillet used to brown the chops, melt *3 tablespoons* of the margarine over high heat. Add *2 cups* of the onions and sauté until onions are dark brown, 5 to 7 minutes, stirring frequently. Stir in the remaining *2 cups* onions and cook and stir 1 to 2 minutes more. Stir in the garlic, remove from heat, and immediately spoon mixture evenly over the chops. Pour the stock around the edges. Seal pan tightly with aluminum foil and bake at 400° until meat is cooked through and tender, about 30 minutes.

Remove from oven and serve immediately with rice or mashed potatoes, spooning gravy over the meat and rice or potatoes.

ALLIE AND ETELL'S RECIPE

Fresh Hot Pepper Pork Roast
(Rôti de Cochon avec Piments Forts Frais)

Makes 6 to 8 main-dish servings

Allie was an outdoor person at heart and preferred to be outside working and playing with the boys. But as the third child and second girl—and with Darilee, the eldest girl, having the responsibility for baby-sitting—she had to begin helping Mom with the cooking when she was six years old. Then, when Allie was fourteen, Mom was con-fined to bed for a year with a back problem, and Allie took over all Mom's jobs—cooking, cleaning, and doing the laundry. "I wasn't afraid to take over. I knew I could do it because I had been helping Mom for years. I cooked everything from chicken to turtle, which meant I also had to kill and clean the chickens and clean the turtle."

Allie's pork roast is stuffed with fresh hot peppers. Mom stuffed fresh peppers in her pork roasts, too; she raised cayenne, bird's-eye, and other hot peppers, though not jalapeños. The roast is wonderfully peppery hot. One of our reliable tasters took a bite and said right off, "Hello, mouth!" If you think you can't take the heat, cut back on either the fresh or the ground peppers—but we urge you not to; we would hate for you to miss out on the authentic taste. Serve the roast with something bland like rice or mashed potatoes, spoon the spicy pan gravy on the meat only, and then enjoy the contrasts in spiciness and texture.

Each of the pork roast recipes in the book is different because of the different cuts of meat used and because of the variations in the seasonings and cooking methods. Allie's roast is the spiciest, and the vegetables in her gravy maintain a nice crunchiness. Season it a day ahead, cover well, and refrigerate until ready to cook.

1 (4½-pound) bone-in Boston butt (shoulder) pork roast

Stuffing:
1 tablespoon plus 2 teaspoons minced garlic
1 tablespoon plus 1½ teaspoons salt
2¼ teaspoons ground red pepper (preferably cayenne)
1 teaspoon sugar
2 teaspoons coarsely chopped fresh hot peppers, such
     as cayenne or jalapeño peppers (see **Note**)

⅔ cup vegetable oil, plus about ½ cup if needed
2 cups chopped onions
1 cup chopped green bell peppers
4 cups plus 3 tablespoons, *in all*, water
1 tablespoon all-purpose flour
Hot **Basic Cooked Rice** (page 252), mashed
     potatoes, or **Smothered Potatoes** (page 299),
     optional

NOTE: Fresh peppers can vary significantly in heat value, so start with one-half the amount called for, then taste before adding more. Fresh jalapeños are preferred; if you have to use pickled ones, rinse as much vinegar from them as possible.

Place the roast, fat side up, in a very large bowl or pan suitable for refrigerating. With a sharp knife, cut 8 to 12 deep slits in the top of the meat to form pockets about 1½ inches long, making the slits as deep as possible without going through to the bottom. Also make 1 or 2 pockets in each end. **NOTE:** If your roast is meatier on the side opposite the fat cap, cut pockets on both sides of the roast, making sure the meatier side contains most of the stuffing.

In a small bowl, combine all the stuffing ingredients except the fresh peppers, mixing well. Set aside about 2 tablespoons of the stuffing mixture. Spoon some of the remaining mixture into each pocket, rubbing it in by hand to the depth of the pocket and using it all. Rub the reserved 2 tablespoons stuffing over the outside of the roast, working it into all folds and openings. Place at least one piece of fresh pepper in each pocket, using all the pepper pieces. Cover well and refrigerate until ready to bake, preferably overnight.

In a heavy ovenproof 8-quart pan or large Dutch oven, heat the ⅔ cup of oil over high heat until hot, about 3 minutes. Carefully slip the roast into the hot oil and carefully turn it over to coat all sides, ending with the fat side down. Reduce heat to medium and cook without turning until browned on the bottom, about 3 minutes. **NOTE:** Reduce heat further if any garlic from the stuffing falls into the oil and browns to a very dark color. Turn meat over and continue cooking until all remaining surfaces are well browned, about 10 minutes, turning meat about every 3 minutes and scraping sediment as necessary from the pan bottom. Remove any very dark sediment from the pan as the meat is browning and reserve it.

Remove from heat and scrape the pan bottom well with a metal spatula. Turn roast fat side up, transfer pan to a 450° oven, and bake about 10 minutes. Reduce oven setting to 275°, remove pan from oven, and transfer roast momentarily to a platter. Pour the hot oil from the pan into a large glass measuring cup and return ½ cup oil and as much browned sediment as possible back to the pan, including any reserved very dark sediment. **NOTE:** If oil contains any bitter-tasting sediment, discard, and use ½ cup fresh oil.

Return roast to the pan, fat side up. Add the onions and bell peppers around the roast. Pour *1 cup* of the water around the roast and a little over the top. Return pan to the 275° oven and bake just until meat is tender and juices run clear, about 2 hours and 30 minutes, adding *1 cup* more water after the first 30 minutes. Do not overcook.

NOTE: Cooking time will vary according to the thickness of the roast. An easy way to test for doneness is to insert a skewer into the thickest part of the meat and then withdraw it; the first juices will probably run clear whether or not the meat is done. Wait a few seconds, then check again; if the juices still run clear, the roast is done. Or, use a meat thermometer to measure the internal temperature: Insert the probe into the densest part of the meat, making sure not to touch a bone. When done, the temperature should read between 160° and 170°. Be sure to take a reading in at least two places.

Remove pan from oven and transfer roast to a serving platter. Cover roast loosely with aluminum foil and let sit at least 15 to 20 minutes before carving.

Skim off most of the fat from the pan. (We skimmed about ¼ cup, but the amount will vary depending on the fat content of the meat and you will need some fat left in the drippings.) Add *2 cups* more water to the pan, stirring well. Place the pan over high heat and bring to a boil. Meanwhile, in a small bowl blend together the remaining *3 tablespoons* water and the flour until smooth. When the liquid in the pan has reached a boil, gradually stir in the flour mixture. Continue cooking about 15 minutes more, stirring almost constantly. Remove from heat.

For each serving, allow a slice of roast and a portion of pan gravy spooned over rice, mashed potatoes, or smothered potatoes, if desired.

Stuffed Pork Pot Roast
(Rôti de Cochon Piqûre à l'Ail)

Makes 4 to 6 main-dish servings

The family ate pork more often than beef—almost as often as chicken, according to Paul—because it was more available. The Prudhommes held their own boucheries only a couple of times a year, but Mom and Dad grouped together with relatives and friends to stagger all their boucheries throughout the fall, winter, and early spring. The family prepared enough cured pork (like salt meat, andouille, tasso, and smoked pork sausage) during the boucherie to last until the next fresh pork was available. In addition, Dad would occasionally kill just one or two smaller hogs to provide fresh meat for several days and supplement the larder of cured pork.

When Paul tasted Bobby's pork roast and pan gravy, he said, "This gravy brings back strong and very old memories! It's a taste I had often with pork roast at home when I was growing up." Bobby loves pork: "I can eat pork three times a day, seven days a week— and I used to before I began really watching my weight." His roast and pan gravy are delicious with **Sweet and Seasoned Potato Salad** *(page 327), or with rice, or the Prudhomme way—with both!*

Stuff the roast at least one day ahead, preferably three to four days before cooking, then cover well, and refrigerate until ready to cook. If you stuff it several days ahead, you'll want to be doubly sure the meat is very fresh and has never been frozen.

Seasoning mix:
2½ teaspoons salt
2½ teaspoons ground red pepper (preferably cayenne)
1¼ teaspoons black pepper

2 tablespoons unsalted butter
1 cup finely chopped onions
1 tablespoon minced garlic

¾ cup finely chopped green bell peppers
1 (3½- to 4-pound) bone-in pork sirloin roast
2 tablespoons pork lard or vegetable oil
About 8 cups, *in all*, **Basic Pork Stock** (page 18)
Hot **Basic Cooked Rice** (page 252) and/or **Sweet
    and Seasoned Potato Salad** (page 327), optional

Combine the seasoning mix ingredients thoroughly in a small bowl.

In a large skillet, heat the butter over medium heat until half melted. Add the onions and *1 tablespoon plus 1 teaspoon* of the seasoning mix; sauté about 3 minutes, stirring and scraping pan bottom frequently. Add the garlic and sauté just until garlic is lightly cooked, about 1 minute more, stirring and scraping pan bottom almost constantly. Remove from heat and let cool thoroughly, about 15 minutes, then stir in the bell peppers. Set aside.

Place the roast, fat side up, on a flat surface or in a pan suitable for refrigerating. With a sharp knife, form pockets by cutting 10 to 14 deep slits about 2 inches long in the top of the meat, and 1 or 2 slits in each end, being careful not to cut through to the bottom of the roast. Make the slits lengthwise so that when the roast is carved, each piece will contain some of the stuffing. Stuff the pockets with the vegetable mixture, using it all. **NOTE**: Once all the pockets are stuffed, be sure to pack any stuffing that may have fallen out firmly back into the pockets; you do not want the stuffing to fall into the oil when you brown the meat later.

Sprinkle the remaining *2¼ teaspoons* seasoning mix evenly over all sides of the roast, patting it in by hand. Cover well and refrigerate overnight or preferably for 3 to 4 days. Keep refrigerated until ready to bake.

In a heavy 6-quart saucepan or large Dutch oven, heat the lard or oil over high heat until hot, about 2 minutes. Place the roast, fat side down, in the pan; turn heat to medium and cook until meat is very well browned on the underside, about 8 minutes. Turn meat and continue browning all sides, about 10 minutes more, scraping pan bottom as needed. Prop up the roast to brown the ends and any angles of meat, too. Reduce heat if sediment gets very dark brown.

Remove pan from heat and transfer roast momentarily to a platter. Drain fat from pan, leaving as much brown sediment in the pan as possible. Add 2 *cups* of the stock to the pan and scrape the pan bottom clean of sediment. Return the roast and its drippings to the pan; cover and bring liquid to a boil over high heat. Place lid slightly askew and cook about 50 minutes, turning meat about every 10 minutes, and adding *1 cup* more stock after about 20 minutes, when the liquid in the pan bottom has reduced and thickened.

Now add *1 cup* more stock and make sure the roast is fat side up; re-cover pan tightly, reduce heat to low, and cook just until meat is tender and juices run clear, about 35 minutes more, adding *1 cup* more stock or water every 10 to 15 minutes, as the gravy continues to reduce and thicken. If necessary, add more stock or water near the end of the cooking time so the gravy yield is about 2 cups. Do not overcook meat. **NOTE**: The cooking time will vary according to the thickness of the roast. An easy way to check for doneness is to insert a skewer into the thickest part of a meat and then withdraw it; the first juices will probably run clear whether or not the meat is done. Wait a few seconds, then check again; if the juices still run clear, the roast is done. Or, use a meat thermometer to measure the internal temperature: Insert the probe into the densest part of the meat, making sure not to touch a bone. When done, the temperature should read between 160° and 170°. Be sure to take a reading in at least two places.

Remove from heat and let sit 15 to 20 minutes before carving. For each serving, allow a slice of roast and a portion of rice and/or potato salad, if desired, topped with the pan gravy.

 ABEL AND JO'S RECIPE

Smothered Stuffed Pork Backbone Roast
(Rôti de Reintier de Cochon Piqûre à l'Ail et Etouffé)

Makes 10 to 12 main-dish servings

"Each time we butchered," Abel explains, "Mom cooked a pork backbone roast like this, but it was big, about one and a half feet long. She

stuffed it with garlic, salt, black pepper, and red pepper, and roasted it in the oven just like we do today—except she used a wood-burning stove."

A pork backbone roast makes a beautiful presentation, and it's tender and juicy. If you don't live in the country where everyone knows what a pork backbone roast is and where it's readily available, you may have to special-order it from your butcher; it's worth doing! Ask for a pork saddle roast, which means it contains the backbone and the pork loins on each side of the backbone. Request it with the rind on; it has a unique and wonderful taste of its own.

Abel and Jo get their backbone roasts fresh from a slaughterhouse. The fresher the roast, of course, the better it will taste. Season the roast a day ahead. You will need a sturdy food injector, and it's a good idea to have an ice pick handy to make holes through the rind or the dense meat so you don't risk breaking the food injector needle. A standard food injector available from many cooking-supply stores or "gourmet" shops works fine for most of the recipes in this book, but a heavy-duty food injector—one in which the plastic device that holds the needle in place is sturdier than it is on smaller injectors—is needed for this thick, densely meated roast. For this recipe, we used what we call our "Cajun deluxe" model food injector, which we found at a veterinarians' supply store. (It's used for giving shots to big animals like horses.) The cylinder should hold at least 2 ounces (60cc), and the needle should be at least 2 to 3 inches long, with the eye or eyes as large as possible.

Unless you're an old hand at this, we suggest you wear old clothes or a smock-style apron when injecting the roast. Cover the roast well and refrigerate until ready to cook.

1 (7½- to 8-pound) pork saddle roast with rind left on
    (preferred), or substitute a bone-in center-cut pork loin roast

Seasoning mix:
    2½ teaspoons salt
    1¼ teaspoons ground red pepper (preferably cayenne)
    1¼ teaspoons black pepper

3 tablespoons unsalted butter
2 cups very finely chopped onions, *in all*
¾ cup very finely chopped celery, *in all*

¼ cup minced garlic
About 10 cups, *in all*, **Basic Pork Stock** (page 18)
2 tablespoons Worcestershire sauce
2 tablespoons **Ground Hot Pepper Vinegar**, mostly
    peppers (page 357; see **Note**)
¾ cup very finely chopped green bell peppers
Additional salt for the gravy, optional

Note: If your Ground Hot Pepper Vinegar is very hot, use your own judgment on how much to use.

Place the roast in a shallow pan suitable for refrigerating.

Combine the seasoning mix ingredients thoroughly in a small bowl and season the meat lightly and evenly with *1 teaspoon* of the mixture. Reserve the remaining seasoning mix.

In a 2-quart saucepan, heat the butter over high heat until half melted. Add *1 cup* of the onions and sauté until onions start getting soft, about 2 minutes, stirring occasionally. Add ¼ *cup* of the celery, the garlic, and the remaining *1 tablespoon plus 1 teaspoon* seasoning mix; cook until garlic is lightly browned, about 2 minutes, stirring and scraping pan bottom frequently. Turn heat to low and stir in ½ *cup* of the stock and the Worcestershire; then add the Ground Hot Pepper Vinegar (use mostly peppers with just a little vinegar). Cook about 2 minutes more, stirring constantly. Remove from heat and immediately transfer mixture to a food processor or blender; process until mixture becomes a *very* smooth purée, about 3 minutes, pushing sides down as needed. (It's extremely important to make the purée as smooth as possible so the injector needle will not clog up.)

Transfer the purée to a 1-cup measuring cup or small deep bowl, preferably with a pouring spout. While the purée is still hot, fill a food injector and inject the roast with the purée as deeply as possible, or to the bone, making the injections about 2 inches apart and in a fairly precise zigzag pattern so the seasoning will be distributed evenly. Rub any last bit of purée that won't go through the injector needle over the surface of the roast.

Note: If the injector needle gets clogged, reheat the purée with a little more stock or water, or process it in the blender again. If you are unable to find an injector with a needle large enough to handle the purée, make narrow, deep holes in the meat with a narrow-bladed knife and use your fingers to rub the purée to the bottom of the holes. Cover the roast well and refrigerate until ready to bake, preferably overnight.

Place the roast, rind or fat side up, in a heavy 15 × 11-inch roasting pan, a heavy ovenproof 10-quart pan, or a large Dutch oven. Pour *4 cups* of the stock around the roast. Bake uncovered at 500° until roast is well browned on top and bottom, about 30 minutes per side, turning the roast once. (If your oven size permits, you can brown the ends, too, about 10 minutes on each end.) Reduce oven setting to 275°, turn meat again to rind or fat side up, and continue cooking just until meat is tender and juices run clear, about 2 hours, adding *4 cups* more stock after about 1 hour. Do not overcook.

NOTE: Cooking time will vary according to the thickness of the roast. An easy way to test for doneness is to insert a skewer into the thickest part of the meat and then withdraw it; the first juices will probably run clear whether or not the meat is done. Wait a few seconds, then check again; if the juices still run clear, the roast is done. Or, use a meat thermometer to measure the internal temperature: Insert the probe into the densest part of the meat, making sure not to touch a bone. When done, the temperature should read between 160° and 170°. Be sure to take a reading in at least two places.

Remove pan from oven and transfer roast to a serving platter; cover roast loosely with aluminum foil and let sit at least 15 to 20 minutes before carving.

Place the pan with the drippings on the stove top and taste the sediment on the pan bottom. If it tastes burned or bitter, pour drippings into a large saucepan without scraping pan. If the flavor is good, scrape as much browned matter from the pan bottom as possible. Add to the drippings *1 cup* stock, *1 cup* onions, *½ cup* celery, and the bell peppers. Bring to a boil over high heat, stirring and scraping pan bottom frequently. Continue cooking until the onions are tender but still a little crunchy, about 10 minutes more, stirring and scraping pan bottom frequently. Remove from heat and skim off fat; add salt to gravy, if needed.

Carve the roast and serve immediately with the pan gravy.

ELDEN AND ODELIA MAE'S RECIPE

Cankton Stuffed Pork Roast
(Rôti de Cochon Piqûre à l'Ail)

Makes 8 to 10 main-dish servings

Odelia Mae so loves to cook that she has three kitchens—two in the house and one in their motor home, and each is fully (abundantly!) equipped. She says, "If you want to make me happy on my birthday or Christmas or Mother's Day, give me another pot or kitchen appliance." Elden also loves to cook, and in the early years of their marriage he did all the cooking while Odelia Mae was working.

Elden and Odelia Mae's roast, named for the small Cajun community where they live, is not very highly seasoned by Cajun standards, but it is delicious by anybody's standards. The Ground Hot Pepper Vinegar and mustard give the gravy a very individual flavor.

Buy the freshest meat you can and be certain it has never been frozen. Season the roast, cover well, and refrigerate for three to four days before cooking. It's essential to begin with very fresh meat when you season it several days ahead.

Stuffing:
1 cup finely chopped onions
⅓ cup plus 1 tablespoon finely chopped garlic
2 tablespoons **Ground Hot Pepper Vinegar,**
    peppers only (page 357; see **Note**)
2 tablespoons prepared mustard
2 tablespoons Worcestershire sauce
1 tablespoon plus ½ teaspoon ground red pepper
    (preferably cayenne)
1½ teaspoons sugar
1½ teaspoons black pepper
1 teaspoon salt
⅔ cup finely chopped green bell peppers

160

4 tablespoons unsalted butter
1 (8-pound) lean pork blade shoulder roast

Seasoned pepper vinegar:
1 tablespoon Ground Hot Pepper Vinegar; use both vinegar and
    peppers (page 357; see **Note**)
1 tablespoon sugar
2½ teaspoons salt
1 teaspoon black pepper
1 teaspoon prepared mustard
1 teaspoon Worcestershire sauce

1 cup very coarsely chopped onions
1 cup very coarsely chopped celery
1 cup very coarsely chopped green bell peppers
6 cups, *in all*, water
1 tablespoon all-purpose flour
Hot **Basic Cooked Rice** (page 252) or mashed potatoes, optional

Note: If your Ground Hot Pepper Vinegar is very hot, use your own judgment on how much of the peppers and vinegar to use each time. Or, if you like excitement, increase the amount of peppers!

In a medium-size bowl, combine all the stuffing ingredients except the bell peppers. In a large skillet, heat the butter over high heat until half melted. Add the stuffing mixture and sauté about 5 minutes, stirring and scraping pan bottom occasionally. Remove from heat and let cool thoroughly, about 15 minutes, then stir in the bell peppers.

    Place the roast, meatier side up, in a very large bowl or pan suitable for refrigerating. (Usually, on a blade roast, this is the side opposite the fat cap.) With a large sharp knife, cut about 8 deep slits to form pockets about 1½ inches long in the surface of the meat. Cut the slits to the bone, or as deep as possible without cutting through to the bottom of the meat. Make them in the direction opposite (at a right angle) to the direction in which the meat will be carved, so each slice will contain stuffing. Make 2 or 3 additional slits horizontally at each end of the meat and about 8 slits in the less meaty side.

Starting on the meatier side, fill each pocket well with the stuffing mixture, using it all and using most of it in the meatier side. Then stuff the ends and the underside of the roast. Rub any excess stuffing over the surface. In a small bowl, combine the seasoned pepper vinegar ingredients, mixing well. Rub the mixture thoroughly on all sides of the roast and into any pockets or folds of meat. Cover the roast well and refrigerate for several hours, preferably 3 to 4 days. Keep refrigerated until ready to bake.

Place the roast, fat side up, in a heavy ovenproof 8-quart pan or large Dutch oven. Add the onions, celery, bell peppers, and 4 *cups* of the water around the meat. Cover pan and bake at 450° for 30 minutes. Reduce heat to 275° and continue baking covered just until meat is tender and juices run clear, about 3 hours. Do not overcook.

NOTE: The cooking time will vary according to the thickness of the roast. An easy way to check for doneness is to insert a skewer into the thickest part of the meat and then withdraw it; the first juices will probably run clear whether or not the meat is done. Wait a few seconds, then check again; if the juices still run clear, the roast is done. Or, use a meat thermometer to measure the internal temperature: Insert the probe into the densest part of the meat, making sure not to touch a bone. When done, the temperature should read between 160° and 170°. Be sure to take a reading in at least two places.

Remove cover, turn oven setting to 450°, and cook until fat on top of roast is a crusty brown, about 8 minutes. Remove from oven and transfer roast to a serving platter. Cover roast loosely with aluminum foil and set aside for at least 15 to 20 minutes before carving.

Skim off most of the fat from the pan. (We skimmed about 1½ cups, but the amount will vary depending on the fat content of the meat and you will need some fat left in the drippings.) Place pan over high heat and cook until liquid reduces and thickens, about 10 minutes, scraping sides and pan bottom almost constantly to dissolve all browned sediment.

Meanwhile, transfer about 3 tablespoons of the liquid from the pan to a small bowl and mix with the flour, stirring until smooth. When the pan drippings have cooked about 10 minutes, gradually add the flour mixture, stirring until well blended. Stir in the remaining 2 *cups* water and bring to a boil, stirring occasionally. Reduce heat and simmer about 15 minutes more, stirring occasionally. Remove from heat and serve immediately. (Or, you may let the gravy sit about 10 minutes, then skim off the fat.)

For each serving, allow a slice of roast and a portion of rice or potatoes, if desired, topped with the pan gravy.

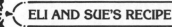

ELI AND SUE'S RECIPE

Stuffed Pork Roast with Dipping Gravy
(Rôti de Cochon Piqûre à l'Ail)

Makes 8 to 10 main-dish servings

About every other Sunday was like Christmas at the Prudhomme house, according to Eli: "All the married brothers and sisters and our aunts and uncles and their kids came over. Mom prepared a feast— with gumbo, pork, beef, chicken, and loads of vegetables and desserts. No one brought a covered dish—that just wasn't done in Cajun culture. When we visited a relative or friends, they fed us and we did the same for them. But the women all helped Mom with the cooking. It was just that you didn't take food with you to someone's house. Lots of times the relatives spent the Saturday night before Sunday with us; the house would be so full that we'd say, 'When you fall asleep, we're going to prop you up against the wall.' But we always had room for everyone—we'd just pull the top mattresses off the beds and make pallets on the floor."

Eli and Sue's roast has a wonderful dipping gravy to serve in individual ramekins. Serve the roast and gravy with **Crusty Houseboat Biscuits** *(page 22) and fresh vegetables. Stuff the roast a day ahead, cover well, and refrigerate until ready to cook.*

Stuffing:
½ cup very finely chopped onions
½ cup very finely chopped green bell peppers
¼ cup minced garlic

1 tablespoon **Ground Hot Pepper Vinegar,** vinegar
    only (page 357; see **Note**)
1 teaspoon **Ground Hot Pepper Vinegar,** peppers
    only (page 357; see **Note**)
1 tablespoon salt
1 tablespoon prepared mustard
1 teaspoon black pepper
¼ teaspoon ground red pepper (preferably cayenne)

1 (5½-pound) boneless Boston butt (shoulder) pork roast
1 tablespoon sugar
2 cups chopped onions
2 cups chopped green bell peppers
2 tablespoons minced garlic
1 tablespoon **Ground Hot Pepper Vinegar,** vinegar
    only (page 357; see **Note**)
½ teaspoon **Ground Hot Pepper Vinegar,** peppers
    only (page 357; see **Note**)
4 cups, *in all*, water
1 teaspoon all-purpose flour

Note: If your Ground Hot Pepper Vinegar is very hot, use your own judgment on how much of the vinegar and peppers to use each time.

In a medium-size bowl, combine the stuffing ingredients, mixing thoroughly.

Place the roast, fat side up, in a very large bowl or pan suitable for refrigerating. With a small sharp knife, cut 10 to 12 deep slits in the top of the meat to form pockets about 1½ inches long, being careful not to cut through to the bottom. Cut the slits in the direction opposite (at a right angle) to the direction in which the roast will be carved, so all slices will contain stuffing. Fill the pockets with some of the stuffing mixture, packing it tightly and using as much as possible; rub the outside of the roast thoroughly with any excess. Sprinkle the sugar over all the roast and rub it in well. Turn the roast stuffed side up, cover well, and refrigerate until ready to cook, preferably overnight.

Place the roast, fat side up, and any drippings in a heavy ovenproof 8-quart pan or large Dutch oven. Sprinkle the onions, bell peppers, garlic, the 1 tablespoon Ground Hot Pepper Vinegar (vinegar only), and the ½ teaspoon Ground Hot Pepper Vinegar peppers evenly over the meat. Add 2 *cups* of the water around the sides of the meat. Cover pan and place in a 375° oven. Immediately reduce oven setting to 300° and bake until tender and juices run clear, about 3 hours and 45 minutes. Do not overcook.

NOTE: The cooking time will vary according to the thickness of the roast. An easy way to check for doneness is to insert a skewer into the thickest part of the meat and then withdraw it; the first juices will probably run clear whether or not the meat is done. Wait a few seconds, then check again; if the juices still run clear, the roast is done. Or, use a meat thermometer to measure the internal temperature: Insert the probe into the densest part of the meat; when done, the temperature should read between 160° and 170°. Be sure to take a reading in at least two places.

Remove cover from pan and push any vegetables on top of the meat into the liquid. Turn oven to highest setting and continue baking roast uncovered just until browned on top, about 10 minutes more. **NOTE**: The browning time will vary greatly depending on how high your oven temperature can be set, placement of the oven rack, and source of the heat in relation to the top of the roast—so watch carefully. The browning is done fast at high heat so the meat will dry out as little as possible. If the top hasn't browned after 20 minutes, remove from oven so roast won't overcook.

Transfer roast to a platter, leaving vegetables and drippings in the pan. Cover roast loosely with aluminum foil and set aside for at least 15 to 20 minutes before carving.

Place the pan with the drippings over high heat. Cook until almost all the liquid has cooked away, about 20 minutes, stirring occasionally. Remove from heat. Skim off most of the fat from the pan. (We skimmed about ¼ cup, but the amount will vary depending on the fat content of the meat and you will need some fat left in the drippings.) Then transfer about 3 tablespoons of the liquid from the pan to a small bowl, add the flour, and stir until smooth. Return pan to high heat; when liquid reaches a boil, gradually add the flour mixture, stirring until well blended. Add the remaining 2 *cups* water and return to a boil, stirring frequently. Continue cooking and stirring about 5 minutes more. Remove from heat and skim.

Carve the roast and serve immediately. Serve the gravy in individual ramekins.

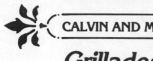

CALVIN AND MARIE'S RECIPE

Grillades

Makes 4 pints

At a boucherie, six hogs might be killed to provide fresh meat for several weeks and to prepare enough smoked, cured, and canned meats to last for many months. Most of the meat was smoked or cured, but Mom and Dad Prudhomme canned very lean strips of pork, which they called "grillades" (pronounced gree-yahds*). To the family, the word means small pieces of boneless meat, and they can be freshly cooked, as in Malcolm and Versie's* **Marinated and Smothered Grillades** *(see next recipe), or canned, as in this recipe. In New Orleans, grillades is the name of a classic dish of veal (not pork) in gravy that is served with grits.*

Mom and Dad used the leanest pork for canned grillades. The meat was cut from the bones and the bones with any remaining meat and fat went to make salt meat or **Ti Salé** *(page 171). The family cooked the grillades outdoors in a huge cast-iron pot over a wood fire, stirring the meat with a clean shovel. Then they placed the grillades in jars and poured hot lard over them, covering the meat completely. The lard preserves the meat by sealing it away from oxygen. Dad and Mom sometimes made over 200 jars of grillades during a boucherie. (Boucheries could last for several days because there was so much work to do to prepare the cured and canned meats.)*

Paul says that canned grillades are traditional Cajun history and that in France they would be called a "confit." And he says that when Cajuns make canned fruit, they call it "confiture." (In France, confiture is jam.) Mom used canned grillades in tomato gravy, and the children often took grillade-and-biscuit sandwiches to school for lunch.

The meat the Prudhommes used for canned grillades was always from a freshly slaughtered animal, and the lard was freshly rendered as well. This was important for preserving the meat, so for best results, use the freshest meat and lard possible. (Fresh duck fat works well also.) We have given you the traditional procedure for the cooking and canning of grillades, but we recommend that they be kept refrig-

erated and used within two weeks. Calvin and Marie say refrigerated lard left over from canning grillades is excellent for making gravy— just strain it first.

You can use grillades immediately after cooking; they're delicious with grits or rice, and they make wonderful sandwiches. To use canned grillades, just remove the amount you need and warm to melt the lard. Then drain and eat as is or add to a red sauce or a gravy.

You will need four wide-mouth pint-size canning jars with metal rings and brand-new self-sealing lids, all in perfect condition. We prefer to use pint jars so there is less handling of the contents once the jar is open.

This dish is cooked for fairly long periods of time over high heat. If your gas burner or electric cooking element produces a very high heat, or if your pot is not a heavy one, you will need to adjust the temperature down.

1 tablespoon plus 1½ teaspoons ground red pepper
    (preferably cayenne)
1 tablespoon salt
1 (5¼-pound) boneless Boston butt (shoulder) pork
    roast, cut into 2-inch squares 1 inch thick (see **NOTE**)
4 cups, *in all*, very fresh (and never previously used)
    pork lard or duck fat

NOTE: Cut the meat across the grain as much as possible so it won't be stringy. Cut the pieces evenly thick and leave the fat on the meat.

Submerge four freshly scrubbed wide-mouth pint-size jars in water and sterilize by boiling as directed by the manufacturer, but for a minimum of 15 to 20 minutes. Leave jars in hot water until ready to fill. Wash and boil lids and rings according to manufacturer's directions.

Combine the red pepper and salt in a small bowl, mixing well. Place the meat on a flat surface and sprinkle it evenly with the seasoning mixture, working it in with your hands and using it all.

Place the meat in a heavy 8-quart pan or large Dutch oven. Add *1 cup* of the lard and cook over high heat until all pieces of meat are cooked through and are very crisp and brown and only a tiny bit of clear steam comes from the pan when you stir. (Stir, then wait a few seconds to see if steam rises and, if so, whether it is whitish or clear.) The browning will take about 50 minutes; stir occasionally and scrape pan bottom well each time. (**NOTE**: Especially during the first half of cooking, whitish steam will constantly rise from the pan as you stir. The presence of white steam—versus clear steam— means there is still a lot of moisture in the meat and it needs further cooking. By the end of the cooking time, there will be a dramatic decrease in the amount of steam and if steam is present, it will look clear.) The finished meat should be well done but still moist inside. Once it's crisp, cut a piece open to make the final judgment on doneness.

Add the remaining *3 cups* lard and stir well. Continue cooking just until the lard is very hot, about 4 minutes more, stirring occasionally. Remove from heat and let cool about 5 minutes.

Meanwhile, remove the jars from the hot water and place them upside down to drain on a clean dry towel. Then, while the lard is still very hot (it has to be hot to settle around the meat properly), spoon equal portions of the meat into each very hot jar, packing it just lightly (so the lard will seep down between the pieces of meat) with the back of the spoon. (You may have a little meat left over—a perfect snack for the cook.)

Immediately ladle the hot lard over the top of the meat in each jar, leaving headspace of ½ inch and making sure all the meat is completely submerged. (It's fine to ladle some of the sediment into the jars, too.) Wait a few seconds to make sure all the meat stays totally submerged. If not, remove one or more pieces so there's room for all the meat to be completely covered.

Promptly wipe the rims well with a clean, damp cloth and place hot lids on top with sealing compound down; screw on metal rings firmly but not too tightly. Place jars upright and at least 2 inches apart on a wooden surface or folded dish towels to cool slightly at room temperature, away from drafts. Then label and date jars and refrigerate. **NOTE**: To avoid breakage, line refrigerator shelf with a folded towel. Place the hot jars about 2 inches apart on the towel and wait until the jars are cool to the touch before removing the towel.

Use the grillades within two weeks, using up one jar completely before opening the next.

To serve, remove from the jar the amount of grillades desired and heat the meat lightly. Grillades are good as is with grits or rice, and they make fine sandwiches, or use them in a red gravy. Since the meat has a coating of lard or duck fat on it, it can be heated easily in an ungreased pan. If you use grillades in a gravy, heat the pieces enough to melt off the lard or fat before adding them to the gravy. **NOTE**: As you take the meat from each jar, make sure the remaining pieces in the jar are completely covered again with lard.

MALCOLM AND VERSIE'S RECIPE

Marinated and Smothered Grillades in Rusty Gravy
(Grillades Amarinées et Etouffées)

Makes 4 to 6 main-dish servings

Malcolm is the only one of the boys who just does not like to cook; he will grill or smoke meats outside, but, as Versie says, "the only thing he will do in the kitchen is fix bacon and eggs." All the family say about Malcolm, "He's not a cook; he's a salesman!" But he knows what's good. When Versie cooked her marinated grillades for the cookbook, Malcolm took a bite and said, "Now, that's Cajun!" And Paul said, "That's exactly how I remember them."

Season the meat one to two days ahead, cover well, and refrigerate until ready to cook. This dish is cooked for fairly long periods of time over high heat. If your gas burner or electric cooking element produces a very high heat, or if your pot is not a heavy one, you will need to adjust the temperature down.

Seasoning mix:
1 tablespoon ground red pepper (preferably cayenne)
2½ teaspoons salt
1½ teaspoons garlic powder

3½ pounds boneless Boston butt (shoulder) pork
  steaks about ¾ inch thick, cut into 12 pieces
  (don't trim fat)
⅓ cup vegetable oil
About 3 cups, *in all,* water
2½ cups finely chopped onions
1 teaspoon coarsely chopped garlic
Hot **Basic Cooked Rice** (page 252)

Combine the seasoning mix ingredients thoroughly in a small bowl. Place the meat in a large bowl or a pan suitable for refrigerating and sprinkle evenly with the seasoning mix, pressing it in by hand and using it all. Cover and refrigerate until ready to cook, preferably for 1 to 2 days.

In a heavy 12-quart pan or large Dutch oven, with as broad a bottom as possible, heat the oil over high heat until hot, about 3 minutes. Carefully slip the meat into the hot oil, with as many pieces as possible in contact with the pan bottom. Cook without turning the meat or stirring it until the underside of the meat is crusty brown, about 10 minutes. **Note**: This thorough browning of the meat is a very important step—the beginning of the smothering process—that results in a delicious "rusty gravy." While browning the meat, don't scrape the pan bottom clean of sediment unless absolutely necessary; try reducing the heat first.

Turn the meat over, again arranging it in a single layer, and cook, with little or no scraping of the pan bottom, until all the pieces are well browned and crusty, about 10 minutes more, turning them over only occasionally to brown all surfaces well. Cut in half any pieces that curl up. The sediment in the pan should be a rusty color by now.

Remove from heat and pour off all but about 2 tablespoons of fat from the pan, leaving as much sediment as possible. Add ¼ *cup* of the water to the pan. Holding the meat firmly with a fork or tongs, rub the meat against the pan bottom to dissolve some but not all the sediment. Return the pan to high heat and cook about 3 minutes, continuing to rub the meat on the pan bottom occasionally.

Now add the onions; cook until most of the liquid has evaporated, about 5 minutes, stirring almost constantly and scraping pan bottom clean. (Rotate pan if sediment is building up only in certain spots.) Stir in ¼ *cup* more water and the garlic; reduce heat to medium and cook about 2 minutes, arranging meat in a single layer and scraping pan bottom as needed. Add ¼ *cup* more water and cook and stir about 1 minute. Add another ¼ *cup* water and cook and stir about 2 minutes. Then add another ¼ *cup* water, coating all pieces of the meat thoroughly with the gravy as you stir and scrape the pan bottom well.

Arrange meat in a single layer again and now cover the pan; reduce heat to low and cook about 10 minutes without stirring. Add 1½ *cups* more water, stirring and scraping pan bottom well; re-cover pan and cook about 20 minutes without stirring. Stir well and turn meat, re-cover pan, and continue cooking until meat is very tender, about 45 minutes more, stirring and turning meat once or twice. **NOTE**: If necessary, add a little more water toward the end of cooking time so the gravy will yield about 1½ cups.

Remove from heat and skim off fat. Serve immediately over rice.

CALVIN AND MARIE'S RECIPE

Ti Salé

Makes 4 quarts

When the family had a boucherie and killed several hogs, they prepared four or five different types of cured pork. One was salt meat, or salt pork, primarily pieces of fat with some lean streaks (there might be a few bones in them), that was cured with salt. Ti salé, (pronounced tee sah-lay) is salt pork, too, but it is made in small quantities and red pepper is mixed in with the salt. Ti salé literally means "small salty." It's part of Cajun history.

Dad was most likely to make ti salé when he killed just one or two smaller hogs occasionally during the year, to provide fresh meat for a few days and to restock the supply of cured meats. He always added red pepper to the cure salt, and the family used up these small amounts of peppery salt pork within a few weeks. Abel says Dad used all the leftover scraps of fat and of meaty bones from the butchering

171

to make ti salé, so unlike salt pork today, it did have bones.

According to Calvin, the family didn't use "table" salt for curing. They used a coarser salt similar to kosher salt, and Paul and Calvin believe it preserved the meat better. Moreover, the meat the family used was extremely fresh (the hog had just been slaughtered).

In our recipe, we call for keeping the ti salé refrigerated and using it within two weeks. A quart jar of ti salé is a good gift for friends who have become addicted to Cajun cooking! Use the freshest meat possible, and do not reduce the amount of salt called for, since it is the salt that preserves the meat. Our recipe also calls for meaty ribs, since we feel today's cooks probably would prefer a meatier seasoning meat than Dad made.

Before using the cured ti salé, rinse it well with water, then boil it in water several times to remove most of the salt. Boil it at least three times—each time in fresh water—to bring the salt down to the proper level for dishes like dried beans that need saltiness. Boil the meat four times for dishes requiring less salt. Paul says the family used ti salé as a seasoning meat primarily with dried beans and fresh vegetables, but he, Calvin, Elden, and Abel all agree that "it makes a good red gravy, too!"

You will need four wide-mouth quart-size canning jars and four metal rings and brand-new self-sealing lids, all in perfect condition.

About 2⅓ cups salt, *in all*
About ½ cup, *in all*, ground red pepper (preferably cayenne)
4½ pounds very meaty pork spareribs or short ribs,
    cut into about 2 × 2½-inch pieces; have your
    butcher cut them

Submerge four freshly scrubbed wide-mouth quart-size jars in water and sterilize by boiling as directed by the manufacturer, but for a minimum of 15 to 20 minutes. Leave jars in hot water until just before ready to fill, then drain momentarily on a clean towel. Wash and boil lids and rings according to manufacturer's directions.

In a large mixing bowl, combine 2 *cups* of the salt with ¼ *cup plus 3 tablespoons* of the pepper, mixing well. **NOTE:** Be sure to use this amount of salt. Dredge each piece of meat thoroughly in the seasoning mixture, pressing it in with your hands. Don't shake off excess seasoning—you want all surfaces of each piece coated with as much as possible. After dredging each piece, place it flat in one of the very hot jars, packing the meat tightly and distributing the pieces evenly among the jars. If you run short of the seasoning mixture, make more with the remaining salt and red pepper, using 5 parts salt to 1 part pepper. Don't worry about *overdoing* the seasoning, because you can't! The important thing is to coat thoroughly all surfaces of each piece of meat. Pour any remaining seasoning mixture over the top of the meat.

Then promptly wipe jar rims well with a clean, damp cloth and place hot lids on top with sealing compound down. Screw on metal rings firmly but not too tightly. Let jars cool slightly, then label and date jars. Refrigerate and use within 2 weeks.

NOTE: A brine solution may form around the meat; this is normal, but not necessary for preserving the meat.

ALLIE AND ETELL'S RECIPE

Paunce Bourré

Makes 6 to 8 main-dish servings

Paunce bourré is the Cajun name for stuffed pork stomach, which Mom Prudhomme made when the family slaughtered or had a boucherie. She cooked it in their small smokehouse, hanging the stuffed paunce about six feet above the source of heat, and it stayed in there until it shriveled up, which often took two or three days of smoking.

Allie says the family had paunce bourré for Easter and other holiday meals that coincided with winter and spring boucheries, and occasionally Mom made it as an extra meat for company. Mom and Dad Prudhomme filled the pork stomach until it was round and wouldn't hold any more stuffing, but Allie likes hers not so fully stuffed.

Do try this tasty old Cajun dish. The paunce itself is eaten, too; its smoky taste and somewhat crunchy texture is a nice counterpoint to the stuffing. Serve a pork or beef gravy with it, but don't make the

*gravy with the drippings from the paunce without tasting them first;
they may be too salty or smoky.*

*Store-bought paunces are usually either packed in salt or frozen.
Allie recommends soaking the cleaned paunce in water overnight, especially if it is packed in salt.*

1 (1- to 1¼-pound) whole pork stomach (paunce)
1 pound lean ground pork
1 pound lean ground beef
½ cup chopped onions
½ cup chopped green onions (tops and bottoms)
½ cup chopped green bell peppers
3 tablespoons coarsely chopped fresh parsley
2 tablespoons water
1½ teaspoons salt
1½ teaspoons ground red pepper (preferably cayenne)
1½ teaspoons minced garlic
1 tablespoon white vinegar
Round wooden toothpicks, to close stuffed paunce
Small green wood pieces (pecan preferred), or wood
    pieces or wood chips that have been soaked in water
      1 to 2 hours

Clean the paunce and let it soak overnight in the refrigerator (see
Lagniappe).

In a large mixing bowl, combine the pork, beef, onions, green
onions, bell peppers, parsley, water, salt, red pepper, and garlic; mix
thoroughly with your hands. Set aside.

Drain the paunce and rinse it once more, inside and out, ending
up with the outside (lighter color) out. Pour the vinegar into the
paunce through the largest duct or hole and squish it around to
rinse, then rinse the inside of the paunce with cool running water
again and drain well.

Stuff the paunce through the largest duct with the meat mixture,
using it all. Hold the duct closed and pat the paunce flat to distribute
the stuffing evenly inside. Close both larger ducts with round
wooden toothpicks. (It's not necessary to close the smaller third
duct.)

Fill a broad-bottomed 8-quart saucepan or large Dutch oven with hot tap water 1¾ inches deep. Add the paunce to the pan, place over high heat, and bring water to just below a simmer, about 8 minutes. **NOTE**: Don't let the water boil, or the paunce may burst. Reduce heat to keep the water just steaming hot, but not hot enough to simmer. With a sharp knife tip, cut a ¼-inch slit in the center of the exposed top of the paunce to let a little juice escape so the paunce won't burst. Cook about 15 minutes. Carefully turn the paunce over and cook about 15 minutes more. Remove from heat and transfer the paunce to a plate.

Pour water from pan and add 1¾ inches fresh water. Place the paunce in the pan again and return the water to the just steaming-hot level; continue cooking in the hot (not simmering) water for about 30 minutes, turning meat over occasionally. (This procedure both tenderizes the paunce and removes more salt.) Remove from heat and drain the paunce well.

Meanwhile, build a charcoal fire in a smoker. Just before smoking the paunce, add several pieces of green wood, or soaked wood or wood chips, to the coals. When the wood catches fire, quench the flames with a small amount of water sprinkled directly on the wood. (If the wood starts blazing, quench the flames with a little more water as necessary.) Place the paunce on the smoker rack and smoke for about 1 hour, turning every 10 minutes or so, and making sure the paunce isn't burning. Check periodically to be certain the wood is smoking heavily but not flaming up; if flaming, quench the flames with sprinkles of water; continue to add wood as needed (you need constant smoke).

Remove the paunce from the smoker and transfer it to an ungreased 11 × 17-inch roasting pan. Bake the paunce at 350° for about 30 minutes or until done and skin is tender. Test by pricking skin with a fork in several places; the fork should come out easily. Remove from oven and serve immediately, sliced crosswise.

· · · · · · · · · · · · · ·**LAGNIAPPE**· · · · · · · · · · · · · ·

Follow the instructions on the next page for rinsing the paunce, which you will probably buy turned inside out. If not, turn it inside out through the largest duct or hole. (The smooth, lighter-colored side with fat along the edges is the outside.) When spread out, the paunce will look like this:

· ·

RIGHT SIDE OUT **INSIDE OUT**

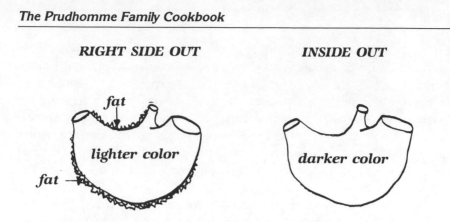

Rinse the paunce under warm running water, scraping surface well with a paring knife to remove any salt, any orange fat (which is attached to surface and can be scraped off readily without piercing any membrane), or any other suspect matter which can easily be scraped off, again without piercing through the membrane. You may see what appear to be some patches of yellowish skin—don't remove these.

Locate the largest duct (there is a large duct at either end and a small one at the upper middle) and carefully turn the paunce *right* side out, so the lighter, smoother side is out. Scrape the fat from the edges with a paring knife or pull it off with your fingers. Also remove any pockets of fat that are near the upper rim under the surface membranes, being careful not to pierce through the stomach wall. It's fine to leave small remnants of fat on the outside of the stomach, but remove large pieces of fat.

If the paunce is not packed in salt: Rinse it well inside and out and end up with it turned right side (lighter color) out. Rinse the paunce a day ahead, cover it with water and refrigerate overnight, covered.

If the paunce is packed in salt: Rinse it well inside and out, then repeat the thorough rinsing procedure again, inside and out, to remove all traces of salt. After rinsing well, turn the paunce right side (lighter color) out. Cover with water and refrigerate overnight, covered.

Hog's Head Cheese
(Fromage de Tête de Cochon)

Makes about 5½ pounds

Paul feels strongly that this recipe is important, both for historical reasons and because it tastes so good. It calls for using a hog's head, for the same reasons, though there are other ways to make the dish. When the family killed hogs, every single scrap of the animals was used in some way (even hooves and bones boiled with lye to make soap!). Calvin says, "The only thing we lost was the 'squeal.'" The heads were always used to make hog's head cheese, or "headcheese."

Elden and Odelia Mae definitely do not think that you can substitute another meat for the hog's head. They believe the finished dish will neither jell correctly nor taste the same. Paul's reaction to their headcheese was, "Ah, if only all hog's head cheese were this good!" It is *terrific*—wonderfully seasoned, lean, shredded meat, rather than the gelatin-like headcheese you get in delicatessens. They make it just like Mom Prudhomme did, but they do cook the meat in a pressure cooker—it's much faster and Elden and Odelia Mae feel it gives the meat a better flavor. If you don't have a large pressure cooker, you can use a stockpot. Boil the meat in the stock uncovered until all of it is very tender and falling away from the bones.

Cajuns eat hog's head cheese only on the day it's made because the taste is so fabulous when it's fresh. You can refrigerate leftovers to use the next day.

Elden and Odelia Mae serve hog's head cheese with baked sweet potatoes, the way Mom did. It's also great as a party food (what a conversation piece!), on toast for breakfast, or on crackers any time of the day or night.

1 (12- to 14-pound) trimmed hog's head, sawed into
    12 or more pieces (see **Note**)
3½ pounds meaty pork shank pieces
4 tablespoons salt, *in all*

2 tablespoons plus 2 teaspoons, *in all*, ground red
    pepper (preferably cayenne)
1 tablespoon plus 1 teaspoon black pepper, *in all*
2 tablespoons **Ground Hot Pepper Vinegar,**
    peppers only (page 357)
About 3½ quarts **Basic Pork** (preferred) or **Beef
    Stock** (page 18)
3 cups coarsely chopped onions
⅓ cup peeled garlic cloves (about 1½ ounces)
4 cups very finely chopped green onions (tops and bottoms)
¾ cup very finely chopped fresh parsley

NOTE: Ask the butcher to saw the head into pieces and to trim it
thoroughly. Be sure to explain that it is to be used for making headcheese. If possible, purchase a fresh (never frozen) head. You won't
find a hog's head in a supermarket! Country meat markets, really
good meat markets in cities, and specialized pork butchers will understand what you need.

Trim *any and all* hair (including the entire hair follicle) from the
pieces of head, leaving on as much fat as possible. Do the same with
the shank meat. (If in doubt about whether what you see are hair
follicles, trim off everything you think *might* be.)

Rinse each piece of head and shank meat very thoroughly with
cool tap water and trim away any hair you may have missed.

Place the pieces of head and shank meat in a 12-quart pressure
cooker, then add *3 tablespoons* of the salt, *1 tablespoon* of the red
pepper, *2 teaspoons* of the black pepper, and the vinegar peppers.
Pour enough stock into the pan to cover the meat, if possible, but be
certain the liquid reaches no higher than 1 inch from the pan rim.
Add the onions and garlic cloves. Seal the pressure cooker and place
over high heat. Let pressure build up to 15 pounds, about 40 minutes. Adjust heat to maintain a 15-pound pressure and cook for 1
hour. Remove from heat and let pressure decrease completely before
removing lid, about 1 hour.

Remove lid. With a slotted spoon transfer meat and any vegetables clinging to it to a large bowl or pan, discarding any bones that
have no meat or fat. Place any large clumps of fat without any meat
or bones in a separate large bowl and set aside.

Strain the stock through a mesh strainer into another large bowl and set aside. Discard any obvious bones from the vegetables in the strainer and place the strained vegetables in the first bowl with the meat. (Discard any residue at the bottom of the strainer that may have tiny bone chips in it.)

Remove all large clumps of fat from the meat, placing them in the bowl with the other reserved fat. Then pick through all the fat and discard any rind, gristle, or tiny bone chips. Set fat aside.

Before proceeding, it's helpful to keep in mind that your goal is to end up with one bowl of very thoroughly picked over and shredded meat and vegetables. While accomplishing this, you will also find more fat in the meat; add it to the bowl of reserved fat. Using your fingers, shred the meat finely, while searching meticulously for all tiny bones, minute bone chips, gristle, rind, cartilage, or any other slightly gritty or tough matter, both in the meat and in the vegetables. Continue working with the meat, shredding it more and more finely each time, and continuing to search for and discard bones and similar matter.

After working with the meat for several minutes, you will be literally squeezing it through your fingers; when you're finished, the meat will be very finely shredded, tender, and mushy. (You can speed up the procedure by transferring picked-over meat and vegetables to a clean bowl, then repeating the procedure again and again, continuing to change bowls and working with the meat until you feel absolutely certain that you've found and discarded everything that must be eliminated.) This procedure is requisite and requires careful attention as well as quite a bit of time. Odelia Mae takes from 30 minutes to an hour to do it.

Measure out 1 cup of the reserved picked-over fat and set aside. (Discard the remaining fat or save it to render for lard.)

Place the meat mixture in a heavy 6-quart saucepan or large Dutch oven. Add the remaining *1 tablespoon* salt, *1 tablespoon plus 2 teaspoons* red pepper, and *2 teaspoons* black pepper, working the seasoning into the meat by hand until thoroughly mixed and continuing to look for and remove bones or other tough matter. Add the 1 cup reserved fat, the green onions, and parsley, mixing by hand until well blended.

Stir the reserved stock. Measure out 1½ cups and add it to the meat mixture; mix well by hand. (Use the remaining stock in another recipe.)

Place the pan over high heat and cook about 15 minutes, stirring and scraping pan bottom almost constantly. Continue to search for bones, gristle, and other such matter in the meat. Remove from heat and let sit about 5 minutes, then stir and scrape pan bottom well.

Spoon equal portions of the mixture into two ungreased 11 × 7-inch pans, distributing the mixture evenly in the pans. Set aside until thoroughly cooled to room temperature, about 1 hour. Serve immediately, cut into pieces about 1 inch thick and 2½ inches square. (The yield will be about 24 squares.)

Refrigerate leftovers and use the next day. Serve leftovers cool, not cold.

BLACKENING

About Blackening

I created the blackening cooking method, using an intensely hot cast-iron skillet, to try to capture the taste of fish or meat cooked directly over an open fire.

Blackening changes the texture of fish and meat and provides a building of natural tastes that can't be duplicated any other way. Butter and herbs and spices are key elements. They allow blackening to reach its ultimate potential by forming a barrier between the food and the very hot skillet. And, the extreme heat evaporates the surface juices of the fish or meat; this keeps the food literally suspended slightly off the skillet, which makes the surface of the buttered and seasoned fish or meat taste sweet.

The blackening process concentrates the outer fibers into a crust and accents the taste in the same way that the reduction of a stock or of cream accents taste. Inside, blackened fish and meat are wonderfully juicy and tender because the blackened surfaces have sealed in the juices.

We've learned a great deal about blackening in the seven years since I first cooked blackened redfish. Because of the enormous popularity of blackened fish and meat across the nation, and because some people have misunderstood the process, I felt I should pass on to you all the information that is helpful for home and commercial blackening:

1. Blackening should be done either outdoors or in a commercial kitchen. The process creates an incredible amount of smoke that will set off your own and your neighbors' smoke alarms. People with really well-installed commercial hood vents at home have gotten away with blackening in their own kitchens. They are privileged! Don't push your luck.

2. A butane burner or gas grill will produce enough heat to heat the skillet to the proper level. You can use a charcoal grill if you add 12 to 14 chunks (not chips) of hickory or other hardwood to the coals and continue to add more wood as it burns up. In addition, when using charcoal, you can heat the skillet on a conventional stove burner in your kitchen and then carefully carry the very hot skillet out to the hot grill.

3. Cast iron is the only suitable material for a blackening skillet.

4. The skillet must be dry when heated; do not put in butter or oil.

5. The skillet must be heated over very high heat until it is extremely hot—just short of the point at which you see white ash or a white spot forming in the skillet bottom. The ideal temperature, about 500°, produces the sweet crust on the outside and the moist, tender inside of blackened fish and meat.

6. Allow the skillet to reheat between batches. This will take only a few seconds if your heat source is intense or you are cooking only one piece of fish or meat at a time.

7. The fish or meat should be at room temperature.

8. Dipping the food in butter and then sprinkling on the herbs and spices are essential steps. This is how the barrier between the hot skillet and the food is made.

9. The seasoning mixture should be sprinkled on evenly (as you would salt). If too much is present, it destroys the method of cooking. Blackened fish and meat are not spicy; if you use the right seasoning mixture and use the correct amount, the result is a sweet, smoky-tasting crust.

10. When the fish or meat is first put in the pan, flames may flare up because of the intense heat. And, when you pour on the teaspoon of butter (both times), there may be flames. If they don't die out immediately, cover the pan for thirty seconds to smother them.

11. When cooking more than one batch of fish or meat, wipe the skillet thoroughly with a thick cotton cloth after each of the first three batches to remove all burned particles and fat, or these will produce a burned taste. After the third batch, scrape the skillet bottom with a flat-edged spatula and turn the skillet, face down, over the source of heat for three to four minutes to burn it out. Then rewipe with a thick cotton cloth. (Use tongs to handle the wiping cloth and work quickly—the skillet will be extremely hot.)

12. If you're blackening for a commercial kitchen, go directly from the skillet to the plate. If you lay the fish or meat on any other surface without thoroughly wiping the surface *each* time you lift a piece, particles will collect and eventually make the later cooked pieces taste overseasoned, salty, and bitter.

13. After cooking, clean the skillet by burning it out. When the skillet has cooled, wipe it clean, and rub it with vegetable oil. Store in a dry place.

14. Blackening is not a suitable method for cooking beef beyond medium. Before the inside can cook to medium-well or well done, the meat surface will burn (that is, taste of ash and be bitter), not blacken (that is, taste sweet and as if it were cooked over wood).

PAUL AND K'S RECIPE

Blackened Redfish

Makes 6 main-dish servings

I've included blackened redfish in this book, even though it's in my book Chef Paul Prudhomme's Louisiana Kitchen, *because we've learned more about blackening and want to pass on that information. And, because of the popularity of the blackening method, we've added three new blackened recipes.*

Before beginning to cook any of these recipes, read **About Blackening** *(page 182).*

Blackened redfish makes an extraordinary main course, but it is also wonderful served as an hors-d'oeuvre—just cut the fish into bite-size pieces after *you blacken it.*

6 (8- to 10-ounce) redfish fillets or other firm-fleshed
    fish fillets. You can use pompano, tilefish, golden
    tile, red snapper, walleye, or sac-à-lait fillets, or
    tuna or salmon steaks, or any favorite, local
    firm-fleshed fish. The pieces must be cut about
    ½ inch thick (see **Note**)
Seasoning mix:
1 tablespoon sweet paprika
2½ teaspoons salt
1 teaspoon onion powder

1 teaspoon garlic powder

1 teaspoon ground red pepper (preferably cayenne)

¾ teaspoon white pepper

¾ teaspoon black pepper

½ teaspoon dried thyme leaves

½ teaspoon dried oregano leaves

¾ pound (3 sticks) unsalted butter, melted and kept
warm in a skillet

NOTE: Redfish, pompano, and tuna are ideal for this method of cooking. If you use tilefish, you may have to split the fillets in half horizontally to have the proper thickness. Any firm-fleshed fish will work wonderfully, so use your best local freshwater or saltwater fish. Whatever fish you use, the fillets or steaks must not be more than ¾ inch thick.

Let the fish come to room temperature before blackening. Thoroughly combine the seasoning mix ingredients in a small bowl.

Heat a large cast-iron skillet over very high heat until it is extremely hot and just short of the point at which you see white ash or a white spot forming in the skillet bottom, about 8 minutes. (The time will vary according to the intensity of the heat source.)

Meanwhile, pour 2 tablespoons melted butter in each of 6 small ramekins; set aside and keep warm. In a warm place, reserve the remaining butter in its skillet. Heat the serving plates in a 250° oven.

Just before cooking each piece, dip it in the reserved melted butter so that both sides are well coated, then sprinkle some of the seasoning mix evenly on each side. (If you lay the fish on a plate or other surface to season it, be sure the surface is warm so the butter won't congeal and stick to the surface instead of to the fish. Wipe the surface clean after seasoning each piece.)

Immediately place the fish in the hot skillet (cook only 1 piece at a time). Pour about 1 teaspoon melted butter on top of the fish (be careful, as the butter may flame up). Cook, uncovered, over the same high heat until the underside forms a crust, about 2 minutes (the time will vary according to the thickness of the fish and the heat of the skillet or fire). Turn the fish over and pour about 1 teaspoon more butter on top; cook just until it is done (flaky and white, but still very moist inside), about 2 minutes more. (With a little practice, you can judge doneness by feel—the fish flesh will "give" when you press it lightly with one finger; if you pressed it a little harder, the meat would break apart or flake.)

Serve each piece crustier side up while piping hot. Clean the skillet after cooking (see page 184) and repeat the blackening procedure for the remaining servings.

To serve, place one piece of blackened fish and a ramekin of butter on each heated serving plate. If you serve several pieces on a platter, do not stack the fish.

PAUL AND K'S RECIPE

Blackened Pork Chops

Makes 6 to 9 main-dish servings

Blackened pork chops are wonderful with **Candied Yams** *(page 282 or 283), and they make superb hors-d'oeuvre—just cut the blackened chops into bite-size pieces.*

18 (4- to 5-ounce) pork chops suitable for broiling,
       cut ½ to ¾ inch thick
   Seasoning mix:
   1 tablespoon salt
   1 tablespoon plus 2 teaspoons white pepper
   1 tablespoon plus ¾ teaspoon black pepper
   2½ teaspoons dry mustard
   2½ teaspoons ground red pepper
        (preferably cayenne)
   2 teaspoons garlic powder
   ¾ teaspoon dried thyme leaves

¾ pound (3 sticks) unsalted butter, melted and kept
       warm in a skillet

Let the chops come to room temperature before blackening. Combine the seasoning mix ingredients thoroughly in a medium-size bowl.

Heat a large cast-iron skillet over very high heat until it is extremely hot and just short of the point at which you see white ash or a white spot forming in the skillet bottom, about 8 minutes. (The time will vary according to the intensity of the heat source.)

Heat the serving plates in a 250° oven.

Just before cooking each chop, dip it in the melted butter so that both sides are well coated, then sprinkle each side generously and evenly with the seasoning mix (use *between ¼ and ½ teaspoon* on each side), patting it in with your hands. (If you lay the chop on a plate or other surface to season it, be sure the surface is warm so the butter won't congeal and stick to the surface instead of to the chop. Wipe the surface clean after seasoning each chop. Use any remaining seasoning mix in another recipe.)

Immediately place the chop in the hot skillet. If the chop is very lean, pour about 1 teaspoon butter on top. (Be careful, as the butter may flame up.) If you cook more than 1 chop at a time, place each chop in the skillet before buttering and seasoning another one.

Cook uncovered over the same high heat until the underside forms a crust, about 2 minutes (the time will vary according to the thickness of the chops and the heat of the skillet or fire). Turn the chops over and pour about 1 teaspoon more butter on top of each, if needed. Cook just until meat is done, about 2 minutes more. Serve the chops crustier side up while piping hot.

Clean the skillet after cooking each batch (see page 184) and repeat the blackening procedure with the remaining chops.

To serve, place 2 or 3 chops on each heated serving plate. If you use a serving platter, do not stack the chops.

Blackened Chicken

Makes 8 main-dish servings

16 (3-ounce) skinless boned chicken breasts, about ½
      to ¾ inch thick, or 8 (10-ounce) bone-in leg-
      thigh pieces, or a combination of these (see **NOTE**)

Seasoning mix:

2 tablespoons salt
1½ teaspoons garlic powder
1½ teaspoons black pepper
1 teaspoon white pepper
1 teaspoon onion powder
1 teaspoon ground cumin
½ teaspoon ground red pepper (preferably cayenne)
½ teaspoon sweet paprika

¾ pound (3 sticks) unsalted butter, melted and kept
      warm in a skillet

NOTE: Skin the leg-thigh pieces, then bone each piece along the length of the two bones, leaving meat in one piece. Trim off excess fat. Pound each breast or leg-thigh fillet to ½ inch thick.

Let the chicken come to room temperature before blackening. Thoroughly combine the seasoning mix ingredients in a small bowl.

Heat a large cast-iron skillet over very high heat until it is extremely hot and just short of the point at which you see white ash or a white spot forming in the skillet bottom, about 8 minutes. (The time will vary according to the intensity of the heat source.)

Heat the serving plates in a 250° oven.

Just before cooking each piece of chicken, dip it in the melted butter so that both sides are well coated, then sprinkle each fillet evenly with the seasoning mix, using about a *rounded ½ teaspoon* on each, and patting it in with your hands. (If you lay the fillet on a plate or other surface to season it, be sure the surface is warm so the butter won't congeal and stick to the surface instead of to the meat. Wipe the surface clean after seasoning each fillet. Use any remaining seasoning mix in another recipe.)

Immediately place the fillet skinned side down in the hot skillet, making sure all meat folds are opened up and the meat is lying flat. Pour about 1 teaspoon butter on top of the fillet (be careful, as the butter may flame up). If you cook more than 1 fillet at a time, place each fillet in the skillet before buttering and seasoning another one.

Cook uncovered over the same high heat until the underside forms a crust, about 2 minutes. (The time will vary according to the thickness of the fillets and the heat of the skillet or fire; watch the meat and you'll see a white line coming up the side as it cooks.) Turn the fillets over and pour about 1 teaspoon more melted butter on top of each. Cook just until meat is cooked through, about 2 minutes more. Serve the chicken fillets crustier side up while piping hot.

Clean the skillet after cooking each batch (see page 184) and repeat the blackening procedure with the remaining chicken fillets.

To serve, place 2 breast fillets or 1 leg-thigh fillet on each heated serving plate. If you use a large serving platter, do not stack the fillets.

PAUL AND K'S RECIPE

Blackened Hamburgers

Makes 6 main-dish servings

Season the meat and form the hamburger patties several hours before cooking. Blackened hamburgers are great with Creole mustard and all the traditional trimmings.

Seasoning mix:
1 tablespoon plus 1 teaspoon ground red pepper (preferably
    cayenne)
1 tablespoon salt
1 tablespoon black pepper
2 teaspoons white pepper
1½ teaspoons garlic powder
1½ teaspoons ground cumin
1½ teaspoons dried thyme leaves
1 teaspoon onion powder

2 pounds best-quality ground beef
⅜ pound (1½ sticks) unsalted butter, melted and
    kept warm in a skillet
6 **Golden Yeast Rolls** (page 25) or hamburger buns,
    or 12 slices **Homemade Yeast Bread** (page 28),
    optional

Combine the seasoning mix ingredients in a medium-size bowl, mixing well. Place the meat in a large bowl and add *3 tablespoons* of the seasoning mix; mix by hand until thoroughly blended. Form the meat into 6 patties, each ¾ inch thick. Cover patties and refrigerate.

Let patties come to room temperature before blackening.

Heat a large cast-iron skillet over very high heat until it is extremely hot and just short of the point at which you see white ash or a white spot forming in the skillet bottom, about 8 minutes. (The time will vary according to the intensity of the heat source.)

Heat the serving plates in a 250° oven.

Just before cooking each patty, dip it in the melted butter so that both sides are well coated, then sprinkle each side evenly with a *rounded ¼ teaspoon* of the seasoning mix, patting it in with your hands. (If you lay the meat on a plate or other surface to season it, be sure the surface is warm so the butter won't congeal and stick to the surface instead of to the meat. Wipe the surface clean after seasoning each patty. Use the remaining seasoning mix in another recipe.)

Immediately place the patty in the hot skillet. (If you cook more than 1 patty at a time, place each one in the skillet before buttering and seasoning another.) Cook uncovered over the same high heat until the underside forms a thick crust, about 3 minutes (the time will vary according to the heat of the skillet or fire). Turn the patties over and cook just until meat is cooked to medium, about 2 minutes more. (If you prefer meat cooked medium-well or well done, remove the patties from the skillet and place them on a *heated* plate for a minute or two; the patties will cook a little more from residual heat.)

Serve each patty crustier side up while piping hot. Clean the skillet after cooking each batch (see page 184) and repeat the blackening procedure with the remaining patties.

To serve the hamburgers, sandwich them in Golden Yeast Rolls, regular buns, or slices of Yeast Bread. If you serve several hamburgers on a platter, do not stack them.

GUMBOS, SOUPS & STEWS

GOMBOS, SOUPES ET FRICASSÉES

Shrimp and Okra Gumbo
(Gombo de Chevrettes et Gombo Févi)

Makes 12 main-dish or 18 appetizer servings

Gumbo was not an everyday dish for the family. Mom made it for holidays, sometimes on Sundays, most often in winter when it was cold, and for special company. "Gumbo Night" was an occasion. Mom cooked a big pot of gumbo for supper and invited family and friends. She also served rice, potato salad, and baked sweet potatoes, but gumbo was the star attraction. It was a real party, since supper was usually just fresh-baked bread with butter, preserves or syrup, and milk.

Because the family rarely had seafood, Mom never made shrimp gumbo, but she made crawfish gumbo and often made her gumbos with okra. There are infinite varieties of gumbo (and each can be an unforgettable experience), made with meat, poultry, game, or fish and/ or shellfish—including chicken, guinea hen, duck, rabbit, squirrel, blackbird, pork sausage, beef, shrimp, crabmeat, oysters, crawfish, fish. Some are made with thickening agents, including roux, okra, and gumbo filé (filé powder), and some without.

Paul says, "Gumbo's a taste, a feeling, a party. I love it; I grew up on it. Mom made chicken and andouille gumbo, crawfish gumbo, dried shrimp gumbo, guinea hen gumbo, rabbit gumbo, squirrel gumbo, blackbird gumbo, and other game gumbos. I never saw hard crabs (shell and all) in gumbo until I was a teenager visiting New Orleans, and I never made a fresh shrimp gumbo or a beef gumbo until I moved to New Orleans when I was about eighteen years old."

Malcolm and Versie often make this gumbo for family and friends. You can serve it in the traditional way over rice, but we like this one even better served just as is. If you make the gumbo ahead, don't add the shrimp until you reheat it; then cook just until the shrimp are pink and plump.

This dish is cooked for fairly long periods of time over high heat. If

your gas burner or electric cooking element produces a very high heat, or if your pot is not a heavy one, you will need to adjust the temperature down.

3 pounds peeled small shrimp
1 tablespoon plus 2¼ teaspoons salt, *in all*
2 teaspoons, *in all*, ground red pepper (preferably cayenne)
½ teaspoon garlic powder
2 cups finely chopped onions, *in all*
½ cup finely chopped green bell peppers
1 cup vegetable oil, *in all*
1 cup all-purpose flour
1½ pounds okra, sliced ¼ inch thick (about 1½
     quarts sliced; see **NOTE**)
1½ cups peeled and chopped tomatoes
3 quarts, *in all*, **Basic Seafood Stock** (page 18)
1½ teaspoons very finely chopped garlic
1 cup chopped green onions (tops only)

NOTE: Versie suggests wiping the okra with a dry kitchen towel instead of washing it, to keep the okra from getting slimy.

Place the shrimp in a large bowl. Sprinkle with *1 tablespoon* of the salt, *1 teaspoon* of the red pepper, and the garlic powder. Stir well, cover, and refrigerate until ready to use.

In a medium-size bowl, combine *1 cup* of the onions with the bell peppers and set aside.

Heat *½ cup* of the oil in a 2-quart cast-iron Dutch oven over high heat until oil is hot and just short of smoking, about 4 minutes. Using a long-handled metal whisk or wooden spoon, very gradually stir the flour into the hot oil. Cook, whisking constantly or stirring briskly, until roux is medium red-brown, 3 to 4 minutes, being careful not to let mixture scorch or splash on your skin. Reduce heat to low and cook until roux is dark red-brown, 1 to 2 minutes more, whisking or stirring constantly. Remove from heat and immediately add the onion and bell pepper mixture, stirring with a wooden spoon until well mixed. Continue stirring until roux stops getting darker, about 2 minutes more. Set aside.

✳See page 12 for more about making roux.

In a 6-quart saucepan or large Dutch oven, combine the remaining ½ *cup* oil with the okra, tomatoes, 1¼ *teaspoons* of the salt, the remaining *1 cup* onions, and *1 teaspoon* red pepper. Place over high heat and cook about 20 minutes, until sticking is excessive, stirring frequently (almost constantly toward end of cooking time) and scraping pan bottom well each time. Add ½ *cup* of the stock and cook and stir about 5 minutes more. (The procedure of stirring and scraping the pan bottom is a major factor in making this dish so good!)

Add 3½ *cups* of the stock and stir until all sediment on pan bottom is dissolved. Bring mixture to a boil, then add the roux by spoonfuls to the boiling stock, stirring until roux is blended in before adding more. Add the remaining *2 quarts* stock, the chopped garlic, and the remaining *1 teaspoon* salt, and return mixture to a boil. Reduce heat and simmer about 40 minutes, stirring occasionally. Stir in the green onions and cook about 5 minutes, stirring occasionally.

Now turn heat to high and stir in the shrimp; cook just until gumbo comes to a simmer and shrimp are pink and plump, stirring occasionally. Do not overcook shrimp. Remove from heat and serve immediately.

Serve 1½ cups gumbo as a main course; 1 cup as an appetizer.

ELI AND SUE'S RECIPE

Chicken and Okra Gumbo
(Gombo de Poule et Gombo Févi)

Makes 6 main-dish servings

In Cajun country, dances are held in several places in each community every Saturday night. It's been this way for as long as anyone can remember. Paul remembers that when he was a young boy, his older brothers and sisters who were married and had children would drop off their kids to stay with Mom and Paul while they went to the dance. As soon as the grown-ups were out the door, Mom and Paul would start making a big pot of gumbo—usually chicken and andouille or chicken with okra. When the gumbo was ready, they just set it on the back of the wood-burning stove and it stayed warm until the dancers returned late at night to pick up their children. All the brothers and sisters knew what was waiting for them on the back burner after the dance. (You know, this might be a terrific way for parents of teenagers to make sure their children get home on time after dating: Have that big pot of gumbo on the back burner!)

Sue, who is not Cajun, has learned a lot about cooking from Eli (she and Eli married after Mom and Dad had died) and from Elden and Odelia Mae, who live just across the road. But this recipe is her very own, and it's really good. It's an unusually thick gumbo, almost like a gravy, with both roux and okra used as thickeners. Paul remembers Mom Prudhomme cooking chicken and okra gumbo and he says she cooked her okra exactly the way Sue does in this recipe— covered for part of the time and then cooked until a lot, but not all, of the okra is browned. This method makes the okra break down better so that it thickens more effectively.

Mom used pork lard to make her roux for chicken and okra gumbo, and that's what Sue prefers, too. Season the chicken the day before and cover and refrigerate until ready to use.

1 (5- to 6-pound) stewing chicken, cut up (use the
    giblets, too)

  Seasoning mix:
    1 tablespoon plus 1¾ teaspoons salt
    1¾ teaspoons garlic powder
    1¾ teaspoons ground red pepper (preferably cayenne)
    1¾ teaspoons black pepper

About 1½ cups pork lard, chicken fat, or vegetable
    oil, *in all*
1½ pounds sliced okra, *in all*, about 2 quarts sliced
½ cup canned tomato sauce
1 cup all-purpose flour
About 3 quarts, *in all*, **Basic Chicken Stock** (page 18)

1 cup chopped onions
1 cup chopped green bell peppers
¾ cup chopped celery
½ pound andouille smoked sausage (preferred) or
    any other good smoked pure pork sausage, such
    as Polish sausage (kielbasa), cut into ½-inch
    slices
3 ounces chopped tasso (preferred) or other smoked
    ham (preferably Cure 81), ¾ cup chopped
1½ teaspoons minced garlic
1 bay leaf
3 hard-boiled eggs
¾ cup chopped green onions (tops only)
3 tablespoons finely chopped fresh parsley
1½ cups hot **Basic Cooked Rice** (page 252)
Gumbo filé (filé powder), optional

Remove excess fat from the chicken pieces and excess skin from around the neck area. Set aside fat and skin trimmings. Place chicken pieces and giblets in a very large bowl.

Combine the seasoning mix ingredients thoroughly in a small bowl. Sprinkle the chicken pieces and giblets with *1 tablespoon plus 2 teaspoons* of the mix, working it in with your hands. (Reserve remaining mix to finish the dish.) Cover and refrigerate overnight.

Slice the reserved chicken fat and skin trimmings into ½-inch pieces to yield about 1 cup. (If necessary, make up the balance with chicken fat, pork lard, or vegetable oil.) Place the fat and skin mixture in a 4-quart saucepan. Cook over high heat until about half the mixture is rendered into fat, about 2 minutes, stirring occasionally. (If half the mixture is lard or oil, heat mixture until hot.) Add *half* the okra to the pan, stirring well. Cover pan tightly and reduce heat to low; cook about 15 minutes, stirring occasionally and scraping pan bottom well. Remove lid and stir well. Increase heat to high and cook uncovered until most of the okra is well browned but some is still green, about 10 minutes, stirring occasionally and scraping pan bottom well. (Stir more frequently toward end of cooking time.) Remove from heat and stir in the tomato sauce. Cover pan and set aside while frying the chicken.

Heat fat or oil ⅝ inch deep in a large skillet over high heat just until it starts to smoke, 4 to 6 minutes. Meanwhile, combine *2 teaspoons* of the seasoning mix with the flour in a paper or plastic bag, mixing well. Just before frying each batch of chicken pieces and giblets, add them to the flour and shake until well coated. Fry the chicken in the hot oil, meaty pieces first with skin side down, until golden brown on both sides, about 10 minutes total. Drain on paper towels and set aside. **NOTE**: Reserve ¼ cup of the seasoned flour to make the roux.

Remove the skillet from heat and let sit about 5 minutes. Spoon out 2 tablespoons of the fat (but not any browned sediment) and place the 2 tablespoons in an 8-inch cast-iron skillet. (Discard remaining fat.) Heat the fat over high heat just until it begins to smoke, about 3 minutes. With a long-handled metal whisk, whisk in the reserved ¼ cup seasoned flour; cook until roux is medium red-brown, about 2 minutes, whisking constantly and being careful not to let it scorch or splash on your skin. Reduce heat to low and continue cooking until roux is dark red-brown, about 1 minute more, whisking constantly. Remove from heat and continue stirring until roux stops getting darker, 2 to 3 minutes.

✱See page 12 for more about making roux.

Meanwhile, in an 8-quart saucepan or large Dutch oven, bring *1 quart* of the stock to a boil over high heat. Add the hot roux by spoonfuls to the boiling stock, stirring until well blended before adding more. Add *1 quart* more stock and the reserved okra-tomato sauce mixture, stirring well. Add the chicken pieces and giblets, cover pan and bring to a boil, stirring occasionally and scraping pan bottom to make sure mixture doesn't scorch. Remove cover and continue boiling about 15 minutes, stirring and scraping occasionally and being careful not to let it scorch.

Now add the onions, bell peppers, celery, andouille, tasso, garlic, and bay leaf, stirring well. Reduce heat and simmer about 20 minutes, stirring frequently and scraping well each time. Skim fat from surface as it develops. Add the *remaining* okra and *2 cups* more stock and return mixture to a boil over high heat. Reduce heat and simmer about 20 minutes, stirring and scraping frequently.

Next add the hard-boiled eggs, green onions, parsley, and the remaining 1 *tablespoon* seasoning mix. Cook until chicken is done and tender, about 20 minutes more, stirring and scraping frequently. **NOTE**: If your gumbo is very, very thick, thin it with about 2 cups more stock or water; but, remember, Sue's gumbo is unusually thick—and it's quite a nice variation! Remove from heat and serve immediately.

To serve, mound ¼ cup rice in the middle of each large serving bowl. Pour 1 to 1½ cups gumbo around the rice and arrange a piece of chicken and half an egg on top. Sprinkle gumbo filé on top, if desired.

·············**LAGNIAPPE**·············
A stewing chicken, especially the dark meat, is never as tender as a fryer. Test stewing chicken for doneness and tenderness by tasting a bite; the meat should not be tough, although it is always firmer than fryer meat.

RALPH AND MARY ANN'S RECIPE

Fresh Fish and Dried Shrimp Gumbo
(Gombo de Poisson Frais et Chevrettes Sèches)

Makes 4 main-dish or 8 appetizer servings

Two of Ralph's favorite things in life are fishing and cooking. He loves to cook the many varieties of fish he catches in gumbos, stews, jambalayas, and gravies.

Ralph was called "Frenchie" when he was a cook in the navy. He started as a mess cook, but he knew how to bake; it took him only about three months to become a baker. Even though he was officially classified as a baker, Ralph figured out ways to cook gumbo for his friends on board ship.

Mom Prudhomme made gumbo with dried shrimp, but not with fresh fish, since she rarely had it. Ralph makes this gumbo with fresh-caught stream bass. If fresh (never frozen) bass isn't available (fresh-water or saltwater are equally good), use any of your favorite local fish that is not oily.

The flavor of fresh fish really complements the dried shrimp. Together they make a light gumbo with a taste that lingers wonderfully in your mouth.

½ cup, packed, dried shrimp (3 ounces)
3 cups hot water, *in all*
½ cup vegetable oil
¾ cup all-purpose flour
2 quarts water
⅓ cup finely chopped onions
⅓ cup finely chopped green bell peppers
¼ cup finely chopped celery
¼ ounce peeled garlic cloves (about 2 large)
½ teaspoon ground red pepper (preferably cayenne)
½ teaspoon black pepper
½ cup finely chopped green onions (tops only)
1 pound freshwater bass fillets (or use fillets of your
    favorite fresh fish), cut into ½-inch squares
Salt to taste
About 2 cups hot **Basic Cooked Rice** (page 252)

In a bowl, soak the shrimp in *2 cups* of the hot water for about 2 minutes. Peel off and discard any shells and place the shrimp in another bowl with the remaining *1 cup* hot water. When all the shrimp are shelled, add the 2 cups "soaking" water to the bowl of shrimp and set aside.

In a large cast-iron skillet, heat the oil over high heat until hot and just short of smoking, about 3 minutes. Using a long-handled metal whisk or wooden spoon, gradually stir the flour into the hot oil, whisking constantly or stirring briskly until smooth. Cook, whisking constantly, until roux is light medium brown, 2 to 3 minutes. Reduce heat to low and continue cooking until roux is medium brown, 1 to 2 minutes more, stirring constantly and making sure it doesn't scorch or splash on your skin. Remove from heat and continue stirring until roux stops getting darker, about 3 minutes. Set aside.

✻ See page 12 for more about making roux.

In a heavy 6-quart saucepan or large Dutch oven, combine the 2 quarts water with the onions, bell peppers, celery, garlic, red and black peppers, the dried shrimp, and 2 cups of the water in which the shrimp were soaked. (Discard remaining shrimp water.) Place over high heat and bring to a boil. Reduce heat and simmer about 25 minutes, stirring occasionally. Add the roux by spoonfuls, blending each spoonful in before adding more. Continue cooking about 45 minutes, stirring occasionally and skimming off any fat as it accumulates on the surface. Add the green onions and fish pieces, turn heat to high, and cook just until the fish is cooked, about 10 minutes more, stirring occasionally. Do not overcook the fish. Skim again and add salt, if needed.

Remove from heat and serve immediately in large soup bowls. Serve about 1½ cups of the gumbo ladled over about ½ cup rice as a main course, being sure to include some of the shrimp and fish in each serving. Serve half that amount for an appetizer.

ELDEN AND ODELIA MAE'S RECIPE

Rabbit, Squirrel, Andouille Smoked Sausage and Tasso Gumbo
(Gombo de Lapin, Écureuil, Saucisse et Tasso)

Makes 10 main-dish servings

Dad didn't really like to hunt with a gun and rarely hunted (the exception was hunting for turtles, which Dad loved to cook) unless the family was spending time in the woods for a special vacation. Then he and friends and the boys in the family set traps for game animals. All the boys hunted occasionally with their slingshots and sometimes set traps for rabbits and squirrels and birds, but only Ralph liked to spend a lot of time hunting in the woods. Game flourished in the forested area behind the Prudhomme home, and Mom cooked the game in many ways: smothered, stewed, in fricassées, and, especially, in gumbos.

Making gumbo is an excellent way to stretch a finite amount of meat to serve many people, so the family had it when there were extra people to feed, but it certainly was not a daily dish. Nowadays, Elden and Odelia Mae make their gumbos with plenty of meat or seafood. This gumbo made with fresh game is really exceptional, and it improves with age. All meat gumbos we are familiar with that don't have okra, or gumbo filé, or seafood in them are better the next day— and even better the day after that. The problem with this gumbo is that you're not likely to get a chance to taste it on the second or third day. It'll all be eaten up the first day!

Elden and Odelia Mae like game, and she cooks rabbits, squirrels, and wild ducks fairly often. You can substitute other game meats, but try to find both rabbit and squirrel to see how good the combination is. If you use other game meats, you may need to cook the gumbo longer to get the meat tender. She makes this gumbo in large quantity to have—you just have to have—leftovers.

Odelia Mae advises that with game squirrel and game rabbit, you must be sure to remove the glands located on each shoulder (each looks like a small lung) and on each leg behind the knee (darker brown). Many people don't know to remove these glands; they make the meat taste too strong and gamy.

*Elden and Odelia Mae serve baked sweet potatoes and potato salad with this gumbo. All the family like to put potato salad in the bowl with gumbo—especially this type made without okra. We like to add **Ground Hot Pepper Vinegar** (page 357) to each bowl. Everyone in the Prudhomme family serves gumbo in extra-large soup bowls plus unlimited refills.*

While we were testing this recipe, our K-Paul's chefs and cooks, who are painfully honest when they critique food, just raved: "It's wonderful!" "It's fabulous!" "It's delicious! All you need with it is a bottle of Tabasco, a cold beer, and a picnic bench!"

Seasoning mix:
2 teaspoons salt
¾ teaspoon ground red pepper (preferably cayenne)
¾ teaspoon black pepper

1 (2- to 2½-pound) rabbit, cut up
2 squirrels, about 1½ pounds dressed, each cut in 6
    pieces
4 cups very finely chopped onions
1 cup very finely chopped green bell peppers
1¼ cups vegetable oil
2 cups all-purpose flour
2 tablespoons very finely chopped garlic
About 4 quarts hot **Rich Chicken Stock** (page 19)
1 pint **Cajun Home-Canned Spicy Tomatoes** (page
    359)
1 tablespoon **Ground Hot Pepper Vinegar** (page
    357), peppers only, plus more for a condiment
    (see **NOTE**)
1 pound andouille smoked sausage (preferred) or any
    other good smoked pure pork sausage, such as
    Polish sausage (kielbasa), cut into 1-inch pieces
½ pound tasso (preferred) or other smoked ham
    (preferably Cure 81), cut into ½-inch cubes
1½ teaspoons salt
2½ cups finely chopped green onions (tops only)
½ cup finely chopped fresh parsley
Scant 1 tablespoon gumbo filé (filé powder),
    optional, plus more for a condiment
About 3⅓ cups hot **Basic Cooked Rice** (page 252)

NOTE: If your vinegar peppers are very hot, use your judgment on how much to put in. If in doubt, add less, since you can always mix in more at the table.

Thoroughly combine the seasoning mix ingredients in a small bowl. Sprinkle the mix evenly over the rabbit and squirrel pieces, working it in with your hands and using it all. Set aside.

Combine the onions and bell peppers in a large bowl and set aside.

In a very large heavy skillet (preferably cast iron) or a 3-quart cast-iron (preferred) or other heavy Dutch oven with flared sides (this is important to keep roux from scorching), heat the oil over high heat until hot and just short of smoking, about 7 minutes. Using a long-handled metal whisk or wooden spoon, very gradually stir the flour into the hot oil. Cook, whisking constantly or stirring briskly, for about 6 minutes, being careful not to let it scorch or splash on your skin. Reduce heat to low and cook until roux is dark red-brown, 2 to 3 minutes more, whisking or stirring constantly. Remove from heat and immediately add about half the onion and bell pepper mixture; stir constantly with a wooden spoon until roux stops turning dark, 3 to 4 minutes. Stir in the garlic and set aside.

✳ See page 12 for more about making roux.

Place *3 quarts plus 3½ cups* stock in a 10-quart saucepan or large Dutch oven; cover and bring to a boil over high heat. Add the roux by spoonfuls to the boiling stock, stirring until roux is blended in thoroughly before adding more. Add the tomatoes, Ground Hot Pepper Vinegar peppers, the rabbit and squirrel pieces and their juices, and the andouille and tasso, stirring well; cover pan and return to a boil. Put on the lid askew, reduce heat, and simmer about 30 minutes, stirring occasionally.

Now stir in the salt and the remaining onion and bell pepper mixture; return to a boil over high heat, then simmer uncovered until the flavors marry and the meat is tender, about 1 hour, stirring and scraping pan bottom occasionally and skimming any fat from the surface as it develops.

At the end, stir in the green onions and parsley and cook about 5 minutes more (see **Lagniappe**). Stir in the gumbo filé, if desired, or have it available as a condiment on the table to sprinkle on top of the gumbo. Remove from heat and skim. Serve immediately.

To serve, mound about ⅓ cup rice in the center of a large soup bowl; ladle about 1½ cups gumbo broth around the rice and add an assortment of the meats on top. Serve additional Ground Hot Pepper Vinegar and gumbo filé as condiments.

This is super with potato salad on the side or in the gumbo itself.

·············**LAGNIAPPE**·············

At the end of the cooking time, try this experiment, which is a good method to use with any rich soup: Ladle up a cup of gumbo broth and add a little stock or water to the cup with the gumbo. Taste, then compare the taste of it with the broth in the pot. We find that broths can sometimes cook down to be so rich that they actually "lock off" the wonderful flavors you're after. If your sample tastes better than what's in the pot, "open" the broth back up by simply adding stock or water.

RALPH AND MARY ANN'S RECIPE

Red Soup with Rice
(Soupe Rouge avec du Riz)

Makes 8 main-dish servings

Red soup with rice was one of Grandma Prudhomme's two favorite dishes (the other was guinea hen gumbo). Ralph and Mary Ann are still making it. Ralph fondly remembers Grandma cooking at her stove. It was about the size of a 9 × 3-foot table. Ralph and Dad Prudhomme built a platform all the way around so Grandma could get up there and reach more easily to stir her pots. As Ralph says, "She was short, but boy was she a good cook!"

Paul remembers red soup with rice from when he was a child. "It was nice and rich." It's also nice and peppery and homemade tasting.

Seasoning mix:

2½ teaspoons salt

2¼ teaspoons red pepper (preferably cayenne)

2¼ teaspoons black pepper

2 pounds bone-in beef shank, about ¾ inch thick, cut
  into 8 pieces (save bone)

1½ pounds boneless beef brisket, cut into 3-inch
  squares

2 quarts **Basic Beef Stock** (page 18)

3 cups finely chopped onions, *in all*

1 (6-ounce) can tomato paste

½ cup uncooked rice (preferably converted)

½ cup chopped green onions (tops only)

Combine the seasoning mix ingredients thoroughly in a small bowl. Sprinkle the beef shank and beef brisket pieces evenly on both sides with a total of *1 tablespoon plus 1½ teaspoons* of the seasoning mix, patting it in with your hands. Let meat sit at room temperature for about 30 minutes.

In a heavy 8-quart saucepan or large Dutch oven, combine the stock, meats, the bone from the beef shank, *1½ cups* of the onions, the tomato paste, and the remaining *2½ teaspoons* seasoning mix, stirring well. Cover and bring to a boil over high heat. Reduce heat to maintain a strong simmer and cook covered until meat is tender, about 1 hour, stirring occasionally and skimming fat from surface as it accumulates.

Now stir in the rice and the remaining *1½ cups* onions, re-cover pan, and cook until rice is tender, 25 to 30 minutes, stirring occasionally. Skim off fat, then stir in the green onions. Remove from heat and serve immediately, allowing a portion of both meats and about 1 cup of the soup per serving.

ENOLA AND SHELTON'S RECIPE

Alligator Soup
(Soupe de Cocodrie)

Makes 4 main-dish or 6 appetizer servings

Alligators are no longer an endangered species in Louisiana. The state has had a legal alligator hunting season with federal approval since 1975. Legal hunting in Louisiana is considered requisite to control a burgeoning alligator population. (Many people were finding alligators in their swimming pools as well as on canal banks in heavily populated areas.) Alligator season begins the first week of September and runs through the first week of October each year and is strictly regulated by the Louisiana Department of Wildlife and Fisheries. Great precautions are taken to protect the nesting female population. Louisiana also has a growing industry of alligator farms. The farms, too, are strictly regulated by the state, but farm-raised alligators can be harvested and sold, with Wildlife and Fisheries approval, during the closed season.

Ralph remembers once when the family was seining for fish, they caught a four-foot-long alligator, which they put in a water cistern. They fed him well until he was about ten feet long. Then Mom made an alligator feast of him, with alligator sauce piquant, fried alligator, stewed alligator, and smothered alligator. As Ralph says, "Alligator is good eating."

Alligator tail meat, which is the edible part, tastes like a cross between chicken and veal and is very high in protein and relatively low in fat. Paul and K have served alligator sausage and alligator sauce piquant often at their restaurant in New Orleans. Enola and Shelton's alligator soup is a fine way to try alligator meat for the first time. They won first place with the recipe at the Alligator Festival in Franklin, Louisiana, in 1985, and they serve it at their restaurant in Louisiana.

The soup is best if made a few hours ahead and reheated. The recipe calls for cooking for fairly long periods of time over high heat. If your gas burner or electric cooking element produces a very high heat, or if your pot is not a heavy one, you will need to adjust the temperature down.

Seasoning mix:
1 tablespoon plus ½ teaspoon salt
2 teaspoons sweet paprika
1¾ teaspoons ground red pepper (preferably cayenne)
1½ teaspoons garlic powder
1 teaspoon onion powder
1 teaspoon ground cumin
1 teaspoon dried sweet basil leaves
¾ teaspoon white pepper
¾ teaspoon dried thyme leaves
½ teaspoon black pepper
½ teaspoon dried oregano leaves

1 pound boneless alligator tail meat, trimmed of fat
    and pounded to ½ inch thick, then cut into
    about 1-inch squares
½ pound (2 sticks) unsalted butter, *in all*
1¼ cups very finely chopped onions, *in all*
1 cup very finely chopped celery, *in all*
½ cup all-purpose flour
2 cups peeled and chopped tomatoes
1 teaspoon minced garlic
6 cups, *in all*, **Rich Seafood Stock** (page 19)
2 tablespoons dry sherry
2 cups hot **Basic Cooked Rice** (page 252), for main-
    dish servings

Combine the seasoning mix ingredients thoroughly in a small bowl. Season the meat with *1 teaspoon* of the mix, working it in with your hands.

In a 5½-quart saucepan, melt *1 stick* of the butter over high heat until about half melted. Add the alligator meat and cook until meat is well browned and sediment on pan bottom is continuously building up, about 13 minutes, stirring occasionally and scraping pan bottom clean of browned sediment. Remove from heat. With a slotted spoon, transfer meat and any bits of very brown sediment to a bowl and set aside.

Return the pan to high heat and add the remaining *1 stick* butter and ¾ *cup* of the onions; cook about 5 minutes, scraping all browned sediment free from pan bottom and then stirring occasionally. Stir in ½ *cup* of the celery, then gradually add the flour, stirring until well blended. Cook about 2 minutes, stirring and scraping frequently. Stir in the tomatoes, 2 *tablespoons* of the seasoning mix, and the garlic; cook about 4 minutes, stirring almost constantly and scraping any browned sediment from pan bottom as it develops. Add ½ *cup* of the stock and scrape until browned sediment on pan bottom is dissolved. Add ½ *cup* more stock and the remaining 2 *tablespoons plus 1¼ teaspoons* seasoning mix; cook about 2 minutes, stirring and scraping frequently.

Now add the remaining 5 *cups* stock and stir and scrape well. Add the meat and sherry and bring mixture to a boil, stirring and scraping frequently. Reduce heat and simmer about 15 minutes, stirring and scraping occasionally. Add the remaining ½ *cup each* onions and celery. Continue simmering until meat is tender and flavors marry, about 30 minutes more, stirring and scraping pan bottom occasionally. Remove from heat and serve immediately in bowls.

Serve 1½ cups soup over ½ cup rice for a main dish; for an appetizer, serve 1 cup of the soup without rice.

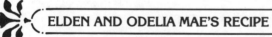

ELDEN AND ODELIA MAE'S RECIPE

Old-Fashioned Pressure Cooker Soup
(Soupe Faite dans un Pressure Cooker)

Makes 8 to 10 main-dish servings

Mom Prudhomme made beef vegetable soup occasionally, as well as **Red Soup with Rice** *(page 206) and chicken soup. Paul says she always added some flour-made ingredient to her chicken soup, like* dumplings or homemade egg noodles. One of Odelia Mae's fondest memories of Mom Prudhomme is of her going out to the garden with her white apron on and coming back to the house with the apron full of fresh vegetables for the family's next meal.

Elden and Odelia Mae have a vegetable garden with lots of varieties of hot peppers and wonderful summer and fall vegetables like mirlitons, tomatoes, green beans, turnips, potatoes, and green onions. Elden is particularly proud of his hot peppers and he and Odelia Mae put up many jars of their **Ground Hot Pepper Vinegar** (page 357) each year. Odelia Mae adds it to many of her recipes.

Her soup has a wonderful assortment of fresh vegetables in it as well as calf or beef leg soup meat. She says soup made with calf leg meat is called "jarret." Odelia loves to cook with a pressure cooker; she has four pressure cookers!

Seasoning mix:
1½ tablespoons salt
1 teaspoon ground red pepper (preferably cayenne)
1 teaspoon black pepper

1 pound bone-in calf or beef leg soup meat, about 1
    inch thick and as meaty as possible
1 pound bone-in calf or beef brisket soup meat, as
    meaty as possible (see **NOTE**)
7 cups water
3 cups coarsely shredded cabbage
3 cups fresh corn kernels cut off the cob (or frozen
    corn kernels)
2 cups very finely chopped onions
1½ cups very finely chopped green onions (tops and
    bottoms)
5 ounces peeled potato, sliced ¼ inch thick and cut
    into ½-inch squares (about 1 cup)
4 ounces peeled white turnips, cut into ½-inch cubes (1 cup)
1 cup peeled and finely sliced carrots
¾ cup **Cajun Home-Canned Spicy Tomatoes** (page 359)
2 ounces green beans, cut into ¾-inch pieces (½ cup)
½ cup canned tomato sauce

211

⅓ cup very finely chopped celery

About 15 strands dry spaghetti, broken into 1-inch pieces

¼ cup uncooked rice (preferably converted)

¼ cup tomato paste

2 tablespoons dried black-eyed peas

1½ teaspoons very finely chopped garlic

1 teaspoon **Ground Hot Pepper Vinegar** (page
    357); use peppers only (see **Note**)

Note: Odelia Mae uses the brisket to add richness to the soup. If the peppers in your Ground Hot Pepper Vinegar are very hot, cut down the amount. You can always add more at the table.

Combine the seasoning mix ingredients thoroughly in a small bowl. Place the meat in a 7-quart pressure cooker and season with the mixture, rubbing it in by hand until meat is well coated, using it all. Add the water, then all the remaining ingredients, stirring well. Seal pressure cooker and place over high heat. Cook until pressure reaches 10 pounds, about 20 minutes. Remove from heat and let pressure reduce to zero. (This will take about 45 minutes.) Remove lid and skim any fat from the surface of the soup. Adjust seasonings if desired and serve immediately.

 MALCOLM AND VERSIE'S RECIPE

Beef Vegetable Soup
(Soupe de Viande de Bête et Légumes)

Makes 6 main-dish servings

When the weather was chilly, Dad Prudhomme wanted homemade beef vegetable soup. The family didn't have fresh beef often, but you could buy a big soupbone with meat for just a few cents. Dad prided himself on the family being self-sufficient. One year, he decided to see how low he could keep the money spent on food. In a year's time, he spent exactly thirty-five cents—he bought a huge, meaty soupbone for Mom to make a big pot of beef vegetable soup.

Before Versie married, her mother did all the cooking and Versie just looked on and "loved to stir the pots." So, after Versie married, she had to learn to cook from an assortment of people—her family, the Prudhomme family, and friends. Versie developed this soup recipe over the years and she uses it as a main course for lunch or a late supper. "C'est bon!" It's even better the second day. And it's great served with hot buttered cornbread.

You can use whatever vegetables you please, but we've given you guidelines for types and amounts.

2 quarts **Rich Beef Stock** (page 19)
2 pounds bone-in beef soup meat, about 1 inch thick,
    cut in 4 to 6 pieces
1 pound bone-in chuck roast, cut into about 1-inch
    cubes (save the bone to add to the soup, too)
1 cup chopped onions
1 cup peeled and chopped tomatoes
½ cup chopped celery
½ cup peeled and coarsely chopped carrots
½ cup canned tomato sauce
¼ cup chopped green bell peppers
1 tablespoon plus 1 teaspoon salt
1 teaspoon finely chopped garlic
½ teaspoon ground red pepper (preferably cayenne)
½ teaspoon black pepper
¾ pound turnips, peeled and cut into ½-inch cubes
    (about 2 cups cubed)
1 cup peeled and coarsely chopped potatoes
1 cup chopped cabbage
½ cup dry twist macaroni (preferably rotini)
6 string beans, trimmed and sliced into 1-inch pieces
    (about ¼ cup sliced)
¼ cup fresh shelled sweet peas
¼ cup chopped green onions (tops only)
About 1 cup hot **Basic Cooked Rice**, optional (page 252)

In a 6-quart saucepan or large Dutch oven, combine the stock, meats, and chuck roast bone; cover and bring to a boil over high heat. Reduce heat and simmer covered for about 45 minutes, stirring occasionally. Turn heat to high and stir in the onions, tomatoes, celery, carrots, tomato sauce, bell peppers, salt, garlic, and red and black peppers. Return soup to a simmer over high heat, then reduce heat and simmer uncovered for about 30 minutes, stirring occasionally.

Now stir in the turnips, potatoes, cabbage, macaroni, beans, and peas; return to simmer over high heat, then reduce heat and simmer until vegetables are tender but still firm, about 30 minutes, stirring occasionally and skimming any fat from surface as it develops. Stir in the green onions and cook about 5 minutes more. Skim any fat again, remove soup from heat, and serve immediately as is or Cajun style, with a tablespoon or two of rice in the bottom of each bowl (just as you would serve gumbo).

PAUL AND K'S RECIPE

Crawfish Bisque
(Bisque d'Écrevisses)

Makes 8 main-dish or 16 appetizer servings

Crawfish bisque is a one-dish meal. The crawfish body shell, referred to as the "head" when you're talking crawfish bisque language, is stuffed here with a cornbread dressing, which serves as the meal's starch. (The bisque is not served over rice.) Classically, most bisques around the world are "white" because they contain cream, but crawfish bisque—which is definitely a Cajun, not Creole, dish—is made with a fairly dark roux and without cream.

In the Prudhomme home, it was understood that the whole family helped make crawfish bisque because, even though it's not difficult to make, it's an all-day project for just one person. The night before the bisque was made, the family would have a much anticipated crawfish boil, which is a wonderful out-of-doors social event in South Louisiana. When everyone had had their fill of boiled crawfish, they set to work preparing crawfish for the bisque.

They had set aside the body shells or heads when they peeled and ate the tails. Now they peeled more tails for the bisque, always saving the wonderful crawfish fat (this is important!) to add richness and flavor to the bisque. Next, they cleaned the heads to be stuffed later with the cornbread dressing. Paul particularly remembers helping to stuff the heads.

Crawfish bisque is one of the most complex dishes we do at Paul and K's restaurant in New Orleans in terms of the number of component parts that make up the wonderful whole. So, what's practical— and really fun, too—is to have the crawfish boil first with friends and family. Then they can help do a great deal of the preparation for the bisque—epecially peeling the crawfish and preparing the heads for baking. They can even help do some of the cooking. At the crawfish boil, boil also the 10 pounds of crawfish for the bisque and get them peeled (reminding those who are peeling them not to eat the tails!). Then peel enough extra crawfish to yield an additional 1 pound (about 2 cups) of tails to put in the bisque at the end. (Or you can buy this extra pound of tails already blanched and peeled; see page 4.)

Another group can assist in preparing the heads and the stuffing: Some can clean the heads; some can make the cornbread for the stuffing; others can make the stuffing itself; and a final group can stuff the heads and bake them. Then, all that's left to do the next day is to make the bisque broth and, when it's finished, add the baked stuffed heads and the whole crawfish tails and heat the assembled bisque.

Of course, you can make and serve the entire crawfish bisque all on the same day. If you plan to do that, allow enough time to let the bisque sit for 2 hours or more, then heat and serve it; if you can possibly fit in the wait, the bisque will benefit a lot. And then pray for leftovers—because they're divine!

Purging the crawfish with salted water is supposed to help flush the mud out of the systems of the live crawfish. It's a controversial procedure: Some people say it's requisite; others say it's not effective. Because it's the traditional thing to do, we chose to do it.

Crawfish boil:
3 gallons water (see **Note**)
1½ pounds unpeeled onions (3 medium), rinsed and quartered

2 lemons, rinsed and halved

1½ to 2 ounces unpeeled garlic (1 large head), rinsed
    and cut crosswise to expose meat

3 large bay leaves

1 tablespoon salt

1½ teaspoons ground red pepper (preferably cayenne)

10 pounds live crawfish, as fresh and lively as possible
    (that is, they should be moving about—they crawl
    backward—and waving their claws around; see **Note**)

1 (1-pound 10-ounce) container salt, *in all*, to purge
    crawfish (about 2¾ cups)

Water, to purge crawfish

> **Seasoning mix:**
>
> 1 tablespoon plus 1 teaspoon salt
>
> 1 tablespoon plus ½ teaspoon ground red pepper (preferably
> cayenne)
>
> 1½ teaspoons sugar
>
> 1½ teaspoons gumbo filé (filé powder)
>
> 1½ teaspoons sweet paprika
>
> 1¼ teaspoons white pepper
>
> 1¼ teaspoons onion powder
>
> 1¼ teaspoons garlic powder
>
> 1¼ teaspoons black pepper
>
> 1¼ teaspoons sweet basil leaves
>
> ½ teaspoon dried thyme leaves

½ pound (2 sticks) plus 2 tablespoons unsalted butter, *in all*

6 cups finely chopped onions, *in all*

4¼ cups finely chopped green bell peppers, *in all*

3¾ cups finely chopped celery, *in all*

¾ cup evaporated milk

1 egg

2½ cups finely crumbled **Bobby's Cornbread** (page 278; see **Note**)

1 pound peeled crawfish tails (in addition to the yield of peeled
    tails from the 10 pounds of crawfish), about 2 cups peeled

½ cup vegetable oil

1 cup all-purpose flour

NOTE: If the live crawfish are muddy, rinse them off with a garden hose or in a bucket or tub before purging. For the stuffing, use the *sweeter* version of Bobby's Cornbread. After boiling the crawfish, reserve 12 cups of the water to use as stock for the bisque.

In a very large pot (at least 6-gallon size), combine the crawfish-boil ingredients; cover and bring to a boil. Remove cover and continue boiling about 15 minutes. Meanwhile, purge the live crawfish. Then, if you need more time to finish purging the crawfish, reduce heat to maintain a slow simmer.

To purge the crawfish: Place the live crawfish in a bucket or tub large enough (at least 5-gallon size) to allow headspace of 6 inches or more above the crawfish. (If you have a large outdoor sink, use it.) Pour about *one third* of the salt over the crawfish and fill the bucket or tub with cool tap water. Let sit about 5 minutes, stirring occasionally (a broom handle works well for this) and removing any very inactive crawfish or ones that may be dead. (Sometimes they play possum. If in doubt, set suspect ones aside and, after a couple of minutes, move them around to see if they move at all, even just a little. Return live ones to the salted water.)

Drain off water and any debris, then add water to rinse out bucket, drain off again, and refill with cool tap water. Pour *one third* more of the salt over the crawfish. Stir well and let sit again about 5 minutes, picking up spoonfuls of the crawfish to find any dead or very inactive ones. Drain bucket well a second time, refill with water, and add the remaining *one-third* salt; repeat procedure of stirring and removing dead crawfish for about 5 more minutes.

Then, with a large spoon, transfer crawfish to a clean container, making a final check to remove any dead ones and draining crawfish well. **NOTE:** You will see with each rinsing that the water will be less muddy. Repeat rinsing procedure as often as necessary to have the final rinse water clear (the later rinsings can be done with or without salt). Even when the water is completely clear, it may still be a fairly dark color—and this is fine.

To boil the crawfish: Bring the crawfish-boil mixture back to a rolling boil and immediately slip the purged crawfish carefully into the boiling mixture; cover pan and return to a boil. As soon as liquid returns to a boil, turn off heat source, leaving pan on burner, and, with a large heat-proof strainer or slotted spoon, quickly transfer crawfish (so they won't overcook) to a large shallow pan to cool.

To finish the stock: Remove lemons from the crawfish liquid (stock) and discard them. Return any vegetables that were spooned out with the crawfish. Return pan to high heat and bring stock to a boil; continue boiling uncovered for 1 hour. Remove from heat and strain stock repeatedly through several thicknesses of cheesecloth (using fresh cheesecloth each time), until stock leaves no residue on the cloth (although it still may *stain* the cloth since the stock is a dark color). This may take 5 to 15 or more strainings. Set aside, or, if making the bisque ahead, cool and refrigerate until ready to use.

NOTE: You can use the delicious inside "goodness" of the garlic and onions from the stock in another dish. And, you will have a lot of leftover stock. If you don't plan to save the excess stock to use in another recipe, just strain enough to yield 12 cups for the bisque. If you do want to save the excess stock, remember that it's already seasoned; you'll need to cut down on the salt, and perhaps the other seasonings as well, in any recipe in which you use the stock.

To peel the crawfish tails: Let crawfish cool slightly, then peel the tails, reserving the body shells. **NOTE**: At this point, don't let the Louisiana language confuse you. The "head" (see Drawing 1) *is* actually the body shell, and up front the crawfish has a real head with its own small shell. We'll call the two together the head-and-body segment to keep things understandable.

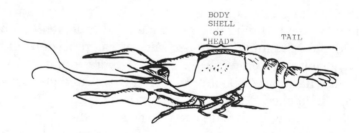

Separate each crawfish tail from the head-and-body segment at the joint where the tail and body meet. To do this, grasp the crawfish body firmly in one hand and the tail in the other and gently twist and pull the tail free. As the tail is separated from the body, you will probably see light yellow-orange, pink, or light-brownish fat at the top of the tail; this is wonderful and will add richness to the bisque, so be sure to leave it attached to the tail.

To peel each tail, hold the end of the tail firmly in one hand and, with the forefinger and thumb of the other hand, peel off the uppermost 2 or 3 rings of shell in a circular fashion. Then squeeze the base of the tail with the fingers of one hand while gently pulling the tail meat in the opposite direction with the other hand—which should make the tail meat pop free in one piece. Place peeled tails in a bowl and refrigerate.

The yield of peeled crawfish tails should be about 1 quart. Reserve any excess fat detached from the juncture between body and tail in a separate bowl; discard any gray or dark matter. If crawfish are lean, you may not have any of this excess fat.

To prepare the "heads" for stuffing: Break the underneath (stomach) section of the head-and-body segment away from the top (back) section by simply pulling the two sections apart with your fingers. From the stomach section, scoop out any fat with your fingers, but not other matter, and place with the other reserved fat; discard the stomach carcass. From the body shell, scoop out any fat and place with the other reserved fat. Refrigerate fat.

Remove the small head shell by holding the body shell with one hand and using the thumb and forefinger of the other hand to gently start a crack underneath one eye. Follow the seam where the head shell is fused to the body shell until the two are separated. Now you have your Louisiana "head" shell on its own, and this is what you stuff. **NOTE**: If the shells are very hard, you can remove the forward small head section by slicing it off with a knife. Each finished head for stuffing should look very similar to the drawings below:

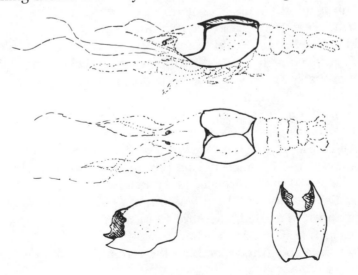

You will have more than enough heads, so don't worry if you ruin a few shells while learning how to prepare them. The yield of heads varies greatly, depending on the size of the crawfish.

Rinse the heads well, being careful to keep them intact. Refrigerate until ready to use.

To make the stuffing: Combine the seasoning mix ingredients thoroughly in a small bowl. In a 5½-quart saucepan or large Dutch oven, melt *4 tablespoons* of the butter over high heat until half melted. Add *1 cup* of the onions and sauté until well browned, 4 to 5 minutes, stirring occasionally. Stir in ¾ *cup* of the bell peppers and ½ *cup* of the celery; cook about 3 minutes, stirring frequently. Add *2½ teaspoons* of the seasoning mix and cook and stir about 1 minute. Add the remaining 1½ *sticks plus 2 tablespoons* butter and stir until melted. Add *4 cups* more onions and any reserved crawfish fat; sauté about 5 minutes, stirring occasionally. Add *2½ cups* more bell peppers and *2¼ cups* more celery; cook about 20 minutes, stirring and scraping pan bottom fairly often. Reduce heat to very low and cook about 30 minutes more, stirring occasionally. Stir in the evaporated milk and remove from heat. Set aside.

In a very large mixing bowl, whisk or stir the egg vigorously a few seconds until frothy. Add the reserved sautéed vegetable and milk mixture, stirring well. Stir in the crumbled cornbread and set aside.

In a food processor, process for a few seconds until minced about two thirds of the tails you got from peeling the 10 pounds of crawfish. (Reserve whole in the refrigerator the remaining one third to add to the bisque.) Add the minced crawfish and *2 tablespoons plus 1 teaspoon* of the seasoning mix to the cornbread mixture, stirring thoroughly. Then stuff the heads; or, if making ahead, cool the stuffing and refrigerate.

To stuff the heads: Stuff the heads (it's easiest to do this by hand) as full as possible with the stuffing, packing it as you go, and mounding a little over the top. Place stuffed heads, stuffing side up, in a greased 13 × 9-inch baking pan or on a greased cookie sheet and bake at 450° until browned and crusty on top, about 30 minutes. (**NOTE:** Baking time will be a few minutes longer if heads are made earlier and refrigerated.) Remove from oven and set aside, or cool and refrigerate if making ahead.

To make the roux: Combine the remaining *1 cup each* of the onions, bell peppers, and celery, and set aside. Have a long-handled wooden spoon handy, even if you're using a metal whisk to make the roux. Heat the oil in a 2-quart cast-iron Dutch oven over high heat until oil is hot and just short of smoking, about 5 minutes. Using a long-handled metal whisk or wooden spoon, gradually stir the flour into the hot oil. Cook, whisking constantly or stirring briskly, until roux is light brown, about 4 minutes. Then reduce heat to medium and continue cooking until roux is medium red-brown, about 1 to 2 minutes more. Remove from heat and with a wooden spoon immediately stir in the reserved onion, bell pepper, and celery mixture. Add 1 *tablespoon* of the seasoning mix and continue stirring until roux stops getting darker, about 3 minutes.

✳See page 12 for more about making roux.

Set aside, or cool thoroughly, and refrigerate if making ahead. (If you make the roux ahead, let it come to room temperature and drain any fat from the surface before using the roux.)

To finish the bisque: In a 6-quart saucepan or large Dutch oven, bring *10 cups* of the strained reserved stock to a boil over high heat. Add the roux by spoonfuls to the boiling stock, stirring or whisking until each addition is well blended before adding more. Add the remaining 2 *tablespoons plus* ¼ *teaspoon* seasoning mix and bring to a boil. Reduce heat and simmer about 30 minutes, stirring frequently and skimming off any fat as it develops. Add the baked stuffed heads and return to a simmer over low heat, stirring gently and occasionally. (**NOTE:** If stuffed heads are cold when you add them, bring broth to a simmer first over *high* heat.) Continue simmering about 15 minutes, stirring as needed so mixture won't stick. Add the remaining 2 *cups* stock.

If serving immediately, also add the reserved one-third peeled crawfish tails from the 10-pound batch of crawfish and the additional 1 pound of peeled crawfish tails. Cook about 10 minutes more, stirring gently and scraping pan bottom as needed. Remove from heat and serve immediately.

If making ahead, remove bisque from heat *after* adding the last 2 cups stock and *before* adding the peeled crawfish tails. With a slotted spoon, remove stuffed heads to a bowl so they won't continue to absorb the bisque broth. Let bisque and heads cool, then cover heads with a clean, damp dish towel so they won't dry out. Refrigerate the heads and bisque until ready to reheat, preferably at least 2 hours. When ready to serve, add the stuffed heads and peeled crawfish tails to the bisque broth and heat just until the broth is hot and the stuffed heads are heated through.

As a main course, serve in bowls, allowing about 2 cups of crawfish bisque with a portion of stuffed heads in it. As an appetizer, serve half that amount in cups. **NOTE:** If there are any people at the table who have never eaten crawfish bisque, tell them to be sure to eat the wonderful stuffing in the heads. Each person can remove the heads to a side dish to make it easier to scoop out the stuffing and then eat it separately or put it back into the bisque. We like to put it back in.

MALCOLM AND VERSIE'S RECIPE

Shrimp Fricassee
(Fricassée de Chevrettes)

Makes 4 main-dish servings

Fricassée (pronounced free-kah-say), or stew, is made with a brown roux that is quite thick. Paul says that, classically, a fricassée is made with cream, but that isn't the way the family made it. And he says the gravy of fricassée is thicker and richer than regular gravies. Versie agrees: "Fricassée has to have a thick roux gravy—so you should use a lot of roux—and you can make it with any meat or shellfish."

Mom Prudhomme served fricassée for special occasions. She made hard-boiled egg, dried shrimp, and potato fricassée, and when she made chicken fricassée, she used an old hen or rooster from the yard.

By the time the younger children were growing up, Mom began to cook seafood, like shrimp, more often. Dad had gotten a truck in 1945, so the family could get to the Louisiana Gulf coast occasionally to visit relatives and seine and fish for seafood. Mom loved shrimp and she usually cooked them in a fricassée.

1 pound peeled small shrimp

    Seasoning mix:
    1½ teaspoons salt
    1 teaspoon ground red pepper (preferably cayenne)
    ½ teaspoon garlic powder
    ½ teaspoon black pepper

¾ cup finely chopped onions
¾ cup finely chopped green bell peppers
⅓ cup vegetable oil
½ cup all-purpose flour
3½ cups **Basic Shrimp Stock** (page 18)
1¾ teaspoons finely chopped garlic
½ teaspoon plus ⅛ teaspoon salt
¼ cup finely chopped green onions (tops only)
3 tablespoons finely chopped fresh parsley
About 3 cups hot **Basic Cooked Rice** (page 252)

Place the shrimp in a large bowl. Combine the seasoning mix ingredients thoroughly in a small bowl. Sprinkle the mix evenly on the shrimp, using it all and stirring well to coat all the shrimp thoroughly. Cover and refrigerate at least 2 hours, preferably overnight.

Combine the onions and bell peppers in a small bowl. Set aside. Have a wooden spoon handy even if you use a metal whisk to stir the roux.

In a 2-quart cast-iron Dutch oven, heat the oil over high heat for about 2 minutes. Using a long-handled metal whisk or wooden spoon, gradually stir the flour into the hot oil. Cook, whisking constantly or stirring briskly, until roux is medium red-brown, about 5 minutes, being careful not to let it scorch or splash on your skin. Reduce heat to low and cook until roux is dark red-brown, about 2 minutes more, whisking or stirring constantly. Remove from heat and with a wooden spoon immediately stir in the reserved onions and bell peppers until well mixed. Continue stirring until roux stops getting darker, 2 to 3 minutes.

✳See page 12 for more about making roux.

In a 4-quart saucepan, bring the stock to a boil over high heat. Add the roux by spoonfuls, stirring until well blended between each addition. Add the garlic and salt and return to a boil. Reduce heat and simmer about 10 minutes, stirring frequently. Stir in the green onions and parsley; cook until mixture starts to get creamy, about 5 minutes, stirring frequently so mixture won't scorch. Add the shrimp and cook just until shrimp are pink and plump, about 3 minutes more, stirring frequently. Do not overcook shrimp. Remove from heat and serve immediately, allowing about ¾ cup rice surrounded by about 1 cup of fricassée.

BOBBY'S RECIPE

Potato Stew with Andouille Smoked Sausage
(Fricassée de Patate Anglaise et Andouille)

Makes 4 to 6 main-dish servings

Mom Prudhomme made potato stew often for dinner at noon. When she made it on a Friday, she omitted the sausage, since the family was Catholic and didn't eat meat on Fridays, and sometimes added hard-boiled eggs instead.

Bobby says Mom also broke fresh eggs into the stew at the end of the cooking and just let them sit until the yolks were firm. Bob does this, too. "That's good eating!" he says.

This is a poor man's stew—nice and thick, you can feed a lot of people with it, it's inexpensive, and really great when the weather is cold.

The roux in this dish was traditionally made with pork lard, but Bobby is a city fellow now and chooses to use margarine.

2 cups chopped onions, *in all*
5 tablespoons margarine
½ cup all-purpose flour

2 tablespoons unsalted butter

1 pound andouille smoked sausage (preferred) or any
    other good smoked pure pork sausage, such as
    Polish sausage (kielbasa), cut into 1-inch slices

1½ quarts **Basic Pork Stock** (page 18)

1 tablespoon minced fresh parsley

1 teaspoon salt

½ teaspoon ground red pepper (preferably cayenne)

½ teaspoon black pepper

3 pounds Idaho potatoes, peeled and sliced crosswise
    ½ inch thick, about 2 quarts sliced

Place *1 cup* of the onions in a bowl. Have a wooden spoon handy even if you use a metal whisk to make the roux.

Heat the margarine in a 2-quart cast-iron Dutch oven over high heat until hot, 2 to 3 minutes. Using a long-handled metal whisk or wooden spoon, gradually stir the flour into the hot margarine. Cook, whisking constantly or stirring briskly, until roux is medium brown, about 5 minutes, being careful not to let it scorch or splash on your skin. Remove from heat and with a wooden spoon immediately stir in the reserved 1 cup onions. Continue stirring until roux stops getting darker, about 3 minutes. Set aside.

✳See page 12 for more about making roux.

In a large skillet, heat the butter over high heat until half melted. Add the andouille and cook about 3 minutes, turning andouille and scraping pan bottom occasionally. Add the remaining *1 cup* onions, turn heat to medium, and continue cooking until andouille and onions are well browned, 6 to 8 minutes, stirring and scraping almost constantly. Remove from heat and set aside.

Bring the stock to a boil in a 4-quart saucepan over high heat. Add the roux by spoonfuls to the boiling stock, stirring until roux is blended in before adding more. Add the reserved andouille and onion mixture (including drippings), the parsley, salt, and red and black peppers. Return mixture to a boil, stirring occasionally. Reduce heat, cover pan, and simmer about 10 minutes, stirring occasionally.

Now add *half* the potatoes, re-cover pan, and return to a boil over high heat; then reduce heat and simmer until potatoes are tender, about 20 minutes more, stirring occasionally. Add the *remaining* potatoes, return to a boil over high heat, then simmer until all potatoes are tender, about 20 minutes more, stirring frequently so mixture doesn't scorch. Remove from heat and serve immediately.

DARILEE AND SAUL'S RECIPE

Pork Backbone Stew
(Fricassée de Reintier de Cochon)

Makes 6 generous main-dish servings

Because Darilee was the oldest child in the family, her job was to baby-sit—and there was always a baby to take care of—so she never had an opportunity really to learn to cook from Mom Prudhomme. She basically learned only a few simple tasks like frying eggs and making mayonnaise at home. So when she married Saul, she didn't know much about cooking and she learned most of her skills from her mother-in-law. (What's ironic is that most of Mom Prudhomme's daughters-in-law learned to cook from her, not from their own mothers!)

Darilee and Saul spent their first three years of married life with his parents; there weren't as many people there as at the Prudhomme home. Darilee stayed with Saul's parents for the birth of both of her and Saul's children, Woodrow and Earl, because Mom Prudhomme had babies of her own and couldn't help Darilee as Saul's mother could.

In 1940 (when Paul was born) Saul and Darilee were again living with Saul's parents and began raising animals. That was when Darilee learned to cook pork backbone stew from her mother-in-law. Mom Prudhomme also made a stew like this; it was her favorite way to cook backbone. It has a wonderful "country gravy" taste.

The fat on fresh pork backbone has a delicious taste and texture. See page 148 for more about backbone.

Seasoning mix:

1 tablespoon plus ½ teaspoon salt
1½ teaspoons black pepper
1 teaspoon ground red pepper (preferably cayenne)

5 pounds pork backbones (have your butcher cut into
    roughly 3-inch squares), bone-in pork loin
    fingers, or country-style pork ribs (preferred), or
    pork neck bones, cut into roughly 3-inch squares
1 cup vegetable oil
1¼ cups plus 2 tablespoons all-purpose flour
About 2½ quarts, *in all*, hot **Rich Pork Stock**
    (page 19)
½ cup finely chopped onions
¼ cup finely chopped celery
½ cup, *in all*, finely chopped green onions (tops only)
½ teaspoon finely chopped garlic
9 cups hot **Basic Cooked Rice** (page 252)

Combine the seasoning mix ingredients thoroughly in a small bowl. Place the meat in a large bowl and sprinkle it evenly on both sides with the seasoning mix, using all the mix and working it in with your hands. Set aside.

    Place the oil in a heavy 8-quart saucepan; heat over high heat about 1 minute. Gradually stir in the flour with a long-handled wooden spoon or metal whisk. Cook about 8 minutes, stirring briskly or whisking constantly and being careful not to let it scorch or splash on your skin. Reduce heat to medium and cook and stir until roux is medium brown, about 2 minutes more, stirring constantly.

✳ See page 12 for more about making roux.

Gradually add *7 cups* of the stock, stirring until well blended. Turn heat to high and add the meat, then the onions, celery, ¼ *cup* of the green onions, and the garlic. Bring to a boil, stirring occasionally. Reduce heat to maintain a strong simmer and partially cover pan, leaving about one third of the pan uncovered; cook about 40 minutes, stirring occasionally.

    Now stir in 2½ *cups* more stock and the remaining ¼ *cup* green onions. Re-cover pan with lid slightly askew, reduce heat to low, and cook until meat is tender, about 35 minutes more, occasionally stirring and scraping pan bottom well. **NOTE**: Add more stock or water if gravy becomes too thick. Remove from heat and serve immediately over rice.

ELDEN AND ODELIA MAE'S RECIPE

Bouilli

Makes 4 main-dish servings

Bouilli (pronounced boo-yee) *is a classic Cajun soup made with the internal organs of beef. Mom Prudhomme made bouilli with almost no meats other than internal organs. (Bouilli and boudin, back when Mom and Dad first married, were made mostly with liver and spleen—that is, with meats you couldn't do anything else with.) What made bouilli so special was that it was always cooked on the day of a boucherie, when everything was as fresh as you can get it—immediately after the animal was killed. Elden and Odelia Mae still make bouilli fairly often; she loves to cook the old Cajun recipes almost as much as she enjoys creating new ones.*

To recapture the special taste of the family bouilli, it's absolutely essential to use very fresh organ meats; they impart the essence, the best taste, of an animal but they age poorly. Paul believes the chief reason people rarely cook with these meats now is that it's so difficult to get them really fresh. But he says, if he could have his choice between very fresh internal organs and other cuts of beef, he'd pick the organ meats for giving the best taste.

For those of you who just can't handle the thought of using spleen or kidney, substitute additional beef. The recipe won't be authentic, but it will still taste wonderful. In some meat markets, especially, of course, in Cajun country in South Louisiana, you can buy a bag of beef "bouilli meat," which is a mixture of organ meats, cleaned and ready to cook. We suggest that you have your butcher clean the kidney, but we've told you how to do it in case you want to learn how the Prudhommes out in the country did it and still do.

Elden and Odelia Mae also take all the meat called for in this recipe, season it well, and cook it in a pot with water, canned tomatoes, potatoes, rice, corn, onions, green onions, parsley, and bell peppers. They say the "old people" used to do this and called the dish "bouillon." Paul says he remembers that the best bouilli he ever tasted was one Mom made the regular way and then added fresh corn to it.

Members of the family define bouilli in different ways: Elden and Odelia Mae say it means mixed meats, to them; Abel and Jo and Paul say it means boiled beef, to them; and one of our Cajun dictionaries says it means a highly seasoned stew of organ meats. We know you'll like this bouilli, no matter how it's defined.

It's very important to use a very rich beef stock.

8 ounces boneless beef rib ends

8 ounces boneless beef sirloin strip

1¼ pounds calf (preferred) or beef heart

4 ounces beef spleen

12 ounces beef kidney

8 ounces calf (preferred) or beef liver

2¼ teaspoons salt

1½ teaspoons ground red pepper (preferably cayenne)

1 teaspoon black pepper

1 tablespoon plus 1 teaspoon **Ground Hot Pepper Vinegar,** vinegar only (page 357)

½ cup all-purpose flour

About ¾ cup plus 1 tablespoon vegetable oil, *in all*

3 cups very finely chopped green onions (tops and bottoms)

2 cups very finely chopped onions

¾ cup very finely chopped green bell peppers

2 tablespoons very finely chopped garlic

5 cups, *in all*, very **Rich Beef Stock** (page 19)

2 teaspoons **Ground Hot Pepper Vinegar,** peppers only (page 357; see **Note**)

About 3 cups hot **Basic Cooked Rice** (page 252)

NOTE: If your Ground Hot Pepper Vinegar peppers are very hot, use your own judgment on how much of the peppers to use. If in doubt, add less, since you can always mix in more at the table. Use the full amount of vinegar.

Trim the fat from the rib ends and sirloin strip; cut the meat into 2½ × 1½ × 1-inch chunks. Place the meat chunks in a large bowl (large enough to hold the other meats, too). Cover and refrigerate.

From the heart, trim away any white blood vessels on the surface, any red meat on the surface that contains a lot of textured blood-vessel network, and any obvious surface membrane, but leave the fat on the heart. Cut the meat into about 1½ × 1 × ¾-inch pieces. Add the heart pieces to the bowl with the rib ends and sirloin and refrigerate.

From the spleen, peel or trim off the silver skin on the surface, leaving on the second, thinner silver skin that is immediately underneath. (This is easiest to do using your fingers—it's like peeling the backing from adhesive-backed paper. Find a place to start peeling and then it's simple to pull off the top layer of silver skin. However, if you just can't seem to find a place that peels off only the top layer, it's all right to take off both skins.) Cut the spleen into about 2 × 1-inch strips. Add the spleen pieces to the bowl with the other meats.

Prepare the kidney as follows, keeping in mind that your goal is to remove all fat or suet, all gristle, and the intricate duct system through which urine passed or was collected. It's very important to remove any questionable matter, or your house will smell like a high school gymnasium! In order to expose the parts needing to be trimmed, use a small, sharp paring knife to cut the kidney crosswise into slices roughly ¾ inch thick or less. Then use your fingers and the knife to uncover the ductwork in each piece and tease away the meat from the ducts, trimming off the skin that formed the walls around the tiny ducts and anything whitish and/or stringy. If in doubt, trim off more than you think is necessary. By the time you are finished, many of the pieces will be quite small. Trim off the suet and all adjacent gristle.

This preparation of the kidney is the only tedious part of making bouilli, and it may take you 20 minutes or so to do it. Place the kidney meat in the bowl with the other meats.

If the liver is ⅜ inch thick or less, cut it into 3½ × 2-inch pieces and place with other meats. If it is more than ⅜ inch thick, pound it to ⅜ inch, then cut it into pieces of similar size. Place the pounded liver in a separate bowl from the other meats because it must be handled gently so it won't fall apart.

Thoroughly rinse each piece of the mixed meats, including the unpounded liver, under cool running water. Drain well and set aside in a large clean bowl. Then, if the liver was pounded, rinse it gently, drain well, and add it to the bowl with the other meats.

In a small bowl, combine the salt and red and black peppers, mixing well; add the mixture and the Ground Hot Pepper Vinegar (vinegar only) to the meats and mix well by hand. Take out the pieces of liver and transfer to a separate bowl. Cover both bowls and refrigerate for about 1 hour.

Remove the liver from the refrigerator. Place the flour in a shallow pan and set aside. In a large skillet, heat ½ *cup* of the oil over high heat about 1 minute. Just before frying, dredge the liver in the flour, shake off excess, and fry in a single layer in the hot oil until browned on both sides, about 2 minutes per side. Do not overcook. Remove skillet from heat and transfer liver to a plate; set aside. Let skillet sit a minute or two, then drain and discard the oil, leaving as much browned sediment in the pan as possible.

In a 5½-quart saucepan or large Dutch oven, heat the remaining ¼ *cup plus 1 tablespoon* oil over high heat for about 1 minute. Add the reserved brown sediment from cooking the liver and all the meats except the liver, stirring well. Cover pan with a loose-fitting lid or one placed slightly askew (so steam can escape) and cook about 20 minutes, stirring occasionally and scraping the pan bottom well each time. Add the green onions, onions, bell peppers, and garlic, stirring well; cook uncovered about 7 minutes, stirring frequently.

Now add *3 cups* of the stock and the Ground Hot Pepper Vinegar peppers, stirring well; reduce heat to medium high, re-cover pan, and cook about 45 minutes, stirring occasionally and scraping pan bottom well each time. Add the remaining *2 cups* stock. If all the meat is tender, add the liver, reduce heat, and simmer uncovered about 5 minutes more, stirring occasionally. If meat is *not* tender, cover pan and simmer until tender, stirring occasionally; then add the liver and cook about 5 minutes more. Remove from heat and serve immediately.

For each serving allow about ⅔ cup rice topped with about ⅔ cup meat and 1 cup of the broth.

JAMBALAYAS & BOUDINS

ELDEN AND ODELIA MAE'S RECIPE

Shrimp and Crabmeat Jambalaya
(Jambalaya de Chevrettes et Viande de Crabe)

Makes 3 to 4 main-dish or 6 to 8 appetizer servings

When the older children were young, the Prudhomme family almost never had shrimp, crabmeat, or oysters; the area of Cajun country where they have always lived is not close to the Louisiana Gulf coast. Dad had two uncles who lived in Hackberry, Louisiana, very near the Gulf, but it was too long a trip to go by horse and wagon. One of Dad's brothers had a car and he did go to the coast occasionally and bring back oysters, shrimp, and saltwater fish. Fresh seafood was a really special treat.

Later, after Dad got a truck in 1945, Mom and Dad and the children got to visit their cousins on the coast every now and then. They took some of the foods they had grown or made on the farm—especially sweet potatoes and sausages and other preserved meats. While they were there, all the family would seine for shrimp, blue crabs, and a variety of saltwater fish, and they went out in a boat to the oyster reefs offshore and harvested oysters. All the boys in the family remember vividly the cookouts they had on the beach after catching all that seafood. Everyone helped do the cooking, and Ralph, Abel, Bob, and Paul particularly, remember boiling the crabs and shrimp and frying some of the fish and making a stew with the rest. And Mom canned some of the seafood to take back home to the country.

After Elden and Odelia Mae married, they lived for almost thirty years in New Orleans, and they often brought seafood home to the family. When they moved back to the country, they bought a seafood market and Odelia Mae ran it for years. They really love to cook with seafood; Odelia Mae makes seafood gumbos, seafood stuffed mirlitons and eggplant, and seafood jambalayas.

This flavorful jambalaya is unusual in that it contains neither smoked meats nor a lot of pepper heat—both of which are present in most Cajun jambalayas—unless you add the optional fresh peppers *from the Ground Hot Pepper Vinegar. If you do use these peppers, you will notice as you eat the jambalaya that they produce heat toward the front of your mouth. Dried ground peppers produce heat more in the middle and back of the mouth—a little note on how we taste.*

Seasoning mix:
¾ teaspoon salt
¾ teaspoon ground red pepper (preferably cayenne)
½ teaspoon black pepper

1 pound peeled small shrimp
4 tablespoons unsalted butter
1 (8-ounce) can tomato sauce
2 cups very finely chopped onions
1 cup very finely chopped green onions (tops and bottoms)
½ cup very finely chopped green bell peppers
¼ cup very finely chopped fresh parsley
2 tablespoons very finely chopped garlic
2 bay leaves
¼ teaspoon dried thyme leaves
2 cups **Basic Seafood Stock** (page 18)
1 cup uncooked rice (preferably converted)
About 1 teaspoon **Ground Hot Pepper Vinegar**
    (page 357), optional; use peppers only (see **NOTE**)
1 teaspoon salt
½ teaspoon black pepper
½ pound crabmeat, picked over

NOTE: Use your own judgment in adjusting the amount of peppers, depending on the heat level of the peppers that were used to make the vinegar. (We used between 1 teaspoon and 1 tablespoon as we retested this dish on more than one occasion because the heat of the peppers varied considerably from one batch of pepper vinegar to the next.) If in doubt, use only a small amount because, in this particular dish, the ground peppers will affect any leftover jambalaya, making it get significantly hotter as it sits. You can always add more vinegar peppers at the table.

Combine the seasoning mix ingredients thoroughly in a small bowl. Place the shrimp in a medium-size bowl, sprinkle the seasoning mix on them, and work it in with your hands, using it all. Cover and refrigerate until ready to use.

Melt the butter in a 6-quart saucepan or large Dutch oven over high heat. Stir in the tomato sauce and cook until the tomato is noticeably darker and the butter clearly separates out of the mixture, making large puddles of red oil, about 8 minutes; stir almost constantly so mixture doesn't scorch. Stir in the onions, green onions, bell peppers, parsley, garlic, bay leaves, and thyme; cook about 2 minutes, stirring constantly. Stir in the stock and rice and cook about 2 minutes more, stirring once or twice. Stir in the vinegar peppers, if desired, and the salt and black pepper. Bring to a simmer, then reduce heat to a slow simmer; cover pan and cook about 15 minutes without stirring.

Now add the shrimp and crabmeat, stirring and scraping pan bottom well. Re-cover pan and remove from heat. Let sit covered about 10 minutes to let the flavors marry, the shrimp cook, and the rice get tender but still firm. Stir well, remove bay leaves, and serve immediately.

To serve, allow 1½ to 2 cups on a heated serving plate for a main course or about ¾ cup for an appetizer.

DARILEE AND SAUL'S RECIPE

Ground Beef, Andouille Smoked Sausage and Cabbage Jambalaya

Makes 6 main-dish or 20 side-dish servings

This is a very meaty jambalaya, lightly flavored with cabbage—and it's good! Darilee and Saul learned to make this unusual jambalaya from Earl, their son, and they like it as a change from traditional jambalayas. Darilee loves to make jambalaya, especially with seafood and crawfish, on their frequent camping trips. She and Saul love to camp almost as much as Calvin and Marie do. They belong to the Good Sam Camping Club. Saul and Darilee have an old camper and Calvin and Marie have a new motor home, so when they go camping together, Saul always says to Darilee, "Well, looks like the poor are going to mix with the rich."

This dish is cooked for fairly long periods of time over high heat. If your gas burner or electric cooking element produces a very high heat, or if your pot is not a heavy one, you will need to adjust the temperature down.

1 tablespoon vegetable oil
1½ pounds ground beef
¾ pound andouille smoked sausage (preferred) or
    any other good smoked pure pork sausage, such
    as Polish sausage (kielbasa), cut into ¾-inch
    slices
1 tablespoon salt
1 teaspoon ground red pepper (preferably cayenne)
¾ teaspoon black pepper
2 cups chopped green bell peppers
1½ cups chopped onions
1 cup chopped celery
1 cup chopped green onions (tops only)
½ cup, packed, chopped fresh parsley
1 tablespoon minced garlic
1¼ cups **Cajun Home-Canned Spicy Tomatoes**
    (page 359)
7 cups coarsely chopped cabbage
4¾ cups, *in all*, **Basic Beef** or **Pork Stock** (page 18)
2 cups uncooked rice (preferably converted)

Place the oil in a heavy 6-quart saucepan or large Dutch oven. Add the beef and place over high heat, breaking meat up into small chunks. Add the sausage and cook until the ground beef is browned, about 4 minutes, stirring occasionally and continuing to break up meat chunks. Stir in the salt and red and black peppers; cook about 2 minutes, stirring occasionally. Add the bell peppers, onions, celery, green onions, parsley, and garlic; cook about 5 minutes, stirring occasionally. Add the tomatoes and cook and stir about 2 minutes more.

Now add the cabbage and do not stir. Cover pan and cook about 25 minutes, stirring only occasionally after mixture on the bottom of the pan has browned and then scraping pan bottom well. Stir in *1½ cups* of the stock, scraping pan bottom until all browned sediment is dissolved. Cook uncovered about 15 minutes, stirring and scraping occasionally. Add *1½ cups* more stock, stirring until all sediment is dissolved from pan bottom, then stir in the *remaining 1¾ cups* stock. Add the rice, stirring well.

Cover pan, reduce heat to very low, and cook about 25 minutes. Check after about 20 minutes to make sure mixture isn't scorching. Remove pan from heat and let sit covered until rice is tender but still a bit crunchy, about 25 minutes more. Stir well and serve immediately.

Serve about 1½ cups of the jambalaya as a main course, about ½ cup as a side dish.

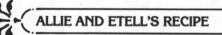

ALLIE AND ETELL'S RECIPE

Crawfish Boudin
(Boudin d'Écrevisses)

Makes about 2¾ pounds or 12 snack or lunch servings

Allie says the family always made boudins when they butchered hogs or had boucheries. They cleaned the pork intestines to use as natural casings for boudins and sausages like andouille. Mom never made crawfish boudin, but she did make **Garfish Boulettes** *(page 68), and the two mixtures are quite similar.*

Boudin is a Cajun sausage with rice mixed into the stuffing. It is traditionally made with pork, but in recent years crawfish and other seafood boudins have become quite popular.

Boudin is wonderful as an appetizer, snack, or lunch; or, if made into small links, it makes really special hors-d'oeuvre. Mom and Dad made red boudin and white boudin long before they had their grocery store, and they made it to sell after they opened the store. Paul says that, at home, the finished boudin was heated in water in a large, cast-iron Dutch oven over a fire outside in the yard. They refrigerated what wasn't eaten right away and, the next day, they split the leftover links lengthwise and fried them (the casings pop off) for breakfast— delicious! All the children loved boudin for breakfast and snacks.

In making this crawfish boudin, use any filling—that last bit that won't go through the sausage funnel—to make absolutely wonderful fried crawfish patties (recipe follows). You may even want to reserve some of the filling for this purpose, as Allie does.

For crawfish boudin, you will need a device for stuffing the sausage, such as a meat grinder with a sausage stuffing attachment, or a food processor with a sausage "horn," or a sausage funnel for stuffing the casings. (In the early days, for traditional boudins, Mom and Dad used a cow's horn with the tip cut off, a boudinière, to stuff the casings.) You may want to have handy something like a fry-basket to lower the boudin into the hot water for poaching and to lift it out.

1 small package 37-millimeter size natural hog
    casings
2 pounds peeled crawfish tails, coarsely chopped
2 teaspoons salt
1½ teaspoons red pepper (preferably cayenne)
¾ teaspoon black pepper
¼ cup vegetable oil
1 cup chopped onions
⅛ teaspoon minced garlic
1 cup chopped green onions (tops only)
¼ cup coarsely chopped fresh parsley
3 cups hot **Basic Cooked Rice** (page 252; see **NOTE**)
Water to heat the boudin

NOTE: For best results, use freshly made rice instead of leftovers.

Assemble the equipment you'll need for stuffing the boudin, then prepare the casings (see **Lagniappe**).

Place the crawfish in a large bowl and sprinkle the salt and red and black peppers on top; mix well. Set aside.

Place the oil, onions, and garlic in a 4-quart saucepan over medium-low heat; sauté about 5 minutes, stirring occasionally. Stir in the green onions and parsley; cook about 5 minutes, stirring frequently. Stir in the crawfish and cook about 20 minutes more, stirring occasionally. Remove from heat and stir in the rice, mixing thoroughly.

While the mixture is still hot, fill the casings and, if desired, make links by carefully twisting the sausage two or three turns at the points where you want the links to be. A 4-inch link is a good size for snacks or lunch. You may want to make smaller links for appetizers and hors-d'oeuvre.

Carefully place the boudin, coiled loosely in a single layer, in an 8-quart, or larger, broad-bottomed saucepan or Dutch oven. Cover the boudin with water. Heat over high heat until water reaches 180° (just below a simmer). Reduce heat to maintain a temperature between 175° and 185° (still just below a simmer) and continue cooking until the boudin is heated through and the flavors marry, 15 to 20 minutes. (Do not let the water reach a simmer, or the casings may burst.) Drain and serve immediately. Or fry as you fry the patties (see below), leaving casings on. For each serving, allow about one 4-inch piece. Depending on individual preference, the casings are eaten or removed as the boudin is eaten.

If you don't plan to serve the poached boudin right away, immediately pack it very loosely in Ziploc bags and give it an ice-water bath for 1 hour and 30 minutes (or until a thermometer inserted into the thickest part of a link reads 40° or less) to cool it down as quickly as possible, making sure the ice water comes in contact with all surfaces of each bag. Then refrigerate. **NOTE:** The boudin is poached first, then cooled down as quickly as possible, to give it a longer shelf-life. Reheat in 175° to 185° (hot, but not simmering) water as directed above.

Fried Crawfish Patties

½ cup leftover filling for each patty
Vegetable oil for frying

Shape each ¼ cup of filling into a 3-inch patty about ½ inch thick.

In a large skillet over high heat, heat oil ¼ inch deep until it sizzles when a drop of water is sprinkled in it. Fry the patties in the hot oil until dark golden brown on both sides, about 4 minutes total, turning at least once. Drain on paper towels and also blot tops of patties with paper towels. Serve immediately.

NOTE: Any leftover boiled boudin—hot or chilled—can be cut into desired lengths and fried in the same manner. You need not slice links open to fry them. As they cook, the casings will shrink and may even split, but they'll surely taste good, no matter what.

· · · · · · · · · · · · · ·LAGNIAPPE· · · · · · · · · · · · · ·
You can use the following instructions for preparing and filling sausage casings to make any kind of homemade sausage.
· ·

To prepare casings: Choose long pieces of casing, so you have more control over the size of links you make. Prepare casings not more than one hour ahead. Let casings soak in cool water about 5 minutes to remove the salt on the outer surface. (Soaking much longer than 5 minutes will tenderize the casings too much and make them more likely to break while being filled.) Rinse under cool running water.

To flush salt out of the inside, hold one end of a casing in place on a faucet nozzle and turn on cold tap water to fill the casing with water. Look for water leaking from holes in the casing; if you spot any holes, discard that piece or cut it at that point. Remove casing from faucet and gently squeeze out water. You need to rinse the inside only once.

Cover the rinsed, drained casings and refrigerate until ready to use. If you don't use all of the casings, drain them well and cover with several tablespoons of salt to coat thoroughly; then refrigerate or freeze. Casings will keep several months.

To fill casings: If possible, enlist a helper. Place a large pan under the stuffing tube to catch the filled casings and any excess stuffing. Carefully slip the entire length of one casing onto the tube or the end of the sausage funnel and then ease about 1 inch of casing back off the tube. Fill the casing with about 2 inches of stuffing, then tie a knot in the filled end, making sure no air bubbles form. Continue filling casing until quite firm but not popping full (the filling will swell during poaching) and then knot the end.

One person should handle the casing, holding it level with the stuffing tube and keeping large air bubbles from forming by working the stuffing into place by hand as the casing fills. Meanwhile, the other person feeds the stuffing into the machine, using a constant, slow pressure. If any large air bubbles form, prick a tiny hole in each bubble with a pin or pointed knife tip. If casing bursts, simply tie it off at that point and start filling a new length of casing. Once the casing is filled, you can leave the boudin as is or form it into links as described in the recipe.

 DARILEE AND SAUL'S RECIPE

Boudin Blanc
(Boudin)

Makes about 5 pounds or about 15 snack or lunch servings

Cajun boudin blanc is a white pork sausage with rice mixed into the stuffing. Boudin rouge, red boudin (see page 246), contains fresh pork blood; otherwise, the recipe is essentially the same as for boudin blanc, which Cajuns always call simply "boudin."

Up until Saul was forty years old, his family and the Prudhommes cooked the meat for boudin outdoors in big pots over a wood fire.

242

Saul learned how to make boudin from his dad and from Dad Prud-homme, and he is justly famous in the Opelousas area for his excep-tional ability as a sausage and boudin maker. He and Darilee have sold their boudins and sausages in their grocery store in Opelousas for years. Everyone knows to get to the store early when Saul is making sausages. Calvin says that when Mom Prudhomme's brother, Walter LeDoux, made boudin, he would be up to his elbows in the pot when he mixed the meat and seasonings. Whenever the Prudhomme family had boudin, Mom always fried what was left over the next morning for breakfast.

Darilee and Saul say boudin alone is great, but it's also "très bon" with saltines and cold beer. It makes a wonderful snack or breakfast food, and it's ideal to serve at parties. You can also use the cooked stuffing as a side dish or to stuff meat and fowl. (The recipe yields about 2½ quarts.)

Excess filling—that last bit that won't go through the sausage funnel—is great spread on crackers or French bread. And leftover boudin can be used to spice up winter soups or can be made into fried patties (page 245).

To make the boudin, you will need a meat grinder with a sausage stuffing attachment, or a food processor with a sausage "horn," or a sausage funnel for stuffing the casings. You may want to have handy something like a fry-basket to lower the boudin into the hot water for poaching and to lift it out.

1½ pounds bone-in pork shoulder steak, about 1 inch
    thick, cut into about 4 pieces (one or more
    pieces will contain bone)
¼ pound pork liver, coarsely chopped (see **NOTE**)
1 small package 37-millimeter-size natural hog casings
About 2½ quarts, *in all*, **Basic Pork Stock** (page 18)
6 to 9 cups hot **Basic Cooked Rice** (page 252; see **NOTE**)
1 cup minced onions
1 cup finely chopped green onions (tops only)
¼ cup finely chopped fresh parsley
1 tablespoon minced garlic
About 1 tablespoon, *in all*, ground red pepper
    (preferably cayenne)
2 teaspoons salt

1½ teaspoons black pepper
Water to heat the boudin

NOTE: If you can't obtain very fresh (and never frozen) liver, it's best to omit it from the recipe because if it's not fresh, the liver taste will dominate all the other flavors. For best results, use freshly made rice instead of leftovers.

Place the steak, liver, and 7 *cups* of the stock in a 4-quart saucepan. Cover pan and bring to a boil over high heat, stirring once or twice. Remove cover and continue boiling about 15 minutes, stirring occasionally and skimming off any foam. Reduce heat to maintain a strong simmer, cover pan with lid askew, and simmer until meat falls away from the bones, about 2 hours, stirring occasionally. (**NOTE:** Add more stock or water toward the end of cooking time if meat is not almost completely covered with liquid.) Remove from heat.

Meanwhile, assemble the equipment you'll need for grinding the meat and stuffing the boudin, then prepare the casings (see **Lagniappe**, page 241).

Use a slotted spoon to transfer the meat and any pieces of fat to a large bowl. Strain the stock that the meat was cooked in and reserve 2 cups. If necessary, add more stock or water to make up the balance. Set aside.

Remove any bones from the meat (look for *small* bones as well as the obvious large ones). Grind the meat and fat in a meat grinder using a coarse grinding disc (one with about ⅜-inch holes) and place in a large bowl. Stir in *6 cups* of the rice, the onions, green onions, parsley, garlic, 2½ *teaspoons* of the red pepper, the salt, and black pepper, mixing well. Taste and add more red pepper if the red pepper taste isn't clearly present. Stir in the reserved 2 *cups* stock, mixing well. If the mixture is very moist but not runny, it's ready to be stuffed into the casings. If the mixture is runny, stir in more rice, *1 to 3 cups*, one at a time. If the mixture is too dry, add more stock, just a little at a time, so you won't overdo it.

While the mixture is still hot, fill the casings and, if desired, make links by carefully twisting the sausage two or three turns at the points where you want the links to be. A 4-inch link is a good size for snacks or lunch. You may want to make smaller links for appetizers and hors-d'oeuvre.

Carefully place the boudin, coiled loosely in a single layer, in an 8-quart, or larger, broad-bottomed saucepan or Dutch oven. Cover the boudin with water and heat over high heat until water reaches 180° (just below a simmer). Reduce heat to maintain a temperature between 175° and 185° (still just below a simmer) and continue cooking until the boudin is heated through and the flavors marry, 15 to 20 minutes. (Do not let the water reach a simmer, or the casings may burst.) Drain and let sit about 15 minutes before slicing. Then serve immediately or fry as you fry the patties (see below), leaving casings on. For each serving, allow about one 4-inch piece. Depending on individual preference, the casings are eaten or removed as the boudin is eaten.

If you don't plan to serve the boudin right away, immediately pack it very loosely in Ziploc bags and give it an ice-water bath for 1 hour and 30 minutes (or until a thermometer inserted into the thickest part of a link reads 40° or less) to cool it down as quickly as possible, making sure the ice water comes in contact with all surfaces of each bag. Then refrigerate. **NOTE:** The boudin is poached first, then cooled down as quickly as possible, to give it a longer shelf-life. Reheat in 175° to 185° (hot, but not simmering) water as directed above.

Fried Boudin Patties

½ cup leftover chilled stuffing for each patty
Vegetable oil for frying

Shape each ½ cup of filling into a 3½-inch patty about ¾ inch thick.

In a large skillet over high heat, heat oil ¼ inch deep until it sizzles when a drop of water is sprinkled in it. Fry the patties in the hot oil until crisp and brown, about 1 minute per side. (It helps to use 2 spatulas to hold patty securely while turning.) Drain on paper towels and also blot tops of patties with paper towels. Serve immediately.

NOTE: If stuffing isn't well chilled, it will break apart and make a fantastic fried rice! Any leftover boiled boudin—hot or chilled—can be cut into desired lengths and fried in the same manner. You need not slice links open to fry them. As they cook, the casings will shrink and may even split, but that will not affect the wonderful taste.

PAUL AND K'S RECIPE

Red Boudin

*Makes about 5½ pounds or about 26 snack
or lunch servings.*

This is a recipe that Paul feels is important to put in the book for historical reasons. Very few people will be able to make red boudin, or blood sausage, because there are almost no sources for purchasing fresh pork blood. There is little demand for red boudin, and small meat-packing plants, because of the great expense involved, are rarely able to comply with federal and state regulations for handling the fresh blood for commercial use. (Louisiana does have three commercial meat companies that have state approval to handle and sell it.)

The family made red boudin only during a butchering or for a boucherie, because the blood has to be extremely fresh—just as they made **Bouilli** *(page 228) only when they butchered because the organ meats also must be extremely fresh. Cajun families who still do their own butchering continue to make red boudin at boucheries. This is really the only place to find it; we were unable to find any stores even in Cajun country that still sell red boudin. So visit a Cajun family during a boucherie; not only will you get to taste red boudin, you will also surely "pass a good time"!*

What you can *do with this recipe is use it to make a white boudin similar to Darilee and Saul's* **Boudin Blanc** *(see preceding recipe). The ingredients are different enough in the two recipes so that you will get two different (and both delicious) versions of white boudin. Just follow* this red boudin recipe exactly, omitting the pork blood.

To make the boudin, you will need a meat grinder with a sausage-stuffing attachment, or a food processor with a sausage "horn," or a sausage funnel for stuffing the casings. You may want to have handy something like a fry-basket to lower the boudin into the hot water for poaching and to lift it out.

About 2½ quarts, *in all*, **Basic Pork Stock** (page 18)
1 (2-pound) bone-in pork shoulder steak
5 cups chopped onions
2 tablespoons, *in all*, ground red pepper (preferably
    cayenne)
1 tablespoon plus 1½ teaspoons minced garlic
1 tablespoon plus 1¼ teaspoons salt, *in all*
1 small package 37-millimeter-size natural hog
    casings
¼ pound pork liver (see **NOTE**)
7 cups hot **Basic Cooked Rice** (page 252; see **NOTE**)
2 cups chopped green onions (tops only)
½ cup minced fresh parsley
2 teaspoons garlic powder
2½ cups fresh pork blood (see **NOTE**)

NOTE: If you can't obtain very fresh (and never frozen) pork liver, it's best to omit it from the recipe; if it's not absolutely fresh, the liver taste will dominate all the other flavors. For best results, use freshly made rice instead of leftovers. Keep your container of pork blood very well iced, but don't freeze it; use within a few hours.

In an 8-quart saucepan or large Dutch oven, combine 2 *quarts* of the stock, the steak, onions, 2½ *teaspoons* of the red pepper, the minced garlic, and 1 *tablespoon* of the salt. Bring to a boil over high heat. Continue boiling about 1 hour and 30 minutes, stirring occasionally and turning the meat over occasionally if it is not totally submerged in liquid. **NOTE:** Add more stock or water toward the end of cooking time if meat is not almost completely covered with liquid.

Meanwhile, assemble the equipment you'll need for grinding the meat and stuffing the boudin, then prepare the casings (see **Lag-niappe**, page 241).

Transfer meat to a bowl to cool, leaving the pot with the boiling stock over high heat. Add the liver to the pot and cook about 3 minutes, turning meat over once if it's not totally submerged in liquid. Remove from heat, remove liver, and set aside. Strain the stock, reserving it and the strained onions and garlic separately.

Cut the pork meat and liver into about 2-inch cubes. (Discard bones or use them to make stock for another recipe.) Grind the meat and fat in a meat grinder, using a coarse grinding disc (one with about ⅜-inch holes). In a very large bowl or a 15½ × 10½-inch pan, combine the meat, rice, reserved onions and garlic, green onions, parsley, garlic powder, 1 cup of the reserved stock, and the remaining *1 tablespoon plus ½ teaspoon* red pepper and *1¼ teaspoons* salt, mixing thoroughly. The mixture should be moist and taste red peppery; if the red pepper taste isn't clearly present, add more. If the mixture isn't moist, add a little stock or water, but don't make the mixture runny. If you stuff the casings at this point, you will have a white boudin. Or stir in the pork blood, mixing well.

While the mixture is still hot, fill the casings and, if desired, make links by carefully twisting the sausage two or three turns at the points where you want the links to be. A 4-inch link is a good size for snacks or lunch. You may want to make smaller links for appetizers and hors-d'oeuvre.

Carefully place the boudin, coiled loosely in a single layer, in an 8-quart, or larger, broad-bottomed saucepan or Dutch oven. Cover the boudin with the reserved *2 cups* stock; add water if necessary to cover. Heat over high heat until water reaches 180° (just below a simmer). Reduce heat to maintain a temperature between 175° and 185° (still just below a simmer) and continue cooking until the boudin is heated through and the flavors marry, 15 to 20 minutes. (Do not let the water reach a simmer, or the casings may burst.) Drain and let sit about 15 minutes before slicing. Then serve immediately. For each serving, allow about one 4-inch piece. Depending on individual preference, the casings are eaten or removed as the boudin is eaten.

If you don't plan to serve the boudin right away, immediately pack it very loosely in Ziploc bags and give it an ice-water bath for 1 hour and 30 minutes (or until a thermometer inserted into the thickest part of a link reads 40° or less) to cool it down as quickly as possible, making sure the ice water comes in contact with all surfaces of each bag. Then refrigerate. **NOTE**: The boudin is poached first, then cooled down as quickly as possible, to give it a longer shelf-life. Reheat in 175° to 185° (hot, but not simmering) water as directed above.

RICE, DRESSINGS & STUFFINGS

RIZ ET FARRES

Basic Cooked Rice

The proportions of ingredients change when you make different amounts of basic cooked rice, so we have given you three formulas, which yield 6, 9, and 12 cups, respectively.

If you make this ahead of time and store it, omit the bell peppers—they tend to sour quickly. Use chicken stock if you are serving the rice with a chicken dish, seafood stock with a seafood dish, beef with a beef dish. . . .

When it's done, serve the rice immediately if you can. However, you can count on the rice staying hot for about 45 minutes and warm for about 2 hours. To reheat cold rice made ahead, or leftover rice, either use a double boiler or warm it in a skillet with unsalted butter.

Basic Cooked Rice to make 6 cups

2 cups uncooked rice (preferably converted)
2½ cups **Basic Stock** (page 17)
1½ tablespoons unsalted butter (preferred) or
      margarine, melted
1½ tablespoons very finely chopped onions
1½ tablespoons very finely chopped celery
1½ tablespoons very finely chopped green bell
      peppers, optional
½ teaspoon salt
⅛ teaspoon garlic powder
A pinch each of white pepper, ground red pepper
      (preferably cayenne), and black pepper

In a 5 × 9 × 2½-inch loaf pan, combine all ingredients; mix well. Seal pan snugly with aluminum foil. Bake at 350° until rice is tender, about 1 hour and 10 minutes.

Basic Cooked Rice to make 9 cups

3 cups uncooked rice (preferably converted)
3⅔ cups **Basic Stock** (page 17)
3 tablespoons unsalted butter (preferred) or margarine, melted
2 tablespoons very finely chopped onions
2 tablespoons very finely chopped celery
2 tablespoons very finely chopped green bell peppers, optional
1 teaspoon salt
¼ teaspoon garlic powder
2 pinches each of white pepper, ground red pepper
    (preferably cayenne), and black pepper

In a 13 × 9-inch baking pan, combine all ingredients; mix well. Seal pan snugly with aluminum foil. Bake at 350° until rice is tender, about 1 hour and 10 minutes.

Basic Cooked Rice to make 12 cups

4 cups uncooked rice (preferably converted)
5 cups **Basic Stock** (page 17)
4 tablespoons unsalted butter (preferred) or
    margarine, melted
3 tablespoons very finely chopped onions
3 tablespoons very finely chopped celery
3 tablespoons very finely chopped green bell peppers, optional
1 teaspoon salt
¼ teaspoon garlic powder
¼ teaspoon ground red pepper (preferably cayenne)
⅛ teaspoon white pepper
⅛ teaspoon black pepper

In a 13 × 9-inch baking pan, combine all ingredients; mix well. Seal pan snugly with aluminum foil. Bake at 350° until rice is tender, about 1 hour and 10 minutes.

MALCOLM AND VERSIE'S RECIPE

Greasy Rice
(Riz à la Graisse)

Makes 3 to 4 snack or light supper servings

All the family remember Mom Prudhomme's greasy rice (they still call it "riz à la graisse") as a mixture of leftover rice, green onion tops, parsley, and a little pork lard. When the children cooked it, and Mom wasn't watching, they added an egg or two. (For a long time, the family rarely ate the eggs their chickens laid; Mom and Dad gave them to the faculty of the Catholic school as payment for tuition for the children.) Calvin and Darilee thought the addition of eggs made the dish wonderful!

By the time Paul came along, Mom used rice, eggs, green onions, and some kind of smoked fat, like rendered bacon or ham or tasso fat—or, if none of these was available, pork lard.

Malcolm and Versie's greasy rice is an example of simple farm cooking—"how the old country people do it." Versie prefers not to use green onion tops in her greasy rice, and she sometimes omits the eggs and just fries the rice and seasonings in hot bacon drippings. Riz à la graisse makes a perfect snack or light supper, and it's good served at room temperature.

¼ pound bacon (about 5 slices)
1 tablespoon vegetable oil
3 cups cold **Basic Cooked Rice** (preferred; page
    252) or other cooked rice (see **Note**)
About ⅓ teaspoon salt, *in all*
About ⅓ teaspoon black pepper, *in all*
3 large eggs, well beaten

Note: Leftover rice is perfect for this dish. If you're making Basic Cooked Rice from scratch for it, use pork, chicken, or beef stock to cook it. If you want, add 2 thinly sliced green onions with some of their green tops when you add salt and pepper.

Fry the bacon in a large heavy skillet until crisp. Drain on paper towels, then crumble and set aside. Pour the hot bacon fat into a glass measuring cup and return 2 tablespoons of it to the skillet. Add the vegetable oil and place over medium heat. Add the rice and ¼ *teaspoon each* of the salt and black pepper. Cook, stirring frequently, until the rice sizzles and some of the rice kernels on the bottom start jumping in the pan when left unstirred a few seconds, about 4 minutes. Add the eggs and cook until eggs are set and mixture starts drying out a little, about 2 minutes more, stirring constantly. Remove from heat and continue stirring a few seconds. Serve immediately on heated serving plates with a portion of the crumbled bacon sprinkled on top. If desired, season with additional salt and pepper at the table.

ENOLA AND SHELTON'S RECIPE

Hot Cajun Rice and Shrimp

Makes 4 lunch or 8 appetizer or side-dish servings

Enola's children loved to visit Mom and Dad Prudhomme and they spent lots of time with them. (Enola worked in the family store for a time after Abel bought it from Mom and Dad, and her children often spent the day with Mom and Dad while she worked.) There was a shed in Mom and Dad's backyard; the children loved to climb to the top of it and jump off. Mom let the girls play with her costume jewelry, and she made special jewelry for all the grandchildren. She used the wishbones of very small birds like quail, dried them well, and painted them with nail polish.

Dad Prudhomme called Enola's daughter, Annette, "radoteur" (Cajun for somebody who talks too much); she chattered all day long. It's Annette's husband, Chris Oncale, who taught Enola how to cook this well-seasoned rice and shrimp dish (just moderately spicy). Mom Prudhomme rarely had fresh shrimp to cook with in the old days, but she often used dried shrimp. Enola began cooking with Mom when she was twelve years old. She's always loved to cook—so now she has a restaurant!

Hot Cajun rice and shrimp is quite different from a traditional Cajun jambalaya. It has fresh peppers and mushrooms and no tomatoes or tomato sauce. It makes a fine side dish to serve with pan-fried fish, candied yams, and potato salad. Or you can serve it as an appetizer or light lunch. We like to use a rich seafood stock in the dish to give the rice plenty of flavor.

Seasoning mix:

1¾ teaspoons salt
½ teaspoon onion powder
½ teaspoon garlic powder
½ teaspoon ground red pepper (preferably cayenne)
¼ teaspoon white pepper
¼ teaspoon black pepper

1½ cups **Rich Seafood Stock** (page 19)
1 cup rice (preferably converted)
1 large bay leaf
¼ pound (1 stick) unsalted butter
1¼ cups chopped onions, *in all*
½ teaspoon minced garlic
½ cup chopped green bell peppers
½ cup chopped green onions (tops only)
1 tablespoon finely chopped jalapeño peppers (see
    Note)
½ pound peeled small shrimp
1¾ cups thinly sliced mushrooms

Note: Fresh jalapeños are preferred; if you have to use pickled ones, rinse as much vinegar from them as possible. If the jalapeños are especially hot, you may want to cut down the amount called for by just a little.

Combine the seasoning mix ingredients thoroughly in a small bowl. In a 1-quart saucepan, combine the stock, rice, bay leaf, and *1 teaspoon* of the seasoning mix, stirring well. Cover and bring to a boil over high heat. Reduce heat to low and cook until rice starts to get tender, 10 to 12 minutes. Remove from heat and set aside, covered.

Meanwhile, in a heavy 3-quart saucepan or Dutch oven, with as broad a bottom as possible, melt the butter over high heat until half melted. Add ¾ *cup* of the onions and sauté until they just start to brown, about 4 minutes, stirring occasionally. Stir in the remaining 2¾ *teaspoons* seasoning mix and the minced garlic; cook about 1 minute, stirring occasionally. Add the bell peppers, green onions, jalapeño peppers, and remaining ½ *cup* onions, stirring well. Cook about 2 minutes, stirring frequently.

Now add the rice, shrimp, and mushrooms, stirring well. Cover, remove from heat, and let sit covered until the rice is tender but still firm and the flavors marry, about 30 minutes. Remove bay leaf before serving.

Serve immediately or at room temperature. Allow 1 cup for lunch servings and ½ cup for appetizer or side-dish servings.

Rice and Mirliton Dressing
(Farre de Riz et Mirliton)

Makes 12 side-dish servings

Mirlitons grew wild where the family lived and Mom Prudhomme loved them. She stuffed them with dressings, used them in rice dressings, and canned and pickled them. Mom made rice dressing more often than cornbread dressing—occasionally on weekdays as well as on Sundays and holidays. She liked to make rice dressing with pork or beef liver, and if she had neither of these, she used chicken livers and gizzards.

Calvin and Marie always have mirlitons in their garden, and she feels they do something special for rice dressing. Calvin loves rice— prepared any way, but especially rice dressing. He'd just as soon have rice with every meal. If you ask him about Cajuns and their love for rice, he'll laugh and say, "Anything a Cajun cooks tastes better with rice. That's why we make a lot of gravy with almost everything—we want gravy to put on that rice!"

Marie's rice dressing is quite rich, and it's good even at room temperature. We tested it with both rich and regular (basic) stocks, and rich stocks gave the best results.

2½ pounds mirlitons (chayotes)

Seasoning mix:
1 tablespoon plus ½ teaspoon salt
1 teaspoon ground red pepper (preferably cayenne)
¾ teaspoon black pepper

¼ cup vegetable oil
1½ cups, *in all*, finely chopped onions
½ pound ground pork
½ pound ground beef
1 teaspoon minced garlic
1 cup finely chopped celery
1 cup finely chopped green bell peppers
2½ cups, *in all*, **Rich Beef Stock** (preferred), or
    Rich Pork or **Chicken Stock** (page 19)
¾ cup chopped green onions (tops only)
½ cup chopped fresh parsley
6 cups warm **Basic Cooked Rice** (page 252)

Boil the mirlitons just until fork tender. Cool, then cut each in half lengthwise; peel and remove seed (eat it, it's delicious, or save to put in a salad), then finely chop the pulp.

Thoroughly combine the seasoning mix ingredients in a small bowl and set aside.

In a 6-quart saucepan or large Dutch oven, with as broad a bottom as possible, combine the oil, mirlitons, and ¾ *cup* of the onions. Place over high heat and cook until most of the mirlitons and onions are browned, about 30 minutes, stirring occasionally. Add the pork and cook 2 to 3 minutes, breaking up chunks of meat and scraping pan bottom well. Add the beef, breaking up chunks. Stir in the seasoning mix and the garlic; cook about 3 minutes, stirring and scraping pan bottom frequently and breaking up any remaining chunks of meat.

Now add the remaining ¾ *cup* onions, the celery, bell peppers, and ½ *cup* of the stock, stirring well and scraping pan bottom clean. Reduce heat to low and cook about 15 minutes, stirring and scraping occasionally. Add the remaining 2 *cups* stock, the green onions, and parsley, stirring well; bring to a boil over high heat. Stir in the rice, mixing well. Remove from heat, cover, and let sit about 20 minutes. Stir well before serving, allowing about ⅔ cup per person.

ELI AND SUE'S RECIPE

Bell Peppers Stuffed with Rice Dressing
(Piments Doux Bourrés)

Makes 12 main-dish servings

Eli says all the children learned to work hard by the example Dad and Mom set for them. In addition to all the work Dad Prudhomme did as a sharecropper and to provide for a family of fourteen, he also worked for other farmers in their rice and cotton fields in the evening, on weekends, and after his seasonal crops were in. He was paid either with a share of the farmers' crops or cash. Dad had his own black-smith shop and made all his tools for the farm; he repaired his own tools and some of his friends' tools. And he was the family dentist and barber, as well as the barber for the nearby town of Lawtell, Loui-siana.

Dad had a pair of dentist's pliers that he used to pull the chil-dren's troublesome teeth, and he had some old hair clippers that the boys all remember were particularly dull. Eli says the clippers "kind of halfway cut your hair, and Dad kind of pulled the rest out." Elden remembers that if the boys complained about Dad pulling their hair, he'd say, "Hey, you have to suffer to be pretty!"

Dad had the barber shop in Lawtell for several years. He cut hair on Friday nights and all day on Saturdays, charging fifteen cents for a haircut and ten cents for a shave. Elden says Dad sometimes made eighteen to twenty dollars on a weekend. He left the house early on Saturday morning and cut hair and gave shaves straight on through the day without stopping for lunch or dinner. Mom loaded up the children in the wagon and went in to Lawtell to pick Dad up. Sometimes the children held a coal-oil lamp for Dad to see to cut hair by, and he kept on cutting until there was no one left waiting in line— sometimes until ten or eleven at night.

Mom Prudhomme made rice dressing fairly often, since rice was a staple crop. Eli and Sue use their rice dressing not only to stuff bell peppers, but also to stuff fowl and to serve as a side dish.

First seasoning mix:
1¼ teaspoons salt
1 teaspoon black pepper
½ teaspoon garlic powder
½ teaspoon ground red pepper (preferably cayenne)

¾ pound chicken gizzards
½ pound chicken hearts
¼ pound chicken livers

Second seasoning mix:
1 whole bay leaf
2 teaspoons salt
1 teaspoon ground red pepper (preferably cayenne)
1 teaspoon black pepper
½ teaspoon white pepper
½ teaspoon garlic powder

1 pound ground beef
¾ pound ground pork
1¾ cups very finely chopped onions
½ cup very finely chopped green bell peppers
¼ cup very finely chopped celery
1 tablespoon minced garlic

1½ teaspoons **Ground Hot Pepper Vinegar,**
    peppers only (page 357) (see **Note**)
About 2 cups, *in all*, **Basic Beef** or **Chicken Stock**
    (page 18), plus about 3 cups stock (or water), to
    set peppers in while baking
6 tablespoons unsalted butter, *in all*
1½ cups finely chopped green onions (tops only)
½ cup finely chopped fresh parsley
5 cups warm **Basic Cooked Rice** (page 252)
2 tablespoons very fine dry bread crumbs
12 medium, well-shaped green bell peppers, about 6
    ounces each (select peppers that will easily sit up
    on end)
Poorman's Gravy (page 340)

Note: If your Ground Hot Pepper Vinegar peppers are very hot, use your own judgment on how much of the peppers to use. If in doubt, add less since you can always add more at the table.

    To prepare the rice dressing: Combine the first seasoning mix ingredients thoroughly in a small bowl and set aside.

    With a sharp paring knife, peel off the silver skin from each gizzard and trim the hard fibrous connection between the two halves. Grind the gizzards, hearts, and livers in a meat grinder with a fine grinding disk (one with about ⅛-inch holes), or chop the giblets very finely. Add the reserved seasoning mix to the giblets, stirring well and using it all. Set aside.

    Thoroughly combine the second seasoning mix ingredients in a small bowl and set aside.

    In a very large cast-iron or other heavy skillet, brown the beef and pork over high heat, stirring frequently and breaking up meat chunks. Sprinkle the reserved second seasoning mix over the meat and cook about 3 minutes, stirring constantly. Remove and discard the bay leaf (Eli and Sue like just a hint of the bay leaf flavor), then cook about 2 minutes more, stirring constantly. Reduce heat to medium and cook about 5 minutes, stirring frequently and scraping pan bottom well. Add the giblets to the skillet, stirring well; cook about 4 minutes, stirring almost constantly.

Now stir in the onions, bell peppers, celery, garlic, Ground Hot Pepper Vinegar peppers, and ¼ *cup* of the stock. Cook until mixture is dry and sticking excessively, about 10 minutes, stirring and scraping pan bottom frequently. Add *4 tablespoons* of the butter; cook about 3 minutes, stirring and scraping frequently. Stir in the green onions, parsley, and ½ *cup* more stock, scraping pan bottom until sediment is dissolved. Stir in ½ *cup* more stock and cook and stir about 2 minutes more. At this point there should be little if any liquid in the pan bottom; if there is liquid remaining, let the mixture cook longer.

Add the rice, stirring very well, and remove from heat. Set aside. **NOTE**: The yield of the rice dressing is about 9½ cups. For stuffing bell peppers, the dressing must be quite moist, but not runny, as it will dry out some while baking. If necessary, add more stock or water to the dressing, about ¼ cup at a time.

To prepare the peppers: Cut the stems and tops from the bell peppers (cut down about ¾ inch from the top), and core and seed the peppers. Discard tops.

Stuff the hot rice dressing into the bell peppers, packing it tightly as you go and mounding the tops slightly. Place peppers upright in an ungreased 13 × 9-inch baking pan, arranging peppers so they fit fairly snugly together. Let stuffing cool about 5 minutes, then press it down a little more with palm of hand or fingertips and sprinkle the bread crumbs evenly on top. Dot tops with the remaining 2 *tablespoons* butter. Add about ¾-inch stock or water around the peppers.

Bake uncovered at 375° for 30 minutes. Then cover pan tightly with aluminum foil and continue baking until bell peppers are tender but still firm, about 30 minutes more. Remove from oven and serve immediately with Poorman's Gravy spooned over the top.

PAUL AND K'S RECIPE

Oyster Dressing

Makes about 9 cups

This dressing is used in **Turducken** *(page 109), and it can be used to stuff other fowl or as a side dish.*

2 pounds small to medium shucked oysters, in their liquor
4 cups cold water

> **Seasoning mix:**
> 2 teaspoons salt
> 2 teaspoons garlic powder
> 2 teaspoons ground red pepper (preferably cayenne)
> 2 teaspoons sweet paprika
> 2 teaspoons black pepper
> 1 teaspoon onion powder
> 1 teaspoon dried oregano leaves
> 1 teaspoon dried thyme leaves

¾ pound (3 sticks) plus 2 tablespoons margarine, *in all*
6 cups chopped onions, *in all*
4 cups chopped celery, *in all*
4 cups chopped green bell peppers, *in all*
1 tablespoon plus 1 teaspoon minced garlic
2 cups chopped green onions, *in all* (tops only)
2 cups very finely chopped fresh parsley, *in all*
8 small bay leaves
About 4½ cups very fine dry bread crumbs, *in all*
4 tablespoons unsalted butter

Combine the oysters, oyster liquor, and water; stir and refrigerate at least 1 hour. Strain and reserve the oysters and 4 cups of the oyster water separately; refrigerate again until ready to use.

In a medium-size bowl, combine the seasoning mix ingredients; mix well. Set aside.

Place *1 stick plus 2 tablespoons* of the margarine in a heavy 8-quart saucepan or large Dutch oven over high heat. When margarine is half melted, add *3 cups* of the onions, *2 cups* of the celery, and *2 cups* of the bell peppers; sauté until onions are well browned, about 30 minutes, stirring occasionally. Stir in *3 tablespoons* of the seasoning mix and the garlic. Reduce heat to low and cook about 4 minutes, stirring and scraping pan bottom occasionally. Add the remaining *2 sticks* margarine, *3 cups* onions, *2 cups* celery, and *2 cups* bell peppers, *1 cup* of the green onions, *1 cup* of the parsley, and the bay leaves. Turn heat to high, stirring until margarine is melted; cook until vegetables are tender but still a little crunchy, about 10 minutes, stirring occasionally.

Now stir in the reserved 4 cups oyster water and cook about 15 minutes, stirring occasionally. Stir in the remaining *1 tablespoon plus 1 teaspoon* seasoning mix and enough bread crumbs (start with *4 cups*, but you may need a little more) to make a fairly moist but not runny dressing. Remove from heat.

Drain oysters well and stir them into the dressing. Spoon dressing into an ungreased 15 × 11-inch baking pan (preferably *not* a nonstick type) and bake uncovered in a 350° oven until well browned, about 1 hour, stirring only after a dark crust builds up (30 to 45 minutes). Then remove from oven and stir thoroughly but gently so oysters won't break apart, scraping browned parts from pan bottom and sides into the mixture. Discard bay leaves.

Add the butter and the remaining *1 cup* green onions and *1 cup* parsley, stirring well. Serve as desired. **NOTE:** Be certain to let the dressing cool, then refrigerate it and chill it well, before using it to stuff fowl.

Andouille Smoked Sausage Dressing

Makes about 10 cups

This dressing is used in **Turducken** *(page 109)*, *and it can be used to stuff other fowl or as a side dish.*

If you are making the dressing to use in Turducken, you need to make two batches.

This dish is cooked for fairly long periods of time over high heat. If your gas burner or electric cooking element produces a very high heat, or if your pot is not a heavy one, you will need to adjust the temperature down.

¼ pound (1 stick) plus 2 tablespoons margarine
8 cups chopped onions, *in all*
4 cups chopped celery, *in all*
4 cups chopped green bell peppers, *in all*
2½ pounds andouille smoked sausage (preferred) or
     any other good smoked pure pork sausage, such
     as Polish sausage (kielbasa), ground
¼ pound (1 stick) unsalted butter
¼ cup minced garlic
¼ cup sweet paprika
2 tablespoons Tabasco sauce
¾ teaspoon salt
4 cups **Basic Chicken Stock** (page 18; see **Note**)
About 5 cups, *in all*, very fine dry unseasoned bread
     crumbs (preferably French bread; see **Note**)

Note: If you are making this dressing for Turducken, you will need to make it quite stiff (stiffer than for a normal stuffing or side dish) by adding a few more bread crumbs, since the dressing tends to absorb juices from the fowl. If you are also preparing other components for the Turducken at the same time as you're making the dressing, you may want to use the larger (2-gallon yield) stock that accompanies the Turducken recipe (page 115). If the sausage is very fatty, you may need more bread crumbs to take up the fat.

In a heavy 8-quart saucepan or large Dutch oven, with as broad a bottom as possible, melt the margarine over high heat until almost melted. Add 4 *cups* of the onions, 2 *cups* of the celery, and 2 *cups* of the bell peppers. Sauté until mixture is well browned, about 35 minutes, stirring and scraping pan bottom occasionally (more often toward the end of cooking time). Remove pan from heat momentarily and add the andouille, stirring well. Return pan to high heat and cook until meat is well browned, about 20 minutes, stirring and scraping pan bottom frequently as browned sediment develops (stir and scrape almost constantly toward the end of the browning period).

Stir in the butter, then add the remaining 4 *cups* onions, 2 *cups* celery, and 2 *cups* bell peppers, and the garlic, paprika, Tabasco, and salt, stirring well. Reduce heat to low and cook until the last vegetables added are tender but still a little crisp, about 15 minutes, stirring and scraping pan bottom frequently.

Stir in the stock and bring to a boil over high heat, stirring and scraping occasionally. Continue boiling until the fat rises to the top and coats most of the surface (until the water evaporates), about 5 minutes, stirring occasionally. Reduce heat to low and stir in the bread crumbs, starting with 4 *cups* and adding more, if necessary, so the final mixture is still very moist but not runny; soak up large puddles of fat with additional bread crumbs. (**NOTE**: If you are making the dressing for Turducken, start with 4½ *cups* bread crumbs; you still may need to add more to make the dressing fairly stiff, so it won't be runny by the time the Turducken has finished roasting.) Remove from heat.

Transfer mixture to an ungreased 15 × 11-inch baking pan (preferably *not* a nonstick type). Bake uncovered in a 425° oven until mixture is well browned throughout, about 1 hour and 30 minutes. Stir and scrape pan bottom well every 15 to 20 minutes, but only after you've allowed the mixture to brown well on top. During the last half of baking time, the mixture should be allowed to stick to the sides and bottom of the pan before stirring.

Serve as desired. **Note**: Be certain to let the dressing cool, then refrigerate it and chill it well, before using it to stuff fowl.

PAUL AND K'S RECIPE

Cornbread Dressing

Makes about 16 cups

This dressing is used in **Turducken** *(page 109) or it can be served as is. If you prefer a less sweet dressing, make the cornbread with only ½ cup sugar.*

1½ pounds turkey, duck, or chicken giblets

> **Seasoning mix:**
> 1 tablespoon plus 1 teaspoon salt
> 1 tablespoon white pepper
> 2 teaspoons ground red pepper (preferably cayenne)
> 2 teaspoons black pepper
> 2 teaspoons dried oregano leaves
> 1 teaspoon onion powder
> 1 teaspoon dried thyme leaves

¼ pound (1 stick) plus 2 tablespoons unsalted butter
4 tablespoons margarine
1½ cups finely chopped onions, *in all*
1½ cups finely chopped green bell peppers, *in all*
1 cup finely chopped celery, *in all*
2 tablespoons minced garlic
3 large bay leaves
2 cups **Basic Chicken Stock** (page 18; see **Note**)
2 tablespoons Tabasco sauce
10 cups finely crumbled **Paul and K's Cornbread**
       (recipe follows)
2 (12-ounce) cans evaporated milk (3 cups)
6 eggs, beaten

Note: If you are making this dressing for Turducken and you're also preparing other components for that recipe at the same time, you may want to use the larger (2-gallon yield) stock that accompanies the Turducken recipe (page 115).

Boil the giblets in water until tender, about 1 hour. Drain the giblets and grind (preferably) or very finely chop them. (The water will make excellent stock if you use it right away, but don't save it or freeze it. Stock made with livers does not hold well.)

Thoroughly combine the seasoning mix ingredients in a medium-size bowl and set aside.

In a 5½-quart saucepan, heat the butter and margarine over high heat until half melted. Add *1 cup* of the onions, *1 cup* of the bell peppers, *½ cup* of the celery, and the garlic and bay leaves. Sauté about 2 minutes, stirring occasionally. Add the seasoning mix and continue cooking about 5 minutes, stirring and scraping pan bottom frequently. Stir in the remaining *½ cup* onions, *½ cup* bell peppers, and *½ cup* celery, the stock, giblets, and Tabasco; cook about 5 minutes more, stirring frequently. Remove from heat.

Add the cornbread, milk, and eggs, stirring well. Spoon the dressing into two greased 13 × 9-inch baking pans (preferably *not* nonstick types), spreading the mixture evenly in the pans. Bake at 350° until browned on top, 35 to 40 minutes. Remove from oven and discard bay leaves.

Serve as desired. **NOTE**: Be certain to let the dressing cool, then refrigerate it and chill it well, before using it to stuff fowl.

Paul and K's Cornbread

2⅔ cups all-purpose flour

1⅓ cups yellow cornmeal

1⅓ cups sugar (or reduce sugar to ½ cup)

1 cup corn flour (see **NOTE**)

3 tablespoons plus 1 teaspoon baking powder

1 teaspoon salt

2⅔ cups milk

¼ pound (1 stick) plus 2 tablespoons unsalted butter,
    melted

2 eggs, beaten

NOTE: Corn flour is available at most health food stores.

In a very large bowl, combine the flour, cornmeal, sugar, corn flour, baking powder, and salt; mix until thoroughly blended, breaking up any lumps. In a large bowl, combine the milk, butter, and eggs and add the mixture to the dry ingredients; blend just until mixed and large lumps are dissolved. Do not overbeat.

Pour mixture into a greased 13 × 9-inch baking pan (preferably *not* a nonstick type) and bake at 350° until golden brown, 50 to 55 minutes. Remove from pan and serve immediately. Makes 8 or more portions, or about 16 cups finely crumbled cornbread.

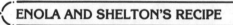

ENOLA AND SHELTON'S RECIPE

Cornbread Dressing
(Farre de Pain de Maïs et Viande Moulue)

Makes about a dozen ¾-cup side-dish servings or 10 cups

Dad Prudhomme planted many acres of corn each year. The family ate it fresh in season, but they took a lot of corn to the mill to be ground into cornmeal, corn flour, and grits or to be mashed for feed for the chickens. And a great part of it was stored and dried on the cob to be used to feed the larger animals—hogs, cattle, horses, and mules. The miller took a percentage of the corn he ground as payment for milling it. Paul says the animals had other feed as well—Dad planted beans between the corn rows for the hogs—but at some times of the year, there was nothing for the animals except corn.

The freshly ground cornmeal and corn flour that Mom cooked with are quite different from the commercial cornmeal available in supermarkets today. The corn flavor is much fresher and stronger, and the granules are larger and coarser, which contributes to the fuller corn taste. Most of the family still cook with freshly ground cornmeal today. It is far superior to store-bought cornmeal and is widely available in Cajun country and rural areas of Louisiana.

Enola says that Versie gave her this recipe for cornbread and ground-beef dressing years ago. She loves it and even won a cooking contest with it. The dressing has a traditional homey Cajun taste, and it's deliciously peppery and very meaty. (And, we discovered, it tastes really good with a little evaporated milk on top.) Enola serves it with barbecued chicken or beef or pork roasts, with candied yams on the side.

You can make the cornbread a day ahead and store it covered at room temperature until ready to use.

5 cups crumbled **Enola and Shelton's Cornbread**
    (recipe follows)
¼ pound beef liver, cut into 2 to 3 pieces
Water to cover liver
3½ cups, *in all*, **Rich Chicken Stock** (page 19)
7 slices stale white bread
3 eggs, beaten

    Seasoning mix:
    1 tablespoon plus 1½ teaspoons salt
    1 tablespoon plus 1 teaspoon ground red pepper (preferably
        cayenne)
    2 teaspoons black pepper

¼ pound (1 stick) unsalted butter
2 cups finely chopped onions
1 cup finely chopped green bell peppers
2 teaspoons minced garlic
1 cup finely chopped green onions (tops only)
¼ cup finely chopped fresh parsley
2 pounds ground beef chuck

Make the cornbread.

Place the liver in a 1-quart saucepan and cover with water. Cover pan and bring to a boil over high heat. Reduce heat and simmer until liver is cooked through, about 10 minutes, turning meat over at least once. Remove from heat, drain well, and process liver in a food processor a few seconds until minced. Set aside.

In a greased 13 × 9-inch baking pan, combine *3 cups* of the stock with the bread, eggs, and cornbread. Mix by hand until all the bread is soggy and crusts are broken into small bits. Set aside.

Combine the seasoning mix ingredients thoroughly in a small bowl.

In a 4-quart saucepan, melt the butter over high heat until half melted. Add the onions and sauté until onions brown, about 6 minutes, stirring occasionally. Add the bell peppers, garlic, and *1 tablespoon* of the seasoning mix; cook about 2 minutes, stirring frequently. Add the green onions and parsley and cook about 1 minute more, stirring constantly. Remove from heat and transfer vegetable mixture with a slotted spoon to a bowl, leaving as much oil in pan as possible.

To the same saucepan, add the ground beef, breaking it up into chunks. Cook over high heat until browned, continuing to break up chunks as meat browns. Add the remaining 2½ *tablespoons* seasoning mix and cook about 3 minutes, stirring frequently. Stir in the minced liver and the remaining ½ *cup* stock and remove from heat. Stir in the vegetable mixture, then add it all to the bread mixture in the baking pan. Stir well, then spread mixture evenly in the pan. Bake at 375° until dressing is browned on top but still moist inside, about 20 minutes. Remove from oven and serve immediately.

Enola and Shelton's Cornbread

1 cup all-purpose flour
1 cup yellow cornmeal
2 teaspoons sugar
1 teaspoon baking powder
1 teaspoon salt
½ teaspoon baking soda
1 cup milk
2 large eggs
4 tablespoons unsalted butter, melted and cooled

In a large bowl, combine the flour, cornmeal, sugar, baking powder, salt, and baking soda, mixing well. In a medium-size bowl, combine the milk, eggs, and butter, mixing well; add to the dry ingredients.

Mix a few seconds just until well blended and any large lumps are dissolved. Do not overbeat.

Pour the batter into a lightly greased 8 × 8-inch baking pan. Bake at 375° until done and lightly browned, about 25 minutes. Remove from oven and immediately turn over onto a plate. Set aside to cool, or, if using the next day, let cool, then cover well and store at room temperature.

You will need only 5 cups of crumbled cornbread for the dressing—which will leave you with 2 generous servings of the bread to enjoy while hot with lots of sweet butter. Or makes 8 servings.

ELDEN AND ODELIA MAE'S RECIPE

Chicken and Oyster Cornbread Dressing
(Farre de Pain de Maïs et Poule avec Huîtres)

Makes 6 to 8 main-dish servings

On the family's infrequent trips to the Louisiana Gulf coast to visit Dad's uncles, the first order of business for him was to get a boat and go out to the oyster reefs. Seining for fish and crabs and shrimp could wait until later. Dad loved oysters. When the men reached a reef, Dad would pluck the oysters up, open them, and slide those meaty, wonderfully flavorful Louisiana oysters into his mouth. When he had eaten his fill, then he would get down to the work of harvesting to carry oysters back to shore. Mom occasionally canned some of them to take home.

Mom made dressing on Sundays and holidays. She served it as a side dish, even though she made some of her dressings very meaty, as all the Prudhomme children and their families still do. The family agree that Mom never made dressing with oysters—oysters never had a chance to end up in a dressing with Dad around.

272

Odelia Mae cooks with all types of seafood, and she often adds it to old Cajun recipes like this chicken and cornbread dressing. Elden kids Odelia Mae about her love for cooking. She often prepares three or more entrées for a weekday meal, and she keeps their freezer loaded with ready-to-serve roasts, wild ducks, and seafood-stuffed mirlitons. He says that if he should outlive Odelia Mae, he'll just eat sandwiches the rest of his life because he's had enough good home-cooked food to last him forever.

This highly seasoned dressing is a dish unto itself; you don't need to serve a meat with it. You can bake the cornbread a day ahead and store it covered at room temperature. You can also cook the chicken and reduce the stock ahead of time.

1 (3- to 3½-pound) whole fryer (see **Note**)

12 cups water

1 medium onion, peeled and coarsely chopped

1 small green bell pepper, coarsely chopped

1 rib celery, coarsely chopped

5 large cloves garlic, peeled

1 tablespoon plus 1 teaspoon salt

1½ teaspoons black pepper

1 teaspoon ground red pepper (preferably cayenne)

1 recipe **Elden and Odelia Mae's Cornbread** (recipe follows)

5 tablespoons unsalted butter

½ cup finely chopped tasso (preferred) or other smoked ham (preferably Cure 81)

1⅔ cups finely chopped green onions (tops and bottoms)

1 cup finely chopped onions

½ cup finely chopped fresh parsley

¼ cup finely chopped green bell peppers

1 tablespoon plus ½ teaspoon finely chopped garlic

1 teaspoon **Ground Hot Pepper Vinegar** (page 357); use peppers only (see **Note**)

20 small to medium shucked oysters, in their liquor, about 12 ounces

2 eggs, beaten

3 hard-boiled eggs, thinly sliced

NOTE: Odelia Mae says to buy as fresh and fatty a fryer as possible. The heat of peppers used to make the Ground Hot Pepper Vinegar varies a lot; if your peppers are mild, use more of them in this dish.

Rinse the fryer thoroughly. Remove and save visible fat. Place the whole fryer, giblets, and the fat in a 6-quart saucepan or large Dutch oven. Add the water, the coarsely chopped onion, bell pepper, and celery, and the garlic cloves, salt, and black and red peppers. Cover pot with lid askew and cook over high heat for about 30 minutes. Turn fryer over and reduce heat to medium low. Cover pan tightly and cook about 1 hour and 15 minutes (no need to stir). Leaving pan over medium-low heat, with a slotted spoon, transfer the chicken and giblets (but not the vegetables) to a large bowl; set aside until cool enough to handle. Increase heat under the chicken stock and vegetables to high and boil until mixture reduces to 4 cups, about 30 minutes. Remove from heat and set aside, unstrained. Meanwhile, bone the chicken and cut meat and giblets into bite-size pieces. Set aside.

In a very large bowl, crumble the cornbread and set aside.

Melt the butter in a large skillet over medium heat. Add the tasso and the finely chopped green onions, onions, parsley, bell peppers, garlic, and the Ground Hot Pepper Vinegar peppers, mixing well; sauté about 5 minutes, stirring occasionally. Turn heat to high and add the reduced unstrained stock; cook about 20 minutes, stirring and scraping frequently so mixture won't scorch. Remove from heat and let cool about 10 minutes.

Add the cooled tasso mixture and the boned chicken meat and giblets to the crumbled cornbread, stirring well. Then add the oysters and their liquor and the raw eggs, mixing well.

Spoon the dressing into a heavy 13 × 9-inch baking pan (it needs to be heavy) that has been greased on the bottom and sides, distributing dressing evenly in the pan. Arrange half the hard-boiled egg slices on top and press them down into the dressing with the back of a spoon, totally covering them with the dressing. Use the remaining egg slices to garnish the surface. Bake at 475° until flavors marry and dressing is browned on top, about 20 minutes. Remove from oven and let sit 10 minutes before serving.

Elden and Odelia Mae's Cornbread

1¼ cups yellow cornmeal
¾ cup plus 2 tablespoons all-purpose flour
2 tablespoons plus 2 teaspoons sugar
1 tablespoon baking powder
1½ teaspoons baking soda
1 teaspoon salt
¾ cup milk
4 tablespoons unsalted butter, melted and cooled
2 large eggs, beaten
3 tablespoons vegetable oil

In a large bowl, combine the cornmeal, flour, sugar, baking powder, baking soda, and salt, mixing well and breaking up any lumps. In a medium-size bowl, thoroughly combine the milk, butter, and eggs and add to the dry ingredients; blend just until mixed and large lumps are dissolved. Do not overbeat.

Place the oil in an 8-inch cast-iron skillet and coat all the pan bottom with it. Add the batter and smooth it out to distribute evenly. Spoon the oil that comes up from around the edges of the pan over the surface of the batter to coat all of it with oil. Bake at 375° until lightly browned but still a hint undercooked, about 20 minutes. (**NOTE**: If you're baking the cornbread to eat as is, rather than to use in the dressing, cook 2 to 3 minutes longer. It makes 8 servings.) Remove cornbread from skillet immediately and set aside to cool; or, if using the next day, let cool, then cover well and store at room temperature.

BOBBY'S RECIPE

Chicken and Cornbread Dressing
(Farre de Pain de Maïs et Poule)

Makes 8 main-dish servings

A favorite Prudhomme family story is the one about Dad and cornbread. A man who had just met Dad, and was really impressed by the size of the Prudhomme family, said to him, "I'll bet it takes a big cornbread to feed your family!" And Dad told him, "No, it doesn't." The man was so taken aback that he just stared for a moment and then he said, "But it has to—with twelve children!" Dad just smiled and said, "It takes three big cornbreads."

Bobby eats cornbread at night with milk, just like the family did at home when he was growing up. He says he's just recently learned to like cornbread as a hot bread along with a meal. (Mom didn't serve it at noon with the family's big meal of the day.)

Bob makes his chicken and cornbread dressing for holidays, so he usually serves other meats and main dishes, too. But we think the dressing can serve well as a main dish, with just a salad and green vegetable.

Season the chicken a day ahead. To save time, you can also make the cornbread a day ahead. Be sure to make the less sweet version of the cornbread. Store it covered at room temperature.

This dish is cooked for fairly long periods of time over high heat. If your gas burner or electric cooking element produces a very high heat, or if your pot is not a heavy one, you will need to adjust the temperature down.

1 (5- to 6-pound) stewing chicken, cut into 14 pieces
   (use the giblets, too)

   Seasoning mix:

   2½ teaspoons salt
   1½ teaspoons garlic powder
   1½ teaspoons ground red pepper (preferably cayenne)

1½ teaspoons sweet paprika
1 teaspoon white pepper
1 teaspoon onion powder
1 teaspoon rubbed sage
1 teaspoon dried sweet basil leaves
¾ teaspoon black pepper
¾ teaspoon dried thyme leaves
½ teaspoon gumbo filé (filé powder)

Vegetable oil for frying
1½ cups all-purpose flour
About 3 quarts, *in all*, **Basic Chicken Stock** (page 18)
1 cup chopped celery, *in all*
5 cups finely crumbled **Bobby's Cornbread** (recipe
　　follows; see **NOTE**)
1 cup finely chopped onions
¾ cup finely chopped green onions (tops and
　　bottoms)
1 egg, beaten
1 hard-boiled egg, chopped
1 teaspoon minced garlic

NOTE: Use the less sweet version, with only 1 tablespoon of sugar in it, for dressings.

Remove all visible fat from the chicken. Combine the seasoning mix ingredients thoroughly in a small bowl. Sprinkle the chicken pieces and giblets on both sides with 2 *tablespoons* of the seasoning mix, patting it in with your hands. Cover and refrigerate until ready to cook, preferably overnight. Reserve leftover seasoning mix to finish the dish.

　　In a very large skillet or deep fryer, heat oil 1 inch deep to 375°, 10 to 12 minutes.

　　Meanwhile, combine 1 *tablespoon* seasoning mix with the flour in a paper or plastic bag. Just before frying, place chicken pieces and giblets in the bag and shake to coat well. Shake off excess flour and fry pieces in batches until dark golden brown on both sides, 8 to 10 minutes per side. As pieces finish browning, transfer them to a heavy

8-quart saucepan or large Dutch oven. Maintain oil's temperature as close to 375° as possible.

When all the chicken has been browned, add ¾ *cup* of the stock and ½ *cup* of the celery to the saucepan. Cover and cook over high heat until sediment that builds up on pan bottom is well browned, 10 to 12 minutes, stirring frequently and scraping pan bottom well each time. Remove cover and add *1 cup* more stock; stir and scrape pan bottom clean. Add *9 cups* more stock and stir, scraping pan bottom well again. Bring to a boil uncovered, stirring occasionally. Continue boiling uncovered until chicken is tender, about 50 minutes, stirring and scraping pan bottom occasionally, and turning meat once or twice if it isn't totally submerged in liquid. (**NOTE**: Add more stock or water if necessary to keep chicken fairly well covered with liquid.) Remove pan from heat and transfer chicken with a slotted spoon to a large bowl. Set aside.

Pour the broth and any sediment from the pan into a quart-size pan or glass measuring cup. Skim fat from broth and pour 3½ cups of the broth into a large mixing bowl. If there is not enough, make up the balance with stock or water, and be sure to include the browned sediment. (Use any leftover broth in another recipe.) To the bowl, add the crumbled cornbread, onions, green onions, the beaten raw egg, the hard-boiled egg, garlic, and the remaining ½ *cup* celery and *1 tablespoon plus 1 teaspoon* seasoning mix, mixing well.

Spoon mixture into an ungreased 13 × 9-inch baking pan, spreading it evenly. Arrange the chicken pieces, skin side up, on top and dribble any drippings over the meat. Bake at 450° until chicken is dark golden brown, 20 to 25 minutes. Remove from oven and serve immediately.

Bobby's Cornbread

6 tablespoons vegetable oil
2 cups yellow cornmeal
1½ cups plus 2 tablespoons all-purpose flour
½ cup sugar for sweetened version, or 1 tablespoon
    sugar for less sweet version
1 tablespoon baking powder

2 teaspoons baking soda
Scant 1½ teaspoons salt
1 cup milk
5 tablespoons unsalted butter, melted and cooled
3 large eggs

Heat a large cast-iron or other heavy ovenproof skillet over high heat about 2 minutes. Add the oil and heat about 2 minutes more. Remove from heat and set aside about 10 minutes.

Meanwhile, in a large bowl, combine the cornmeal, flour, sugar, baking powder, baking soda, and salt, mixing well and breaking up any lumps. In a medium-size bowl, combine the milk, butter, and eggs, mixing until well blended; add the liquid mixture to the dry ingredients and stir just until blended. Add the hot oil and mix just until blended and large lumps are dissolved. Do not overbeat.

Place the unwiped hot skillet over very low heat and pour in the batter, spreading it evenly in the pan. If any oil collects around edges of skillet, spoon it over top of batter. Remove from heat and transfer skillet to oven; bake at 450° until done and brown around edges, about 16 minutes if for dressing, or about 18 minutes if for bread. Remove from oven and immediately turn cornbread over onto a plate.

Serve while hot, or, if using later, let cool, then cover and store at room temperature. Makes 8 to 10 servings or about 9 cups finely crumbled cornbread.

VEGETABLE DISHES

LÉGUMES

ELDEN AND ODELIA MAE'S RECIPE

Candied Yams
(Patates Douces en Candi)

Makes 6 to 8 side-dish servings

The word "yam" is used nationally today as a sort of trademark among produce wholesalers and retailers to identify the moist-fleshed Louisiana sweet potato. (Paul says that for years the family thought the word "yam" meant a good sweet potato.) Louisiana candied yams are a dish that Paul says grew out of the "Yambilee," an Opelousas sweet-potato festival that began in 1945 to celebrate this major Louisiana crop. The annual fall festival features parades, cooking contests, produce displays, and wonderful Louisiana food. Paul says he and all his brothers rode their horses in the parade each year, and the whole family attended. (Mom's brother, Walter LeDoux, was head of the festival for many years.) Mom Prudhomme baked sweet potatoes and made sweet-potato pie long before the festival began, but she learned to make candied yams and **Fried Sweet Potatoes** *(page 290) through the festival.*

Elden and Odelia Mae's candied yams have a rich and dark candylike syrup, and they're a fine example of this classic dish. Elden says the Prudhommes and Odelia Mae's family raised the Puerto Rican variety of sweet potatoes and that they make the best candied yams. It's best to use sweet potatoes in season—July through November—when they're at the peak of flavor.

2½ pounds (about 5 small to medium)
    even-sized sweet potatoes,
    preferably Puerto Rican variety
3 quarts plus ½ cup water, *in all*
1⅓ cups, packed, dark brown sugar
4 tablespoons unsalted butter
1½ teaspoons ground cinnamon
1½ teaspoons vanilla extract

Place the potatoes and *10 cups* of the water in a 5½-quart saucepan. Cover pan with lid askew and cook over high heat until fork tender, about 1 hour. Remove from heat, drain well, and set aside to cool while making the syrup.

Combine the brown sugar, butter, cinnamon, vanilla, and the remaining 2½ *cups* water in a 2-quart saucepan. Bring to a boil over high heat, stirring occasionally. Reduce heat to maintain a simmer and cook about 30 minutes, stirring occasionally.

Meanwhile, peel the potatoes and halve them lengthwise. Place in an ungreased 13 × 9-inch baking pan in a single layer, cut side up.

When the syrup has finished cooking, pour it over the potato halves, coating all the potatoes completely. Bake at 475° until bubbly brown and syrup is heavy, about 35 minutes, basting thoroughly every 15 minutes. Remove from oven, baste once more, and transfer to a serving dish. Let cool at least 15 minutes before serving (so syrup won't burn your mouth!). Serve undrained. These are great as is or at room temperature. (The syrup will thicken a lot as it cools.)

J.C. AND SIS'S RECIPE

Candied Yams
(Patates Douces en Candi)

Makes 6 to 8 side-dish servings

Dad Prudhomme raised two cash crops, sweet potatoes and cotton, and he paid a percentage of the profit to the landowner. He ran the farm exactly like any other business, and at sweet-potato harvest time, the family worked together like a production line in industry.

On harvest days, Paul says, Dad and the boys "plowed the fields with a mule-drawn plow, turning over the soil to expose the potatoes. Then we harvested them on our knees, breaking the potatoes from the vines. We sorted them by size, tossing them in piles on the harvesting rows, between the plant rows. When the harvesting rows were filled, one of the boys came along with crates and loaded the potatoes. Then someone else came along with a mule hooked up to the slide we used for hauling and carried the crates to the head row, the gathering point where the truck from the processing plant would pick them up. One year Dad was recognized by the plant for producing more pounds of sweet potatoes on an acre of land than anyone else in the surrounding parishes."

Sis remembers her mom baking a stove full of sweet potatoes (it was a wood-burning stove) and serving them with homemade sour cream; she still likes them, and candied yams, too, with sour cream. J.C. and Sis's candied yams are delicious hot or at room temperature. They're quite different from Elden and Odelia Mae's recipe; they're not as syrupy and they don't taste the same because of the different cooking procedure. You can cook these candied yams ahead and reheat them just before serving. It's best to use sweet potatoes in season—July through November—when they're at the peak of flavor.

2½ pounds (about 5 small to medium) even-sized
  sweet potatoes, preferably Puerto Rican variety
Butter or margarine to grease potatoes
½ cup sugar
½ cup, packed, light brown sugar
½ cup water
5 tablespoons unsalted butter
½ teaspoon ground cinnamon

Scrub the potatoes well, then dry, and grease them lightly with butter. Place on a cookie sheet and bake at 400° until fork tender, about 1 hour. Remove from oven and, when cool enough to handle, peel and slice them crosswise into about ½-inch-thick pieces. Arrange evenly in an ungreased 11 × 7-inch baking pan and set aside.

Combine the remaining ingredients in a 2-quart saucepan; bring to a boil over high heat, stirring almost constantly. Continue boiling about 2 minutes to thicken the syrup slightly, stirring constantly. Remove from heat and continue stirring a few seconds more. Pour the mixture evenly over the potato slices. Bake at 350° until syrup is bubbly and thick, 30 to 35 minutes, basting once or twice. Remove from oven and let cool at least 15 minutes, so syrup won't burn your mouth. Serve undrained as is or at room temperature.

J.C. AND SIS'S RECIPE

Sweet Squash with Nutmeg and Vanilla
(Ciblème Douce avec Muscade et Vanille)

Makes 4 side-dish servings

Paul says the family grew "tons" of pattypan squash every summer and "no one ever got tired of it because Mom cooked it so many different ways: She fried it; she smothered it; she baked it as pudding with onions, sugar, and vanilla; and she scooped out the pulp and used it to make a stuffing with meat or seafood or other vegetables and then stuffed it back in the shell and baked it."

Sis learned to like vegetables and to cook them from Mom Prud-homme, but she learned to cook meat on her own when she was about ten. Every year after canning season, her mother left home to visit a married daughter for a week of vacation, which left Sis at home with her dad and two brothers. Sis says her dad didn't know how to wash a spoon and didn't want to learn, so she had kitchen duty. She says, "You learn fast like that," and she did.

J.C. and Sis's sweet squash dish is quite rich, and it's great with roast pork. Choose the smallest squash possible because they have fewer and smaller seeds.

About 1 cup water, *in all*
5 cups peeled and chopped small white summer (pattypan) squash
½ cup sugar
4 tablespoons unsalted butter
⅛ teaspoon salt
1 teaspoon vanilla extract
½ teaspoon freshly grated nutmeg

Place ½ *cup* of the water and the squash in a 2-quart saucepan. Cover pan and cook over high heat until water has almost evaporated, about 20 minutes, stirring and scraping pan bottom frequently and being careful not to let squash scorch. If it is not fork tender after about 20 minutes of cooking, add ½ *cup* more water, reduce heat to low, and cook uncovered until squash is tender and water has evaporated. Stir occasionally throughout cooking to break up squash into small pieces.

Add the sugar, butter, and salt, stirring well. Cook about 5 minutes, stirring frequently. Remove from heat and stir in the vanilla and nutmeg. Transfer mixture to an ungreased 1-quart ovenproof casserole. Cover and bake at 400° until brown and bubbly around edges and squash seeds are tender, about 45 minutes. Stir well and serve immediately.

BOBBY'S RECIPE

Fried Okra with Red Onions
(Gombo Févi Frit avec des Oignons Rouges)

Makes 4 to 6 side-dish or to 2 to 3 snack servings

Bobby loves okra "cooked any way and all ways." Mom Prudhomme fried it, boiled it, pickled it, and made okra salad. When she cooked fried okra and onions, Bobby says, "she used green onions, because that's what we raised in the garden, and she fried the tops and bottoms together."

Fried okra and onions makes an excellent side dish with other summer vegetables like corn on the cob, field peas, and sliced garden tomatoes—and be sure to serve hot buttered cornbread, too.

¾ pound untrimmed fresh okra, about 1 quart
About 4½ cups water
1 packed cup thinly sliced red onions separated into rings
6 tablespoons vegetable oil
¼ cup white vinegar
½ teaspoon salt plus a little to sprinkle on the finished okra
½ teaspoon black pepper

Seasoning mix:

2 teaspoons salt

1 teaspoon sweet paprika

½ teaspoon white pepper

½ teaspoon onion powder

½ teaspoon garlic powder

½ teaspoon dry mustard

¼ teaspoon red pepper (preferably cayenne)

¼ teaspoon dried thyme leaves

¼ teaspoon dried sweet basil leaves

½ cup plus 2 tablespoons corn flour (see **NOTE**)

½ cup plus 2 tablespoons yellow cornmeal

Vegetable oil for frying

NOTE: Corn flour is available at health food stores.

Place the okra in a 2-quart saucepan and cover with water. Bring to a boil over high heat, then continue boiling about 5 minutes, stirring occasionally. Cover pan, remove from heat, and let sit about 5 minutes. Drain in colander, then rinse with cool tap water, tossing gently so okra cools thoroughly and being careful to keep each pod intact; drain well.

Place the okra in a medium-size bowl. Add the onions, oil, vinegar, the ½ teaspoon of salt, and the black pepper; mix gently to coat okra and onion rings well. Let sit about 15 minutes. Drain well and remove onions to another bowl. **NOTE:** The drained, seasoned oil and vinegar is good used as a salad dressing or to marinate other vegetables for a salad.

Thoroughly combine the seasoning mix ingredients in a small bowl. Place the corn flour and cornmeal in a pan (pie and cake pans work well) and add the seasoning mix, mixing well.

In a deep skillet or deep fryer, heat oil at least 2 inches deep to 350°. Dredge okra in seasoned flour mixture; turn with a fork to coat thoroughly. Let sit in the flour mixture about 5 minutes. Shake off excess flour and slip okra pods into the hot oil, one at a time and in a single layer, being careful to keep them intact. Fry in batches until very crisp, about 8 minutes, turning at least once. Do not crowd. (Adjust heat as needed to maintain about 350°.) Drain on paper towels.

Dredge the onions in the same flour mixture while the last batch of okra is frying; let sit in mixture about 5 minutes. Fry onions in batches in the hot oil until crisp, about 3 minutes; do not crowd. Drain on paper towels. Salt the okra lightly, then toss with the onions. Serve immediately.

ABEL AND JO'S RECIPE

Smothered Okra and Tomatoes
(Gombo Févi et Tomates Etouffés)

Makes 6 to 8 side-dish servings

Outside of Louisiana, crawfish etouffée and shrimp etouffée are probably the only recognized kinds of etouffée, but in Cajun country, virtually every Cajun family cooks at least one etouffée daily, and it is rarely crawfish or shrimp. "Etouffée" means a smothered dish, and the Prudhomme family, as well as most Cajuns, smother everything possible—meat, game, fish, shellfish (including chicken, duck, turtle, rabbit, squirrel, alligator, frogs' legs, beef, pork, crawfish, shrimp, crabmeat, fish), and vegetables (including potatoes, turnips, eggplant, cabbage, and particularly okra and tomatoes).

Abel and Jo have a long-standing friendly feud about the yard surrounding their house. Abel thinks any area not covered by sidewalk or driveway should be planted with vegetables; Jo wants a beautiful lawn. The truce as it now stands is that the front lawn is off limits for Abel's vegetables, but everything else is fair game—and Abel hasn't missed a square foot. Any spot that has at least a one-foot width of soil is planted with tomatoes, fresh peppers, beans, peas, okra, turnips.

Abel and Jo's smothered okra and tomatoes takes a lot of stirring, but it's really worth it! It's a fine side dish with almost any meat, and it makes a wonderful "Cajun steak"—just spoon it on top of your favorite grilled steak.

This dish is cooked for fairly long periods of time over high heat. If

*your gas burner or electric cooking element produces a very high heat,
or if your pot is not a heavy one, you will need to adjust the temperature down.*

½ cup pork lard, or bacon drippings, or a mixture of
    4 tablespoons each unsalted butter and
    margarine (any of these preferred), or vegetable oil
3 pounds okra, sliced ¼ inch thick (3 quarts sliced)
2 cups finely chopped onions
¾ cup finely chopped green bell peppers
½ cup finely chopped celery
2½ teaspoons salt
1 teaspoon ground red pepper (preferably cayenne)
1 teaspoon minced garlic
4 cups peeled and chopped tomatoes, *in all*
½ cup water

Place the lard or other fat in a heavy 5½-quart saucepan or large
Dutch oven. Add the okra, onions, bell peppers, celery, salt, red pepper, and garlic. Cover pan, place over high heat, and cook about 5
minutes, stirring well every minute or two. Remove cover and cook
about 5 minutes, stirring almost constantly and being sure to scrape
any browned sediment from pan bottom.

Now add *1 cup* of the tomatoes and the water. Cook until mixture is sticking excessively, about 10 minutes, stirring and scraping
almost constantly. This browning process is important to the wonderful flavor of the finished dish. Add *1 cup* more tomatoes and cook
and stir until mixture is sticking excessively again, about 10 minutes.
(**NOTE**: Rotate pan occasionally if mixture always sticks to same
spot.) Add the remaining *2 cups* tomatoes and cook and stir until
mixture is sticking excessively again, about 10 minutes more. Remove from heat and transfer about 5 cups of the okra mixture to a
bowl; set aside.

Stir remaining okra in the saucepan well to dissolve all browned
matter from pan bottom. Place pan over medium heat and cook
until okra is browned and mushy, about 25 minutes, stirring and
scraping frequently. **NOTE**: This final browning is what adds so
much depth of flavor to the dish. If you feel the sticking is getting
out of control, remove pan from heat as needed to let mixture sit a

few seconds; the fat in the pan will help dissolve the sediment. Then stir thoroughly and return to medium heat.

Remove pan from heat and scrape pan bottom well. Stir in the reserved okra mixture, place pan over high heat, and cook and stir until mixture is heated through, 2 to 3 minutes more. Remove from heat and serve immediately.

ELI AND SUE'S RECIPE

Fried Sweet Potatoes
(Patates Douces Frites)

Makes 6 to 8 side-dish servings

Paul says sweet potatoes are so much a part of Cajun culture that they are also a part of songs and dances. At parties and house dances (fais-dodos), there always used to be a sweet-potato dance in which couples started by holding a potato between their foreheads. The aim was to dance and keep that sweet potato up off the floor—NO hands allowed!—no matter where the two of them ended up holding it. It made for some interesting body language. Of course the couple that kept the potato off the floor the longest won a prize.

A song Paul likes to sing while he's cooking, driving, or relaxing is "Lâche Pas la Patate" ("Don't Let Go the Potato"); he likes the message: "Don't let a hot potato go; if you drop it, that's not right; just keep changing hands; it'll cool down; persevere, don't give up—you'll make it!"

Eli and Sue say sweet potatoes are as popular a staple in a Cajun kitchen as rice. They serve fried sweet potatoes for breakfast and as a vegetable or a snack or a dessert.

⅓ cup sugar
1½ teaspoons ground cinnamon
About 2 cups pork lard (preferred) or vegetable oil

3 pounds sweet potatoes, peeled and cut crosswise
　　into slices ⅜ inch thick (see **NOTE**)
About 3 tablespoons unsalted butter, softened, optional

NOTE: Be sure to cut potato slices uniformly thick so they will fry evenly.

In a small bowl combine the sugar and cinnamon, mixing well. Set aside.

In a large deep skillet or deep fryer, heat lard at least 1 inch deep to 300° over high heat; if using oil, heat to 340°. Maintain these temperatures as nearly as possible while frying the potatoes. Add the potato slices to the hot lard in a single layer and fry until slices are soft, bright orange in the center (take out a slice and test it by cutting it in half), and browned on both sides. This takes about 18 minutes, or, if using oil, about 12 minutes. Turn slices occasionally. Drain on paper towels and also blot tops. While still piping hot, rub potato slices with butter, if desired, then sprinkle slices very generously on both sides with the cinnamon sugar. Serve immediately.

BOBBY'S RECIPE

Fried Green Tomatoes
(Tomates Vertes Frites)

Makes 4 to 6 side-dish or 2 to 3 snack servings

The family's summer garden always had to be large enough to supply fresh vegetables all summer and still produce plenty more to can for the winter. The boys remember going out to the garden early in the morning to pick huge washtubs full of tomatoes, okra, cucumbers, butter beans, field peas, corn, and green beans. To bring them all back, they took a mule, hitched to the slide they used to drag heavy loads—a simple raftlike contraption made of wood, with runners underneath.

Green tomatoes had to be picked early, and fresh fried green tomatoes were a favorite. We are fortunate in Louisiana, we have Creole tomatoes, which are incomparable. All green tomatoes have a unique flavor, slightly tart. Buy a variety that is local to your area; it will be better than what the supermarket has (if the supermarket even carries green tomatoes!).

Bobby says he likes fried green tomatoes best for snacking, but sometimes makes a meal of them because he "just loves them." They're a fine side dish against rich food—almost, as Paul puts it, a palate cleanser.

1½ pounds medium to large, very green tomatoes,
    about 3 (preferably Creole)

Seasoning mix:
1¼ teaspoons black pepper
1 teaspoon salt
¾ teaspoon ground red pepper (preferably cayenne)
½ teaspoon garlic powder

1 cup all-purpose flour
½ teaspoon baking powder
Vegetable oil for frying

Trim away stem-end slice from each tomato, as well as a thin slice off the other end, so that all tomato slices will have exposed meat on both sides. Slice tomatoes ¼ inch thick. Place slices on a flat surface in a single layer.

Combine the seasoning mix ingredients thoroughly in a small bowl; sprinkle evenly on both sides of each tomato slice, pressing seasoning in with your hands and using it all. Let tomato slices sit at least 15 minutes.

Meanwhile, combine the flour and baking powder in a pan (pie and cake pans work well), mixing well. In a large skillet, heat oil ½ inch deep over medium heat until hot (until a pinch of flour dropped in sizzles), about 4 minutes. Just before frying, dredge each tomato slice thoroughly in the flour. Shake off excess flour and fry slices in a single layer in the hot oil until browned on both sides, 4 to 6 minutes total. Drain on paper towels. Serve immediately, allowing 3 to 4 slices as a side dish and 6 as a snack.

ALLIE AND ETELL'S RECIPE

Buttery Baked Macaroni and Eggs with Caramelized Onions

Makes 6 to 8 side-dish servings

The family "kind of lived off baked macaroni and eggs during lean times," according to Allie. Although most of the eggs the Prudhommes raised were used to pay tuition for Catholic school for the children, Mom did cook egg dishes when meat was scarce. All the children knew eggs were special. They remember Easter as a great day because each of them got a dozen hard-boiled Easter eggs. In the early years, Mom dyed them with coffee grounds, catalpa leaves, berries, and the dye from bright scraps of fabric. But by the time the younger children were born, Bobby says Mom bought commercial Easter egg dye, and she wrote the children's names and drew flowers on the eggs with a candle. When the family spent Easter with either set of grandparents, Dad packed the several dozen Easter eggs in a large washtub between layers of cotton seeds to cushion them for the bumpy trip by wagon.

Paul says that when he was growing up, the children also had Easter egg fights, and they knew how to make "ringer" fighting eggs— shells filled with hardened wax. But what Paul remembers most about Easter was the forty-day Lenten season that came before. He says Mom attended church every day during Lent, and the family had meatless meals every Wednesday and Friday. Good Friday was strictly observed as a religious holiday and no work of any kind was done on that day.

Allie and Etell's baked macaroni and eggs is wonderfully rich and buttery—definitely good enough for company!

Seasoning mix:
1¾ teaspoons salt
½ teaspoon sugar
½ teaspoon black pepper
½ teaspoon ground red pepper (preferably cayenne)

5 tablespoons unsalted butter, *in all*
2 cups finely chopped onions
1½ teaspoons minced garlic
4 cups water
¼ teaspoon salt
6 ounces macaroni (9-inch-long maccheroncelli),
     broken in half (about 60 strands before they are
     broken)
Butter, to butter pan
2¼ cups plus 2 tablespoons heavy cream
3 hard-boiled eggs, sliced
Extra ground black pepper to sprinkle on each
     serving, optional

Thoroughly combine the seasoning mix ingredients in a small bowl.

Melt *4 tablespoons* of the butter in a large skillet over medium heat until almost melted. Add the onions and sauté until onions just start to brown, about 3 minutes, stirring occasionally. Add the garlic and seasoning mix and sauté until onions are caramelized (well browned but not burned), about 8 minutes more, stirring and scraping pan bottom frequently. Remove from heat and set aside.

In a 3-quart saucepan, combine the water, the remaining *1 tablespoon* butter, and the salt. Place over high heat and bring to a boil. Add the macaroni, stirring well, and cook to al dente stage, about 7 minutes, stirring occasionally; do not overcook. Immediately turn out macaroni into a colander. Rinse first with hot water to wash off starch, then rinse well with cold water to stop the cooking. Rinse until cool to the touch, then drain very well in the colander.

Place the onion mixture in a 13 × 9-inch baking pan that has been well buttered on the sides and bottom. Add the macaroni and the cream, mixing well. Add the hard-boiled eggs, stirring gently so egg yolks don't break up. Be sure all egg slices are moistened and all macaroni strands are down in the liquid (no loops in the air!), if not actually submerged. Bake at 450° until done and brown and bubbly on top, about 30 minutes. Remove from oven and sprinkle black pepper on top, if desired. Serve immediately.

RALPH AND MARY ANN'S RECIPE

Eggplant, Corn and Cheese Casserole
(Casserole de Brème, Maïs et Fromage)

Makes 8 to 10 side-dish servings

If you're ever driving in Cajun country and you smell something wonderful cooking along an isolated stretch of road with no homes and no restaurants in sight, look for an old blue van, then follow your nose. You're sure to find Ralph cooking up something Cajun in the cast-iron pot he keeps in his truck along with onions, garlic, salt, and red pepper. It's a habit he acquired as a youngster when Mom Prudhomme gave him some old pots and spoons. Every time he went hunting or fishing he carried pots and seasonings with him—and he still does that today. He says, "When I catch some fish, all I have to do is get out my pot and seasonings and I'm ready to cook. If I don't catch any fish, I can always pick up a chicken and make a stew or a gumbo."

Mary Ann likes to make this good vegetable-and-cheese casserole for church dinners. You can make the recipe ahead up to the point of baking.

3½ cups peeled and chopped eggplant
2 cups water
¼ pound (1 stick) plus 2 tablespoons unsalted butter
1½ cups finely chopped onions, *in all*
1½ cups fresh corn cut off the cob (preferred; about
    four 8-inch ears) or frozen corn kernels
2 large eggs, beaten
½ cup finely chopped green bell peppers
1 teaspoon minced garlic
½ teaspoon salt
½ teaspoon ground red pepper (preferably cayenne)
¼ teaspoon black pepper

2½ cups grated cheddar cheese, *in all*
1¼ cups very finely ground unsalted saltine cracker
     crumbs, about 4 ounces

Place the eggplant and water in a 2-quart saucepan; cover pan and bring to a boil; reduce heat and simmer until eggplant is tender, about 30 minutes, stirring occasionally. Drain well in a colander with a bowl underneath; reserve in separate containers the eggplant and 1 cup of the eggplant stock.

Heat the butter in a 3-quart saucepan over medium heat until half melted. Add *1 cup* of the onions and sauté until well browned, about 9 minutes, stirring occasionally. Remove pan from heat and transfer onions with a slotted spoon to a bowl. Add the corn to the same pan and return to medium heat. Cook about 8 minutes, stirring frequently and scraping pan bottom well. Remove from heat and stir in the reserved cooked onions, reserved eggplant, and the eggs, mixing well. Add the remaining ½ *cup* onions, the bell peppers, garlic, salt, red and black peppers, *1½ cups* of the cheese, *1 cup* of the cracker crumbs, and the reserved eggplant stock, mixing well.

Pour mixture into an ungreased 8 × 8 × 2-inch baking pan (preferably *not* nonstick type), patting the mixture down evenly in pan. Sprinkle the remaining *1 cup* cheese evenly over the top, then sprinkle the remaining ¼ *cup* cracker crumbs evenly over the cheese. Bake at 350° until crumbs are lightly browned, cheese is melted, and the mixture bubbles around the edges, about 40 minutes. (If you make the mixture ahead and place it in the oven chilled, it will need to bake a few minutes longer.)

Remove casserole from oven, let cool about 10 minutes, and serve immediately.

ELI AND SUE'S RECIPE

Corn Maque Choux
(Maque Choux de Maïs)

Makes 8 to 10 side-dish servings

Corn maque choux was for holidays and occasionally for Sundays and birthdays. Mom made **Chicken Maque Choux** *(page 85) or crawfish maque choux for "maque choux nights," but she usually just roasted freshly picked ears of corn in the oven for everyday meals.*

The boys used leftover corncobs for their game of corncob wars. There were usually a dozen or more boys at the house every day—the brothers brought friends home from school daily—and weekends were like holidays, with forty or fifty people present. The boys divided into two teams, one team positioned in the hayloft of the barn and the other on the ground behind the wagons and other farm equipment. When everyone was in position, the teams assaulted one another with the dried-up corncobs. Paul says, "The game always deteriorated into a war, with both sides soaking the corncobs in water and rolling them in dirt to make more potent weapons—and boy, did they sting when they hit you!"

Select the freshest corn possible for this sweet, highly seasoned, and delicious dish. Very fresh corn not only tastes better, but it also gives off more starch, and an essential part of the taste of corn maque choux is the browned starch that forms on the pan bottom during cooking.

This dish is cooked for fairly long periods of time over high heat. If your gas burner or electric cooking element produces a very high heat, or if your pot is not a heavy one, you will need to adjust the temperature down.

¼ pound (1 stick) unsalted butter
7 cups fresh corn cut off the cob (preferred; about
     seventeen 8-inch ears) or frozen corn kernels
1 cup finely chopped onions
1 cup finely chopped green bell peppers

1 cup **Basic Chicken, Pork** or **Beef Stock** (page 18)
2 teaspoons sweet paprika
1½ teaspoons salt
1 teaspoon ground red pepper (preferably cayenne)
1 teaspoon black pepper
1 large bay leaf
2 egg yolks, beaten
1 cup milk
¼ cup sugar

In a heavy 5½-quart saucepan or large Dutch oven, combine the butter, corn, onions, bell peppers, stock, paprika, salt, red and black peppers, and bay leaf. Place over high heat and cook until butter is melted and liquid comes to a boil, stirring and scraping pan bottom occasionally. Stir well, then cover pan, and cook about 4 minutes without stirring. Remove cover and stir and scrape pan bottom well; continue cooking uncovered about 5 minutes, stirring and scraping only after a very thin brown crust develops and starts sticking on the pan bottom (it can easily be scraped off); then scrape well. **NOTE**: If your corn is not very fresh, it may not give off enough starch to form much of a crust.

Remove and discard the bay leaf (Eli and Sue like just a hint of bay leaf flavor). Continue cooking over high heat until the mixture is fairly dry or sticking excessively, about 12 minutes, stirring and scraping pan bottom as needed. Reduce heat to very low.

In a small bowl, stir together the egg yolks and milk until very frothy, then immediately, but *gradually,* add the mixture to the corn, stirring briskly so the eggs won't scramble. Increase heat back to high and bring the mixture to a boil, stirring and scraping pan bottom occasionally.

Now stir in the sugar, cover pan, reduce heat to medium low, and cook until flavors marry and corn is cooked, about 20 minutes more, stirring and scraping only enough to make sure mixture doesn't scorch, and then scraping pan bottom clean. **NOTE**: Reduce heat if sticking becomes excessive.

Remove from heat and serve immediately.

RALPH AND MARY ANN'S RECIPE

Smothered Potatoes
(Patates Etouffées)

Makes 8 to 10 side-dish servings

Ralph asked Mom Prudhomme once why she always scorched the potatoes when she made smothered potatoes. She said the first time she did it wasn't on purpose. She was busy changing diapers and fixing bottles for five babies and toddlers, as well as cooking, and by the time she checked back on the potatoes, they were stuck to the bottom of the pot. Everyone thought they tasted great, so she kept on making them that way and they became a family favorite.

Ralph began cooking with Mom Prudhomme when Allie got married: "I was about twelve years old when I became Mom's helper with the cooking and the washing. I liked the cooking, but washing was a big chore. Mom washed for the fourteen of us plus her two brothers who worked in a department store. (They had to wear starched white shirts every day!) We washed on a scrub board and we didn't have running water—we carried water up from a nearby stream. Mom mixed up cornstarch for starch and she ironed with black cast-iron irons that she heated on the wood stove. We learned to work hard when we were young, and that helped us all after we were grown and had to earn a living."

Ralph and Mary Ann's smothered potatoes are delicious. He loves to spread them on Mary Ann's homemade yeast rolls to make a potato sandwich.

This dish is cooked for fairly long periods of time over high heat. If your gas burner or electric cooking element produces a very high heat, or if your pot is not a heavy one, you will need to adjust the temperature down.

⅓ cup vegetable oil
3 pounds potatoes, peeled, sliced ¼ inch thick, and
    cut into about 1-inch squares
1½ cups very finely chopped onions

2 teaspoons salt
½ teaspoon black pepper
½ teaspoon minced garlic
¼ teaspoon white pepper
1½ cups, *in all*, **Rich Stock** (preferred; page 19) or
    water (see **NOTE**)
½ cup finely chopped green onions (tops only)

NOTE: Use chicken stock if you're serving the potatoes with a chicken dish, beef stock with a beef dish, and so on.

In a very large skillet (preferably cast iron), heat the oil over high heat about 1 minute. Add the potatoes, onions, salt, black pepper, garlic, and white pepper, stirring well. Cook about 10 minutes, stirring and scraping pan bottom well only when mixture is browning and starting to stick excessively, but doing so each time that occurs. (It's this sticking process that makes these potatoes special, so be sure to let the mixture stick before you stir!)

Reduce heat to low and cook until mixture is mottled brown throughout, about 20 minutes, stirring and scraping only occasionally. Add ½ *cup* of the stock and scrape pan bottom well; cook about 5 minutes, stirring only once or twice. Add ½ *cup* more stock and cook about 5 minutes, stirring and scraping well and breaking up half of the potato pieces, if not already broken up, so the potatoes are half creamed, half lumpy. Add the remaining ½ *cup* stock and the green onions, stirring well. Cook about 5 minutes more, stirring and scraping occasionally. Remove from heat and serve immediately.

ABEL AND JO'S RECIPE

Smothered Potatoes and Turnips
(Patates et Navets Etouffés)

Makes 6 to 8 side-dish servings

Abel says Dad and Mom Prudhomme were far better organized than we are today. The family never ran out of potatoes because Dad planted a spring and a fall crop, and he did the same with other vegetables. The whole family worked together to can vegetables each season to use out of season or when the garden was damaged by drought or floods. Elden remembers that when Mom needed potatoes from the garden she just used a large spoon to dig around each plant. She never took more than two potatoes from a stalk and she always packed the soil back down around the plants so they would continue to produce.

Abel and Jo's smothered potatoes and turnips is a great recipe to try if you've always thought you didn't like turnips. It's wonderful. Use the freshest turnips possible; very fresh ones will really make a difference. Mom Prudhomme served this dish with smothered chicken or smothered beef and rice, and Abel likes it with red beans and rice.

Jo smothers vegetables and meats in cast-iron pots. She says, "There's something about an iron pot—it cooks better."

This dish is cooked for fairly long periods of time over high heat. If your gas burner or electric cooking element produces a very high heat, or if your pot is not a heavy one, you will need to adjust the temperature down.

1 cup vegetable oil

3½ pounds potatoes, peeled and cut into 1-inch
    cubes, about 10 cups cubed

1½ pounds white turnips, peeled and cut into ½-inch
    cubes, about 4 cups cubed

1½ cups finely chopped onions

½ cup finely chopped celery

2 teaspoons salt

1 teaspoon ground red pepper (preferably cayenne)
¼ teaspoon black pepper
1 cup chopped green onions (tops and bottoms)
¼ cup chopped fresh parsley
About 1 cup, *in all*, **Basic Pork** or **Chicken Stock**
    (preferred; page 18), or water

In a 7½-quart cast-iron (preferred) or other large Dutch oven, combine the oil, potatoes, turnips, onions, celery, salt, and red and black peppers. Place over high heat and cook about 10 minutes, stirring occasionally. Cover pan and cook until potatoes and turnips are tender but still firm, about 25 minutes, stirring only occasionally at first, then almost constantly during second half of cooking time, and scraping pan bottom well each time. **NOTE:** Be sure to let browned sediment stick each time before you stir, but don't let it scorch; the browned matter is what makes this dish so good! If you're not sure whether the mixture is browning or scorching, take a little of the browned mixture out of the pan, cool a few seconds, and taste it—any scorched mixture will *taste* scorched. If this happens, change pans without stirring or scraping pan bottom. Or if sticking becomes so excessive that you feel you're losing control, remove the pan from heat and scrape the pan clean; if necessary, then add ½ *cup* of stock or water at a time to scrape clean any trouble spots. However, don't scrape bottom if mixture looks scorched; rather, pour mixture into a clean pan without scraping. Then return this pan to high heat.

When potatoes and turnips are tender, stir in the green onions, parsley, and ¼ *cup* stock or water. Reduce heat to low and cook about 3 minutes more, stirring almost constantly and scraping the pan bottom as clean as possible. Remove from heat and serve immediately. The finished dish should be lumpy, with lots of brown creamy parts.

Smothered Turnips with Fresh Pork
(Navets Etouffés avec Viande de Cochon Frais)

Makes 10 to 12 side-dish servings

When Marie married Calvin, the only thing she knew how to cook was fried chicken. An elderly black lady who lived nearby offered to teach her how to smother vegetables and meats and make stews and bake cakes. In addition, Mom Prudhomme and Calvin both taught her some basic cooking skills.

Calvin and Marie live in the city, but they still have a farm in the country where they keep cattle and other animals. Calvin says now that he's retired, he and Marie stay on the go with their camping friends and he no longer slaughters his own animals and dresses out and freezes the meat. But up until a couple of years ago, they grew all their vegetables and raised animals for pork and beef.

The turnips in this dish aren't smothered in the sense that we normally mean in Cajun cooking—that is, letting them stick to the pan bottom often and get very brown. The turnips don't brown at all, but they're really good. K thinks they're fabulous—the best turnips she's ever had. Be sure to use the freshest turnips you can find because very fresh ones will make a noticeable difference.

This dish is cooked for fairly long periods of time over high heat. If your gas burner or electric cooking element produces a very high heat, or if your pot is not a heavy one, you will need to adjust the temperature down.

2 cups **Rich Pork Stock** (page 19)
¾ pound boneless pork meat, cut into bite-size
    pieces, with a little fat left on
5 quarts peeled and thinly sliced white turnips (about
    15 to 17 medium-size turnips)
¾ cup vegetable oil
¼ cup sugar
2 teaspoons salt

1 teaspoon black pepper
½ teaspoon ground red pepper (preferably cayenne)
½ teaspoon white vinegar

Place the stock and meat in a heavy 7-quart saucepan (cast iron preferred) or large Dutch oven. Cover pan and bring to a boil over high heat. Stir well, then reduce heat to low and cook about 15 minutes without stirring. Stir well, then add the turnips, oil, sugar, salt, and black and red peppers. Cover pan and place over high heat; cook about 20 minutes, stirring occasionally.

Now remove lid and stir in the vinegar; continue cooking, uncovered, until turnip pieces are tender but still somewhat firm and most of the liquid has evaporated, about 30 minutes, stirring occasionally and scraping pan bottom well. (Stir and scrape more often toward end of cooking time.) Remove from heat and serve immediately.

ABEL AND JOE'S RECIPE

Black-Eyed Peas with Slab Bacon and Tasso
(Fèves de Black-Eye avec Béquine et Tasso)

Makes 8 to 10 side-dish servings

Black-eyed peas were a traditional New Year's Day dish (they were supposed to bring good health and good luck), along with smothered cabbage and coleslaw (to ensure wealth) and pork roast (which just tasted wonderful). (Paul says the boys cut cabbage leaves into the shape and size of dollar bills and put them in their wallets, hoping they would miraculously turn into real bills.) Those were the traditional dishes, but the table was loaded with other food as well—including beef, chicken, duck, vegetables, and lots of desserts. Abel remembers the family spending New Year's Day with Mom Prud-

homme's family when he was quite young (when the older children were small, the family went to Dad's parents), but by the time he was a teenager, all the family gathered at the Prudhomme home for New Year's each year.

Abel and Jo's black-eyed peas are creamy and wonderfully peppery, and the two meats make a good contrast in taste—the slab bacon with the peas is delicious, and then the bites of tasso and peas are a completely different taste treat.

Paul says the family didn't cook peas and beans with stock, but they got the same effect because they usually cooked them for long periods of time with seasoning meats like salt meat, andouille, and tasso.

2 quarts plus 1½ cups **Basic Pork** (preferred) or
    Chicken Stock (page 18)
1 pound dried black-eyed peas (not soaked)
½ pound slab bacon, cut into 1-inch cubes (1½ cups cubed)
¼ pound tasso (preferred) or other smoked ham
    (preferably Cure 81), cut into 1-inch cubes (1 cup cubed)
1½ cups finely chopped onions
½ cup finely chopped green bell peppers
¼ cup finely chopped celery
1 teaspoon minced garlic
1¾ teaspoons salt
½ teaspoon ground red pepper (preferably cayenne)

In a 5½-quart saucepan or large Dutch oven, combine the stock, peas, bacon, tasso, onions, bell peppers, celery, and garlic. Cover pan and bring to a boil over high heat, stirring occasionally so peas don't stick. Put lid askew and continue boiling about 5 minutes.

Stir well, reduce heat to maintain a simmer, and re-cover pan with lid askew. Simmer about 1 hour, stirring occasionally (more often toward the end of cooking time so the mixture doesn't scorch). Stir in the salt and pepper, re-cover pan, and simmer about 30 minutes, stirring frequently and being careful the mixture doesn't scorch. If it does scorch, do not stir; change to a new pan.

Remove cover and simmer until creamy thick, about 10 minutes more, stirring as necessary. Remove from heat and serve immediately.

DARILEE AND SAUL'S RECIPE

Fresh Purple-Hull Peas

Makes 14 to 16 side-dish or
6 to 8 main-dish servings with rice

Saul's garden is always picture perfect, with never a weed anywhere. He plants a spring and a fall garden with wonderful vegetables and lots of varieties of fresh hot peppers—his specialty. He and Darilee supply Paul and K with pepper plants. K is the gardener and has a fine green thumb for peppers and flowering plants. They use many of the fresh peppers at their restaurant in New Orleans.

Darilee and Saul's purple-hull peas are delicious served with sliced garden tomatoes. Purple-hull peas are southern field peas with a very short shelf-life, so it will be quite difficult to find them fresh outside the South. In an emergency—or, as Paul says, for a "pea attack north of the Mason-Dixon Line"—we recommend frozen field peas, frozen purple-hull peas, or frozen crowder peas. Several nationwide supermarket chains carry all three types frozen. You will need about 1½ pounds of frozen peas to yield 5 cups.

This dish is cooked for fairly long periods of time over high heat. If your gas burner or electric cooking element produces a very high heat, or if your pot is not a heavy one, you will need to adjust the temperature down.

3 pounds purple-hull peas, shelled (about 5 cups
    shelled)
About 4 quarts, *in all*, **Rich Chicken** or **Pork Stock**
    (page 19)
1 cup chopped onions
1 cup chopped celery
1 cup chopped green bell peppers
1 cup chopped green onions (tops only)
¼ pound (1 stick) unsalted butter
½ cup chopped fresh parsley
2¼ teaspoons salt

¾ teaspoon black pepper
½ teaspoon ground red pepper (preferably cayenne)
6 to 8 cups hot **Basic Cooked Rice** (page 252), if
    serving as a main dish

In a heavy 5½-quart saucepan or large Dutch oven, combine the peas
with *5 cups* of the stock. Place over high heat and bring to a boil,
stirring frequently and scraping pan bottom well. Continue boiling
about 25 minutes, stirring and scraping frequently so peas won't
stick. Stir in *2 cups* more stock and return to a boil, stirring frequently. Continue boiling about 15 minutes, stirring and scraping
frequently. Add *2 cups* more stock; cook and stir about 15 minutes.
Add *2 cups* more stock; cook and stir until pea centers and hulls are
tender, about 20 minutes. **NOTE**: Continue adding stock or water, 1
to 2 cups at a time, if peas require longer cooking to make them
tender.

Now stir in *2 cups* more stock and the onions, celery, bell peppers, green onions, butter, parsley, salt, and black and red peppers;
return to a boil, stirring and scraping frequently. Reduce heat and
simmer until vegetables are tender and liquid has thickened, about
35 minutes more, stirring and scraping frequently. **NOTE**: If peas
stick, do *not* stir. Immediately remove from heat and change to another pot without scraping any scorched peas into the mixture.

Remove from heat and serve immediately as is for a side dish; or,
if serving as a main dish, allow for each serving 1 cup peas over 1
cup rice.

ELI AND SUE'S RECIPE

Fresh Butter Beans
(Fèves Plattes Fraîches)

Makes 4 to 6 side-dish servings

To the children, summer was the best season—no school and lots of daylight hours left to play after all the chores were finished. Mom Prudhomme absolutely forbade swimming, which made it all the more appealing. (She had never been taught to swim, and she really believed it was dangerous.) The boys had Dad clip their hair really short in summer. He didn't know why, but the boys knew it had to dry fast so Mom and Dad wouldn't know they had been swimming.

Some days, after dinner, when the weather was just too hot to do anything, Mom and Dad lay down for a nap, and the boys sneaked off to the nearby bayou under the railroad trestle. Most of them learned to swim fairly well. (Years later, Calvin used to joke in Mom's presence that "it was hell learning to swim in a number-three wash-tub.") Ralph says he and Elden and J.C. just jumped in and learned; Abel says he learned with his black friends; and Bobby says he learned to swim with Eli (Eli says Bobby came close to drowning them both), using syrup buckets and gallon jugs as floats. Bobby says, "The floats worked fine until they slid to your feet. Then you sank head first with your feet floating on top, and you had to fight your way back upright."

Fresh young butter beans—limas—taste like a summer day; there's no other fair description. Eli and Sue's recipe is terrific for a side dish, but they like to serve the butter beans over rice. With rice, a pound of butter beans in the shell will make 2 to 3 main-dish servings or 6 to 7 side-dish servings.

¼ pound (1 stick) unsalted butter
2 tablespoons pork lard (preferred) or chicken fat
2 cups very finely chopped onions
2 teaspoons salt
1 teaspoon minced garlic

308

¾ teaspoon ground red pepper (preferably cayenne)
½ teaspoon black pepper
1 pound unshelled fresh butter (lima) beans (3¼
     cups shelled)
About 6 cups, *in all*, **Rich Chicken Stock** (page 19)
2 tablespoons sugar
Hot **Basic Cooked Rice** (page 252), optional

Melt the butter with the lard in a heavy 5½-quart saucepan or large
Dutch oven over high heat. Add the onions, salt, garlic, and red and
black peppers; cook about 2 minutes, stirring occasionally. Add the
beans, stirring well. Reduce heat to low and cook until a thin layer of
starch sticks to the pan bottom (it should be easy to scrape off), 25
to 30 minutes, stirring occasionally and scraping pan bottom well
each time. Be sure to cook the beans to this sticking stage; it's an
important step in breaking the starch out of the beans. Add *1 cup* of
the stock, stirring and scraping pan bottom well. Cook about 15
minutes, stirring and scraping occasionally so beans won't scorch.
NOTE: If they do scorch, do not stir; change to a new pan.

Now add *2 cups* more stock and bring to a boil over high heat,
stirring occasionally. Reduce heat and simmer about 20 minutes,
stirring and scraping pan bottom occasionally (more frequently
toward the end of cooking time). Stir in *1½ cups* more stock and the
sugar. Return to a boil over high heat, then reduce heat, and simmer
until beans are tender, about 20 minutes more, stirring and scraping
frequently so beans won't scorch. If necessary, add more stock or
water, 1 cup at a time, and continue cooking until done.

Remove from heat and serve immediately as is or over rice. **NOTE**:
The beans thicken quickly once removed from heat; if necessary, thin
them with more stock or water.

ELI AND SUE'S RECIPE

Dried Baby Lima Beans with Salt Meat

(Ti Fèves Plattes Sèches avec Viande Salée)

Makes 6 to 8 main-dish servings

Eli and Sue serve these well-seasoned, slightly sweet, and country-style small butter beans over rice or **Crusty Houseboat Biscuits** *(page 22). Cajuns serve dried beans along with lots of other food, such as baked sweet potatoes, other vegetables, and homemade breads.*

When you cook dried beans, you should always be aware of two things: First, the cooking time can vary by an hour or more from batch to batch with the same type of bean because of the age of the beans—and it's virtually impossible to know the age of dried beans. So always cook dried beans of all types until tender and don't worry about exact times given in recipes. Second, the consistency of dried-bean dishes can range from that of a soup to thick baked beans, depending on how long you wait to add more stock or water as you're cooking the starch out of the beans. If you want a soup-like consistency and like the beans to break up and not stay whole, wait as long as possible before adding more liquid. Conversely, if you like the consistency of thick baked beans and want the beans to stay whole, add liquid sooner and more frequently. Either method gives excellent results.

This dish is cooked for fairly long periods of time over high heat. If your gas burner or electric cooking element produces a very high heat, or if your pot is not a heavy one, you will need to adjust the temperature down.

4 cups water
1 pound salt pork (with as much lean as possible),
     cut into 1½-inch cubes (preferred), or substitute
     coarsely chopped bacon or tasso, whole ham
     hocks, or diced andouille smoked sausage

About 7 quarts, *in all*, **Basic Pork Stock** (preferred;
    page 18) or water
1 pound dried baby lima beans (small butter beans),
    rinsed and sorted
1½ cups finely chopped onions
½ cup finely chopped green bell peppers
5 large peeled garlic cloves, a scant ⅛ cup
2 tablespoons sugar
2 tablespoons pork lard (preferred) or chicken fat
¾ teaspoon salt
1½ teaspoons black pepper
½ teaspoon ground red pepper (preferably cayenne)
Hot **Basic Cooked Rice** (page 252) or **Crusty
    Houseboat Biscuits** (page 22), optional

Bring the 4 cups water to a boil in a 2-quart saucepan over high heat. Add the salt meat, cover pan with lid askew, and boil about 15 minutes. (If you use bacon, tasso, ham hocks, or andouille, omit this step.) Remove from heat and drain well.

Place the salt meat and *2 quarts* of the stock in a 5½-quart saucepan or large Dutch oven. Cover and bring to a boil over high heat; reduce heat and simmer about 15 minutes. Add the beans, cover pan, and return to high heat; bring to a boil, stirring once or twice so beans won't stick. Remove cover and continue boiling until hulls and centers of beans are very tender, about 1 hour and 30 minutes, stirring and scraping pan bottom frequently (more often toward end of cooking time) so beans won't scorch. **NOTE:** If they do scorch, change to a new pan without stirring.

Now add more stock or water, about *2 cups* at a time, as liquid evaporates to a level at which beans are not well covered and/or as liquid becomes thick and creamy like split pea soup. **NOTE:** You will need to add *10 to 14 cups* more stock, 2 cups at a time, every 10 to 25 minutes, depending on how fast evaporation occurs. This will vary according to the surface area of your pan and the heat of the stove's burner.

To finish, add *1 cup* more stock and the onions, bell peppers, garlic cloves, sugar, lard, salt, and black and red peppers. Bring to a boil, then reduce heat, and simmer until vegetables are tender, flavors marry, and sauce is creamy, about 45 minutes more, stirring and scraping pan bottom as needed. If mixture gets too thick, add more stock or water.

Remove from heat and mash the garlic cloves into the beans. Add salt, if desired, but taste with a bite of the salt meat first so you won't add too much. Serve immediately on plates or in bowls, spooning the beans over rice or biscuits, if desired, and making sure all servings get some of the salt meat. **NOTE**: Once the beans are removed from heat, they tend to thicken quickly; if needed, stir in more stock or water.

BOBBY'S RECIPE

Dried Pinto Beans with Andouille Smoked Sausage
(Fèves Caille Sèches avec Andouille)

Makes 6 main-dish servings

The family had dried beans several times a week as well as on weekends and holidays, according to Paul, who says they're a staple in Cajun homes. Bobby says he loves all the good starchy foods like pinto beans and red beans and lima beans. He serves them on rice "for lunch or dinner, in summer or winter." Although Bobby didn't ever cook with Mom Prudhomme, he says he learned the "taste" of her dishes at various stages when he ran by the stove and stuck his finger in the pot for a quick taste of whatever was cooking.

Bobby thinks andouille smoked sausage makes the best seasoning meat for dried beans; he likes it better than salt meat. In the early days when the family made andouille, it was strictly a seasoning meat made from the intestines of pigs—what's used today for natural sausage casings—and few people ate it. But today andouille is an intensely smoked, highly seasoned pure pork sausage that is absolutely wonderful! It still makes an excellent seasoning meat, but it's delicious baked or grilled and it makes a po boy that will "wow" you!

Bobby serves his delicious and hearty pinto beans with andouille over rice and just serves sliced garden tomatoes and fried or boiled okra on the side.

This dish is cooked for fairly long periods of time over high heat. If your gas burner or electric cooking element produces a very high heat, or if your pot is not a heavy one, you will need to adjust the temperature down.

1 pound dried pinto beans, soaked overnight and
    drained
About 4 quarts, *in all*, **Basic Pork Stock** (preferred;
    page 18) or water
1½ pounds andouille smoked sausage (preferred) or
    any other good smoked pure pork sausage, such
    as Polish sausage (kielbasa), cut into 6 pieces
1½ cups chopped onions
1 cup chopped green bell peppers
1 tablespoon sugar
2 teaspoons salt
1 teaspoon black pepper
1 teaspoon minced garlic
About 4½ cups hot **Basic Cooked Rice** (page 252)

In a heavy 5½-quart saucepan or large Dutch oven, combine the beans with *6 cups* of the stock. Cover pan, place over high heat, and bring to a boil, stirring occasionally so beans won't stick. Remove cover and continue boiling until the liquid barely covers the beans, about 35 minutes, stirring and scraping pan bottom frequently. Stir in *2 cups* more stock; cook until liquid has again reduced enough that some of the beans are not covered, about 20 minutes, stirring and scraping the pan bottom frequently so the beans won't scorch. **NOTE**: If they do scorch, do not stir; change to a new pan.

Continue adding stock *2 cups* at a time and then cooking about 20 minutes after each addition, until beans are very tender and don't taste starchy, stirring and scraping pan bottom frequently, especially toward the end of cooking time. **NOTE**: This will amount to about 1 hour more cooking time and you will need to add about *6 cups* more stock.

Now add *1 cup* more stock and the andouille, onions, bell peppers, sugar, salt, black pepper, and garlic. Bring to a boil, stirring frequently. Reduce heat and simmer until flavors marry, about 30 minutes more, stirring and scraping the pan bottom frequently so the beans won't scorch. If you like your beans more soupy, add about *1 cup* more stock during the last 10 or 15 minutes of cooking. Serve immediately.

To serve, allow about ¾ cup rice mounded in the center of a large plate, surrounded by about 1½ cups of the beans. Place a piece of sausage on top of each serving.

ABEL AND JO'S RECIPE

Red Beans with Salt Meat and Tasso
(Fèves Rouges avec Viande Salée et Tasso)

Makes 6 to 8 main-dish servings

Paul explains that "when I was growing up in Cajun country, red beans were just another dried bean, like pinto beans and lima beans—and Cajuns loved dried beans. But when I moved to New Orleans, I discovered that red beans were a cultural phenomenon, a tradition dating back for hundreds of years."

Red beans and rice is the traditional Monday meal in New Orleans. Monday was always washday and the family cook, or the lady of the house, could put on a pot of red beans to cook and then get on with her washing while the beans simmered for hours with little or no attention. When the washing was done, the beans were ready to eat.

In New Orleans, red beans are cooked with ham or smoked pork sausage, or both, and the dish is considered Creole, not Cajun. But as Louisiana food has grown in popularity throughout the country— with the focus on Cajun food—the distinctions between Cajun and Creole have almost vanished. "Classic" Creole red beans are now seasoned in a classic Cajun way, and in Cajun country, red beans are claimed as a good "traditional" Cajun dish. What they are, in fact, is a fine example of Louisiana cooking.

Red beans were the only beans the family bought; they raised their own limas, pintos, butter beans, and black-eyed peas. Abel and Jo season their red beans with salt pork and tasso. Tasso, known as Cajun ham, is lean strips of intensely smoked, wonderfully seasoned pork that is popular as a seasoning meat in Southeast Louisiana. The tasso the family made was almost like beef jerky, and it was an excellent seasoning meat for robust dishes like dried beans and gumbos. The tasso of today, however, is often a sophisticated smoked ham that can be used in light cream sauces as well as in heartier dishes.

This dish is cooked for fairly long periods of time over high heat. If your gas burner or electric cooking element produces a very high heat, or if your pot is not a heavy one, you will need to adjust the temperature down.

1 pound dried red kidney beans
Water to cover the beans
¾ pound salt pork (with as much lean as possible),
    cut into 1-inch squares about ½ inch thick
    (preferred), or coarsely chopped bacon, or a
    good-quality smoked pure pork sausage, such as
    andouille or Polish sausage (kielbasa)
4 cups water
About 5 quarts, *in all*, **Basic Chicken Stock**
    (preferred; page 18) or water
¾ pound tasso (preferred) or other smoked ham
    (preferably Cure 81), cut into ½-inch cubes
2½ cups finely chopped onions
1½ cups finely chopped green bell peppers
1 cup finely chopped celery
1 teaspoon minced garlic
1 cup finely chopped green onions (tops and
    bottoms)
¼ cup chopped fresh parsley
Salt to taste
About 6 cups hot **Basic Cooked Rice** (page 252)

Cover the beans with water at least 3 inches above the beans; soak overnight. Drain.

Place the salt pork in a 2-quart saucepan with the 4 cups water. Place over high heat and bring to a boil. (If you use bacon or sausage, omit this step.) Reduce heat to maintain a strong simmer and cook about 15 minutes. Remove from heat, drain well, and set aside.

In a heavy 5½-quart saucepan or large Dutch oven, combine the beans with *7 cups* of the stock. Place over high heat and bring to a boil, stirring frequently and scraping pan bottom well so the beans won't stick. Continue boiling until the liquid barely covers the beans, about 25 minutes, stirring and scraping frequently so beans won't scorch. **NOTE**: If they do scorch, change to a new pan without stirring.

Stir in *2 cups* more stock and return to a boil, stirring frequently. Continue boiling until liquid has again reduced enough that it barely covers the beans, about 15 minutes, stirring and scraping pan bottom frequently. Add *2 cups* more stock; cook and stir about 15 minutes. Add *3 cups* more stock; cook and stir until beans (both centers and hulls) are very tender and don't taste starchy, 30 to 40 minutes. **NOTE**: If beans require longer cooking to tenderize them, continue adding stock or water as needed, 1 to 2 cups at a time.

Now stir in *2 cups* more stock and add the tasso, onions, bell peppers, celery, and garlic. Return to a boil and cook about 10 minutes, stirring occasionally. Add the reserved salt pork (or the bacon or sausage) and continue cooking over high heat about 15 minutes, stirring occasionally. Reduce heat to a simmer and cook until flavors marry, about 30 minutes, stirring and scraping pan bottom frequently.

Finally, stir in the green onions and parsley and add more stock or water if you want the beans juicier; continue cooking about 10 minutes more, stirring frequently and being careful not to let the beans scorch. Remove from heat and add salt, if needed. (But remember, if you eat the salt pork with the beans, the dish will taste saltier.) Serve immediately.

To serve, allow about ¾ cup rice mounded in the center of a large plate, surrounded by about 1½ cups of red beans, salt pork, and tasso.

SALADS

SALADES

RALPH AND MARY ANN'S RECIPE

Okra Salad
(Salade de Gombo Févi)

Makes 4 to 6 side-dish servings

Ralph says that both Dad and Mom were outgoing and friendly, they had lots of friends, and they visited back and forth really often. One of Ralph's favorite memories of Dad is riding with him to the forest in the mule-drawn wagon to get firewood. Dad liked to stop along the road to talk to people they met on the way home. He'd just stop the mules and start talking. The male was a big white mule named Tom, and Liza, the female, was red. But when these two were hitched to the wagon, Dad couldn't talk for long because Liza would kick the wagon when he made her stop. Pretty soon he'd have to say, "Tonnerre, mais faudra on gone!" ("Thunder, we have to go!") Ralph says he always wanted to get on home, so if the mule didn't kick, he'd tell her, "Come on, Liza—kick!"

Ralph and Mary Ann make okra salad just like Mom did. She made it often when okra was fresh in the garden during the summer. The okra in this salad is slippery—but delicious!

¾ pound untrimmed fresh okra, about 1 quart
Water to cover okra
1 cup thinly sliced onions, separated into rings
¼ cup plus 2 tablespoons vegetable oil
¼ cup white vinegar
About ¾ teaspoon salt, *in all*
About ¾ teaspoon black pepper, *in all*

Place the okra in a 2-quart saucepan and cover with water. Bring to a boil over high heat, then continue boiling about 5 minutes, stirring occasionally. Cover pan, remove from heat, and let sit about 5 minutes. Drain in a colander, then rinse with cool tap water, tossing gently so okra will cool thoroughly and being careful to keep pods intact. Drain well.

Place okra in a medium-size bowl. Add the onions, oil, vinegar, and ½ *teaspoon each* of the salt and pepper; mix gently to coat okra and onion rings well. Let sit about 15 minutes to let flavors marry. Sprinkle on a little additional salt and pepper just before serving.

RALPH AND MARY ANN'S RECIPE

Warm Beet Salad
(Salade de Betterave Chaude)

Makes 8 side-dish servings

Ralph loves to tell stories about the family while he was growing up. He didn't really leave home until he went into the navy. When he came back, he lived at home again for a time, so he has lots of stories to tell. Once, when he and a group of friends, including one or two brothers, were walking into town to go to a dance, a skunk sprayed the air near them. It wasn't a direct hit, so the guys kept on walking, which wasn't too smart. When they got to the dance, everyone got this huge whiff of skunk scent. The party was over for them before it began; they all had to turn around and head for home.

Dad Prudhomme grew beets in the garden, and what Paul remembers best about beets is that they were wonderful when fresh and horrible if canned. (He was served canned ones at public school.) The family always grew onions, too, but only green onions. When Mom made beet salad, she used the white part of the green onions, which makes slices that look like slices of pearl onions. You might want to try this for a variation of Ralph and Mary Ann's beet salad; the taste of the salad as well as the look will change somewhat.

This is a fresh, light salad that Ralph and Mary Ann always serve warm.

319

2½ pounds young beets, trimmed (but not peeled),
　　and rinsed well
Water to cover beets
⅓ cup sugar
⅓ cup white vinegar
1 tablespoon vegetable oil
1½ cups thinly sliced onions, separated into rings
1¾ teaspoons salt
¼ teaspoon black pepper

Place the beets in a 4-quart saucepan and cover with water; cover pan and bring to a boil over high heat. Place lid askew, reduce heat if necessary to keep from boiling over, and continue boiling until beets are tender, about 30 minutes. Remove from heat and drain in a colander; let sit in cool tap water until cool enough to handle, then drain well, peel, and slice ¼ inch thick. Place slices in a large serving bowl and set aside.

In an 8-inch skillet, combine the sugar, vinegar, and oil. Place over high heat and cook about 2 minutes, stirring constantly. Add the remaining ingredients; cook until onions are tender but still quite firm and some of the liquid has evaporated, about 4 minutes, stirring frequently. Remove from heat and pour mixture over the beets, stirring gently to mix well. Serve immediately.

ALLIE AND ETELL'S RECIPE

Carrot, Apple and Raisin Salad
(Salade de Carotte, Pomme et Raisin)

Makes 6 side-dish servings

Allie says the family always had carrots in the garden. Mom usually cooked them in stews, or she smothered them, or served them raw. Carrot salad, though, was a holiday dish.

Allie believes strongly in the work ethic. She believes God put every-one on this earth for some reason, and she believes he put her here to work. When she was six years old, she began to help Mom at home, and before she was a teenager she spent long periods of time with Mom's mother and two of her aunts helping them take care of babies and cook and clean. She says that even today, with only Etell and her at home, she's still a compulsive worker. But she has learned to relax and have a good time. She's great fun to be around—always so happy and outgoing.

Allie loves this carrot salad; it's an excellent side dish to serve with rich Cajun food. For a nice variation, use a crunchy, tangy green apple, like a Granny Smith, and use sweet baby carrots and golden seedless raisins.

2½ cups unpeeled and grated red Delicious apples
2½ cups grated carrots
½ cup seedless raisins
¾ cup **Seasoned Mayonnaise** (page 334)

Combine all ingredients in a large bowl, mixing well. Cover and re-frigerate until well chilled, about 2 hours.

ENOLA AND SHELTON'S RECIPE

Coleslaw
(Choucroute)

Makes 8 to 10 side-dish servings

Enola says that by the time she came along the family was well into the modern world. They had a washing machine that ran on gasoline and started with a foot pedal like a motorcycle, and they had a coal-oil refrigerator. But they still lived off the land, growing virtually all their own food. They had a year-round garden and, in the fall and winter, when there was fresh cabbage, Enola says coleslaw was a favorite, though it wasn't a staple like potato salad.

Mom made coleslaw using only the ingredients she had on hand—cabbage, carrots, vinegar, salt and pepper. Enola says the family never bought apples except at Christmas, and raisins were bought only for **Mom's Dry Fruit Cake** *(page 419). But Enola loves to add lots of ingredients to her coleslaw, and she often serves it as a side dish at her restaurant.*

3 cups finely shredded cabbage (combination of
    purple and green preferred)
2 cups chopped red apples (cored but not peeled)
2 cups grated carrots
1 cup plus 2 tablespoons **Basic Homemade
    Mayonnaise** (page 332)
½ cup seedless raisins
2 tablespoons finely chopped onions
2 tablespoons finely chopped green onions (tops only)
½ teaspoon salt
½ teaspoon black pepper

Combine all the ingredients in a large bowl, mixing well. Cover and refrigerate until well chilled, about 2 hours.

BOBBY'S RECIPE

Bobby's Sweet Pea Salad
(Salade de Petits Pois)

Makes 4 side-dish servings

The family grew green peas in their winter garden, and Mom always cooked them with a little sugar. They always used the peas fresh; they just never could grow enough of them to can them. Mom didn't make sweet pea salad; J.C. and Sis say it was their daughter Pat who introduced the family to pea salad.

Bobby's recipe is quite different from Calvin and Marie's (see next recipe), so we've given you both. Crisp crackers taste great with this salad.

5 cups water, to cook fresh peas

2¼ pounds unshelled fresh green peas, a generous 3 cups shelled (preferred); or 1 (17-ounce) can small sweet peas, well drained

1 tablespoon sugar, to cook fresh peas

1 cup finely chopped red onions

2 hard-boiled eggs, chopped

½ cup **Seasoned Mayonnaise** (page 334)

1 teaspoon salt

1 teaspoon black pepper

If using fresh peas, bring 5 cups of water to a boil in a 2-quart saucepan. Add the peas and sugar. Cover and return to a boil. Reduce heat, remove lid, and simmer until peas are tender but still firm, about 11 minutes. Remove from heat and immediately drain in a colander. Let cool about 10 minutes.

If using canned peas, do not cook.

Combine all the ingredients in a medium-size bowl, mixing well. Serve warm; or refrigerate until well chilled, at least 2 hours, before serving.

CALVIN AND MARIE'S RECIPE

Calvin and Marie's Sweet Pea Salad
(Salade de Petits Pois)

Makes 4 side-dish servings

Calvin says he just has to have a little garden—he loves to work in it, and he and Marie love to cook and eat the fresh vegetables. After

Calvin and Marie married, they often went to visit the family, and by the time Paul was about nine years old and Calvin and Marie were living in the country, they would take Paul back home with them to spend a week every now and then. Marie loved to cook his favorite dishes for him.

Calvin and Marie serve their sweet pea salad alongside rich dishes and meat, and rice and gravy. Their original recipe called for canned small peas, but fresh peas of any size are even better. This sweet pea salad is quite different from Bobby's (see preceding recipe), so we've given you both.

2¼ pounds unshelled fresh green peas (generous 3
    cups shelled), or 1 (17-ounce) can small sweet
    peas, well drained
5 cups water, to cook fresh peas
1 tablespoon sugar, to cook fresh peas
¾ cup plus 2 tablespoons **Basic Homemade**
    Mayonnaise (page 332)
½ cup very finely chopped onions
⅓ cup very finely chopped celery
¼ cup very finely chopped green bell peppers
¼ cup very finely chopped sweet gherkin pickles
¼ cup very finely chopped green olives stuffed with pimentos
1½ teaspoons salt
½ teaspoon black pepper
¼ teaspoon ground red pepper (preferably cayenne)
2 hard-boiled eggs, thinly sliced

If using fresh peas, bring 5 cups of water to a boil in a 2-quart saucepan. Add the shelled peas and sugar; cover and return to a boil. Reduce heat and simmer uncovered until peas are tender but still firm, about 11 minutes. Remove from heat and drain immediately in a colander; let cool 10 minutes.

If using canned peas, do not cook.

In a medium-size bowl, combine the peas with all the remaining ingredients except the eggs, mixing thoroughly. Add the eggs and stir gently so egg slices won't break up. Refrigerate until well chilled, at least 2 hours, before serving.

Cajun Macaroni Salad
(Salade de Macaroni)

Makes 6 to 8 side-dish servings

Bobby never cooked with Mom Prudhomme; he was strictly an out-door kid. He was ill quite often with asthma and pneumonia when he was very young, so when he finally outgrew those early illnesses, he spent every waking moment outdoors. What Paul remembers most about Bobby is that he was always in motion; he wanted to be the fastest at everything—eating, working, doing schoolwork. And he loved to work with the animals—feeding them, driving the mules, helping take care of newborn animals.

Bobby says that even though he didn't cook with Mom, he watched her cook and learned most of what he knows about cooking from her anyway. He cooks his meats and vegetables the way she did. Macaroni salad is kind of a new dish for the family. Mom usually baked macaroni and she didn't use it in salads. Bob's macaroni salad is similar to her potato salad, though he actually learned how to make it from his son, Wesley. The original recipe calls for regular mayonnaise, but we've given it extra spice by using Ground Hot Pepper Vinegar Mayonnaise.

Bobby serves his macaroni salad well chilled, and he says to serve it with anything that would taste good with potato salad. You will need to make the Ground Hot Pepper Vinegar Mayonnaise (add the optional sugar) at least two days ahead to give it time to mellow properly.

2 quarts water
3 cups 1-inch long shell macaroni (about 7 ounces)
1 recipe **Ground Hot Pepper Vinegar Mayonnaise**
    (page 335; see **NOTE**)
½ cup plus 2 tablespoons very finely chopped red onions
½ cup plus 2 tablespoons very finely chopped green bell peppers

3 hard-boiled eggs, chopped
¾ teaspoon black pepper
½ teaspoon salt

Note: Be sure to add the optional sugar.

Place the water in a 3-quart saucepan and bring to a rapid boil over high heat. Add the macaroni, stirring well, and cook just until tender, about 10 minutes, stirring occasionally. Immediately drain macaroni in a colander. Rinse first with hot water to wash off the starch, then rinse well with cold water to stop the cooking. Rinse until cool to the touch, then drain well.

   In a large bowl, combine the macaroni with the remaining ingredients, mixing thoroughly. Serve immediately, or refrigerate and serve well chilled. **Note:** If the ground hot peppers in the mayonnaise are mild, you may want to mix more peppers into the salad, but not more vinegar.

DARILEE AND SAUL'S RECIPE

Creamy Hard-Boiled Egg Potato Salad
(Salade Crèmeuse de Patate Anglaise et Oeuf Bouilli)

Makes 8 to 10 side-dish servings

In 1984, Darilee won first place with this recipe in a cooking competition at the Washington, Louisiana, "May Festival." Darilee learned to make potato salad from Saul's mother. She taught both Mom Prudhomme and Paul how to make the hard-boiled egg mayonnaise she uses in her own potato salad. It makes a really nice side dish, and it makes a wonderful sandwich, too. (Cajuns like potato sandwiches!) Darilee serves her salad while it's still warm, but it's terrific any way you serve it.

2 pounds red potatoes, peeled and cut into ¾-inch
    cubes
4 hard-boiled eggs, halved and yolks separated from
    whites
1 recipe **Hard-Boiled Egg Mayonnaise** (page 333)
2 tablespoons warm water
1 tablespoon plus 1 teaspoon prepared mustard
1½ teaspoons salt
1½ teaspoons black pepper
½ cup finely chopped onions
¼ cup finely chopped green bell peppers

Boil the potatoes until tender.

Meanwhile, place the egg yolks in a medium-size bowl and mash well. Add the mayonnaise, water, mustard, salt, and pepper, mixing well. Set aside. Finely chop the egg whites and set aside.

When potatoes are cooked, drain them well and place in a large bowl while still hot. Add the onions, bell peppers, egg whites, and mayonnaise mixture, mixing well and breaking up some of the potatoes so the finished salad will be creamy textured with some lumps in it. Serve immediately.

ABEL AND JO'S RECIPE

Sweet and Seasoned Potato Salad
(Salade Douce et Assaisonnée de Patate Anglaise)

Makes 8 to 10 side-dish servings

Potato salad was a Sunday and a special-occasion dish. During the week, Mom usually smothered or mashed potatoes, or cooked them in stews. Potato salad meant homemade mayonnaise, which everybody loved. Abel and Jo serve their potato salad warm, but it's great cold, too. It has a rich, light yellow-orange color and tastes quite different from Darilee and Saul's (see preceding recipe), so try them both.

Jo's mother had her own variation of potato salad. She boiled potatoes and beets together, which made the potatoes red. Then, while the potatoes and beets were still hot, she diced them and added onions (which had been sautéed in pork lard) and vinegar, salt, and black pepper. We think this would make a pretty Christmas salad, especially if you added bright green chopped bell peppers and/or pickle relish.

2 pounds red potatoes, peeled and cut into ¾-inch
    cubes
4 hard-boiled eggs, chopped
¼ cup (not too well drained) sweet pickle relish
1 teaspoon prepared mustard
1 teaspoon salt
½ teaspoon ground red pepper (preferably cayenne)
¼ teaspoon black pepper
2 cups **Seasoned Mayonnaise** (page 334)

Boil the potatoes until tender. Drain well and, while still hot, place in a large bowl. Add the remaining ingredients and mix well. Serve warm.

MAYONNAISES, SAUCES & GRAVIES

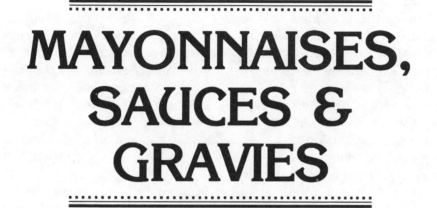

MAYONNAISES ET SAUCES

ALLIE AND ETELL'S RECIPE

Basic Homemade Mayonnaise

Makes about 2½ cups

While the family thinks of Darilee as the mayonnaise maker of the family, Allie and Paul say everyone else took their turns, too. Since Darilee was the one who took care of her younger brothers and sisters for Mom Prudhomme, sitting down and stirring together the mayonnaise was a welcome respite for her. Allie says the women in the family sat together and talked on Sunday mornings while they made mayonnaise. They made it every Sunday, and for holidays and family gatherings, to use in potato salad. It was a special-occasion food and everyone looked forward to it. Allie says she will always associate homemade mayonnaise with the good talks the women had together on those early Sunday mornings.

The family had fresh eggs from the yard hens they raised, and if you've ever been fortunate enough to have a good country, brown egg, you know that the yolk is a deep orange, not the pale yellow of eggs we buy in supermarkets. So the homemade mayonnaise they made was a beautiful, rich deep yellow-orange.

Allie's basic mayonnaise is lemony delicious, just great in potato salads (pages 326 and 327). It's easy to make by hand if you have a helper to take turns stirring with you. Or you can make it in a food processor. (We found it difficult to make this one come together right using an electric blender.) The handmade version yields about a quarter cup less than the machine-made, but it has a deeper, better flavor, so we recommend it.

4 large to extra-large egg yolks
2 cups corn oil (preferred) or other vegetable oil
1 tablespoon plus 1½ teaspoons lemon juice
2 teaspoons white vinegar
½ teaspoon plus a pinch of salt
¼ teaspoon black pepper
3 tablespoons water, if using a food processor

To make by hand: In a large bowl, beat the egg yolks vigorously with a metal whisk until very frothy, about 45 seconds. Very gradually add *1 cup* of the oil, 2 to 3 tablespoons at a time, whisking until oil is incorporated before adding more. Whisk in the lemon juice, vinegar, salt, and pepper, then very gradually add the remaining *1 cup* oil. Refrigerate at least 30 minutes before serving. Makes 2⅓ cups.

To make in a food processor: Place the egg yolks, lemon juice, vinegar, and the 3 tablespoons water in a food processor and blend about 30 seconds. With the machine still running, gradually add the oil in a thin steady stream. When the mixture becomes thick and creamy, add the salt and pepper, and process until mixture is well blended, about 1 minute, pushing the sides down once or twice with a rubber spatula. Refrigerate at least 30 minutes before serving. Makes a generous 2½ cups.

DARILEE AND SAUL'S RECIPE

Hard-Boiled Egg Mayonnaise
(Mayonnaise d'Oeuf Bouilli)

Makes 1¼ cups

Saul's family taught Darilee how to make this different mayonnaise, and she in turn taught both Mom Prudhomme and Paul. Mom used mayonnaise only in potato salad. She always made it first without salt and pepper, then added the salt and pepper to the salad after the mayonnaise was stirred in.

If you don't usually make homemade mayonnaise, you must treat yourself to a batch. And then it's difficult to settle for store-bought; there is no comparison. You can make wonderful variations by adding stock or seafood or special vinegars or seasonings.

It's fun and quite fast to make this by hand, especially if you have someone who will take turns with you on the stirring. Darilee says you have to remember to "stir fast-fast!" to keep the mayonnaise from getting too thick.

3 hard-boiled egg yolks, still warm
1 raw egg yolk
1 tablespoon white vinegar
1 cup vegetable oil

In a large mixing bowl, mash the cooked yolks very well with a fork. Add the raw yolk and vinegar and beat with a metal whisk or large spoon for a few seconds until very creamy. Gradually add the oil in a thin steady stream, whisking constantly or stirring briskly and making sure all the oil is incorporated before adding more. Refrigerate for at least 30 minutes before serving.

PAUL AND K'S RECIPE

Seasoned Mayonnaise

Makes about 2½ cups

This mayonnaise isn't hot; it's an all-purpose mayonnaise with a nice little zing! Try it in **Sweet and Seasoned Potato Salad** *(page 327) and in* **Bobby's Sweet Pea Salad** *(page 322).*

3 egg yolks
1 egg
1 tablespoon white vinegar
1 tablespoon lemon juice
1 teaspoon salt
1 teaspoon dry mustard
1 teaspoon ground red pepper (preferably cayenne)
2 cups vegetable oil

Place all the ingredients except the oil in a food processor and process about 30 seconds. With the machine still running, gradually add the oil in a thin steady stream; blend until well mixed, pushing sides down once or twice with a rubber spatula. Refrigerate for at least 30 minutes before serving.

PAUL AND K'S RECIPE

Ground Hot Pepper Vinegar Mayonnaise

Makes about 1⅔ cups

This mayonnaise is wonderful from the moment it's made, but it's even better if allowed to mellow for three or four days. Be sure to add the sugar if you're serving it with **Cajun Fried Crawfish** *(page 56) or in* **Cajun Macaroni Salad** *(page 325). It also wakes up "slow sandwiches" and "pale po boys."*

3 tablespoons **Ground Hot Pepper Vinegar** (page
   357); use half peppers, half vinegar (see **NOTE**)
1 egg
2 tablespoons finely chopped onions
1 tablespoon sugar, optional
¾ teaspoon salt
1½ cups vegetable oil

NOTE: If your Ground Hot Pepper Vinegar is very hot, use your own judgment on how much of the peppers to use, but do not cut down on the amount of vinegar.

Place all the ingredients except the oil in an electric blender and blend a few seconds. With machine still running, add the oil in a thin steady stream; blend thoroughly. Refrigerate for several hours before using, preferably 3 to 4 days. This will keep for up to 3 weeks refrigerated.

CALVIN AND MARIE'S RECIPE

Barbecue Sauce
(Sauce de Barbaqueue)

Makes from 3½ to 7 cups

When the older children were still youngsters, Mom and Dad would invite family and friends over and they barbecued the old-fashioned country way: The men went to the woods and dug a pit in the ground. They placed wood in the pit and burned it to make coals—and they also put in green wood and continued to add it throughout the barbecue to make smoke. When the coals were ready, they placed chicken wire above the coals and put the prepared meat on the wire to cook.

Because they barbecued only for special occasions—especially New Year's Day—there were always about thirty-five people present. So Dad would cook a side of beef, a small hog, and a goat or sheep. He prepared the meat by stuffing it with seasoning vegetables and spices and rubbing seasonings all over the surface. Then he put the seasoned meats in gunnysacks or grass sacks that had been thoroughly washed and dipped in barbecue sauce. He wrapped wire around the sacks before placing them in the pit on the grill.

Later, when the family had grown quite large and several of the oldest children were married and had children of their own, the family would meet for New Year's Day and family reunions in the park in Opelousas, and Dad used conventional barbecue pits to cook the meat, usually a goat and several chickens. Dad preferred to make his own barbecue sauce; he usually used onions, bell peppers, garlic, a little vinegar and sugar, but the ingredients varied depending on what there was at home at the time—because you didn't just run out to the store the way we do today.

Calvin remembers gathering at Mom's parents' home to kill a calf to barbecue. Everyone was there—extended family and lots of friends. He says that back then people only barbecued on really special occasions like New Year's Day, the Fourth of July, and weddings. Now barbecues are almost routine, on weekends and even weekdays.

Calvin began making his own barbecue sauce because the store-bought ones just weren't like the barbecue sauce he remembers from home. He usually makes it in great quantity and puts it up in bottles to use throughout the year. His sauce is a lovely blend of hot, sweet, and sour, and it can be used for barbecuing chicken, hamburgers, ribs, chops, or other cuts of pork or beef (Calvin's favorite is pork). And it's good brushed on meats before they are roasted or baked.

Calvin uses the oil that rises to the top of the sauce to baste the meat as it cooks. When it is done or just short of done, he transfers the meat to a heavy saucepan, covers it with the rich sauce, then covers the pan and lets it sit about 20 minutes before serving.

The yield of the recipe varies from about 3½ to 7 cups, depending on how long and hard you boil the sauce.

We've given you a delicious **Lagniappe:** Malcolm and Versie's method for seasoning chicken for grilling or barbecuing.

1 medium-size lemon, washed well, cut in quarters,
    and seeded
Heaping 2 cups finely chopped onions
2 (8-ounce) cans tomato sauce
2 cups vegetable oil
Heaping 1 cup finely chopped green bell peppers
1 cup catsup
⅔ cup Worcestershire sauce
Heaping ½ cup finely chopped celery
¼ cup finely chopped garlic
¼ cup prepared mustard
4 tablespoons unsalted butter
1 tablespoon plus 1 teaspoon ground red pepper
    (preferably cayenne)
2½ teaspoons salt
½ teaspoon black pepper

Mince the lemon finely by hand or in a blender or food processor. Place the processed lemon and the remaining ingredients in a heavy 12-quart saucepan. (Be sure to use a very large pan so the sauce won't spatter the stove and the kitchen.) Place the mixture over high heat and bring to a rolling, spattering boil, stirring occasionally. Continue boiling about 10 minutes, stirring frequently and scraping pan bottom well so mixture doesn't scorch.

Reduce heat to maintain a simmer (mixture should still be spattering, with lots of small bubbles on the surface). Cook about 20 minutes more to let the flavors marry, or until the oil is dark red. The mixture should leave a very fine layer of sediment on the bottom of the pan that can be easily scraped off; stir and scrape the pan bottom almost constantly. (Don't be surprised—the oil will continuously separate out of the mixture.) Remove from heat and use immediately, or let cool and refrigerate until ready to use.

· · · · · · · · · · · · · · ·**LAGNIAPPE**· · · · · · · · · · · · · · ·

Malcolm and Versie's excellent Cajun grilled chicken is a bonus recipe for using the barbecue sauce.

Malcolm is the only one of the Prudhomme boys who doesn't love to cook; he limits his cooking to grilling and smoking meats outdoors. His grilled chicken is peppery hot and really delicious and is extra special basted with the oil that collects on top of the barbecue sauce. Serve the hot sauce along with the grilled chicken.

Malcolm cuts three (4- to 4½-pound) fryers in half and pats on a seasoning mixture made of ¼ cup salt, 2 tablespoons ground red pepper (preferably cayenne), and 2 teaspoons garlic powder. Then he seals the chickens in a closed container or plastic bags and refrigerates them for one to two days before grilling, with the grill lid *closed.* He usually bastes the chickens with a generous amount of melted margarine, but the oil that forms on top of the barbecue sauce is great for basting (or you can use a milder mixture of the oil and margarine).

PAUL AND K'S RECIPE

Béarnaise Sauce

Makes about 2 cups

Use this rich but wonderfully light sauce on top of **Chicken Chartres** *(page 90) or with broiled, baked, or fried chicken, seafood, veal, beef, or pork. And it's really special to use over poached eggs for a brunch dish.*

1 pound unsalted butter
6 tablespoons margarine
3 tablespoons plus 2 teaspoons white wine, *in all*
1 teaspoon dried tarragon leaves
¼ teaspoon salt
⅛ teaspoon ground red pepper (preferably cayenne)
4 egg yolks
2½ teaspoons lemon juice
1 teaspoon Tabasco sauce
1 teaspoon Worcestershire sauce

Melt the butter and margarine in a 1-quart saucepan over low heat. Raise heat and bring to a rapid boil. Remove from heat and cool about 5 minutes. Skim froth from the top and discard. Pour butter into a large glass measuring cup and set aside.

In a separate 1-quart saucepan, combine *3 tablespoons* of the wine, the tarragon, salt, and pepper. Cook over high heat until most of the liquid has evaporated, about 2 minutes, stirring occasionally. Let cool about 5 minutes.

In a medium-size stainless-steel mixing bowl or the top of a double boiler, combine the remaining 2 *teaspoons* wine, the cooled tarragon mixture, and all the remaining ingredients except the butter mixture. Mix together with a metal whisk until frothy, about 1 minute.

Place bowl over a pan of slowly simmering, not boiling, water. (Bowl must never touch the water.) Vigorously whisk egg mixture, picking up the bowl frequently to let the steam escape; whip until the egg mixture is very light and creamy and has a sheen, 5 to 7 minutes. (This amount of beating is important so that the cooked eggs will better be able to hold the butter.) Remove bowl from the pan of hot water. Gradually ladle about ¼ cup of the butter mixture (use the top butterfat, not the butter solids on the bottom) into the egg mixture while vigorously whipping the sauce. Make sure the butter you add is well mixed into the sauce before adding more. Continue gradually adding the surface butterfat until you've added about 1 cup.

So that you can get to the butter solids, ladle out and reserve about ½ cup surface butterfat in a separate container. (The butter solids add flavor and also thin the sauce.) Gradually ladle all but ⅓ cup of the bottom solids into the sauce, whisking well. (Use any remaining bottom solids in another dish.) Then gradually whisk in enough of the reserved top butterfat to produce a fairly thick sauce. The butterfat thickens the sauce, so you may not need to use it all. Keep the sauce in a warm place until ready to serve.

ELI AND SUE'S RECIPE

Poorman's Gravy

Makes 3½ to 4 cups

Eli says Ralph is the storyteller in the family, but that he usually tells stories about everyone but himself. So Eli thought we should hear a good story about Ralph. When Ralph came back from the navy, he moved back home with the family. Eli was about thirteen at the time. One day, when Mom and Dad Prudhomme were away and Eli and Bobby and several friends were playing at home, they all decided they wanted something to eat. And Ralph could cook; they knew he loved to cook. So the boys woke Ralph up in midafternoon (he'd been out really late the night before) and asked him to make them some pan-

cakes. Ralph got up and started making pancakes, and the boys all sat down and ate their fill of them, with homemade butter and syrup. When they'd had enough, they got up from the table. But Ralph was still making pancakes and he told them, "Oh, no! You woke me up to make pancakes, and now you're going to eat every single pancake I cook." And they did! And they never woke him up again to cook for them. Mom never understood why they were all feeling pretty bad that night and didn't want anything to eat for supper.

This recipe of Eli and Sue's for gravy is unusually simple and little work is required, which Sue really appreciated when we asked her for it. She had minced so many seasoning vegetables in preparation for cooking for the cookbook—and had helped Elden and Odelia Mae with mincing vegetables for their recipes (just as Odelia Mae helped Eli and Sue)—that, Eli says, Sue woke him up in the middle of the night talking in her sleep about chopping seasonings!

Mom made poorman's gravy—the family called it roux gravy— often at noon to serve over rice and potatoes. Eli and Sue also like to serve it over biscuits, and it's excellent over their **Bell Peppers Stuffed with Rice Dressing** *(page 259). This is a good country gravy that tastes best if you use a rich stock that's been made with well-browned chicken bones, but the family always made it with water, not stock.*

6 tablespoons chicken fat or pork lard (preferred) or
    vegetable oil
½ cup plus 3 tablespoons all-purpose flour
1 cup chopped green onions (tops only)
4 cups hot **Rich Chicken Stock** (preferred; page 19)
    or water
1 teaspoon salt
¾ teaspoon black pepper

Have a wooden spoon handy even if you're using a metal whisk to make the roux, just in case you need to switch to it quickly to stir.

In a 2-quart cast-iron Dutch oven, heat the fat over high heat about 1 minute. Gradually stir the flour into the hot oil. Cook, whisking constantly or stirring briskly, until roux is medium brown, about 5 minutes, being careful not to let it scorch or splash on your skin. Remove from heat and continue whisking or stirring about 1 minute.

✳See page 12 for more about making roux.

Add the green onions, whisking a few seconds, then slowly whisk in the stock (it will steam up), then the salt and pepper and continue stirring until smooth. Place over high heat and bring to a boil, stirring once or twice. Reduce heat and simmer about 15 minutes, stirring occasionally. Remove from heat and serve immediately.

PAUL AND K'S RECIPE

Sweet-Potato Eggplant Gravy

Makes about 6 cups

This gravy is delicious on **Turducken** *(page 109) or other baked or roasted fowl. It is cooked for fairly long periods of time over high heat; if your gas burner or electric cooking element produces a very high heat, or if your pot is not a heavy one, you will need to adjust the temperature down.*

Seasoning Mix:
1 tablespoon salt
1 tablespoon white pepper
1 tablespoon ground red pepper (preferably cayenne)
2 teaspoons dry mustard
1 teaspoon dried thyme leaves

1 cup chicken fat or vegetable oil (see **Note**)
8 cups, *in all*, peeled and chopped eggplant, about
    1¾ pounds
3 cups chopped onions
2 cups peeled and *finely* chopped sweet potatoes
2 teaspoons minced garlic
2 bay leaves

4 quarts, *in all*, **Basic Chicken Stock** (page 18; see
    Note)
1 cup, packed, dark brown sugar, *in all*
2 cups peeled and chopped sweet potatoes
2 tablespoons Grand Marnier
1 cup finely chopped green onions (tops only)

Note: If you are making the gravy to serve on Turducken, substitute
1 cup drippings from the Turducken, plus excess duck skin from
boning the duck (see **Turducken** recipe, page 113) for the 1 cup
chicken fat or vegetable oil. If you're also making all the dressings
for the Turducken yourself, you may want to make the large-yield
stock recipe (page 115).

Combine the seasoning mix ingredients thoroughly in a small bowl,
breaking up any lumps.

    Place the chicken fat or vegetable oil (or drippings and duck skin
from the Turducken) in a 5½-quart saucepan or large Dutch oven
over high heat. Add *6 cups* of the eggplant and sauté until eggplant
starts to get soft, translucent, and brown, about 5 minutes, stirring
and scraping pan bottom occasionally. Add the onions and the remaining *2 cups* eggplant, stirring until pan bottom is clean of sediment. Cook until the mixture starts to turn brown from all the
sediment scraped into it, 10 to 12 minutes, still stirring and scraping
pan bottom frequently.

    Add the 2 cups finely chopped sweet potatoes; continue cooking
about 4 minutes, stirring and scraping pan bottom almost constantly. Stir in the garlic, bay leaves, and *3 tablespoons* of the seasoning mix; stir well, scraping pan bottom if needed.

    Stir in *2 cups* of the stock and cook about 2 minutes, scraping
pan bottom clean. Add *2 cups* more stock; cook about 5 minutes,
stirring occasionally and scraping pan bottom well each time. Stir in
½ *cup* of the brown sugar and cook about 2 minutes, stirring and
scraping occasionally. Add another *2 cups* stock and cook about 10
minutes, stirring occasionally. (**Note:** The continuous addition of
small amounts of stock yields a richer gravy than if you added all the
stock at once. This is because the smaller amounts evaporate more
quickly and you get a better reduction.) Add the remaining ½ *cup*
brown sugar and *2 cups* more stock; cook about 10 minutes, stirring

occasionally. Add another 2 *cups* stock and cook about 15 minutes more, stirring occasionally. Now reduce heat to low and simmer about 15 minutes. Stir in another 2 *cups* stock and simmer about 5 minutes more.

Remove from heat and strain well, forcing as much liquid as possible through the strainer. Place the strained gravy in a 4-quart saucepan. Add the 2 cups chopped sweet potatoes and 2 *cups* of the stock; bring to a boil over high heat, then reduce heat and simmer about 1 hour, skimming off any froth and fat as it develops.

Next, stir in the Grand Marnier and continue simmering about 10 minutes, stirring occasionally. Add the green onions, *1 teaspoon* more seasoning mix, and the remaining 2 *cups* stock. (Use remaining seasoning mix in another recipe.) Bring gravy to a boil over high heat, then reduce heat, and simmer until the gravy reduces to about 6 cups, about 25 minutes more, stirring occasionally.

CANNED & PICKLED FOODS

MANGER ENCAINÉ ET CORNICHONS

Home Canning Notes

You'll find home canning is quite easy and very rewarding, but it does require very careful attention to cleanliness and moving quickly every step along the way to avoid any sources of contamination. Follow these guidelines closely and you'll be thrilled with your new talent and the results of your labor!

In making these canning recipes, you will be using a "boiling water-bath" method. (Exceptions to this are Blackberry Jelly, which is not processed—or heated—once packed into jars, and Pickled Beets and Eggs, which are refrigerated and used within a short period of time.) This procedure is used when relatively short-term processing at the temperature of boiling water (212° F.) is required. (The other major method of canning is the "steam-pressure method," used for low-acid foods. These foods require processing for longer periods and at much higher temperatures than that of boiling water.) Both methods, when done properly, result in sterilized foods sealed in airtight containers.

The following are important principles for successful home canning when using the boiling water-bath method:

1. Select the freshest products possible and ones at their peak of quality.

2. Can the food within a few hours of procuring, and, if at all possible, within two hours. Store food in a cool place until ready to can. If food was gathered during the heat of the day, it should be spread out to cool until it is no longer warm to the touch before canning.

3. Wash all food thoroughly (even food to be peeled), removing every trace of soil or other impurities. Store in very clean containers until ready to use.

4. Never reduce or dilute the amount of acid, such as vinegar or lemon, in a recipe.

5. To cook the food, use only stainless-steel, unchipped enamel, or Pyrex pots and utensils.

6. Use only jars made especially for home canning. You may re-use jars and metal rings if in good condition, but use self-sealing (flat, with sealing compound) lids only once. Discard any jars with irregularities at the mouth (such as cracks, chips, and bumps in the glass); likewise, discard any dented metal rings or lids that are defective in any way. Otherwise, you may not get an airtight seal. (Faulty seals are a major cause of spoilage in home-canned food.) Sterilize new and used jars by boiling as directed by the manufacturer, but for a minimum of 15 to 20 minutes. Wash and boil lids and rings according to manufacturer's directions. (**NOTE:** Lids with sealing compound may need boiling or holding in boiling water for a specific time; this procedure and the time requirements vary with the manufacturer.) We advise having at least one extra jar and its closures sterilized and ready in case the yield is larger than expected or any other problems occur at the last moment.

7. Glass jars (and their contents) must be hot when filled, to avoid breakage when jars are placed in the canner. Place jars on a wooden surface or on folded towels to fill.

8. When filling the jars with whole or sliced raw vegetables (but not ground ones), pack the vegetables snugly, since the food will shrink a little during processing. When pouring hot liquid over vegetables, use sufficient liquid to expel all air from spaces within the packed mixture; let liquid seep a minute, then add more liquid, leaving appropriate headspace (see recipes) and making sure vegetables are submerged in liquid. When closing each jar, place lid on with the sealing compound next to the glass.

9. Once jars are filled, it is important to process them immediately in a water-bath canner or deep pot as directed in the recipe. Have the water in the canner hot, but not boiling, when jars are placed in it, again to avoid breakage. Start to count processing time once water in the canner reaches a rolling boil. Once processed, remove jars immediately from the canner to cool. Then, when cooled thoroughly, test for an airtight seal by pressing down center of each lid. Lid should stay down. **NOTE:** If it doesn't, use the food in that jar immediately. And, if liquid was lost during processing, use that food immediately.

10. Do not turn processed jars upside down or attempt to tighten the metal rings, or you may lose the airtight seal.

11. If there are any signs of spoilage, *do not taste* contents of jar; discard in such a way that neither people nor animals can eat the spoiled food. Botulism, a serious and sometimes deadly form of food poisoning that is both odorless and tasteless, may be present.

Carefully examine each jar before opening and after opening for signs of spoilage. If the airtight seal has been lost (if lid comes off without having to pry it), discard jar and food *without* tasting. Likewise, if you observe cloudy liquid, a bad odor, a marked change in the appearance or consistency of the canned food, bulging jar lids or rings, or a leak, discard jar and food *without* tasting. If no signs of

High-Altitude Canning Chart*

For Processing Foods in a Water-Bath Canner: All processing times given in this book are for altitudes of sea level up to about 1,000 feet. If you live at an altitude of 1,000 feet or higher, consult the chart below to determine how many minutes to **add** to the processing time stated in the recipe.

Altitude	Increase in processing time if the time called for is:	
	20 minutes or less	*More than 20 minutes*
1,000 feet	1 minute	2 minutes
2,000 feet	2 minutes	4 minutes
3,000 feet	3 minutes	6 minutes
4,000 feet	4 minutes	8 minutes
5,000 feet	5 minutes	10 minutes
6,000 feet	6 minutes	12 minutes
7,000 feet	7 minutes	14 minutes
8,000 feet	8 minutes	16 minutes
9,000 feet	9 minutes	18 minutes
10,000 feet	10 minutes	20 minutes

*United States Department of Agriculture, Publication Number 2254, 1984, Louisiana State University Agricultural Center, and Louisiana Cooperative Extension Service.

spoilage are present, but you notice an off taste or observe anything at all that makes you even slightly hesitant, discard jar and food.

12. Properly canned food (with an airtight seal) that has been stored upright in a cool, dark, and dry place should retain its quality for at least a year, but, again, be alert for any signs of spoilage.

NOTE: These guidelines were developed specifically for the recipes in this book. Other canning recipes may often require different procedures. There are several reliable sources for more information about canning and pickling, such as booklets from the U.S. Government Printing Office or your county or state cooperative extension office. Special thanks to the Louisiana Cooperative Extension Service, St. Landry Parish Office, for reviewing our canning and pickling information.

J.C. AND SIS'S RECIPE

Fig Preserves
(Confiture aux Figues)

Makes 2 pints

If you are making these preserves to use in J.C. and Sis's **Fig Sweet-Dough Pie** *(page 388), you will have enough for two pies. Cook the preserves exactly as directed to the point at which you would spoon them into the canning jars, but, instead, spoon them into two prepared pie shells and bake. (If you want to make only one pie, process the other pint of preserves as described below.)*

Select firm ripe figs that are as fresh and unblemished as possible. Be sure to read the **Home Canning Notes** *before you begin.*

3 pounds firm ripe figs, about 9 cups
4 cups sugar
1 cup water
½ to 1 teaspoon lemon juice or 1 slice of lemon *per* pint, if canning

349

If canning, assemble all utensils before starting. You will need a water-bath canner with a rack and lid or a very deep pot with rack and lid; the pot must be deep enough to cover the upright jars (sitting on the rack) with 1 to 2 inches of water and still allow space for brisk boiling once the pan is covered. And you'll need two freshly scrubbed pint-size canning jars, metal rings, brand-new self-sealing lids, and a few clean dish towels. Fill the canner or pot with water and bring to a near boil (this takes quite a bit of time!) before beginning to fill the jars with the preserves. Have extra boiling water ready in case you need to add more water to the canner once the jars are in it.

In another pot, submerge the clean jars in water and sterilize by boiling as directed by the manufacturer, but for a minimum of 15 to 20 minutes. Leave jars in the hot water until ready to fill. Wash and boil lids and rings according to manufacturer's directions.

Wash the figs thoroughly in a large bowl or pot of cool tap water, removing any blemishes. Drain well, then wash again. Drain well and trim off stems.

Combine all the ingredients (except the lemon juice or lemon slices, if canning) in a 5½-quart stainless-steel, unchipped enamel, or Pyrex saucepan. Bring to a boil over high heat, stirring occasionally. Continue boiling while you skim off all the thick yellowish foam from the surface of the mixture. (This will take roughly 10 minutes to do because the yellow foam continues to develop. A less dense purple foam—actually just lots of bigger boiling bubbles—may also develop; this is easy to distinguish from the thick yellowish foam and does not require skimming.)

Reduce heat to medium and cook about 50 minutes, stirring and scraping pan bottom occasionally (more often toward end of cooking time) so mixture doesn't scorch. Skim any additional yellowish foam as it develops. (**NOTE**: If mixture gets very thick and you still have additional cooking time, add 2 to 4 tablespoons more water, as needed. If it rained right before the figs were picked, they will be juicier and you probably won't need this extra water.) By the end of the cooking time, the mixture should be very thick, and most, if not all, of the figs should be reduced to a purée. Remove from heat. If canning the preserves, stir in the lemon juice or lemon slices.

Place the very hot jars on a wooden surface or folded towels and immediately spoon the hot fig mixture into the jars up to ½ inch from the rims, packing the mixture down fairly tightly. (If using lemon slices, be sure to put a slice in each jar.) Let jars sit just a few seconds to let preserves settle and expel air bubbles. Then promptly wipe rims well with a clean, damp cloth and place hot lids on top with sealing compound down; screw on metal rings firmly but not too tightly.

Immediately place filled jars upright on the rack in the water-bath canner, or deep pot, filled with hot but not boiling water. Arrange jars so they don't touch each other or sides of pot. If necessary, add boiling water around but not on jars to cover jar tops by 1 to 2 inches. Cover pan and bring water to a rolling boil over high heat. Then boil 45 minutes for pints or 50 minutes for a quart jar (or as directed on the **High-Altitude Canning Chart,** page 348, if you live at a 1,000-foot or higher altitude). Immediately remove jars with canning tongs and place upright and at least 2 inches apart on a wooden surface or on folded dish towels to cool at room temperature, away from drafts. Do not cover jars.

Once jars are completely cooled, test for an airtight seal by pressing down center of each lid. Lid should stay down. Label and date jars, then store upright in a cool, dark, and dry room or pantry.

The preserves are ready to use immediately. Refrigerate after opening.

(ELDEN AND ODELIA MAE'S RECIPE

Blackberry Jelly
(Gelée de Mures d'Éronce)

Makes 3 to 5 pints

Select berries at their peak of quality and can them as soon as possible. Do not double the recipe. If you wish to make more, do so in separate batches. The yield of the recipe varies depending on the juiciness of the berries, so have 5 pint jars and lids ready, just in case.

*Be sure to read the **Home Canning Notes** before you begin.*

2 quarts firm ripe blackberries (2½ pounds picked
    over)
About 8 to 10 cups sugar
1 tablespoon orange juice
1 teaspoon orange zest
2 pinches of salt
1 (3-ounce) pouch liquid fruit pectin

Assemble all utensils before starting. You will need 5 freshly
scrubbed pint-size canning jars, metal rings, brand-new self-sealing
lids, and a few clean dish towels. You will also need a very clean
stainless-steel, unchipped enamel, or Pyrex ladle (scald it well), and
it's helpful to have a wide-mouthed funnel (also clean and scalded),
too, to fill the jars. Submerge the clean jars in water and sterilize by
boiling as directed by the manufacturer, but for a minimum of 15 to
20 minutes. Leave jars in the hot water until ready to fill. Wash and
boil lids and rings according to manufacturer's directions.

Wash the berries in cold running water and discard any bruised
berries or ones with decay or other imperfections. Remove any stems
or caps. Process the blackberries in a food processor a few seconds
until puréed. Strain purée through a strainer or dense cheesecloth.
Measure the yield: You should have 4 to 5 cups strained purée.

In an 8-quart stainless-steel, unchipped enamel, or Pyrex saucepan or large Dutch oven, combine the purée and exactly twice that
amount of sugar, the orange juice, orange zest, and salt, stirring
well. Bring to a rolling boil over high heat, stirring frequently. Stir in
the pectin and return to a rolling boil that cannot be stirred down,
then boil exactly 1 minute, stirring constantly.

Remove the jelly mixture from heat; let sit just a few seconds,
then, working as quickly as possible, skim all foam from surface.
(Don't be surprised—you may need to skim off a cup or more.) Immediately ladle the hot mixture into the very hot jars, leaving headspace of ⅛ inch; skim any bubbles from the surface of liquid with a
teaspoon. (**NOTE**: If your last jar is only partially full, seal it as directed below, and, once cooled, refrigerate and use within a few
days.) Then promptly wipe rims well with a clean, damp cloth and
place hot lids on top with sealing compound down; screw on metal
rings firmly but not too tightly.

Place jars upright and at least 2 inches apart on a wooden surface or on folded dish towels to cool undisturbed overnight (to avoid breaking gel), at room temperature and away from drafts. Once jars are completely cooled, test for an airtight seal by pressing down center of each lid. Lid should stay down. Label and date jars, then store upright in a cool, dark, and dry room or pantry. Refrigerate after opening.

ALLIE AND ETELL'S RECIPE

Pickled Eggs and Beets
(Cornichon de Betterave et Oeuf)

Makes 1 quart

Select very fresh ingredients and wash each thoroughly, even those to be peeled, removing every trace of soil or other impurities.

You will need a 1-quart canning jar in which to store the eggs and beets and a new self-sealing lid and metal ring to close the jar, all in perfect condition.

1 pound unpeeled trimmed beets, about 1 quart
Water, to cover beets and eggs
7 large eggs
1¼ cups white distilled vinegar (see **Note**)
½ cup chopped onion
½ teaspoon minced garlic
1 teaspoon salt
1 teaspoon sugar (see **Note**)
½ teaspoon ground red pepper (preferably cayenne)

Note: If you prefer a less vinegary taste, increase the amount of sugar used, but don't decrease the amount of vinegar used and don't dilute the vinegar.

353

Submerge a freshly scrubbed 1-quart canning jar in water and sterilize by boiling as directed by the manufacturer, but for a minimum of 15 to 20 minutes. Leave jar in the hot water until ready to fill. Wash and boil lid and ring according to manufacturer's directions.

Place the beets in a large saucepan and cover with water. Cover pan and bring to a boil over high heat. Place lid askew and continue boiling until the beets are tender, about 25 minutes. Drain off hot water from pan, then cover beets with cool tap water.

Meanwhile, place the eggs in a separate saucepan and cover with water. Cover pan and bring to a boil over high heat. Continue boiling for 5 minutes. Remove from heat and let sit covered for 15 minutes. (This procedure keeps eggs from having a green color around the yolks.) Then drain and cover with cool tap water.

When eggs are thoroughly cooled, peel them and set aside in a bowl. When beets are cool enough to handle, peel and cut them into slices ¼ inch thick; set aside in a separate bowl.

In a 1-quart stainless-steel, unchipped enamel, or Pyrex saucepan, combine the vinegar, onions, and garlic; bring to a boil over high heat. Remove from heat and strain the vinegar into a bowl. Return vinegar to the pan and set aside. Reserve the onion and garlic separately.

In the very hot jar, place 4 of the eggs, then half of the beets, then half of the strained onion and garlic. Then in the same order add the remaining 3 eggs, beets, and onion and garlic, leaving headspace of 1 inch. (You may have to leave out a few slices of beets, but press food down in the jar to see if all of it can fit.) Add the salt, sugar, and pepper over the top; you don't need to stir.

Return the hot strained vinegar to a boil, then pour it into the jar up to ½ inch from the rim; press the beets and onions down into the liquid and remove any vegetables that won't stay totally submerged. Then promptly wipe rim well with a clean, damp cloth and place hot lid on top with sealing compound down; screw on metal ring firmly but not too tightly. Place upright on a wooden surface or on folded dish towels to cool at room temperature, away from drafts, just until glass feels cool to touch. Label and date jar, then refrigerate.

Refrigerate for several days, preferably 3 weeks, before eating. These eggs and beets should keep well for 1 month beyond the 3-week aging period if prepared as directed and stored in the refrigerator, and if food is kept submerged in the liquid.

Pickled Green Cherry Tomatoes

Makes 2 pints

Be sure to let the pickled green tomatoes age at least 48 hours before using. They make a great martini garnish, and we love to serve them alongside red beans and rice and other dried-bean dishes. They're also an excellent garnish for almost any salad or appetizer.

It's important for best flavor to select cherry tomatoes that are totally green, with no red, white, or yellow coloration.

Be sure to read the **Home Canning Notes** *before you begin.*

1 pound small, very green, and unblemished cherry
    tomatoes, washed thoroughly and stems
    removed, about 1 quart
8 washed and peeled pearl onions or 8 washed and
    trimmed bulbs from green onions (each
    trimmed bulb should be about 1 inch long)
4 fresh unblemished cayenne or jalapeño peppers,
    washed thoroughly, trimmed of stems but not
    seeded, and cut in half lengthwise
1½ cups water
1½ cups white distilled vinegar (see **NOTE**)

NOTE: For safety reasons, be sure not to decrease the proportion of vinegar to water. If you like a less vinegary taste, leave the amount of vinegar the same and add some sugar.

Assemble all utensils before starting. You will need a water-bath canner with a rack and lid or a very deep pot with rack and lid; the pot must be deep enough to cover the upright jars (sitting on the rack) with 1 to 2 inches of water and still allow space for brisk boiling once the pan is covered. And you'll need 2 freshly scrubbed pint-size canning jars, metal rings, brand-new self-sealing lids, and a few clean dish towels. Fill the canner or pot with water and bring to a near boil (this takes quite a bit of time!) before beginning to fill the jars with food. Have extra boiling water ready in case you need to add more water to the canner once the jars are in it.

Submerge the clean jars in water and sterilize by boiling as directed by the manufacturer, but for a minimum of 15 to 20 minutes. Leave jars in the hot water until ready to fill. Wash and boil lids and rings according to manufacturer's directions.

Trim any bruises, decay, or other imperfections from the tomatoes, onions, and peppers.

Combine the water and vinegar in a 2-quart stainless-steel, unchipped enamel, or Pyrex saucepan. Bring to a boil over high heat. Add the onions and peppers; boil about 6 minutes. Remove from heat and set aside.

Fill each very hot jar with the tomatoes, up to 1 inch from the rims, packing snugly. Using a slotted spoon, place half the peppers and onions from the vinegar mixture into each jar, pressing vegetables down to ½ inch from rims. Return water and vinegar to a boil, then pour vinegar mixture over the tomatoes, leaving headspace of ½ inch and pushing vegetables down into the liquid. Then promptly wipe rims well with a clean, damp cloth and place hot lids on top with sealing compound down; screw on metal rings firmly but not too tightly.

Immediately place filled jars upright on the rack in the water-bath canner, or deep pot, filled with hot but not boiling water. Arrange jars so they don't touch each other or sides of pot. If necessary, add boiling water around but not on jars to cover jar tops by 1 to 2 inches. Cover pot and bring water to a rolling boil over high heat. Then boil 35 minutes for pints, 45 minutes for a quart jar (or as directed on the **High-Altitude Canning Chart,** page 348, if you live at a 1,000-foot or higher altitude).

Immediately remove jars with canning tongs and place upright and at least 2 inches apart on a wooden surface or on folded dish towels to cool at room temperature, away from drafts. Do not cover. Once jars are completely cooled, test for an airtight seal by pressing down center of each lid. Lid should stay down. Label and date jars, then store upright in a cool, dark, and dry room or pantry.

Store at least 48 hours before using. Refrigerate after opening.

Ground Hot Pepper Vinegar
(Vinaigre de Piment Fort Moulu)

Makes 2 pints

Select firm peppers that are as fresh and unblemished as possible. Green and/or red ones work equally well. Cayennes are probably the least hot and the most flavorful, but you can substitute Tabasco, jalapeño, bird's-eye, or other fresh peppers, or any combination. Elden grinds or minces his peppers, but if you prefer you can chop them. (Allie, for example, coarsely chops hers.)

Ground Hot Pepper Vinegar is used as a condiment—for example, with gumbos, jambalayas, and dried-bean dishes—but it's also wonderful cooked into sauces and other foods, used as a marinade, and added to salad dressings. Experiment with it!

Be sure to read the **Home Canning Notes** *before you begin.*

1¼ pounds cayenne or other hot peppers, washed
    thoroughly, trimmed of stems, but not seeded
2½ cups white distilled vinegar (see **NOTE**)
1 tablespoon salt

NOTE: For safety reasons, be sure to use undiluted vinegar and do not decrease the amount of vinegar.

Assemble all utensils before starting. You will need a water-bath canner with a rack and lid or a very deep pot with rack and lid. It must be deep enough to cover the upright jars (sitting on the rack) with 1 to 2 inches of water and still allow space for brisk boiling once the pan is covered. And you'll need 2 freshly scrubbed pint-size canning jars, metal rings, brand-new self-sealing lids, and a few clean dish towels. Fill the canner or pot with water and bring to a near boil (this takes quite a bit of time!) before beginning to fill the jars. Have extra boiling water ready in case you need to add more water to the canner once the jars are in it.

357

Submerge the clean jars in water and sterilize by boiling as directed by the manufacturer, but for a minimum of 15 to 20 minutes. Leave jars in the hot water until ready to fill. Wash and boil lids and rings according to manufacturer's directions.

Trim any bruises, decay, or other imperfections from the peppers. Process the peppers in a food processor a few seconds until minced. Set aside.

Bring the vinegar to a boil in a 1-quart saucepan over high heat. Meanwhile, spoon half the minced peppers into each of the very hot jars up to no higher than 1½ inches from the rims, without packing peppers down tightly. Add 1½ teaspoons salt to each jar, then pour the boiling vinegar over the peppers, leaving headspace of ½ inch and pushing peppers down if necessary to cover with the liquid. After a minute, check to make sure liquid is still up to ½ inch from the rim; if not, add more. Then promptly wipe rims well with a clean, damp cloth and place hot lids on top with sealing compound down; screw on metal rings firmly but not too tightly.

Immediately place filled jars upright on a rack in the water-bath canner, or deep pot, filled with hot but not boiling water. Arrange jars so they don't touch each other or sides of pot. If necessary, add boiling water around but not on jars to cover jar tops by 1 to 2 inches. Cover pan and bring water to a rolling boil over high heat. Then boil 10 minutes for pints, 20 minutes for a quart jar (or as directed on the **High-Altitude Canning Chart,** page 348, if you live at a 1,000-foot or higher altitude). Immediately remove jars with canning tongs and place upright and at least 2 inches apart on a wooden surface or on folded dish towels to cool at room temperature, away from drafts. Do not cover.

Once jars are completely cooled, test for an airtight seal by pressing down center of each lid. Lid should stay down. Label and date jars, then store upright in a cool, dark, and dry room or pantry.

Store at least 48 hours, preferably 2 weeks, before using. Refrigerate after opening.

DARILEE AND SAUL'S RECIPE

Cajun Home-Canned Spicy Tomatoes

Makes 3 to 6 pints

Cayennes are probably the least hot and the most flavorful peppers to use for our spicy tomatoes, but you can substitute Tabasco, jalapeño, bird's-eye, or other fresh peppers, or any combination of them. Darilee likes to use green cayennes, but red ones are fine, too. No matter what type of fresh peppers you choose, select firm, unblemished ones at their peak of freshness.

Spicy tomatoes can be used as a condiment, but they are also wonderful cooked in any recipes in which you normally use cooked tomatoes.

The yield of this recipe may vary from 3 to 6 pints, because tomatoes differ significantly in their moisture content. So, be prepared for 6 pints, just in case.

Be sure to read the **Home Canning Notes** *before you begin.*

6½ pounds vine-ripened tomatoes (about 20 medium
    size), thoroughly washed, peeled, and cored
2½ cups chopped onions
4¼ ounces green or red cayenne peppers (preferred),
    in all, or other hot peppers, thoroughly washed,
    trimmed of all blemishes, then minced (¾ cup
    minced)
2 teaspoons finely chopped garlic
1 tablespoon salt
1 to 2 tablespoons lemon juice (see **NOTE**)

NOTE: Some tomatoes have a low acid level. If the tomatoes you use are low-acid, or if you're not sure of the acid level, for safety reasons it's important to add at least *1 teaspoon lemon juice per pint* to bring the acid content up.

Assemble all utensils before starting. You will need a water-bath canner with a rack and lid or a very deep pot with rack and lid; the pot must be deep enough to cover the upright jars (sitting on the rack) with 1 to 2 inches of water and still allow space for brisk boiling once the pan is covered. And you'll need 6 freshly scrubbed pint-size canning jars, metal rings, brand-new self-sealing lids, and a few clean dish towels. **NOTE**: If you choose to use a combination of pint and quart jars, you will need to process pint jars separately from quart jars. Fill the canner or pot with water and bring to a near boil (this takes quite a bit of time!) before beginning to fill the jars with food. Have extra boiling water ready in case you need to add more water to the canner once the jars are in it.

Trim any bruises, decay, hard whitish areas, or other imperfections from the tomatoes and place in a food processor, breaking up the tomatoes with your hands in order to feel for hard parts to discard. Process tomatoes to a smooth purée, about 1 minute. (If your processor is fairly small, do this in batches.) Transfer the purée to a 5½-quart stainless-steel, unchipped enamel, or Pyrex saucepan or large Dutch oven, leaving 1 cup of the purée in the processor.

To the processor add the onions, about *half* of the cayenne peppers, and the garlic; process until puréed, about 1 minute, pushing sides down with a rubber spatula. Add the purée mixture to the saucepan with the tomato purée; then add the *remaining* minced cayenne peppers and salt, stirring well. Place over medium-high heat and cook until mixture reduces to a thick tomato sauce, about 1 hour and 10 minutes, stirring occasionally and skimming off any foam as it develops. Adjust heat to maintain a simmer and, toward the end of cooking time, stir and scrape pan bottom almost constantly so mixture won't scorch.

Meanwhile, submerge the clean jars in water and sterilize by boiling as directed by the manufacturer, but for a minimum of 15 to 20 minutes. Leave jars in the hot water until ready to fill. Wash and boil lids and rings according to manufacturer's directions.

As soon as the tomato mixture has finished cooking, skim any remaining foam from surface and immediately ladle mixture into the very hot jars, leaving headspace of ½ inch. (**NOTE**: If the last jar is more than half full, but not quite full, add boiling water up to ½ inch from rim. If the last jar is less than half full, cap the jar as directed below, and once cooled slightly, refrigerate and use within a day or two.) Add the lemon juice, if needed. Then promptly wipe rims well with a clean, damp cloth and place hot lids on top with sealing compound down; screw on metal rings firmly but not too tightly.

Immediately place filled jars upright on the rack in the water-bath container, or deep pot, filled with hot but not boiling water. Arrange jars so they don't touch each other or sides of pot. If necessary, add boiling water around but not on jars to cover jar tops by 1 to 2 inches. Cover pan and bring water to a rolling boil over high heat. Then boil 35 minutes for pints, 45 minutes for quarts (or as directed on the **High-Altitude Canning Chart,** page 348, if you live at a 1,000-foot or higher altitude).

Immediately remove jars with canning tongs and place upright and at least 2 inches apart on a wooden surface or on folded dish towels to cool at room temperature, away from drafts. Do not cover jars. Once jars are completely cooled, test for an airtight seal by pressing down center of each lid. Lid should stay down. Label and date jars, then store upright in a cool, dark, and dry room or pantry.

ALLIE AND ETELL'S RECIPE

Bread and Butter Pickles

Makes 3 pints

Select firm cucumbers (the smaller ones are firmer and prettier and better tasting) and onions that are as fresh and unblemished as possible.

Be sure to read the **Home Canning Notes** *before you begin.*

1½ pounds cucumbers (small ones preferred)
Pickling lime and water (read directions on package)
1 quart ice
About 2 quarts cold water
1½ cups white distilled vinegar (see **NOTE**)
1 cup water
¾ pound small onions (use ones with about the same
    diameter as the cucumbers you're using),
    scrubbed, peeled, and cut into slices ½ inch
    thick (about 2 cups sliced)
1¾ cups sugar
1 tablespoon pickling spice
1½ teaspoons ground red pepper (preferably
    cayenne), optional

NOTE: For safety reasons, be sure not to decrease the proportion of vinegar to water. If you like a less vinegary taste, leave the amount of vinegar the same and add some sugar.

Wash cucumbers thoroughly. Trim away any bruises, decay, or other imperfections and trim tip ends. Score through the skins lengthwise with fork tines, then cut cucumbers into slices ⅛ inch thick. Place them in a large crock or a glass or stoneware bowl and soak, refrigerated, overnight in pickling lime and water as directed on the pickling lime package. **NOTE**: Use crockery or stoneware made in the United States; some foreign-made crockery and stoneware contain dangerous levels of lead.

    Remove cucumbers from refrigerator and drain in a colander, rinsing off as much lime solution as possible with cool tap water. Place in a large bowl; fill bowl with water and swirl cucumbers to wash off as much remaining lime as possible, separating slices that are stuck together. Repeat procedure at least twice and as often as necessary to wash away all the lime; drain well.

    Place cucumbers in a large clean bowl. Cover with the ice and enough cold water to submerge cucumbers. Refrigerate for 3 hours. Remove from refrigerator, drain well, and let come to room temperature, about 30 minutes.

    Meanwhile, assemble all utensils. You will need a water-bath canner with a rack and lid or a very deep pot with rack and lid. The pot must be deep enough to cover the upright jars (sitting on the rack) with 1 to 2 inches of water and still allow space for brisk boiling once the pan is covered. And you'll need 3 freshly scrubbed pint-size canning jars, metal rings, brand-new self-sealing lids, and a few clean dish towels. **NOTE**: If you choose to use a combination of pint and quart jars, you will need to process pint jars separately from quart jars. Fill the canner or pot with water and bring to a near boil (this takes quite a bit of time!) before beginning to fill the jars with food. Have extra boiling water ready in case you need to add more water to the canner once the jars are in it.

Submerge the clean jars in water and sterilize by boiling as directed by the manufacturer, but for a minimum of 15 to 20 minutes. Leave jars in the hot water until ready to fill. Wash and boil lids and rings according to manufacturer's directions.

Combine the vinegar, the 1 cup water, the onions, sugar, pickling spice, and red pepper, if desired, in a 2-quart stainless-steel, unchipped enamel, or Pyrex saucepan. Stir well, cover pan, and bring to a boil over high heat. Remove cover and continue boiling until liquid has slightly thickened, about 8 minutes, stirring occasionally and separating onions into rings as you stir. Remove from heat and immediately strain with a bowl beneath the strainer to catch the liquid. Set aside strained onion mixture. Return vinegar mixture to the pan and slowly return it to a boil over low heat.

Meanwhile, fill each very hot jar with about 2 tablespoons of the onion mixture, then add ⅓ cup of the cucumbers. Continue filling jars, alternating between onion mixture and cucumbers, until jars are filled to no higher than 1 inch from the rims; pack food down tightly if necessary so more will fit. (You may have a few cucumbers left over.) Slowly pour the boiling vinegar mixture over the cucumbers and onions, leaving headspace of ½ inch and pushing vegetables down to cover them with the liquid. After a few seconds, check to make sure liquid is still up to ½ inch from the rim; if not, add more. Then promptly wipe rims well with a clean, damp cloth and place hot lids on top with sealing compound down; screw on metal rings firmly but not too tightly. **NOTE**: If you don't have enough liquid to fill the last jar, quickly boil more vinegar and add it.

Immediately place filled jars upright on a rack in the water-bath canner, or deep pot, filled with hot but not boiling water. Arrange jars so they don't touch each other or sides of pot. If necessary, add boiling water around but not on jars to cover jar tops by 1 to 2 inches. Cover pan and bring water to a rolling boil over high heat. Then boil 10 minutes for pints, 20 minutes for quarts (or as directed on the **High-Altitude Canning Chart,** page 348, if you live at a 1,000-foot or higher altitude).

Immediately remove jars with canning tongs and place upright and at least 2 inches apart on a wooden surface or on folded dish towels to cool at room temperature, away from drafts. Do not cover jars. Once jars are completely cooled, test for an airtight seal by pressing down center of each lid. Lid should stay down. Label and date jars, then store upright in a cool, dark, and dry room or pantry.

Store at least 48 hours, preferably 2 weeks, before using. Refrigerate after opening.

BEVERAGES

BOISSONS

PAUL AND K'S RECIPE

Anisette

Makes about 4 quarts

Mom Prudhomme always made anisette for the family to drink as part of the New Year's Day celebration. She made two kinds—one with alcohol and one without. The grown-ups got the alcoholic anisette and the children got the nonalcoholic.

Alcoholic anisette is a really refreshing "sipping" drink—even for people who don't like licorice. What is surprising is that these very simple ingredients develop into a drink with multiple tastes. The anisette dominates your taste buds and clears away other tastes, so it's a nice palate cleanser—and it's also creamy smooth.

For a really smashing variation for an after dinner drink (you guys ignore the pink Cadillac color), fold in about an equal amount of whipped cream and serve "neat," well chilled and in small glasses. To flavor whipped cream for a dessert topping, fold about 1 tablespoon of anisette into ½ pint of heavy cream, whipped.

Alcoholic anisette tastes best if aged at least six weeks before serving.

6 quarts water
6 cups sugar
3 cups sour mash whiskey
1 tablespoon vanilla extract
1 teaspoon anise oil (see **NOTE**)
1 teaspoon red food coloring
A tub full of ice, to cool down anisette quickly after
    bottling

NOTE: Anise oil and anise extract are not the same. Be sure to use the *oil*; it's available at many health food stores.

Assemble all utensils before starting so you can bottle the anisette quickly once it's prepared. (Don't use any plastic utensils because anise oil might mar them.) You will need 4 freshly scrubbed quart-size canning jars and metal rings in good condition and 4 brand-new self-sealing lids. You will also need tongs to remove the jars from the hot water you sterilize them in, a very clean ladle (scald it well), and a few clean dish towels.

Submerge the clean jars in water and sterilize by boiling 15 to 20 minutes. Leave jars in the hot water until ready to use. Wash and boil lids and rings according to manufacturer's directions.

In a 12-quart stock or soup pot, combine the water and sugar. Bring to a boil over high heat, stirring until sugar is dissolved. Reduce heat and simmer until liquid reduces to 3 quarts plus 1 cup (you'll have to measure to be sure), about 1 hour and 20 minutes, stirring occasionally. Remove from heat.

Stir in the whiskey, vanilla, anise oil, and food coloring. Place the very hot jars on a wooden surface or folded towels and immediately pour the anisette into the jars up to ½ inch from the tops. Wipe rims well with a clean, damp cloth and place hot lids on top with sealing compound down; screw on metal rings firmly but not too tightly. Immediately place jars upright in a sink that has been lined with a damp dishcloth (so the hot jars won't slide or break by touching the cold sink). Slowly fill the sink by running cool tap water around but not on jars until most, if not all, of the liquid in the jars is surrounded by water. (Cover the jars entirely if your sink is deep enough.) Let jars sit in the water until cool to the touch, about 5 minutes, then place them upright in a tub of ice, with ice to top of jars, to cool the anisette as quickly as possible. Once contents of jars are well chilled, about 1 hour, remove jars from ice. Label and date jars, then store upright in a cool, dark, and dry room or pantry.

Store at least 6 weeks before using. Serve "neat," well chilled and in small glasses, or serve on the rocks. Anisette keeps well for several months if refrigerated or held in a cool, dark, and dry place.

Nonalcoholic Anisette

Makes 3 quarts

Nonalcoholic anisette tastes best if aged at least two weeks before serving.

1 gallon water
6 cups sugar
1 tablespoon vanilla extract
1 teaspoon anise oil (see **NOTE**)
½ teaspoon red food coloring
A tub full of ice, to cool down anisette quickly after
    bottling

NOTE: Anise oil and anise extract are not the same. Be sure to use the *oil*; it's available at many health food stores.

Assemble all utensils before starting so you can bottle the anisette quickly once it's prepared. (Don't use any plastic utensils because anise oil might mar them.) You will need 3 freshly scrubbed quart-size canning jars and metal rings in good condition and 3 brand-new self-sealing lids. You will also need tongs to remove the jars from the hot water you sterilize them in, a very clean ladle (scald it well), and a few clean dish towels.

Submerge the clean jars in water and sterilize by boiling 15 to 20 minutes. Leave jars in the hot water until ready to use. Wash and boil lids and rings according to manufacturer's directions.

In a 12-quart stock or soup pot, combine the water and sugar. Bring to a boil over high heat, stirring until sugar is dissolved. Continue boiling until liquid reduces to 3 quarts (you'll have to measure to be sure), about 45 to 50 minutes, stirring occasionally. Remove from heat.

Stir in the vanilla, anise oil, and food coloring. Place the very hot jars on a wooden surface or folded towels and immediately pour the anisette into the jars up to about 1 inch from the tops. Wipe rims well with a clean, damp cloth and place hot lids on top with sealing compound down; screw on metal rings firmly but not too tightly. Immediately place jars upright in a sink that has been lined with a damp dishcloth (so the hot jars won't slide or break by touching the cold sink). Slowly fill the sink by running cool tap water around but not on jars until most, if not all, of the liquid in the jars is surrounded by water. (Cover the jars entirely if your sink is deep enough.) Let jars sit in the water until cool to the touch, about 5 minutes, then place them upright in a tub of ice, with ice to top of jars, to cool the anisette as quickly as possible. Once contents of jars are well chilled, about 1 hour, remove jars from ice. Label and date jars, then refrigerate for at least 2 weeks before serving.

Serve over ice. Nonalcoholic anisette will keep for at least 6 months if refrigerated.

PAUL AND K'S RECIPE

Cherry-Flavored Anisette

Makes 3 quarts

We created this mildly flavored anise drink expressly for the cookbook because we had some anise extract handy and it was cherry season!

Cherry-flavored anisette tastes best if aged at least one month, preferably two, before serving.

4 quarts water
2 quarts plus 1½ cups pitted fresh cherries (preferably Bing)
2½ cups sugar
2 tablespoons plus 2 teaspoons anise extract, *in all* (see **NOTE**)
4 cups sour mash whiskey
2 teaspoons vanilla extract
A tub full of ice, to cool down anisette quickly after bottling

NOTE: Anise extract and anise oil are not the same. Be sure to use the *extract* for this recipe.

Assemble all utensils before starting so you can bottle the anisette quickly once it's prepared. (Don't use any plastic utensils because anise extract might mar them.) You will need 3 freshly scrubbed quart-size canning jars and metal rings in good condition and 3 brand-new self-sealing lids. You will also need tongs to remove the jars from the hot water you sterilize them in, a very clean ladle (scald it well), and a few clean dish towels.

Submerge the clean jars in water and sterilize by boiling 15 to 20 minutes. Leave jars in the hot water until ready to use. Wash and boil lids and rings according to manufacturer's directions.

In an 8-quart saucepan or large Dutch oven, combine the water, cherries, sugar, and *1 tablespoon* of the anise extract. Bring to a boil over high heat. Reduce heat and simmer until liquid reduces to 9 cups (you'll have to measure to be sure), about 2 hours. (You don't need to stir.) Remove pan from heat. With a slotted spoon, remove cherries from liquid (leave liquid in the pan) and put cherries through a food mill.

Return cherries to the liquid in pan. With a metal whisk, whisk in the whiskey, vanilla, and the remaining *1 tablespoon plus 2 teaspoons* anise extract. Place the very hot jars on a wooden surface or folded towels and immediately pour the anisette into the jars up to about a inch from the tops. Wipe rims well with a clean, damp cloth and place hot lids on top with sealing compound down; screw on metal rings firmly but not too tightly.

Immediately place jars upright in a sink that has been lined with a damp dishcloth (so the hot jars won't slide or break by touching the cold sink). Slowly fill the sink by running cool tap water around but not on jars until most, if not all, of the liquid in the jars is surrounded by water. (Cover the jars completely if your sink is deep enough.) Let jars sit in the water until cool to the touch, about 5 minutes, then place them upright in a tub of ice, with ice to top of jars, to cool the anisette as quickly as possible. Once contents of jars are well chilled, about 1 hour, remove jars from ice. Label and date jars.

Refrigerate at least one month (preferably two) before serving. Serve on the rocks. This anisette keeps well for several months if refrigerated.

PAUL AND K'S RECIPE

Cherry Bounce

Makes 1 quart

Mom Prudhomme used to make cherry bounce to "sip on" at New Year's and other special times. She used the pits of wild cherries from trees that still grow all over Louisiana. The cherries are wonderful when they're ripe, but the trees don't bear each year and the season is quite short. For testing this recipe, we used fresh Bing cherry pits, but cherry pits from any edible cherries as well as from Louisiana's wild cherry trees will do.

Cherry bounce tastes best if aged at least six months to let the cherry flavor develop fully.

About 1¼ cups cherry pits (preferably Bing)
2 tablespoons sugar
About 3 cups sour mash whiskey

Submerge a freshly scrubbed quart-size canning jar in water and sterilize it by boiling 15 to 20 minutes. Wash and boil lid and ring according to manufacturer's directions.

Place the hot jar on a wooden surface or folded towel and add to the jar the pits and sugar. Fill jar to 1 inch from the top with whiskey. Wipe rim well with a clean, damp cloth and place hot lid on top with sealing compound down; screw on metal ring firmly but not too tightly. Let cool on the wooden surface or folded dish towel until thoroughly cooled. Label and date jar. Age at least 6 months in a cool, dark, and dry place, then strain out pits and it's ready to serve.

DESSERTS & SWEETS

SWEETS

MANGER DOUX

ALLIE AND ETELL'S RECIPE

Bread Pudding
(Poudine au Pain)

Makes 8 to 10 servings

The family had bread pudding only for Sunday dinner and special occasions like birthdays. Allie began making it when she was a young girl helping Mom with the cooking. Back then she made bread pudding with homemade bread—and she thinks it's really good like that—but she makes it with store-bought bread now because it's so quick and easy and she can stir it up often.

Allie says you can add raisins, roasted pecans, or other nuts or coconut to the recipe, but she likes to make bread pudding plain because that's the way she's always done it. It's not "plain" tasting, however—it's creamy rich and delicious.

¼ pound (1 stick) unsalted butter, softened
1 cup plus 2 tablespoons sugar
2 (12-ounce) cans evaporated milk (3 cups)
3 eggs
2 teaspoons vanilla extract
1 teaspoon ground cinnamon
¾ teaspoon ground nutmeg
½ teaspoon salt
¼ teaspoon cream of tartar
¼ teaspoon ground ginger
7 slices stale (preferred) white sandwich bread, toasted

Place the butter and sugar in a large bowl of an electric mixer and beat on medium speed until creamed, about 5 minutes, pushing sides down with a rubber spatula. Add the milk, eggs, vanilla, cinnamon, nutmeg, salt, cream of tartar, and ginger, beating on low speed until batter is thoroughly blended, about 3 minutes, and pushing sides down as needed.

374

Line the bottom of an ungreased 8 × 8-inch baking pan evenly with the toasted bread, breaking it into small pieces. Pour the mixture over the bread and let sit for about 1 hour, patting down the bread that floats up occasionally.

Bake at 450° until very well browned and the mixture shakes like a bowl of jelly when the pan is gently shaken back and forth, 20 to 25 minutes. Remove from oven and let cool about 15 minutes before serving.

J.C. and SIS'S RECIPE

Cream Cheese and Roasted Pecan Cookies
(Tit Gâteaux de Crème de Fromage et Pacanes Grillées)

Makes about 4 dozen cookies

*Paul says Mom baked pecan cookies for special occasions. The recipe uses cream cheese, which she made regularly because the family always kept at least one milk cow. Mom held the fresh milk in large crockery bowls and made clabbered milk by letting it sit at room temperature until a thick, curdlike substance formed on top. The family liked the clabber, or caille, with **Couche-Couche** (page 30), but sometimes Mom put the caille in a cheesecloth bag and hung it from a limb of the cedar tree in the front yard for about twenty-four hours. After that length of time, the caille had become cottage cheese, a simple farm cheese.*

Mom whipped the cottage cheese with some of the rich, thick cream that formed on top of chilled bowls of fresh cow milk to make a cream farmer cheese. Paul remembers that it was incredible tasting.

Sis says her mom also made homemade cottage cheese, as well as sour cream. Sis's favorite method of cooking is baking, and what she most likes to bake is sweets. She and J.C. both have powerful sweet tooths! These cookies are so special that the bakers at Paul and K's restaurant borrow the recipe regularly to cook them for the restaurant staff.

1½ cups sugar
1 large egg
½ pound (2 sticks) unsalted butter, very soft
1 (3-ounce) package cream cheese, very soft
1 tablespoon Hershey's cocoa
¾ teaspoon salt
2 tablespoons milk
1 teaspoon vanilla extract
2¼ cups all-purpose flour
1½ teaspoons baking powder
2 cups pecan pieces, dry roasted

In a very large mixing bowl, combine the sugar, egg, butter, and cream cheese; stir with a large spoon until mixture is very creamy and the butter and cheese are reduced to very small lumps, about 4 minutes. **NOTE:** Sis says to be sure to use a spoon, not a mixer. Stir in the cocoa and salt, then add the milk and vanilla, stirring until well mixed.

Gradually sift the flour and baking powder into the mixture, about 1 cup at a time, stirring only enough to blend in the flour before adding more; stir just a few seconds more to mix well, then stir in the pecans.

Drop batter by heaping teaspoonfuls onto a greased cookie sheet, about 1 inch apart. Bake at 350° until edges of cookies are brown, 12 to 14 minutes. Immediately remove from pan with a spatula and cool on a wire rack. **NOTE:** The cookies will be quite soft while they're warm and get crisp as they cool.

J.C. AND SIS'S RECIPE

Homemade Cherry Ice Cream
(Crème à la Glace de Merise)

Makes about 1½ quarts

As sharecroppers, Dad and Mom had to raise two cash crops—cotton and sweet potatoes—as well as corn for the animals and year-round vegetables for the family. When the older children were quite small, Dad established a tradition with the cotton crop: When they had picked the first bale of cotton from their land, Dad sold the bale and bought a five-pound stick of cheese. More important, as far as the children were concerned, when the family picked the last bale of cotton, Dad sold the bale and bought the makings for homemade ice cream. The children never grew tired of the tradition—it continued for the youngest children, too—especially the ice cream.

Every year on that day, when the last bale was picked, the children chattered all day, "la crème à la vanille à soir" (vanilla ice cream tonight!). Calvin says that one year some of the children got so carried away with the prospect of ice cream that they quit working and took to playing. Dad had to spank J.C. with a small cotton stalk and the other boys teased him for the rest of the day with "la crème à la tite branche à soir" (small branch ice cream tonight!).

Mom and Dad made homemade ice cream for many years before they ever bought their first ice-cream maker. Ralph and Bobby say the method required a little more work than today's fancy machines, but the ice cream couldn't have been better. Mom stirred together eggs, sugar, milk, and cream, then cooked the mixture and poured it into gallon-size syrup buckets. Dad set three syrup buckets at a time of Mom's ice-cream mixture in a washtub filled with ice and salt, and the children twisted the handles of the buckets back and forth until it froze. Ralph says it took about six gallons for everyone in the family to get enough. That was a lot of twisting of buckets, but everybody helped and took turns.

J.C. and Sis's ice cream has an exceptional taste and texture. We love it made with fresh Bing cherries, but don't hesitate to use your *favorite fresh fruit. Use Sis's recipe as a basic mixture for any flavoring you wish—fresh strawberries or peaches—or add chocolate along with the cherries.*

If you use fresh cherries, you can make the cherry base sauce a day ahead. You need a candy or deep-fry thermometer for cooking the egg-yolk-and-cream mixture.

4 egg yolks
1¼ cups sugar, *in all*
⅛ teaspoon salt
2 cups half-and-half
2 cups heavy cream
4 egg whites, cold
1 teaspoon vanilla extract
1 recipe **Cherry Base Sauce** (preferred; recipe
    follows), or 1 (6-ounce) jar maraschino cherries,
    drained and finely chopped, with juice reserved

In a large mixing bowl, combine the egg yolks, *1 cup* of the sugar, and the salt; beat vigorously with a large spoon until very light colored and creamy, about 6 minutes. Gradually add the half-and-half and cream, mixing until smooth.

Place the egg-yolk-and-cream mixture in the top of a double boiler over boiling water (top pan must never touch the boiling water). Turn heat to medium and cook until mixture reaches 190°, about 11 minutes, stirring constantly. Remove from heat and pour mixture into a large bowl. Let cool slightly, then refrigerate until well chilled, about 2 hours.

Once the mixture is chilled, place the egg whites in a large bowl of an electric mixer and beat on high speed until peaks form, about 2 minutes. Gradually beat in the remaining ¼ *cup* sugar, pushing sides down with a rubber spatula. Pour the chilled egg-yolk-and-cream mixture into the egg whites, stirring well. Stir in the vanilla.

If using fresh cherries, now add *half* the cooled cherry base sauce or, if using maraschino cherries, add *half* the cherries plus all their juice. Freeze in an ice-cream machine according to machine directions for about 10 minutes. Add the *remaining* cherry base sauce, or the *remaining* maraschinos, and freeze until ice cream is hard, about 20 minutes more. Serve immediately.

Cherry Base Sauce

1 pound fresh Bing cherries, *in all*, seeded and cut
    into quarters (a heaping 2½ cups cherry meat)
½ cup sugar
1½ teaspoons vanilla extract

Place *1½ cups* of the cherry meat in a food processor and process about 1 minute until puréed, pushing sides down with a rubber spatula.

    Place the purée in a 1-quart saucepan with the sugar and vanilla, stirring well. Place over high heat and bring to a boil, stirring frequently. Add the remaining *heaping 1 cup* cherry meat and return mixture to a boil, stirring frequently. Cover pan, remove from heat, and let sit about 10 minutes. Remove lid and cool slightly, then refrigerate until ready to use. Makes 1⅔ cups.

J.C. AND SIS'S RECIPE

Fresh Pineapple Delight

Makes 8 to 10 servings

Sis developed her pineapple delight recipe from scratch. Neither her mom nor Mom Prudhomme ever made it, though both families made fresh fruit salad often and they loved sweets. Sis says she named her creation Pineapple Delight because of a neighbor she had who described absolutely everything she liked as a delight.

*   The Prudhomme family and Sis's family always used maraschino cherries in fruit salads because, until recently, they were the only cherries available in small Louisiana towns like Opelousas. But any fresh sweet cherries like Bing cherries, or canned sweet cherries, are fine.*

*   You can make this dessert a day ahead if you like.*

1 (3- to 3½-pound) pineapple (or enough to yield 2 cups
    pineapple purée plus 1 cup chopped pineapple meat)
1½ teaspoons orange zest
½ cup sugar
32 (2½-inch) squares graham crackers, *in all* (9 ounces)
4 tablespoons unsalted butter, very soft
1 cup powdered sugar
2 cups plus 2 tablespoons heavy cream, *in all*
2 tablespoons lemon juice
1½ teaspoons vanilla extract
Pinch of salt
1 (6-ounce) jar maraschino cherries, drained; optional (see **NOTE**)

NOTE: You may use canned pitted black Bing cherries or, to be really special, fresh Bing cherries pitted with that fancy little tool you can buy in "gourmet" shops.

Chill a large bowl of an electric mixer and the beaters in a freezer until well chilled, about 1 hour.

Peel and core the pineapple, then cut the meat into chunks; process just enough in a blender or food processor to yield 2 cups purée. Chop enough additional pineapple to yield 1 cup. (Use remaining pineapple for another dessert.) Place the pineapple purée, chopped pineapple, and orange zest in a medium-size bowl. Stir in the granulated sugar and set aside.

In a separate medium-size bowl, crumble *26 of the graham cracker squares* into small pieces. Set aside.

In a large bowl, combine the butter, powdered sugar, *2 table-spoons* of the cream, and the lemon juice; stir a few seconds until creamy. Set aside.

Place the remaining *2 cups* cream in the chilled bowl and beat on high speed of the electric mixer just until whipped, about 1 minute; do not overbeat. Pour the whipped cream over the butter-and-powdered-sugar mixture. Fold in the reserved crumbled graham crackers. Fold in the pineapple mixture, vanilla, and salt, mixing well.

Spoon mixture into an ungreased 13 × 9-inch pan suitable for use in a freezer, distributing it evenly in pan. Very finely crumble (or grind in a blender) the remaining *6 graham cracker squares* and sprinkle evenly over the pineapple mixture. Garnish the top with the cherries, if desired. Cover and refrigerate until well chilled, about 2 hours. **NOTE**: If you're in a hurry, freeze the pineapple delight for 30 minutes, then transfer to refrigerator and keep refrigerated until ready to serve.

BOBBY'S RECIPE

Creamy Warm Fresh Fruit Salad
(Salade de Fruits Frais Crèmeux)

Makes 3 quarts or about 16 servings

Mom served fruit salad as a dessert, and she made it with a combination of fresh and home-canned fruits. The ingredient that set Mom's recipe apart from today's fruit salads was rich, thick fresh cream—straight from the cow. The cows were milked every morning and evening, and fresh milk that has not been pasteurized or homogenized is unbelievably different from milk sold in supermarkets today. The fresh milk was caught in clean milk pails, carried into the house, poured into large crockery bowls, and put in the icebox (or refrigerator, in later years). After a few hours, the fresh milk formed a very thick cream on top, to a depth of ½ to ¾ of an inch in the bowl. It was so thick that you literally could reach into the center of the bowl with your fingers and pick the cream up intact. The taste was incomparable.

Mom used cream in fruit salads and coffee, and she made homemade sweet butter with it. Bobby remembers her fruit salads vividly, and he makes his just the same way. This is definitely a dessert and not a salad. It is very rich and, as Bobby says, "It don't take much!" When his daughters were youngsters, Bobby and the girls fought each other for the cherries. Mom used maraschino cherries because that was all that was available, but any canned sweet cherries would be fine.

2 tablespoons unsalted butter

1 pound peaches, peeled and chopped (about 2½ cups)

½ pound apricots or plums, peeled and chopped (about 1 cup)

3 cups chopped fresh pineapple, *in all*

1½ cups well-mashed *overripe* bananas (about 3 medium to large)

½ pint heavy cream

½ cup plus 2 tablespoons sugar

1 (14-ounce) can sweetened condensed milk

1 (6-ounce) jar maraschino cherries, drained (reserve liquid), and coarsely chopped (or use canned sweet cherries)

2 cups sliced bananas (about 2 medium)

1 medium to large firm red apple, unpeeled and finely chopped (about 2 cups)

1½ cups whole strawberries, hulled

½ pound pears, peeled and chopped (about 1 cup)

2 large oranges, peeled and separated into segments without membrane (about 1 cup segments)

1 tablespoon orange juice

Place the butter and peaches in a large skillet over medium heat; cook about 5 minutes, stirring frequently. Add the apricots or plums and stir well; cook about 2 minutes, stirring occasionally. Add *1 cup* of the chopped pineapple, the mashed bananas, cream, and sugar; cook about 5 minutes more, stirring occasionally. Remove from heat and stir in the condensed milk and cherry juice (but not the cherries).

In a very large mixing bowl, combine the remaining *2 cups* pineapple, the sliced bananas, apple, strawberries, pears, oranges, cherries, and orange juice. Add the hot cream mixture to the fruit, mixing well. Let sit about 30 minutes at room temperature. Then serve immediately, while still warm, which we think is best. Or refrigerate and serve well chilled. This salad is splendid for a buffet table, leftovers make a lovely breakfast, and try it over ice cream for a decadent variation.

J.C. AND SIS'S RECIPE

Fresh Coconut Pralines
(Pralines au Coco Frais)

Makes about 1½ dozen pralines

Dad Prudhomme planted peanuts (the children had parched peanuts for snacks), which Mom used for making peanut pralines; she only made pecan pralines for very special occasions. Sis prefers making coconut pralines, because J.C. is crazy about coconut. It's worth the extra time and effort to prepare fresh coconut for these unusual, creamy pralines.

*The trickiest thing about pralines is judging the precise moment when they are done (see **Lagniappe**) and then spooning them out quickly so they will harden with just the right texture. Follow the recipe and read the lagniappe carefully, and you should end up with delicious pralines just like Sis makes.*

3 cups, *in all*, lightly packed grated fresh coconut
    (preferred), about 7 ounces (see **NOTE**)
3 cups sugar
1 (12-ounce) can evaporated milk
½ cup milk
4 tablespoons unsalted butter
2 teaspoons vanilla extract

NOTE: You can use packaged coconut flakes, but remember they are sweeter than fresh coconut.

Assemble all the ingredients and utensils before starting to cook. You will need a candy thermometer, a large, heavy-bottomed aluminum pot or skillet with deep sides, a long-handled metal whisk or spoon, 2 large spoons (or an ice-cream scoop with a manual release), and enough lightly buttered cookie sheets to hold at least 18 pralines. Spray the spoons or scoop with vegetable spray or grease them with butter.

Be careful not to get any of the cooked mixture on your skin, as it sticks and can cause serious burns.

Spread *half* the coconut on an ungreased cookie sheet and bake at 350° until toasted, about 10 minutes, stirring fairly often so coconut won't burn. Remove from oven and set aside.

Combine the sugar, evaporated milk, and milk in the pot. Place over high heat and bring to a boil, whisking frequently until sugar dissolves. Then whisk only occasionally until it reaches a boil again. Now reduce heat to medium and cook until mixture reaches the soft-ball stage (240° on candy thermometer), about 24 minutes, whisking constantly. Add the coconut (both the toasted and untoasted), and the butter and vanilla, stirring vigorously for about 1½ minutes (see **Lagniappe** on tests for doneness). Remove pan from heat.

Quickly and carefully drop the batter onto the cookie sheets by heaping spoonfuls, using the second spoon to scoop the batter off the first (or use ice-cream scoop). Each praline patty should be 2 to 3 inches in diameter and about ½ inch thick.

Cool and store in an airtight container, or wrap each praline in plastic wrap or foil.

· · · · · · · · · · · · · ·**·LAGNIAPPE·**· · · · · · · · · · · · ·

To judge doneness, use one or more of the following guides:

· ·

1. The batter will begin forming distinct threads on the sides or bottom of the pan.

2. Near the end of the cooking time, make a test praline every few seconds. The early-test praline will be somewhat runny, very shiny, and somewhat translucent. The ideal praline will have progressed past that stage—it will not be runny and will be less shiny. When cooled, it will be opaque, lusterless, and crumbly instead of chewy.

3. Near the end of the cooking time, drizzle spoonfuls of the mixture across the surface of the mixture. When ready, it will form a neat thread across the surface.

To clean the pot and utensils, boil water in the pot with the utensils in it. This will melt the batter off.

MALCOLM AND VERSIE'S RECIPE

Roasted-Pecan Butter Pecan Pie
(Tarte de Pacanes Grillées Faite en Beurre)

Makes one 8½-inch pie

Mom Prudhomme's mother, Grandma LeDoux, was the pecan pie expert of the family. Her pies were fabulous and reserved for Sunday dinners and holidays. Paul says Mom preferred making fruit pies and sweet potato pie. The family home site didn't have pecan trees on it, but there were a few trees fairly nearby and the children picked up the nuts during late fall for Mom to make cookies, pralines, and holiday fruit cake. The family never had an abundance of pecans, so anything made with them was special.

Malcolm and Versie's pecan pie is delicious; it's not syrupy sweet like many pecan pies. When we tested it for the cookbook, everyone who had tasted it was still asking weeks later, "When will you bake another pecan pie?"

Dough:

1 cup plus 3 tablespoons all-purpose flour, *in all*

½ teaspoon salt

7 tablespoons cold unsalted butter, cut into small
    pieces

¼ cup ice water

Pecan Filling:

½ cup pecan pieces or halves, dry roasted until dark

3 large eggs

1 cup sugar

1 cup dark corn syrup

2 tablespoons unsalted butter, melted and cooled

1½ teaspoons vanilla extract

⅛ teaspoon salt

1 cup pecan halves

For the dough: Sift *1 cup* of the flour and the salt into a large mixing bowl. Add the butter and, working quickly and with a light touch, cut butter into the flour with a spoon and fingertips (or use a pastry cutter) until mixture is the texture of coarse cornmeal. Add the ice water and stir until well blended. Form the dough into a ball and place on a flat surface floured with the remaining *3 tablespoons* flour.

With a floured rolling pin, roll out dough to a thickness of ¼ to ⅛ inch. Place an ungreased 8½-inch round pie pan face down on top of the dough and cut around the pan, leaving a ¾-inch border. Lightly flour the top of the dough and fold it in quarters. Carefully place dough in the pie pan, with the points of the folded dough centered. Unfold dough and line the pan bottom and sides, gently pressing dough into place and draping a little over the rim. Flute the edges (Versie does this so quickly and well!) or trim the edges. Refrigerate prepared pie shell until ready to use.

For the filling: Process the roasted pecans in a food processor until they become a relatively smooth butter, 2 to 3 minutes, scraping sides down as needed with a rubber spatula.

Place the eggs in a medium-size bowl of an electric mixer and beat on high speed a few seconds until frothy. Add the sugar, corn syrup, butter, vanilla, salt, and the pecan butter. Beat on medium speed a few seconds until well mixed, pushing sides down as needed. Stir in the unroasted pecans.

Pour mixture into the prepared pie shell. Place on a cookie sheet and bake at 350° for 40 minutes. Reduce heat to 325° and cook until filling is browned on top and crust on edges is lightly browned, about 40 minutes more. Remove from oven and let cool at least 30 minutes before serving.

Sweet Dough for Pies
(Pâte Douce pour les Tartes)

Makes dough for one 9-inch pie

Once Sis got this pie dough the way she wanted it, we used it for all three of her sweet-dough pies. Make it exactly the same way for each pie.

About 1¼ cups all-purpose flour, *in all*
1 teaspoon baking powder
1 egg
⅓ cup sugar
3 tablespoons cold unsalted butter, cut into very small pieces
3 tablespoons cold milk
½ teaspoon vanilla extract
¼ teaspoon ground nutmeg
⅛ teaspoon ground cinnamon

In a small bowl, sift together *¾ cup plus 2 tablespoons* of the flour and the baking powder. Set aside.

   In a medium-size bowl, combine the egg and sugar; mix with a large spoon until well blended and very frothy, about 1 minute. Add the butter and stir just a few seconds until butter is separated into very small pieces but not creamed into mixture. (Sis says, "The less you fool with dough, the better!") Add the milk, vanilla, ground nutmeg, and cinnamon; stir a few seconds. Add the flour mixture, stirring just until blended.

   Generously flour a flat surface. Divide the dough (it will be very soft) into 1 two-thirds portion and 1 one-third portion; spoon each portion onto the floured surface, keeping them separate. Flour hands liberally with additional flour and roll the larger portion of dough in flour until it no longer sticks to your hands; place it in the center of an ungreased 9-inch pie pan and line the bottom and sides evenly with the dough, pressing dough gently into place. Continue to flour your hands as needed. Gently shake off any excess flour from the pie shell; set aside. Reserve the remaining dough.

Now follow the instructions for filling each pie (fig, fresh peach, or fresh blackberry). Then make the lattice with the reserved one third of the dough this way:

With floured hands, roll the reserved portion of dough in flour until it no longer sticks to your hands, then separate it into 6 equal pieces. With floured hands, place them over the pie as follows: Tease 3 portions of dough into long flat strips and lay them across the pie in one direction. Make strips of the remaining 3 pieces and lay criss-cross on top of the first 3 strips, stretching them to fill any large gaps. (This lattice will look quite roughly done.) Wipe any flour from the pan rim and dab dough strips with a clean dish towel to remove surface flour.

The pie is ready to bake. Follow the instructions in the individual recipes; they are not all identical.

J.C. AND SIS'S RECIPE

Fig Sweet-Dough Pie
(Tarte aux Figues à Pâte Douce)

Makes one 9-inch pie

Fig trees are abundant in South Louisiana. Mom made fresh fig sweet-dough pie often during fig season, and she put up many jars of fig preserves each year. The preserves were the family's favorite sweet to eat with hot breads for breakfast and supper.

*Sis made the Fig Preserves for the cookbook, and she made this pie with the freshly made preserves. Ten of J.C. and Sis's recipes in the cookbook are desserts, and two more, **Candied Yams** (page 283) and **Sweet Squash with Nutmeg and Vanilla** (page 285), are sweet. Sis has firmly convinced us all of the strength of her sweet tooth—and J.C. was awfully pleased that she made so many of the sweets.*

1 recipe **Sweet Dough for Pies** (preceding recipe)
1 pint **Fig Preserves** (page 349)
½ teaspoon freshly grated nutmeg
6 paper-thin slices orange (seeded)
4 paper-thin slices lemon (seeded)
4 tablespoons unsalted butter, melted
¼ cup water
1½ teaspoons vanilla extract
Pinch of salt

Line the pie pan with the dough (page 387) and set aside, reserving one third of the dough.

In a medium-size bowl, combine the Fig Preserves and grated nutmeg. Mash well with a pastry blender until well blended and all large fig lumps are broken up. Add the remaining ingredients, mixing well with a spoon.

To assemble, pour the fig mixture into prepared pie shell and spread evenly over the dough. Distribute the orange and lemon slices evenly so each pie slice will contain some. Then make sure orange and lemon are well coated by pushing them down a bit and spooning some of the fig mixture over them. Cover the filling with the pie-dough lattice (page 388).

Bake at 375° until dark golden brown, about 24 minutes. Remove from oven and cool until firm, about 15 minutes. Serve as is or top with ice cream.

J.C. AND SIS'S RECIPE

Fresh Peach Sweet-Dough Pie
(Tarte aux Pêches Fraîches à Pâte Douce)

Makes one 9-inch pie

Although the family didn't have peach trees on the property they farmed, lots of friends and relatives did, so Mom had fresh or home-

canned peaches for making pies and fruit salad. She made sweet-dough crusts for all her pies and semisweet pie crust for crawfish pie. All the Prudhomme children and their families use sweet-dough crusts, and, like Mom, Paul makes semisweet crusts for crawfish dishes.

When we were cooking with J.C. and Sis for the cookbook, she and Paul sang in French while she made her sweet-dough pies. Sis says she gained three pounds practicing all her recipes, but that she lost the extra pounds when she cooked with us because we made her work so hard.

Our Louisiana peaches are sweet, juicy, and firm textured, but very few are marketed outside the state. So choose peaches that smell wonderfully ripe and be sure to make the pie at least once during the peak of peach season to get the best taste possible.

2 pounds peaches, peeled and quartered
¾ cup sugar
½ cup water
2 teaspoons cornstarch dissolved in 1 tablespoon
　　water
½ teaspoon ground nutmeg
1 recipe **Sweet Dough for Pies** (page 387)

Make the filling first: In a 2-quart saucepan, combine the peaches, sugar, and water. Bring to a boil over high heat, stirring occasionally. Reduce heat to medium and cook until peaches are tender and juice becomes a heavy syrup, about 14 minutes, stirring occasionally and skimming foam from surface as it develops. With pan still over medium heat, skim any remaining foam from surface, then mash peaches with a pastry blender or the back of a large spoon until no large pieces remain. Stir the cornstarch into the peaches, mixing well and mashing the peaches a bit more against the side of the pan until all peach pieces are fairly small. Remove from heat and add the nutmeg, stirring until well blended. Set aside to cool while making the pie shell.

Line the pan with the dough (page 387), reserving one third of the dough. Pour the reserved peach filling into the pie shell, distributing it evenly. Cover the filling with the pie-dough lattice (page 388).

Bake at 375° until crust is dark golden brown, about 24 minutes. Remove from oven and cool until filling is firm, about 45 minutes. Serve as is or top with ice cream.

J.C. AND SIS'S RECIPE

Fresh Blackberry Sweet-Dough Pie
(Tarte aux Mûres d'Éronce Fraîches à Pâte Douce)

Makes one 9-inch pie

Blackberries were one fruit the Prudhomme family could look forward to in great abundance each year. They grow wild and thick in South Louisiana. During the season (mid-June to mid-July), after finishing their evening chores, the children went to pick blackberries for an hour or so. They ate them by the quart as they picked them, and they loved them in sweet-dough pie.

At the peak of the season, Mom, Dad, and the children took a day or two off from regular work and went en masse to pick berries by the gallon. Mom canned them whole in their juice to use for pies and she made blackberry preserves and **Blackberry Jelly** *(page 351).*

This pie recipe won the record for being retested the most often— seven times! We think this might be because it's so good that we kept looking for reasons to retest it. However, blackberries vary greatly from batch to batch in sweetness, juiciness, and pectin content. All these factors affect the thickness of the pie filling, so we've worked out a method to compensate for the variations.

1¼ pounds picked-over blackberries, or 1 quart picked over, *in all*
About 1½ cups sugar, *in all*
Between 4 and 7 tablespoons cornstarch, *in all*
2 tablespoons blackberry-flavored brandy
½ teaspoon ground cinnamon
½ teaspoon ground nutmeg
1 recipe **Sweet Dough for Pies** (page 387)

Make the filling first: Place 2 *cups* of the blackberries in a blender or food processor and process a few seconds until puréed. Strain purée through a mesh strainer into a measuring cup, forcing liquid through with the back of a spoon and extracting as much juice as possible. Discard seeds. (The yield should be between ¾ cup to 1¼ cups strained purée.)

Place the purée in a 2-quart saucepan. Add *1 cup* of the sugar and whisk with a metal whisk until well blended. (If your berries are not very sweet, add ½ *cup* more sugar; if in doubt, add the extra sugar.) Bring to a boil over high heat, stirring almost constantly. Continue boiling until mixture is a syrup, about 5 minutes, stirring almost constantly and scraping pan bottom well.

Meanwhile, in a small bowl, stir together *4 tablespoons* of the cornstarch and the brandy until well blended. After the purée has boiled for about 5 minutes, remove from heat and whisk the cornstarch mixture into the purée; return to high heat and cook just until mixture reaches a boil, whisking constantly and making sure to scrape pan bottom well. Remove from heat and stir in the cinnamon and nutmeg until thoroughly blended.

NOTE: At this point, check thickness of filling; if it isn't syrupy thick, it will not thicken enough during baking to "set up" properly, so you will need to adjust it. If in doubt, check to see if it's thick enough by doing the following: Remove 2 tablespoons of filling to a very small bowl, add 2 berries, and break up berries to release their juice. Place bowl over a larger bowl containing ice and stir a few seconds until mixture comes to room temperature; if this mixture is not a very thick syrup, you will need to add more cornstarch to the main mixture: Dissolve *3 tablespoons* more cornstarch in 1 to 2 tablespoons water; use the least amount of water possible. Then whisk the dissolved cornstarch into the pan of filling; place over high heat and return mixture to a boil, stirring constantly. Remove from heat and set aside while making the pie shell.

If the filling seems thick enough without checking, set aside while making the pie shell.

Line the pie pan with the dough (page 387), reserving one third of the dough. Distribute the reserved 2 *cups* whole blackberries evenly in the bottom of the prepared pie shell. Pour the thickened blackberry purée evenly over the berries, making sure to coat them all well. Cover the filling with the pie-dough lattice (page 388).

Place the pie on a cookie sheet and bake at 375° until crust is dark golden brown, about 24 minutes. Remove from oven and let cool a little before serving. Serve as is or top with ice cream.

MALCOLM AND VERSIE'S RECIPE

Lemon Sweet Pie-Dough Coffee Cake
(Tit Gâteau de Limon)

Makes 1 coffee cake or 10 to 12 servings

All the Prudhommes have a sweet tooth. So does Versie. She likes to bake, especially desserts. The next generation is really interested in sweets, too. Malcolm and Versie's daughter, Brenda, has been a baker in the restaurant business for about five years. She and her husband, Pete Lutzen, who is a chef, work at a restaurant in Portland, Oregon.

Malcolm is an authentic sweet-tooth Prudhomme. He says Versie's coffee cake is "gooood!" for a snack or dessert.

Dough:
¼ pound (1 stick) unsalted butter, softened
½ cup sugar
2 large eggs
¾ teaspoon baking powder
½ teaspoon vanilla extract
½ teaspoon almond extract
1½ cups all-purpose flour

Filling:
1¼ cups warm tap water
1 cup sugar

¼ cup cornstarch
⅛ teaspoon salt
¼ cup lemon juice, freshly squeezed
3 large egg yolks, well beaten
1 tablespoon unsalted butter
2 teaspoons unsalted butter, melted (to brush top of
    cake)

For the dough: In a medium-size bowl of an electric mixer, combine the butter, sugar, eggs, baking powder, vanilla, and almond extract. Beat on low speed a few seconds to blend, then on high speed until light and creamy smooth, about 4 minutes, pushing sides down with a rubber spatula. With machine still running, add the flour by spoonfuls, beating until well blended between additions and pushing sides down as needed. Turn speed to low and beat about 2 minutes more.

Reserve 1 cup of the dough for the topping. Spoon the remaining dough into a greased 11 × 7-inch cake pan (1½ inches deep), spreading the dough evenly over the bottom and up the sides of the pan to about ½ inch from the top edge. (What you are making is a very shallow bowl of the dough.) Set aside.

For the filling: In a 2-quart saucepan, combine the water, sugar, cornstarch, and salt, stirring well. Place over medium heat and cook about 4 minutes, stirring almost constantly. Add the lemon juice and cook for about 2 minutes, stirring constantly. Stir in the egg yolks and the 1 tablespoon butter; cook 3 to 4 minutes more, stirring constantly.

Remove from heat and spoon mixture into the prepared shell, spreading the filling out evenly on top of the dough. Then drop scant teaspoonfuls of the reserved batter close together and evenly over the top of the filling, making about 4 rows across and about 6 rows down.

Bake at 350° until cake is done and well browned on top, about 40 minutes. Remove from oven and, with a pastry brush, brush the top with the melted butter. Let sit at least 40 minutes before cutting. Store leftovers overnight covered and at room temperature. After that, refrigerate.

MALCOLM AND VERSIE'S RECIPE

Fresh Pear Sweet Pie-Dough Coffee Cake
(Tit Gâteau de Poires Fraîches)

Makes 1 coffee cake or 10 to 12 servings

There were pear trees near the family home, and the Prudhomme children picked pears by the bushel during the season. They sneaked a lot of them to eat raw. Mom canned pears for preserves and for sweet-dough pie.

Malcolm and Versie's pear sweet pie-dough cake is rich and buttery. They serve it to special company along with good, strong Louisiana dark-roast coffee.

Dough:
½ pound (2 sticks) unsalted butter, softened (see **NOTE**)
½ cup sugar
2 large eggs
¾ teaspoon baking powder
½ teaspoon vanilla extract
½ teaspoon almond extract
1½ cups all-purpose flour

Filling:
6 cups peeled, cored, and coarsely chopped pears (about 2¾ pounds)
¾ cup sugar
2 tablespoons unsalted butter
2 tablespoons water
1 teaspoon vanilla extract
2 tablespoons unsalted butter, melted (to brush top of cake)

Glaze:
½ cup powdered sugar
About 2½ teaspoons milk, *in all*

NOTE: The dough for this coffee cake should be richer than the one in the preceding recipe, therefore, use ½ pound butter.

For the dough: In a medium-size bowl of an electric mixer, combine the butter, sugar, eggs, baking powder, vanilla, and almond extract. Beat on low speed a few seconds to blend, then on high speed until light and creamy smooth, about 4 minutes, pushing sides down with a rubber spatula. With machine still running, add the flour by spoonfuls, beating until well blended between additions and pushing sides down as needed. Turn speed to low and beat about 2 minutes more.

Reserve 1 cup of the dough for the topping. Spoon the remaining dough into a greased 11 × 7-inch cake pan (1½ inches deep), spreading the dough evenly over the bottom and up the sides of the pan to about ½ inch from the top edge. (What you are making is a very shallow bowl of the dough.) Set aside.

For the filling: In a large skillet, combine the pears, sugar, and the 2 tablespoons *unmelted* butter. Place over medium heat and cook until mixture is browned and fairly dry, about 35 minutes, stirring and scraping pan bottom occasionally and more often toward end of cooking time. (**NOTE:** If mixture gets dry before it browns, add 1 tablespoon of water as needed.) Turn heat to low and add the 2 tablespoons water and the vanilla, stirring well. Cook about 3 minutes more or until mixture is fairly dry again, stirring frequently. Remove from heat and spoon mixture into the prepared shell, spreading the filling out evenly on top of the dough. Then drop scant teaspoonfuls of the reserved batter close together and evenly over the top of the filling, making about 4 rows across and about 6 rows down.

Bake at 350° until cake is done and dark golden brown on top, about 35 minutes. Remove from oven and, with a pastry brush, brush the top with the melted butter. Set aside.

For the glaze: Place the sugar in a small bowl. Stir in 2 *teaspoons* of the milk, mixing a few seconds, just until smooth. Immediately drizzle over the hot cake. (If glaze gets too thick as you drizzle it, add about ½ *teaspoon more* milk.)

Let cake sit 30 minutes before cutting. Store leftovers overnight covered and at room temperature. After that, refrigerate.

ENOLA AND SHELTON'S RECIPE

Apple Cake with Apple Chantilly Cream
(Gâteau aux Pommes)

Makes 1 tube cake

In the early days, the family rarely had fruits like apples, bananas, and oranges except at holiday times, especially Christmas; they didn't grow in the area and Mom and Dad had to buy them at a store. Mom had the fresh fruits that grew nearby, like blackberries, dewberries, mulberries, muscadines, figs, pears, peaches, and persimmons for her fruit salads, canning, and baking, but an apple cake would have been something very special.

Enola's children and everyone else we know who's tasted it love this moist and delicious cake. It's not syrupy sweet, and Enola and Shelton guarantee that it has "no" calories!

Because the cake is very dense, it's best to use a tube pan with a removable bottom so you won't have to turn the pan over to remove the cake.

2 pounds Granny Smith apples (about 5 medium)
3 cups water
Lemon juice, to squeeze on apples
2½ cups sugar, *in all*
¾ pound (3 sticks) unsalted butter
1 teaspoon ground cinnamon
½ teaspoon ground nutmeg
3¼ cups all-purpose flour
1½ teaspoons baking soda
1 teaspoon salt
1 cup coarsely chopped pecans, dry roasted until dark, then cooled
1 teaspoon ground allspice
3 large eggs

1 tablespoon vanilla extract
Butter, to butter cake pan
Flour, to flour cake pan
Glaze (recipe follows)
Icing (recipe follows)
Apple Chantilly Cream (recipe follows)

To make the cake: Peel and core the apples; place the peelings and cores in a 2-quart saucepan with the water. Finely chop the apples and add ½ cup of them to the pan with the peelings and cores. Squeeze lemon juice over the remaining apple pieces and refrigerate until ready to use.

Add ½ *cup* of the sugar to the pan and bring mixture to a boil over high heat, stirring once or twice. Continue boiling until liquid is slightly syrupy, about 25 minutes, stirring occasionally. Remove from heat and strain mixture, extracting as much juice as possible. Discard remaining mixture. The yield of the strained syrup should be about 1 cup; reserve ¼ cup of the syrup in the refrigerator for the chantilly cream.

Return ½ cup of the remaining strained syrup to the pan. (Save any remaining syrup to substitute for some of the water called for in the glaze.) Add the butter, cinnamon, and nutmeg. Cook over high heat just until butter is melted and all ingredients are blended, about 2 minutes, whisking or stirring constantly. Set aside.

In a large bowl, sift together the flour, baking soda, and salt. Stir in the remaining 2 *cups* sugar, the pecans, and allspice, mixing well. Set aside.

In a very large bowl of an electric mixer, beat the eggs on high speed about 1 minute. Add the vanilla, then gradually beat in the reserved butter-and-apple-syrup mixture; continue beating on high speed about 1 minute. Reduce speed to medium and gradually beat in the flour mixture, beating until ingredients are well blended; continue beating about 2 minutes more, pushing sides down with a rubber spatula. Fold in the chopped apples.

Spoon the batter into a greased and lightly floured 10-inch tube pan with a removable bottom. Place in a preheated 425° oven, immediately reduce heat to 375°, and bake until cake is brown and bounces back when lightly pressed, about 1 hour and 10 minutes. Remove from oven and place pan on a wire rack. Let cake sit in pan until thoroughly cooled, about 1 hour, so it won't crack open. (Once the cake is out of the oven, it will continue to cook by residual heat from the pan and from the apples inside.)

However, while the cake is still warm and in the pan, glaze and ice the top. **NOTE:** After about 20 minutes, you may be able to remove, very carefully, the side section of the pan before icing the top, but leave the center tube and bottom section in place until cake is thoroughly cooled. If in doubt, leave side section of pan in place, too.

Serve with a dollop of Apple Chantilly Cream on each slice.

Glaze

½ cup powdered sugar
½ cup leftover strained apple syrup or water (or a mixture of both)
1 teaspoon lemon juice
1 teaspoon vanilla extract

In a 1-quart saucepan, combine the powdered sugar, syrup (or water), and lemon juice, mixing well. Bring to a boil, stirring frequently. Remove from heat and stir in the vanilla. Immediately brush the glaze evenly over the warm cake, making slits in the top of the cake with a knife so glaze can sink in and using all the glaze. Makes about ¾ cup.

Icing

1 heaping cup powdered sugar
4 ounces cream cheese, softened
½ cup coarsely chopped pecans, dry roasted and cooled
4 tablespoons margarine, softened
1 teaspoon vanilla extract

In a medium-size bowl of an electric mixer, combine all the ingredients and beat on low speed until well blended, about 2 minutes, pushing the sides down with a rubber spatula. Immediately spread over the top of the cake. Makes a scant 1½ cups.

Apple Chantilly Cream

⅔ cup heavy cream
1 teaspoon vanilla extract
1 teaspoon brandy
1 teaspoon Grand Marnier
¼ cup sugar
¼ cup reserved apple syrup

Chill a medium-size bowl of an electric mixer and the beaters until very cold. Combine the cream, vanilla, brandy, and Grand Marnier in the chilled bowl and beat with the electric mixer on medium speed about 1 minute. Add the sugar and apple syrup and beat on medium speed just until soft peaks form, about 3 minutes. Do not overbeat. Makes about 2 cups.

DARILEE AND SAUL'S RECIPE

Sweet Memories Pecan Cake
(Gâteau aux Pacanes du Souvenir)

Makes one 4-layer cake

Darilee created this cake during the early years of her marriage when she and Saul lived on some land with a large, productive pecan tree. Paul remembers Darilee's pecan cake vividly from an early age. (Darilee and Saul were married four years before Paul was born.) He liked it so much and remembers it so well that he still uses the memory of the taste of Darilee's pecan cake to create pecan dishes today.

*Because Paul and Enola were fairly close in age, he didn't have a chance to grow up tasting and appreciating her **Roasted Pecan Cake with Roasted Pecan Filling** (next recipe), but Enola's cake is really special, too; you must try both!*

Pecan Filling:

2½ cups, *in all*, pecan pieces, dry roasted until dark, then ground

2 cups sugar

¾ cup milk

5 tablespoons unsalted butter

1 teaspoon vanilla extract

¾ cup canned sweetened condensed milk

Cake:

2½ cups all-purpose flour, sifted

2 tablespoons baking powder

⅛ teaspoon salt

2¼ cups sugar

1 cup heavy cream

3 large eggs

2 tablespoons plus 1½ teaspoons vanilla extract

½ pound (2 sticks) plus 4 tablespoons unsalted
     butter, melted and cooled

Butter and waxed paper to prepare pans

Glaze (recipe follows)

Icing (recipe follows)

For the filling: Set aside *2 tablespoons* of the ground pecans for garnishing the finished cake.

In a heavy 3-quart saucepan or Dutch oven, combine the sugar and fresh milk, stirring with a long-handled wooden spoon until well blended. Add the butter, place over high heat, and bring to a boil, stirring constantly. Add the remaining *2 cups plus 6 tablespoons* pecans and the vanilla. Cook until mixture is thick and is just starting to pull away from the edges of the pan, about 5 minutes, stirring constantly and being careful not to let it splash on your skin. Remove from heat and gradually stir in the condensed milk, mixing until well blended. Set aside.

For the cake: Sift together the flour, baking powder, and salt and set aside.

In a large bowl of an electric mixer, combine the sugar and cream; beat on medium speed a few seconds until well blended, pushing sides down with a rubber spatula. Add *1 cup* of the flour mixture, the eggs, and vanilla; beat on medium speed for about 1 minute, pushing sides down as needed. Add *1 cup* more flour mixture and the butter; beat on low speed until blended, then on high speed for about 2 minutes. Gradually add the *remaining* flour mixture and continue beating on high speed until very smooth and creamy, about 3 minutes more, pushing sides down as needed.

Butter the bottoms and sides of four 9-inch round cake pans 2 inches deep. Cut waxed paper rounds to fit the pans. Line each pan bottom with one of the rounds and butter the tops of the rounds. Spoon about 1½ cups of batter into each pan, spreading batter evenly. Bake, 2 layers at a time, at 350° on the middle rack of the oven until centers spring back when lightly pressed, 18 to 20 minutes. Remove cake from oven and let pans cool on a wire rack for about 5 minutes. Meanwhile, make the glaze.

Run a knife around the sides of each layer and carefully remove layers from the pans. Peel off the waxed paper from the bottoms and place layers on the wire rack. While the cake is still warm, place one layer on a cake platter, brush it with one fourth (about 4½ tablespoons) of the glaze on the top and sides, making a few small slits in layer with a paring knife. Spread one fourth of the filling (about ¾ cup plus 2 tablespoons) evenly on the top but not sides of the layer. **NOTE**: If filling gets too thick as it sits, thin it to spreading consistency with a little more milk or water.

Now place another layer on top of the first and repeat the procedure of glazing, spreading on filling, and adding the next layer on top until all the layers have been glazed and spread with filling, including the top one.

Let cake cool thoroughly, then ice the top and sides. Garnish with the reserved 2 tablespoons ground pecans.

Glaze

1 cup water
½ cup sugar
1 teaspoon vanilla extract

In a small saucepan, combine the water and sugar and bring to a boil. Remove from heat and stir in the vanilla. With a pastry brush,

brush the hot glaze over the surface and a little on the sides of each cake layer, making small slits in the layers with a paring knife so the glaze can sink in and using all the glaze. Makes 1⅛ cups.

Icing

6 egg whites
2 cups sugar
⅔ cup water
1½ teaspoons vanilla extract

Place the egg whites in a large bowl of an electric mixer. Beat on high speed about 1 minute until soft peaks form. Set aside.

Combine the sugar and water in a 2-quart saucepan and bring to a boil over high heat, stirring occasionally. Continue boiling until mixture reaches 230° on a candy thermometer (soft-thread stage), 2 to 3 minutes, stirring almost constantly. Remove from heat and let sit a few seconds until mixture is no longer bubbling, then with the electric mixer on high speed, very gradually beat the syrup mixture into the egg whites. Add the vanilla and continue beating until icing is creamy and thick enough to spread, 5 to 7 minutes more. If icing is not quite thick enough, refrigerate it for a few minutes before using. Makes about 6 cups.

ENOLA AND SHELTON'S RECIPE

Roasted Pecan Cake
with Roasted Pecan Filling
(Gâteau de Pacanes Grillées avec Pacanes pour Mettre entre Ton Gâteau)

Makes one 2-layer cake

When Mom and Dad retired from the family store, they finally had time to enjoy their many grandchildren—they had forty-seven grandchildren! Both Mom and Dad had worked hard all their married life, but they had no trouble learning to take it easy. They had always known how to have a good time and enjoy life.

All the grandchildren loved to go visit with Mom and Dad. Enola's children remember that Dad took them out to gather berries in the spring and to pick up pecans in the fall. He designed simple pecan "picker-uppers" for the grandkids to use; one kind was a stick with a can nailed to the end and the other was a stick with a short forked end. The children could slide the cans along the ground to gather the nuts or push the forked sticks down over the pecans and pick them up that way. Dad liked to use the gadgets, too, as he got older, so he didn't have to bend over.

Enola loved to have her children go gather pecans with Dad so she could use them in her baking. Enola still remembers how Mom roasted pecans outdoors in a cast-iron skillet over a wood fire. She likes to make this roasted pecan cake with its pecan filling because it reminds her of the wonderful taste of Mom's pecan desserts.

The cake has the taste and texture of a homemade country cake— not very sweet, relatively dense, with plenty of flavor.

Butter and waxed paper to prepare cake pans

Cake:
2½ cups all-purpose flour
1 tablespoon baking powder
1⅛ teaspoons salt
1½ cups sugar
¼ pound (1 stick) unsalted butter, very soft
4 tablespoons margarine, very soft
1 cup milk
3 large eggs
1 tablespoon vanilla extract
½ cup chopped pecans, dry roasted

Glaze (recipe follows)
Pecan Filling (recipe follows)
½ cup pecan halves, dry roasted and cooled, to garnish cake

Heavy cream or half-and-half to serve
    under each slice of cake, optional
    (see **Note**)

Note: Allow 2 to 3 tablespoons cream or half-and-half per serving.

Butter the bottoms and sides of two 10-inch round cake pans 2 inches deep. Cut waxed paper rounds to fit the pans. Line each pan bottom with one of the rounds and rub butter on tops of the rounds. Set aside.

In a medium-size bowl, combine the flour, baking powder, and salt, mixing well. Set aside.

In a large bowl of an electric mixer, combine the sugar, butter, and margarine; beat on medium speed until creamed and very light in color, 6 to 8 minutes, pushing sides down with a rubber spatula. Add the milk, eggs, and vanilla; beat on low speed a few seconds so liquid won't splash out of bowl, then on medium speed until butter mixture is reduced to very small lumps, about 3 minutes. Reduce speed to low and gradually add the flour mixture, beating until the dry mixture is blended in and pushing sides down as needed. Increase speed to high and beat about 1 minute. Add the chopped pecans and beat a few seconds more until pecans are mixed in.

Spoon equal portions of the batter into the cake pans, spreading the batter evenly. Bake at 375° on the middle rack of the oven until centers spring back when lightly pressed, 25 to 27 minutes. Remove layers from oven and set pans on a wire rack to cool about 5 minutes. Meanwhile, make the glaze.

Loosen sides of cake with a knife and carefully remove layers from pans. Peel off the waxed paper from the bottoms and place layers on the wire rack. While the cake is still warm, place one layer on a cake platter, brush it with one half (about ⅓ cup) of the glaze on the top and sides, making a few small slits in cake with a paring knife. Glaze the other layer on the wire rack. Cool cake thoroughly, then spread half the filling (scant 1 cup) on the bottom layer. Place the second layer on top and spread the remaining filling over it, letting a little dribble down the sides. Garnish top with pecan halves.

If using cream or half-and-half, spoon 2 to 3 tablespoons on each dessert plate, place a slice of cake on top, and serve immediately.

Glaze

¾ cup water
½ cup powdered sugar
1 teaspoon lemon juice
1 teaspoon vanilla extract

In a 1-quart saucepan, combine the water, sugar, and lemon juice, mixing well. Bring to a boil, stirring frequently. Remove from heat and stir in the vanilla. With a pastry brush, immediately brush the glaze evenly over the tops and a little on the sides of the warm cake layers, making slits in the layers with a paring knife so the glaze can sink in and using it all. Makes about ⅔ cup.

Pecan Filling

1 (14-ounce) can sweetened condensed milk
1 (3-ounce) package cream cheese, very soft
1 teaspoon vanilla extract
¾ cup chopped pecans, dry roasted and cooled

In the top of a double boiler, but not over heat, combine the condensed milk and cream cheese, stirring until mixture is as smooth and creamy as possible, with only tiny lumps of cheese remaining. Place over a pan of simmering (not boiling) water, being sure top pan does not touch water. Cook until mixture is of spreading consistency (it should look like thin mashed potatoes), about 9 minutes, stirring constantly so mixture doesn't scorch. Remove from heat and stir in the vanilla, then the pecans. Use immediately because the filling thickens quickly. If it gets too thick to spread, reheat in the double boiler, adding a little milk or water. Makes a scant 2 cups.

CALVIN AND MARIE'S RECIPE

Double Banana Cake on Cream
(Gâteau de Banane sur la Crème)

Makes one 4-layer cake

Calvin says that when he was a youngster the family almost never bought any food from a store. Mom sometimes bought lemons and ice for iced tea on Sundays, but for daily meals they made do with whatever they had at home. Bananas from the store were special treats only for the children at Christmastime.

Marie learned to make this country-style cake, rich but not sweet, from "Granny," an elderly black lady who taught her how to cook. Marie always makes an extra layer when she bakes a cake so she and Calvin can eat it plain as a lagniappe.

This cake is unusually dense and moist, with a texture like bread pudding. Calvin has noticed that people tease Marie about how heavy the cake is—but then they always ask for seconds! Serving the cake on cream adds richness, but more important is what it does for the banana flavor.

Cake:

2¾ cups all-purpose flour
1 tablespoon baking powder
½ pound (2 sticks) unsalted butter, very soft
2¾ cups sugar
5 large eggs, *in all*
1 cup well-mashed overripe bananas (about 3
    medium)
1 tablespoon vanilla extract
2½ cups milk, *in all*
3 cups coarsely chopped pecans, dry roasted, optional

Butter, to butter cake pans
Flour, to flour cake pans
Banana Filling (recipe follows)

407

Glaze (recipe follows)

½ cup pecan halves, dry roasted, to garnish cake top,
    optional

Heavy cream to serve under each slice of cake (see
    Note)

Note: Allow 2 to 3 tablespoons of cream for each serving.

In a medium-size bowl, sift together the flour and baking powder; set aside.

In a very large bowl of an electric mixer, combine the butter with the sugar; beat on medium-low speed until very light colored and grainy, about 4 minutes, pushing sides down with a rubber spatula. Turn speed to medium and beat 1 egg at a time into the mixture, pushing sides down. Add the bananas and vanilla and beat until very light and creamy, about 4 minutes. With the machine still running, beat in about one fourth of the flour and baking powder mixture, then beat in one fourth of the milk. Continue adding the flour mixture and milk alternately until all is mixed in, then beat about 2 minutes more, pushing sides down. Stir in the pecans, if desired.

Spoon the batter into four 9-inch round cake pans that have been buttered and lightly floured. Each pan should hold about 2¾ cups batter with pecans, or a scant 2½ cups without pecans. Bake at 350°, two layers at a time, on the middle rack of the oven until cake is lightly browned and bounces back when lightly pressed—about 32 minutes with pecans, or about 44 minutes without pecans.

Meanwhile, make the banana filling, then the glaze.

Let layers cool in pans on a wire rack about 10 minutes, then loosen sides of layers with a knife and carefully remove from pans. Place the first layer on a cake platter and the others on the rack to cool. While it is still warm, glaze the bottom layer, using *one fourth* (about 2½ tablespoons) of the glaze; make a few small slits in the layer with a paring knife so filling will sink in, then spread *one fifth* (about ½ cup) of the filling evenly on the top but not sides of the layer. Place another layer on top of the first and repeat the procedure of glazing and spreading on filling until all the layers, including the top one, have been glazed and spread with filling. Then spoon the last *one fifth* of the filling all around the top edge of the cake, letting it dribble down the sides. Garnish top with roasted pecan halves, if desired.

To serve, spoon 2 to 3 tablespoons of heavy cream on each dessert plate, place a fairly thin slice of cake (about 1 inch thick) on top, and serve immediately. Refrigerate leftovers.

Banana Filling

¼ pound (1 stick) unsalted butter
1 cup canned sweetened condensed milk
1 cup milk
1 cup well-mashed overripe bananas (about 3
    medium)
¾ cup sugar
1 tablespoon vanilla extract

In a 3-quart saucepan, combine the butter, condensed milk, fresh milk, bananas, and sugar. Place over high heat and bring to a strong boil, stirring constantly and breaking up any banana lumps. Reduce heat to maintain a simmer and cook until filling has thickened to the consistency of soft pudding, about 30 minutes, stirring constantly so mixture doesn't scorch. Remove from heat and stir in the vanilla.

NOTE: Measure the yield carefully before spreading any filling on the cake. Because the cake has no icing and because the filling itself yields only enough for thin layers, you will need to be fairly precise in using equal portions on each layer. Makes a generous 2½ cups filling.

Glaze

½ cup water
¼ cup sugar
½ teaspoon vanilla extract

Combine the water and sugar in a small saucepan and bring to a boil. Remove from heat and stir in the vanilla. Spread the glaze over the surface and a little on the sides of each layer, using all the glaze. Then just before spreading filling on each layer, make a few slits in each with a paring knife. Makes ½ cup plus 2 tablespoons glaze.

 J.C. AND SIS'S RECIPE

Fresh Strawberry Cake
(Gâteau aux Fraises)

Makes one 6-layer cake

Louisianians are spoiled by the most extraordinary, sweet-tasting strawberries in the world and they won't settle for any other kind. We eat copious amounts of them during the season (March and early April) and buy whole flats of them to make preserves and to freeze for cooking after the short season ends. We hope you are fortunate enough to have access to Louisiana strawberries! If not, use the freshest, sweetest berries you can find for this exceptional and beautiful cake.

Sis says of course she first learned to make cakes from scratch, but that when commercial cake mixes came out, everyone in her generation seemed to think that store-bought cake mix was the only way to make a cake and over the years they just forgot how real homemade cakes tasted. For the cookbook, Sis had to go up to the attic to find this old recipe she had written down forty years ago. We're awfully glad she found it—and so are J.C. and Sis because now they both appreciate again how wonderful cakes are made from scratch.

4 pounds strawberries, *in all* (Louisiana ones
    preferred!), rinsed and hulls removed (about 1
    gallon)
About 4½ cups sugar, *in all*
3 cups all-purpose flour

1 tablespoon baking powder

½ teaspoon plus 1 pinch salt, *in all*

4 large eggs

½ pound (2 sticks) plus 4 tablespoons unsalted
    butter, softened and cut into chunks

1 cup evaporated milk

2 tablespoons plus 1 teaspoon vanilla extract, *in all*

1½ cups heavy cream

⅓ cup powdered sugar

Place a medium-size bowl of an electric mixer in the freezer.

Reserve two or three perfect large strawberries for garnish; refrigerate until ready to use. Place the remaining strawberries in a large mixing bowl and mash with a pastry blender or sturdy spatula until all berries are broken up and mixture is soupy. Stir in 2 *cups* of the sugar. (Add ¼ to ½ cup more sugar if your strawberries are tart.) Refrigerate until ready to use.

In a medium-size bowl, sift together the flour, baking powder, and ½ *teaspoon* of the salt; set aside.

In a large bowl of an electric mixer, combine 2 *cups* of the sugar and the eggs. Beat on low speed until smooth, about 1 minute, pushing sides down with a rubber spatula. Add the butter; beat on low until mixture is creamy and light colored, about 3 minutes. Beat in the milk and 2 *tablespoons* of the vanilla. Gradually add the flour mixture, about 1 cup at a time, beating after each addition just until smooth and pushing sides down as needed. Then beat on high speed about 1 minute more, pushing sides down. Rinse off beaters and place them in the freezer.

Spoon equal amounts of the batter (a generous 1 cup) into six 9-inch round cake pans that have been greased and lightly floured. Spread batter out evenly in each pan. Bake at 350°, 3 at a time, on the middle rack of the oven until centers spring back when lightly pressed, 18 to 20 minutes. Immediately remove cake layers from pans to a wire rack to cool. Bake the three remaining layers as you did the first. If re-using the same pans, first scrub, re-grease, and lightly flour them.

Place one of the baked layers on a cake plate and pierce it several times with a large fork so strawberry juice will sink in. Remove strawberry mixture from refrigerator; stir well and measure out and reserve ½ cup in the refrigerator to use in the icing. Pour a generous 1 cup of the strawberry mixture evenly over the top, but not over the sides, of the first layer, being sure to cover entire top with juice. Place another layer on top of the first, pierce it through with the fork as you did the first, and add another generous cup of the strawberry mixture evenly over the top. Continue in the same fashion until each stacked layer has strawberries on it and all the strawberry mixture is used. Set cake aside.

Place the cream in the chilled mixing bowl. Beat on medium speed of the electric mixer for about 1 minute. Add the powdered sugar, the remaining *1 teaspoon* vanilla, and the pinch of salt. Beat on medium just until stiff, about 2 minutes; do not overbeat. Fold in the reserved ½ cup strawberry mixture until well blended. Then ice the cake on the top and sides with the whipped-cream mixture, using it all. Garnish the center of the cake with the reserved whole strawberries.

Refrigerate at least 1 hour before serving. Refrigerate any leftovers—but we bet you won't ever have leftovers.

MALCOLM AND VERSIE'S RECIPE

Fresh Pineapple Cake
(Gâteau à l'Ananas Frais)

Makes one 4-layer cake

Versie's mom taught her how to make this cake. When Versie tested it for the cookbook, she cut up a fresh pineapple for the first time in her life. She had always used canned pineapple, just as her mom did. Fresh pineapple has become available in rural areas of Louisiana only in the last few years, and Versie was greatly impressed by how much better it tasted. Her mom used round cake pans and often made five or six very thin layers rather than four thicker ones. Versie's way of doing it is a little easier and it makes an extra-special birthday cake.

Pineapple Filling:

1 (4- to 4½-pound) pineapple, or enough to yield 2
    cups minced pineapple meat plus at least ¼ cup
    thin bite-size pineapple pieces to garnish cake
    (see **NOTE**)
1 cup plus 2 tablespoons sugar
2 tablespoons unsalted butter
2 teaspoons cornstarch dissolved in 2 teaspoons water

Cake:

3 cups all-purpose flour
1 tablespoon baking powder
½ teaspoon salt
½ pound (2 sticks) unsalted butter, softened
2 cups sugar
4 eggs, *in all*
1 cup milk, *in all*
2 teaspoons vanilla extract

Glaze (recipe follows)
Icing (recipe follows)

NOTE: Be sure to save the peelings and core to make the glaze.

For the filling: Peel, core, and chop the pineapple; reserve the peelings and core. Process enough of the pineapple meat (about 3 cups chopped) in a food processor to yield 2 cups minced pineapple meat. Transfer to a 2-quart saucepan and set aside. Cut the remaining pineapple into thin bite-size pieces and reserve, refrigerated, to garnish the cake.

Place the saucepan over medium-high heat. Add the sugar and stir well. Cook about 5 minutes, stirring frequently. Add the butter and cook about 2 minutes more, stirring frequently. Remove pan from heat momentarily and stir in the cornstarch, then place pan over high heat and cook until mixture reduces to about 2 cups, 3 to 4 minutes more, stirring constantly. Remove from heat and set aside.

For the cake: Sift the flour, baking powder, and salt together in a medium-size bowl and set aside.

In a large bowl of an electric mixer, combine the butter and sugar; beat on medium speed until light colored and creamy, about 4 minutes, pushing sides down with a rubber spatula. Add *1* of the eggs, ¼ *cup* of the milk, and about *1 cup* of the flour mixture; beat a few seconds on medium until blended. Continue beating, adding 1 egg, ¼ cup milk, and about 1 cup of the flour mixture at a time, beating each time, until all of these ingredients are added and the batter is smooth, light colored, and fluffy, about 3 minutes total. Add the vanilla and beat on medium speed about 2 minutes more.

Grease and lightly flour four 11 × 7-inch baking pans 1½ inches deep. Spoon one fourth of the batter (about 1¾ cups) into each pan and spread it out evenly. Bake at 350°, 2 layers at a time, on the middle rack of the oven until centers spring back when lightly pressed, 22 to 25 minutes. While the first 2 layers are baking, make the glaze.

Remove cake layers from oven as they are done and let pans sit about 5 minutes on a wire rack, then loosen sides with a knife and remove layers from pans to cool on the wire rack. Place one layer on a serving platter and glaze the top and sides. Make a few small slits in the layer with a paring knife and spread one third of the filling (about ⅔ cup) on the top but not sides. Place another cake layer on top and repeat procedure of glazing and spreading on filling; repeat until all layers have been filled and glazed. However, only glaze the top layer, don't spread filling on it.

Let cake cool thoroughly, then ice top and sides of cake. Garnish with the reserved pineapple slices.

Glaze

Reserved pineapple core and peelings
¼ cup sugar
About 6 cups water
1 teaspoon vanilla extract

In a 4-quart saucepan, combine the reserved pineapple core and peelings, sugar, and just enough water to cover ingredients (about 6 cups), stirring well. Bring to a boil over high heat. Continue boiling about 30 minutes, stirring occasionally. Remove from heat and, with a slotted spoon, remove and discard core and peelings. Return pan to high heat and reduce liquid to 1 cup, 6 to 8 minutes. Remove from heat and stir in the vanilla. Strain liquid through cheesecloth, or a mesh strainer lined with paper towels, into a glass measuring cup. With a pastry brush, brush glaze over the surface and on the sides of all the layers a little at a time and using all the glaze.

Icing

1 (8-ounce) package cream cheese, softened
¼ pound (1 stick) unsalted butter, softened
1 teaspoon vanilla extract
1 (16-ounce) box powdered sugar

In a medium-size bowl of an electric mixer, combine the cream cheese and butter; beat on medium speed until creamy, about 1 minute, pushing sides down with a rubber spatula. Beat in the vanilla, then gradually beat in the powdered sugar, beating until very smooth, 2 to 3 minutes, and pushing sides down with the spatula as needed.

J.C. AND SIS'S RECIPE

Fresh Coconut Cake
(Gâteau au Coco Frais)

Makes one 6-layer cake

When J.C. and Sis's children were small, Sis did as many busy mothers do, she switched to using "convenience" foods. When she changed back from canned to fresh coconut to practice this cake for the cookbook, she realized what she had been missing for almost thirty years! She says "it really tastes better to use fresh coconut!"

Sis's mom used to make this cake and Sis has added her own touches over the years. It is absolutely exceptional! Everyone who tasted it hoped it would have to be tested at least thirty times because we all wanted more—every day!

Be sure to use fresh coconut. It is immeasurably better, and you need the coconut milk to make the glaze.

Coconut Filling:

About 3¾ pounds fresh coconuts, or enough to yield 4 cups plus 2
    tablespoons minced coconut meat, *in all* (see **NOTE**)
2½ cups heavy cream
1½ cups sugar
½ pound (2 sticks) unsalted butter
1 tablespoon cornstarch dissolved in 1 tablespoon water
1 teaspoon vanilla extract

Cake:

3 cups all-purpose flour
1 tablespoon baking powder
½ teaspoon salt
2 cups sugar
4 large eggs
½ pound (2 sticks) plus 4 tablespoons unsalted
    butter, softened and cut into chunks
1 cup evaporated milk
1 tablespoon vanilla extract

Coconut-Milk Glaze (recipe follows)
Frosting (recipe follows)

NOTE: Be sure to reserve the coconut milk to make the glaze.

For the filling: Drain the milk from the coconuts by carefully making a hole in each of the three "eyes" of the coconuts with a clean, new, and large nail, an icepick, or a sharp, very sturdy knife point. Strain the milk through cheesecloth or through a fine mesh strainer lined with a paper towel and measure out 1½ cups; if necessary make up the balance with water. Refrigerate until ready to use.

Break coconuts into small pieces with a hammer. Peel the pieces and remove the brown inner skin attached to the white coconut meat. Rinse and drain coconut meat well, then process it in batches in a food processor until minced. You will need *4 cups* minced coconut for the filling plus 2 *tablespoons* to garnish the top of the cake. Set aside. (Use leftover coconut as a snack or in another recipe, such as **Fresh Coconut Pralines,** page 383.)

In a heavy 5½-quart saucepan or large Dutch oven, heat together the cream, sugar, and butter over medium-high heat until mixture reaches a boil, stirring frequently. Add the *4 cups* of minced coconut, stirring well. Cook until mixture reduces to 5 cups, about 15 minutes, stirring almost constantly. Remove from heat and stir in the cornstarch. Place pan over high heat and bring to a boil, stirring constantly. Add the vanilla and cook and stir about 1 minute. Remove from heat and continue stirring a few seconds more. Cool slightly, then refrigerate until well chilled. **NOTE**: Filling will decrease in volume as it cools. Once it is chilled, measure yield and divide by 5 to determine amount to use between cake layers. Keep refrigerated until just before ready to use.

For the cake: In a medium-size bowl, sift together the flour, baking powder, and salt; set aside.

In a large bowl of an electric mixer, combine the sugar and eggs; beat on low speed until smooth, about 1 minute, pushing sides down with a rubber spatula. Add the butter; beat on low until mixture is creamy and light colored, about 3 minutes. Beat in the milk and vanilla. Gradually add the flour mixture, about 1 cup at a time, beating after each addition just until smooth and pushing sides down as needed. Then beat on high speed for about 1 minute more, pushing sides down.

Spoon equal portions of the batter (a slightly mounded 1 cup) into six 8-inch round cake pans that have been greased and lightly floured. Spread batter out evenly in the pans. Bake at 350° on the middle rack of the oven, 3 layers at a time, until centers spring back when lightly pressed, 18 to 20 minutes. Remove from oven and let pans sit about 5 minutes, then loosen sides of cake with a knife and remove layers from pans to a wire rack. Bake the 3 remaining layers. If re-using the same pans, first wash, re-grease, and lightly flour them. Meanwhile, make the glaze.

After the cake layers have cooled about 15 minutes, glaze one layer by brushing glaze over the surface and on the sides with a pastry brush, a little at a time and using one sixth of the glaze (about 2½ tablespoons). Make holes in the cake with a paring knife so glaze can sink in. Immediately (before glazing another layer), spread one fifth of the filling on top of the glazed layer, extending it to about ½ inch from the edge. Then place another layer on top and repeat procedure of glazing and spreading on filling until all the layers are glazed and all but the top layer have filling spread on them.

Let cake cool thoroughly, then frost top and sides. Sprinkle the remaining 2 *tablespoons* minced coconut on top. Let sit 1 hour before slicing.

Coconut-Milk Glaze

1½ cups reserved strained coconut milk (or a mixture
    of coconut milk and water)
⅓ cup sugar
1 teaspoon vanilla extract

Combine the coconut milk and the sugar in a 2-quart saucepan and bring to a boil over high heat, stirring occasionally. Continue boiling until glaze reduces to 1 cup, about 5 minutes, stirring frequently. Remove from heat and stir in the vanilla. Pour into a glass measuring cup and use glaze as directed in the recipe. Makes 1 cup.

Frosting

2 (3-ounce) packages cream cheese, softened
¼ pound (1 stick) unsalted butter, very soft
1 tablespoon vanilla extract
¼ teaspoon salt
2 tablespoons plus 1 teaspoon evaporated milk
1 (1-pound) box powdered sugar, *in all* (4 cups)

Combine the cream cheese, butter, vanilla, and salt in a medium-size bowl of an electric mixer; beat on high speed until creamy, about 1 minute. Turn speed to medium and beat in the milk and *1 cup* of the sugar, pushing sides down with a rubber spatula. Beat in the remaining *3 cups* sugar, 1 cup at a time, mixing until smooth before adding more. If the frosting becomes too thick for the mixer, do the last bit of mixing with a spoon.

ALLIE AND ETELL'S RECIPE

Mom's Dry Fruit Cake
(Gâteau aux Fruits Secs à Mom)

Makes one 9½-inch cake

This recipe was Mom Prudhomme's special dessert for the holidays, which Allie has preserved—an annual tradition the family looked forward to each winter for Christmas and New Year's. Be sure to allow it to age for two to three weeks before serving. None of the Prudhomme children can remember how long Mom aged her fruit cakes; they all say that with her houseful of kids, Mom would have had a difficult time holding on to any food long enough to age it!

Mom used maraschino cherries because that was all she could get, but candied cherries are better. Soak the raisins overnight in the rum before starting this delicious cake. It has that wonderful, familiar flavor of roasted pecans.

1½ cups seedless raisins
2 cups dark rum
1 pound (4 sticks) unsalted butter, *in all*, plus butter
    to grease the pan
3 cups chopped pecans
1 (1-pound) package pitted dates (with or without
    sugar coating), chopped
1¼ pounds marshmallows

2 (6-ounce) jars maraschino cherries, drained and
    stemmed, or 8 ounces candied cherries
1⅓ pounds graham crackers, finely ground

Place the raisins in a large glass or ceramic bowl and pour the rum over them, making sure all raisins are submerged. Cover tightly and let sit overnight at room temperature.

Drain the raisins and set them aside. Reserve the drained rum in a clean, tightly covered glass container to serve over the fruit cake.

In a 5½-quart saucepan, melt 2 *sticks* of the butter over high heat until butter is half melted. Add the pecans and cook until pecans are browned, about 8 minutes, stirring frequently with a sturdy long-handled spoon. Remove from heat and immediately stir in the dates. Add the remaining 2 *sticks* butter and stir until melted.

Add the marshmallows and return pan to high heat; cook until marshmallows are almost melted, about 4 minutes, stirring constantly. Stir in the cherries and raisins and stir constantly until well mixed and marshmallows are totally melted, being careful not to burn yourself. Remove from heat and gradually stir in the graham cracker crumbs, mixing very well and working quickly so mixture won't get too thick to stir.

Spoon the mixture into a 9½-inch tube pan 4 inches deep that has been generously greased with butter, packing the cake mixture firmly in the pan. Cover pan loosely and let cake age, refrigerated, at least 2 to 3 weeks.

When ready to serve the first time, run a knife around edges of pan to loosen cake; remove cake from pan and place on a serving platter to slice. Serve the raisin rum over the top, if desired. Once aged, the cake will last about 6 weeks more if covered well and stored in the refrigerator.

················**LAGNIAPPE**················
To clean the pot and utensils, boil water in the pot with the utensils in it. This will melt the batter.

The Family

Darilee Prudhomme Broussard

June 5, 1919

Darilee Prudhomme Broussard was the second child born to Mom and Dad Prudhomme. (The firstborn child, a son christened Woodrow, died when he was about six months old.) Darilee married Saul Broussard in 1935. Their two sons, Woodrow and Earl, have five children and three grandchildren.

Saul's parents were sharecroppers, just as Mom and Dad were, and Darilee and Saul met when the two families were farming on adjacent properties. They spent the early years of their marriage sharecropping with Saul's parents. Then, when Mom and Dad Prudhomme retired from the family grocery store, Abel and Jo bought the store and hired Darilee and Saul to run it for them. In 1969, Darilee and Saul bought their own grocery store, where Saul became famous for his smoked sausages and boudins. In 1980, Darilee and Saul retired from the store and their son Earl took it over.

All the family considered Darilee and Saul the best dancers in Cajun country, and for many years dancing was their favorite entertainment. Darilee's fondest memory of Dad Prudhomme is that he always got a group together to have a dance or go dancing when Darilee felt she just had to dance.

Both Darilee and Saul always greeted all visitors to their home in Cajun French, and Saul spoke French more often than English. They celebrated their golden wedding anniversary on November 25, 1985. Saul passed away on November 11, 1986. All the family sorely miss his soft-spoken ways and his gentle presence. Darilee lives in Opelousas, Louisiana.

Elden Prudhomme

June 20, 1920

Elden Prudhomme, the third child, married Odelia Mae Darbonne in 1941. They have three living children, Edwin, Debbie, and Charles. (Their son Glenn died when he was a young man.) They have six living grandchildren and six great-grandchildren. (Their grandson, Glenn, Jr., died when he was a teenager.)

As the oldest boy in the family, Elden set the example for his younger brothers and sisters by working hard alongside Dad and Mom on the farm and then later when he worked away from home. He left home to get a job when he was fourteen. When he told Dad he was leaving to make more money, Dad said, "That's fine, son, if that's what you think you should do, but remember that you can always come home if things don't work out."

In the early years of his career, Elden worked in the oil fields, then in about 1940, he went to work in the shipyards in New Orleans. Later, he worked in the construction business for about ten years.

Elden and Odelia Mae met at a Cajun dance. She has a fine reputation as an excellent Cajun cook and has been featured in several regional and national newspapers and periodicals. She loves to cook more than anything!

Elden retired several years ago because of a heart problem—but he just couldn't stay retired. (Eli likes to say, "If Elden has a bad heart, then give me one, because no one can work like him.") He and Odelia Mae own and operate a company that fabricates metal buildings. They live in Cankton, Louisiana. They are Paul's godparents.

Allie Prudhomme Fontenot

August 5, 1921

Allie Prudhomme Fontenot, the fourth child, married Etell Fontenot in 1963. They have one son, Teddy, and Allie has five daughters, Margie, Adele, Bonnie, Penny, and Sheila, from an earlier marriage. They have seventeen grandchildren (soon to be twenty, including a set of twins), and eight great-grandchildren (soon to be ten).

When Allie was a preteen, she spent several years living with Mom's mother and two of her aunts, helping them take care of younger children and do household chores. Allie returned home to help Mom when Bobby was born, and she and Bobby have always had a special relationship because of those early years when she took care of him. Mom called Allie "the radio" because she was either talking or singing—all the time.

After Allie left home, she worked outside her home for about eighteen years while raising her daughters, and her proudest accomplishment is bringing them up virtually on her own.

Allie and Etell met at a Cajun dance. Etell worked as a barber for seventeen years before joining the St. Landry Parish Sheriff's Department, where he has worked for several years. Allie says Etell is a "a Cajun, skin and all, even under his feet." His parents neither spoke nor understood English.

Allie and Etell both love to cook, and he works a lot in his vegetable garden. He plants popcorn (as Dad Prudhomme did) and cotton (both brown and white) so his grandchildren and great-grandchildren will know what it looks like and will understand a significant part of their family history. Allie and Etell live in Port Barre, Louisiana, just down the road from Opelousas.

J.C. Prudhomme

August 23, 1922

J.C. Prudhomme, the fifth child, married Emma Brasseaux in 1945. They have four living children, Sharon, Glenda, Patricia, and James Carroll. (Their son Larry died when he was a young child.) They have thirteen grandchildren and four great-grandchildren.

J.C. began his career in the construction business in 1947 and moved quickly up the ladder from laborer to highly skilled heavy-equipment operator. He was known throughout South Louisiana as one of the finest heavy-equipment men in the state. And even today, many years after his retirement, people still talk about his exceptional ability with construction machinery.

J.C. spent most of his early teen years with Mom's parents, helping them on their farm. The quiet life with his grandparents was in marked contrast to the exuberant family homelife with Mom and Dad and the brothers and sisters, and J.C., perhaps in part because of growing up in that quiet setting, is one of the shyest and most soft-spoken of the family.

J.C. and Sis met when she served him coffee at the coffee shop where she worked—and he said to his friends as he left, "I'm going to marry that girl!" Sis's parents were sharecroppers, too, but her family farmed on land that was about thirty miles from the Prudhomme farm, so she and J.C. didn't meet until they had both left home.

The family say J.C. is the world's best coffee maker and best cornbread maker—no one can touch him! He and Sis are retired now, and they enjoy having lots of time to spend with their children and grandchildren. They live in Opelousas, Louisiana.

Calvin Prudhomme

March 19, 1924

Calvin, the sixth child, married Marie Orgeron in 1945. They have two children, Ray and Bridgette, and four grandchildren.

Calvin left home when he was fifteen to work in the rice fields in Lake Charles, Louisiana. He joined the army in 1942, saw combat and was wounded in World War II, and received a Purple Heart. When he was discharged from the army, he went to work for the Monterey Pipeline Company, beginning as a laborer and moving up to pipeline welder and then inspector. He retired from the company in 1984 after a thirty-seven year career.

Calvin and Marie met at a Cajun dance and got married one year and two months later. Her parents were sharecroppers, too. She says she had everything to learn about cooking when she and Calvin married, since she knew nothing about it. She had superb teachers—Mom Prudhomme and Calvin.

Calvin and Marie have two homes, their primary home in Opelousas, and a farm in the country. In addition, they have a beautiful new motor home. They are avid campers and belong to two camping clubs. They love their retirement. Calvin keeps a small vegetable garden, and they spend most of their time traveling around the country spreading the word about Cajun cooking in campgrounds north and south. Calvin says the good smells of gumbos and jambalayas coming from their camper have led to their making friends with people throughout the United States.

Calvin and Marie rarely visit their farm in the country now and spend most of their time at home in Opelousas when they're not on the road. He says that if he can choose to do anything he wants to, he'll continue to live exactly as he does now.

Ralph Prudhomme

June 1, 1925

Ralph Prudhomme, the seventh child, married Mary Ann Sonnier in 1947, after returning home from the navy. They have three children, Rebecca, Russell, and Brenda, and six grandchildren.

Ralph didn't leave home until he was drafted when he was eighteen. After his three-year stint in the navy, he moved back to the family home, where he lived until he and Mary Ann were married. Ralph worked for twenty years in the oil fields, beginning as a roughneck and ending up as a drilling superintendent. When he left the oil industry, he went into the construction business and worked for many years as a carpenter and welder.

To the younger children, Ralph will always be the lovable, but "mean as the dickens," older brother who sat them on calves and mules and then left them there stranded, hanging on for dear life. He met Mary Ann when she served him a meal at an Opelousas restaurant where she worked. Her parents were sharecroppers, too. The two of them are thoroughly enjoying retirement. Ralph still likes to use his welding and carpentry skills and helps out the family and anyone else who needs repair work done. Mary Ann works part time at their church.

Ralph's two favorite occupations are fishing and cooking—and he does one or both daily. He has an outdoor kitchen, a separate structure that he uses for cleaning and cooking fish and game and for cooking gumbo. He says, modestly, that he's a good cook, adding, "I'm not the best, but I'm in the top ten." (And he's not talking about the family ranking.) Ralph and Mary Ann love having their children and grandchildren over regularly for visits and meals. They live in Port Barre, Louisiana.

Abel Prudhomme

November 27, 1927

Abel Prudhomme, the eighth child, and Josephine Doucet were married in 1947. They have five children, Katherine, Mildred, Wayne, Linn, and Carl, and nine grandchildren.

Abel began working for a seismograph crew of an oil company when he was sixteen, but he continued to live at home and help Dad with the farming. He stayed in the oil industry for many years, beginning as a roughneck and working up through driller to supervisor. In 1958, when Mom and Dad retired from the family store, Abel and Jo bought it, but Abel continued to work in the oil industry until 1967. Then he and Jo ran the store together for about ten years until Abel realized that his heart was in the oil fields, so he sold the store and went back to the business he had begun in as a teenager. When the oil boom slowed dramatically in Louisiana, Abel went to work with Paul, managing Paul's smoked-meat plant in Melville, Louisiana. (Abel had established a fine reputation as a sausage maker when he owned the grocery store in Opelousas.)

Abel says that whenever any of the boys left home to go to work, Dad always told them, "Give the man a full day's work." He says all the children have always lived by that advice from Dad, and they've all been able to get and hold good jobs throughout their lives.

Abel and Jo met when the two families farmed adjacent properties. Her parents were sharecroppers, too. The family says that when Abel fell in love with Jo, he was so smitten, he couldn't do the simplest tasks, and Dad teased him about being so helplessly in love. Allie's pet name for Abel was "suce-fleur," French for hummingbird, because he was such a tiny youngster. He was also very fast, the only one in the family fast enough to get a finger in the pot to taste what Mom was cooking before she could catch him.

Abel and Jo say life is wonderful for them. They have a fine family and are enjoying their later years more and more. They live in Opelousas, Louisiana.

Malcolm Prudhomme

July 25, 1929

Malcolm Prudhomme, the ninth child, and Versie Robin were married in 1951, just two weeks after Malcolm returned home from the Korean War, in which he earned a Purple Heart. They have six children, Ronnie, Brenda, Donna, Steve, Kurt, and Michelle, and seven grandchildren.

Malcolm left home to begin working when he was fifteen and worked in various jobs until he was old enough to enlist in the army at age sixteen. He stayed in the army for ten years, but came home on furloughs often enough to meet, court, and marry Versie. Their first two children were born in Germany, where Malcolm was stationed for several years.

After leaving the army, Malcolm worked in an oil refinery in Texas for four years. Then he returned to Louisiana and went into business for himself, designing and building custom-designed mobile-home porches, steps, and carports. Malcolm is a fine inventor, and has designed and built several innovative deep-fat fryers and cooking-oil filtering machines. He is in partnership now, with the owner of a major fast-food company, in a research and design company that develops new equipment for the restaurant industry and redesigns work areas for commercial kitchens.

Malcolm and Versie met at a Cajun dance. Her parents, too, were share-croppers. Now that all the children are grown and away from home, Versie is working also, managing townhouse rental properties.

All the family laugh and say that Malcolm is a consummate salesman. They say he has always been a great talker (they used to call him "the lawyer"). He is not a cook—he's the only one of the boys who isn't. Malcolm says what he treasures most from others is honesty. He and Versie live in Opelousas, Louisiana.

Enola Prudhomme Prather

January 1, 1932

Enola Prudhomme Prather, the tenth child, married Shelton Prather in 1986. She has five children, Howard, Diane, Sonny, Toni, and Annette, and twelve grandchildren.

Enola worked outside her home for many years while her children were growing up, and most of her jobs were related to the food industry. She worked for several years in Mom and Dad's grocery store, she had a catering company for a number of years, and she managed the food-service operations for the vocational technical school in Opelousas, Louisiana.

In early 1984, Enola opened her own restaurant, Prudhomme's Cajun Café, in Washington, Louisiana, a small, historic town in Cajun country. Shelton and her children and their spouses work there with her. She has just relocated the restaurant, moving it into a much larger place, a renovated country house in Cankton, Louisiana. Her restaurant is a favorite with people who are looking for good Cajun cooking in South Louisiana, and it has just been named one of the top ten restaurants in Louisiana by *Louisiana Life*.

Enola and Shelton met at a Cajun dance. Shelton worked in the oil industry before joining Enola at the café. Enola is active in the state chefs' association, Les Chefs des Cuisines de la Louisianne, and has won numerous cooking awards. She's been featured in many regional and national newspapers and periodicals.

She and Shelton are extremely busy with the restaurant. Enola says that since all her children and their spouses work with her, she gets to be with them and the grandchildren more often than if she were not working. Enola and Shelton live in Cankton, Louisiana.

Eli Prudhomme, Jr.

August 14, 1933

Eli Prudhomme, the eleventh child, married Sue Bloodsworth in 1983. They have two children, Tanya and Kyle, and five more from their first marriages, Donald, David, Aaron, Dexter, and John. Eli has seven grandchildren.

Eli left home to go to work in the oil fields when he was sixteen. He worked in that business for sixteen years, interrupted by two years in the army, nine months of which he served in the Korean War. When he left the oil industry, Eli went on to pipeline construction, and that's what he does today. He learned to do electronics work by reading about it—he loves to read, and he enjoys working with electronic equipment. In addition, he's a fine heavy-equipment operator. He did all the major construction of the bass and bream pond at Paul and K's country house.

Eli says Mom was an avid reader—she was one of the few literate older people in the area—and the children knew that the newspaper was to be delivered directly to her to read before anyone else opened it. Eli's favorite memory of growing up is the way the family shared what they had with families who had less. All the children say they might have been poor in money and material things, but they always had plenty to eat and plenty to share with others who were less fortunate.

Sue is from North Louisiana, and Eli kids her about her "redneck" heritage. She grew up with her grandparents, who owned a farm. (Sue and K are the only spouses of Prudhomme children who are not Cajun.) She's having a great time learning to cook Cajun from Eli and other members of the family.

Eli and Sue have their hands full with their two youngsters, both of whom are real live wires. They live in Cankton, Louisiana.

Bobby Prudhomme

August 6, 1935

Bobby Prudhomme, the twelfth child, is a bachelor now. He has four living children, Veronica, Troy, Bobby Allen, and Angela, and one grandchild. (His son Kurt died when he was a teenager.)

Bobby left home when he was seventeen and began working in the oil fields when he was eighteen. He worked in the oil industry for more than twenty-four years. He began as a roughneck and soon got up to driller. Later, he worked for a company that serviced oil rigs located in the Gulf of Mexico; he was sent out to the rigs to work on repairs and other problems. After leaving the oil business, Bobby moved to North Louisiana and worked in the lumber industry for eight years, operating heavy equipment.

In 1984, Bobby moved to New Orleans to work in Paul's herb and spice company. He is the master blender for the seven Cajun Magic® blends.

Bobby's strongest memory of Dad was of his sternness, tempered by love and fairness. He says if the children did anything wrong, they knew they'd be punished—and they were. But when they were in the right, they knew Dad would always go to bat for them all the way—and he did. All the family remember Bobby as a little daredevil who could be put up to anything. They say he was absolutely fearless.

Bobby lives in New Orleans. He thinks the city's all right, but says he's still a country boy at heart.

Paul Prudhomme

Julu 13, 1940

Paul Prudhomme, the thirteenth and last child, married K Hinrichs in 1979. They have two German Shepherds (Herzog and Ouber), one mastiff (Lancelot), two cats (Thutiy II and Thutmose II), and two parrots (Paco and Sam).

As soon as Paul finished high school, he opened his first restaurant, Big Daddy-O's Patio, a hamburger drive-in restaurant in Opelousas, Louisiana. He was seventeen years old, and he went broke in nine months. But he knew he wanted to cook for a living—he had known that since he was nine. He moved to New Orleans to learn about the restaurant business and worked there for a year before deciding that he wanted to know more about cooking and restaurants than he could learn in New Orleans and Louisiana. He wanted to learn everything he could about the way people cooked everywhere in the country, and other countries, as well.

So he built a camper on the back of his truck and began traveling around the United States, stopping to cook in different places with cooks and chefs of every conceivable educational and ethnic background and experience. He even spent some time on an Indian reservation, just sitting around the first day or so and talking with the women who were cooking until they got accustomed to having him there. Then he asked to cook with them, and he stayed for several days working with them and learning their cooking methods. Paul spent twelve years working all over the United States, a period he refers to as his apprenticeship in the cooking profession.

In 1972, Paul decided to return to Louisiana, realizing that it was after all *the* place to cook. Louisiana's prime produce—fish, seafood, vegetables, everything—is incomparable, and cooks and chefs are held in high esteem. He worked in two or three fine New Orleans restaurants for a number of years before he opened his own French Quarter restaurant, K-Paul's Louisiana Kitchen, in 1979 with K. As word about the restaurant spread, Paul garnered a reputation as one of the four or five top American chefs in regional American cooking.

Paul's cookbook, *Chef Paul Prudhomme's Louisiana Kitchen*, has sold almost 600,000 copies since 1984 and keeps on selling. His 1986 cooking videotapes by the same title made the best-seller lists. Paul and K and the restaurant staff have been invited to cook at national and international functions throughout the country, and they took the whole restaurant "on the road" in 1983 (San Francisco) and 1985 (New York). The restaurant was named one of the top ten in the country by *Nation's Restaurant News* and has won the prestigious Ivy Award from *Restaurants and Institutions*. Paul was the first American-born chef to be awarded the *Mérite Agricole* by the French government. In 1986, Paul was named Chef of the Year by his peer group, the National Chefs' Association.

The family remember Paul as being a "little spoiled" and a "whole lot popular." K was born and grew up in Montana, but she adopted New Orleans as her home when she first moved there in 1969. She and Paul met when they were both working for a local restaurant. She has always run the front of the house at K-Paul's, while Paul heads up the kitchen.

Paul and K stay very busy with all their businesses—including K-Paul's, the herb and spice company, a sidewalk café, a smoked-meat company, and a mail-order company. They live in New Orleans and have a home in the heart of Cajun country, in Palmetto, Louisiana, where they escape from the city as often as they can.

LAGNIAPPE

LOUISIANA FAIRS & FESTIVALS

Louisiana is a festival state—"Laisséz les bons temps rouler!" (Let the good times roll!)—with more festivals and fairs than any other state in the nation. As a special lagniappe, we've provided a year's listing of selected Louisiana festivals—those that celebrate the Cajun heritage and those that celebrate traditional foods and dishes featured in our cookbook. Dates for the festivals can vary somewhat from year to year, so be sure to call the Louisiana Office of Tourism, Louisiana Department of Culture, Recreation, and Tourism, for specific dates, as well as for information on other festivals and fairs. Call TOLL FREE 1-800-33 GUMBO; in Louisiana, call 504-925-3860. Or write to the Louisiana Office of Tourism, P.O. Box 44291, Baton Rouge, LA 70804.

LOUISIANA BOUDIN FESTIVAL, last weekend **January** or first weekend **February,** Broussard, LA

INTERNATIONAL CRAWFISH TASTING/TRADE SHOW, last weekend **February,** Lafayette, LA

CAJUN MARDI GRAS, **February** or **March** (41 days before Easter), Lafayette, LA

COURIR DU MARDI GRAS, **February** or **March** (Sunday before Mardi Gras), Mamou, LA, and Church Point, LA

LA GRANDE BOUCHERIE, first weekend **March,** St. Martinville, LA

AMITE OYSTER DAYS, third weekend **March,** Amite, LA

CRAWFISH FESTIVAL OF ST. BERNARD, first weekend **April,** Chalmette, LA

CATFISH FESTIVAL, second weekend **April,** Winnsboro, LA

PONCHATOULA STRAWBERRY FESTIVAL, second weekend **April,** Ponchatoula, LA

AMERICAN LEGION STRAWBERRY & FOOD FESTIVAL, fourth weekend **April,** Gonzales, LA

CAJUN FOOD AND FUN FESTIVAL, fourth weekend **April,** Welsh, LA

CREOLE FESTIVAL, fourth weekend **April,** Jeanerette, LA

JAZZ & HERITAGE FESTIVAL, last weekend **April** or first weekend **May,** New Orleans, LA

FRENCH ACADIAN MUSIC FESTIVAL, fourth weekend **April,** Abbeville, LA

BLESSING OF THE SHRIMP FLEET, fourth weekend **April,** Chauvin, LA

LOUISIANA PRALINE FESTIVAL, first weekend **May,** Houma, LA

GATOR FESTIVAL, first weekend **May,** Baton Rouge, LA

BREAUX BRIDGE CRAWFISH FESTIVAL, first weekend **May,** Breaux Bridge, LA

TOMATO FESTIVAL, first weekend **May,** Chalmette, LA

ALLONS MANGER FOOD FESTIVAL, first weekend **May,** Belle Rose, LA

THE GREAT AMITE RIVER CATFISH FESTIVAL, third weekend **May,** Denham Springs, LA

PEARL RIVER CATFISH FESTIVAL, third weekend **May,** Pearl River, LA

CAJUN COUNTRY OUTDOOR OPRY, third weekend **May,** Houma, LA

CAJUN MUSIC FESTIVAL, first weekend **June,** Mamou, LA

CAJUN CRAB FESTIVAL, first weekend **June,** Henderson, LA

OKRA FESTIVAL, first weekend **June,** Kenner, LA

TASTE OF LOUISIANA, second weekend **June,** Sulphur, LA

LOUISIANA PEACH FESTIVAL, second and third week **June,** Ruston, LA

JAMBALAYA FESTIVAL, second weekend **June,** Gonzales, LA

BAYOU LACOMBE CRAB FESTIVAL, third weekend **June,** Lacombe, LA

SOUTH LAFOURCHE CAJUN FESTIVAL, third weekend **June,** Galliano, LA

FELICIANA PEACH FESTIVAL, third weekend **June,** Clinton, LA

LOUISIANA CORN FESTIVAL, third weekend **June,** Bunkie, LA

FESTIVAL INTERNATIONAL DE LOUISIANE, last weekend **June,** and first week **July,** Lafayette, LA

CAJUN BASTILLE DAY, second weekend **July,** Baton Rouge, LA

LOUISIANA CATFISH FESTIVAL, second weekend **July,** Des Allemands, LA

LOUISIANA OYSTER FESTIVAL, third weekend **July,** Galliano, LA

ANNUAL BEEF COOK-OFF, fourth weekend **July,** Opelousas, LA

SOUTH LAFOURCHE SEAFOOD FESTIVAL, first weekend **August,** Galliano, LA

DELCAMBRE SHRIMP FESTIVAL, second full week **August,** Delcambre, LA

FÊTE DES ACADIENS, third weekend **August,** Lafayette, LA

CALCASIEU CAJUN FESTIVAL, fourth weekend **August,** Sulphur, LA

LE BAL DE MAISON, last weekend **August,** Lafayette, LA

CAJUN HUNTERS FESTIVAL, last weekend **August,** Cut Off, LA

LOUISIANA SHRIMP AND PETROLEUM FESTIVAL AND FAIR, first weekend **September,** Morgan City, LA

DUCK FESTIVAL, first weekend **September,** Gueydan, LA

KINDER SAUCE PIQUANT & MUSIC FESTIVAL, first weekend **September,** Kinder, LA

ZYDECO FESTIVAL, first weekend **September,** Plaisance, LA

CAJUN DAY FESTIVAL, second weekend **September,** Church Point, LA

CAJUN FESTIVAL, third weekend **September,** Vinton, LA

FROG FESTIVAL, third weekend **September,** Rayne, LA

FESTIVALS ACADIENS, third weekend **September,** Lafayette, LA

SUGAR CANE FESTIVAL, last full week **September,** New Iberia, LA

ST. ANDREW'S CAJUN FESTIVAL, last weekend **September,** Amelia, LA

RACELAND SAUCE PIQUANT FESTIVAL, first weekend **October,** Raceland, LA

ST. PHILOMENA CAJUN COUNTRY FESTIVAL, first weekend **October,** Labadieville, LA

THE GUMBO FESTIVAL, second weekend **October,** Bridge City, LA

LAGNIAPPE ON THE BAYOU, second weekend **October,** Chauvin, LA

SORRENTO BOUCHERIE FESTIVAL, second weekend **October,** Sorrento, LA

INTERNATIONAL RICE FESTIVAL, third weekend **October,** Crowley, LA

INTERNATIONAL ALLIGATOR FESTIVAL, third weekend **October,** Franklin, LA

INTERNATIONAL ACADIAN FESTIVAL, third weekend **October,** Plaquemine, LA

LOUISIANA GUMBO FESTIVAL OF CHACKBAY, third weekend **October,** Chackbay, LA

COCHON DE LAIT FESTIVAL, third weekend **October,** Luling, LA

FRENCH LOUISIANA FESTIVAL, third weekend **October,** Kenner, LA

LA VIE LAFOURCHAISE, third weekend **October,** Raceland, LA

LOUISIANA YAMBILEE, fourth weekend **October,** Opelousas, LA

FRENCH FOOD FESTIVAL, fourth weekend **October,** Larose, LA

ANDOUILLE FESTIVAL, fourth weekend **October,** La Place, LA

VIOLET OYSTER FESTIVAL, fourth weekend **October,** Violet, LA

LOUISIANA SWINE FESTIVAL, last week and weekend **October,** Basile, LA

LOUISIANA PECAN FESTIVAL, first weekend **NOVEMBER,** COLFAX, LA

CHRISTMAS ON THE BAYOU, last Sunday **November,** Lafayette, LA

MERRY CAJUN CHRISTMAS, whole month of **December,** Lafayette, LA

CHRISTMAS COMES ALIVE—An Acadian Christmas, first and second weekends **December,** Lafayette, LA

SANTA ON THE BAYOU, first weekend **December,** Lacombe, LA

Index